Opportunities and Challenges for Blockchain Technology in Autonomous Vehicles

Amit Kumar Tyagi
Vellore Institute of Technolgy, Chennai, India

Gillala Rekha
K. L. University, India

N. Sreenath
Pondicherry Engineering College, India

A volume in the Advances in Data Mining and
Database Management (ADMDM) Book Series

Published in the United States of America by
IGI Global
Engineering Science Reference (an imprint of IGI Global)
701 E. Chocolate Avenue
Hershey PA, USA 17033
Tel: 717-533-8845
Fax: 717-533-8661
E-mail: cust@igi-global.com
Web site: http://www.igi-global.com

Library of Congress Cataloging-in-Publication Data

Names: Tyagi, Amit Kumar, 1988- editor. | Rekha, Gillala, 1981- editor. |
    Sreenath, N., 1965- editor.
Title: Opportunities and challenges for blockchain technology in autonomous
    vehicles / Amit Kumar Tyagi, Gillala Rekha, N Sreenath, editors.
Description: Hershey, PA : Engineering Science Reference, 2020. | Includes
    bibliographical references and index. | Summary: "This book examines the
    applications, approaches, and challenges to using blockchain technology
    in autonomous vehicles"-- Provided by publisher.
Identifiers: LCCN 2019051016 (print) | LCCN 2019051017 (ebook) | ISBN
    9781799832959 (hardcover) | ISBN 9781799832966 (paperback) | ISBN
    9781799832973 (ebook)
Subjects: LCSH: Automated vehicles--Computer programs. | Blockchains
    (Databases)--Industrial applications. | Intelligent transportation
    systems.
Classification: LCC TL152.8 .O67 2020 (print) | LCC TL152.8 (ebook) | DDC
    629.04/6028557--dc23
LC record available at https://lccn.loc.gov/2019051016
LC ebook record available at https://lccn.loc.gov/2019051017

This book is published in the IGI Global book series Advances in Data Mining and Database Management (ADMDM) (ISSN: 2327-1981; eISSN: 2327-199X)

British Cataloguing in Publication Data
A Cataloguing in Publication record for this book is available from the British Library.

For electronic access to this publication, please contact: eresources@igi-global.com.

Advances in Data Mining and Database Management (ADMDM) Book Series

David Taniar
Monash University, Australia

ISSN:2327-1981
EISSN:2327-199X

MISSION

With the large amounts of information available to organizations in today's digital world, there is a need for continual research surrounding emerging methods and tools for collecting, analyzing, and storing data.

The **Advances in Data Mining & Database Management (ADMDM)** series aims to bring together research in information retrieval, data analysis, data warehousing, and related areas in order to become an ideal resource for those working and studying in these fields. IT professionals, software engineers, academicians and upper-level students will find titles within the ADMDM book series particularly useful for staying up-to-date on emerging research, theories, and applications in the fields of data mining and database management.

COVERAGE

- Cluster Analysis
- Information Extraction
- Association Rule Learning
- Data Warehousing
- Web-based information systems
- Heterogeneous and Distributed Databases
- Text Mining
- Web Mining
- Quantitative Structure–Activity Relationship
- Customer Analytics

IGI Global is currently accepting manuscripts for publication within this series. To submit a proposal for a volume in this series, please contact our Acquisition Editors at Acquisitions@igi-global.com or visit: http://www.igi-global.com/publish/.

Titles in this Series

For a list of additional titles in this series, please visit:
http://www.igi-global.com/book-series/advances-data-mining-database-management/37146

Cross-Industry Use of Blockchain Technology and Opportunities for the Future
Idongesit Williams (Aalborg University, Denmark)
Engineering Science Reference • © 2020 • 228pp • H/C (ISBN: 9781799836322) • US $225.00

Applications and Developments in Semantic Process Mining
Kingsley Okoye (University of East London, UK)
Engineering Science Reference • © 2020 • 248pp • H/C (ISBN: 9781799826682) • US $195.00

Challenges and Applications of Data Analytics in Social Perspectives
V. Sathiyamoorthi (Sona College of Technology, India) and Atilla Elci (Aksaray University, Turkey)
Engineering Science Reference • © 2020 • 330pp • H/C (ISBN: 9781799825661) • US $245.00

Handling Priority Inversion in Time-Constrained Distributed Databases
Udai Shanker (Madan Mohan Malaviya University of Technology, India) and Sarvesh Pandey (Madan Mohan Malaviya University of Technology, India)
Engineering Science Reference • © 2020 • 338pp • H/C (ISBN: 9781799824916) • US $225.00

Feature Extraction and Classification Techniques for Text Recognition
Munish Kumar (Maharaja Ranjit Singh Punjab Technical University, India) Manish Kumar Jindal (Panjab University Regional Centre, Muktsar, India) Simpel Rani Jindal (Yadavindera College of Engineering, India) R. K. Sharma (Thapar Institute of Engineering & Technology, India) and Anupam Garg (Bhai Gurdas Institute of Engineering and Technology, India)
Engineering Science Reference • © 2020 • 300pp • H/C (ISBN: 9781799824060) • US $225.00

Neutrosophic Graph Theory and Algorithms
Florentin Smarandache (University of New Mexico, USA) and Said Broumi (Faculty of Science Ben M'Sik, University Hassan II, Morocco)
Engineering Science Reference • © 2020 • 406pp • H/C (ISBN: 9781799813132) • US $245.00

Handbook of Research on Big Data Clustering and Machine Learning
Fausto Pedro Garcia Marquez (Universidad Castilla-La Mancha, Spain)
Engineering Science Reference • © 2020 • 478pp • H/C (ISBN: 9781799801061) • US $285.00

701 East Chocolate Avenue, Hershey, PA 17033, USA
Tel: 717-533-8845 x100 • Fax: 717-533-8661
E-Mail: cust@igi-global.com • www.igi-global.com

Editorial Advisory Board

Table of Contents

Detailed Table of Contents

Information is the input for several transactions in blockchain technology and AI algorithms. Information in the net is scattered everyplace and controlled by totally different stakeholders. The net is hard to authorize or validate. In this chapter, the authors have a tendency to propose a completely unique approach. Bury Planetary Classification System and Ethereum offer safer information storing, sharing, computing within the large-scale net atmosphere. Here the authors have a tendency to square measure desegregation of two key components: 1) blockchain-based information sharing with possession guarantee and trustworthy information sharing within the large-scale atmosphere to make real huge information and 2) AI-based mostly secured computing technology to supply a lot of intelligent security policies to make a trustworthy net. Bury Planetary classification system makes it attainable to distribute high volumes of knowledge with high potency and no duplication.

Chapter 2

Unprecedented advancement in wireless technology, storage, and computing power of portable devices with the gigabyte speed of internet connectivity enables the possibility of communication among machine to machine. IoT has a different way to connect many nodes simultaneously to store, access, and share the information to improve the quality of life by the elimination of the involvement of human. Irrespective of unlimited benefit, IoT has so many issues that arise to eclipse IoT in reality because of its centralized model. Scalability, reliability, privacy, and security challenges are rising because of the huge numbers of IoT nodes, centralized architecture, and complex networks. Centralized architecture may lead to problems like a single point of failure, single way traffic, huge infrastructure cost, privacy, security, and single source of trust. Therefore, to overcome the issues of the centralized infrastructure of the IoT, the authors diverted to decentralized infrastructure. It may be the best decision in terms of performance, reliability, security, privacy, and trust. Blockchain is an influential latest decentralization technology to decentralize computation, process management, and trust. A combination of blockchain with IoT may have the potential to solve scalability, reliability, privacy, and security issues of IoT. This chapter has an overview of some important consensus algorithms, IoT challenges, integration of the blockchain with IoT, its challenges, and future research issues of a combination of blockchain and IoT are also discussed.

    Randhir Kumar, National Institute of Technology, Raipur, India
    Rakesh Tripathi, National Institute of Technology, Raipur, India

There are many critical applications working with blockchain-based technology including the financial sector, healthcare, and supply chain management. The fundamental application of blockchain is Bitcoin, which was primarily designed for the financial value transfer. Owing to the feature of decentralized storage structure, immutability, integrity, availability, and reliability of transactions, the blockchain has become the need of the current industry like VANET. However, presently, not much work has been done in order to mitigate the redundancy in the distributed ledger. Hence, the authors arrive at the intelligible conclusion to detect a similar transaction that can mitigate the redundancy of transaction in a distributed ledger. In this chapter, they are addressing two main challenges in blockchain technology: firstly, how to minimize the storage size of blockchain distributed ledger and, secondly, detecting the similar transaction in the distributed ledger to mitigate the redundancy. To detect similar transaction from the distributed ledger they have applied the average hash technique.

    Keesara Sravanthi Reddy, IT Department, Vallurupalli Nageswara Rao Vignana Jyothi
        Institute of Engineering and Technology, India

Due to recent development in technology and smart devices in people's lives, their lives are becoming easier and safer. One of popular examples in todays is parking (i.e., people find free parking space without moving a long distance or consuming more time or fuel over the road network). Today many automated companies are designing vehicles, but we are still unable to get automatic parking system in an area. Finding free parking slot/space has a probability of revealing user's privacy (i.e., either by service provider to third party/attacker or submitted information [user personal information] can be hacked by an attacker [via performing attacks like Man in Middle, Denial of Service, etc.]). Hence, privacy is a main issue in parking. Providing sufficient privacy in parking to vehicle users is a primary concern of this chapter. For that, this chapter used the blockchain technology to avoid privacy issues (raised in parking searching). Blockchain technology makes reservation of parking slot transparent, decentralized, and secure (privacy-preserved).

    Devesh Kumar Srivastava, SCIT, Manipal University, Jaipur, India
    Saksham Birendra Bhatt, SCIT, Manipal University, Jaipur, India
    Divyangana, SCIT, Manipal University, Jaipur, India

Blockchain could be called a string of blocks that acts like a ledger that is also distributed. Members in a defined P2P network are given access to the blockchain and can create new blocks. When the data is stored in a blockchain, changing it becomes virtually impossible. The data stored within blocks is timestamped to avoid tampering. Blockchain has applications in numerous fields like IoT, digital currency, financial services, reputation systems, smart contracts, security services, etc. If any virtual or real asset transaction is happening online, blockchain technology can be easily applied to optimize and secure the transaction better. Blockchain-based applications bring controversies, and yet many exceptional and diverse use-cases have been found for blockchain in both financial and non-financial sectors. Although it holds immense promise, it doesn't come without risks and uncertainties. This chapter elucidates the growing risks and uncertainties which accompany the use of blockchain in automated systems.

Chapter 6

Blockchain is the upcoming new information technology that could have quite a lot of significant future applications. In this chapter, the communication network for the reliable environment of intelligent vehicle systems is considered along with how the blockchain technology generates trust network among intelligent vehicles. It also discusses different factors that are effecting or motivating automotive industry, data-driven intelligent transportation system (D2ITS), structure of VANET, framework of intelligent vehicle data sharing based on blockchain used for intelligent vehicle communication and decentralized autonomous vehicles (DAV) network. It also talks about the different ways the autonomous vehicles use blockchain. Block-VN distributed architecture is discussed in detail. The different challenges of research and privacy and security of vehicular network are discussed.

Chapter 7

The chapter suggests an iterative social system in which individuals and totals use a development, watch its arranged and unintended outcomes, and after that, build new improvements. Blockchain development has the potential to construct productivity, capability, straight imposition, and disintermediation in shared worth or information exchange. This chapter proposes how the blockchain will be implemented in developing and non-developing countries. These countries can use the blockchain for financial services, transportation, healthcare, e-marketplace, etc. And what is the risk and danger of using blockchain in non-developed countries?

    Priti Gupta, Banaras Hindu University, India

    Abhishek Kumar, Banaras Hindu University, India

    Achintya Singhal, Banaras Hindu University, India

    Shantanu Saurabh, The Maharaja Sayajirao University of Baroda, India

    V. D. Ambeth Kumar, Department of Computer Science and Engineering, Panimalar
        Engineering College, Anna University, Chennai, India

Blockchain provides innovative ideas for storing information, executing transactions, performing functions, creating trust in an open environment, etc. Even though cryptographers, mathematicians, and coders have been trying to bring the most trustable protocols to get authentication guarantee over various systems, blockchain technology is secure with no central authority in an open network system because of a large distributed network of independent users. If anyone tries to change the blockchain database, the current hash will also change, which does not match with the previous hash. In this way, blockchain creates privacy and trust in digital data by removing malleability attacks. In this chapter, security and privacy on the blockchain has been focused. The safety and privacy of blockchain are mainly engrossed on two things: firstly, uncovering few attacks suffered by blockchain systems and, secondly, putting specific and advanced proposals against such attacks.

    Brahim Lejdel, Univeristy of El Oued, El Oued, Algeria

In the near future, the electric vehicle (EV) will be the most used in the word. Thus, the energy management of its battery is the most attractive subject specialty in the last decade. Thus, if a driver uses an electric vehicle, he wants to find an optimal method that can optimize the energy battery of its electric vehicle. In this chapter, the authors propose a new concept of the smart electric vehicle (SEV) that can manage, control, and optimize the energy of its battery, in condition to satisfy the drivers' and passengers' comfort. Thus, they use a hybrid approach based on the multi-agent system and the genetic algorithm (MAS-GA).

    Arnab Kumar Show, Banaras Hindu University, India

    Abhishek Kumar, Banaras Hindu University, India

    Achintya Singhal, Banaras Hindu University, India

    Gayathri N., Galgotias University, India

    K. Vengatesan, Sanjivani College of Engineering, Savitribai Phule University, India

The autonomous industry has rapidly grown for self-driving cars. The main purpose of autonomous industry is trying to give all types of security, privacy, secured traffic information to the self-driving cars. Blockchain is another newly established secured technology. The main aim of this technology is to provide more secured, convenient online transactions. By using this new technology, the autonomous industry can easily provide more suitable, safe, efficient transportation to the passengers and secured traffic information to the vehicles. This information can easily gather by the roadside units or by the passing vehicles. Also, the economical transactions can be possible more efficiently since blockchain technology allows peer-to-peer communications between nodes, and it also eliminates the need of the third party.

This chapter proposes a concept of how the autonomous industry can provide more adequate, proper, and safe transportation with the help of blockchain. It also examines for the possibility that autonomous vehicles can become the future of transportation.

Chapter 11

Jenila Livingston L. M., Vellore Institute of Technology, India
Ashutosh Satapathy, Vellore Institute of Technology, India
Agnel Livingston L. G. X., St. Xavier's Catholic College of Engineering, India
Merlin Livingston L. M., Jeppiaar Institute of Technology, India

In secure multi-party computation (SMC), multiple distributed parties jointly carry out the computation over their confidential data without compromising data security and privacy. It is a new emerging cryptographic technique used in huge applications such as electronic auction bidding, electronic voting, protecting personal information, secure transaction processing, privacy preserving data mining, and privacy preserving cooperative control of connected autonomous vehicles. This chapter presents two model paradigms of SMC (i.e., ideal model prototype and real model prototype). It also deals with the type and applications of adversaries, properties, and the techniques of SMC. The three prime types of SMC techniques such as randomization, cryptographic techniques using oblivious transfer, and anonymization methods are discussed and illustrated by protective procedures with suitable examples. Finally, autonomous vehicle interaction leveraged with blockchain technology to store and use vehicle data without any human interaction is also discussed.

Chapter 12

Siddharth M. Nair, Vellore Institute of Technology, Chennai, India
Varsha Ramesh, Vellore Institute of Technology, Chennai, India
Amit Kumar Tyagi, Vellore Institute of Technology, Chennai, India

The major issues and challenges in blockchain over internet of things are security, privacy, and usability. Confidentiality, authentication, and control are the challenges faced in security issue. Hence, this chapter will discuss the challenges and opportunities from the prospective of security and privacy of data in blockchain (with respect to security and privacy community point of view). Furthermore, the authors will provide some future trends that blockchain technology may adapt in the near future (in brief).

Chapter 13

Abhishek Bhattacharya, Independent Researcher, India

The world is going digital, and the wave of automation is sweeping across all facets of our corporate and personal lives. Industry 4.0 is all about leveraging IoT (internet of things) devices to facilitate further the process of automation that helps all organisations to rapidly scale by leveraging technology. The amount of data and information generated by the connected things is being harnessed with the help of advanced algorithm empowered analytics to induce intelligence into all the actions undertaken for the functioning of these connected devices. This chapter is geared towards giving a representative outlook on the concepts of blockchain that see a base in the concepts of cybersecurity. Further to that, this chapter explores the very imminent use cases of what we call the Industry 4.0. This includes use cases from remmitance, insurance, governance, internet of things (IoT), and supply chain, including the kinds of challenges we currently face.

Chapter 14

Blockchain as a service has evolved significantly from where it started as an underlying technology for Bitcoin cryptocurrency when introduced in 2008. Realization of the immense opportunities this technology possesses encouraged the development of several other Blockchain solutions such as Ethereum, which focused more on the unique competencies much beyond just the digital currency. In this chapter, the authors provided insights into the unmatchable capabilities of Blockchain to evade cyber-attacks that can facilitate a much-needed push for the scalable operation of autonomous vehicles by providing a safer and trustable ecosystem through smart contracts. The chapter also discusses the integration of Ethereum Blockchain with Confidential Consortium Framework (CFF) to overcome the shortcomings of Blockchain in terms of speed and volume. Towards the end, they talked about some of the modern technologies such as IoT and AI that can be benefitted by Blockchain.

Chapter 15

Clinical research comprises participation from patients. Often there are concerns of enrolment from patients. Hence, it has to face various challenges related to personal data, such as data sharing, privacy and reproducibility, etc. Patients and researchers need to track a set plan called study protocol. This protocol spans through various stages such as registration, collection and analysis of data, report generation, and finally, results in publication of findings. The Blockchain technology has emerged as one of the possible solutions to these challenges. It has a potential to address all the problem associated with clinical research. It provides the comfort for building transparent, secure services relying on trusted third party. This technology enables one to share the control of the data, security, and the parameters with a single patient or a group of patients or any other stakeholders of clinical trial. This chapter addresses the use of blockchain in execution of secure and trusted clinical trials.

Preface

The Blockchain is the best new tool of the decade. However, at the beginning of 2019, this subject is still experiencing a severe lack of understanding and awareness on the part of the general public. This is a problematic starting point for the full success of its evolution. As a revolutionary technology, Blockchain provides a practical solution to enable a secure and decentralized public ledger that a huge plethora of exciting new technology applications in several areas, such as the Internet of Things (IoT), Cyber-Physical Systems, Manufacturing, and Supply-Chain Management, etc. Blockchain technology has infiltrated all areas of our lives, from manufacturing to healthcare and beyond. Cybersecurity is an industry that has been significantly affected by this technology and maybe more so in the future. Blockchain Technology is defined as a decentralized system of distributed registers that are used to record data transactions on multiple computers. The reason this technology has gained popularity is that you can put any digital asset or transaction in the blocking chain, the industry does not matter. Blockchain technology can be used to prevent any data breach, identity theft, cyber-attacks or criminal acts in transactions. This ensures that data remains private and secure. We extend this concept for Automated Vehicles and attract researcher's attention (from around the globe) for overcoming issues and challenges and suggest useful solutions for the Future Vehicles of Tomorrow.

Building trust in machines and in people is always an essential requirement. A new concept for building trust (as distributed and de-centralized network) was coined in 2008 in form of cryptocurrency, i.e., as Bitcoin. Today's use of Blockchain concept has been moved to several revolutions. For example, Blockchain 1.0 is related to launching of Bitcoin (a New Cryptocurrency), Blockchain 2.0 is related to Ethereum Rise (as Smart Contracts), Blockchain 3.0 is related to next Generation Technology without mining-DApps, in last Blockchain 4.0 is related to making Blockchain concept usable in Industry (i.e., for real-world's applications). However, there is more to Blockchain technology than Bitcoin Cryptocurrency due to having secured, trusted and privacy preserved network/ tarnation. Generally, transactions stored in Blockchains (or blocks) are more secured than data stored in traditional databases (each block in a Blockchain is having information/ address about previous and next blocks). Such transactions cannot be altered, there is transparency in the transaction between the parties using the Blockchain (every peer node contains every transaction's record in a Blockchain). In other words, concept of cryptocurrency was coined by Blockchain technology, after that, many cryptocurrency flows into the market. But today's Blockchain is being used in different sectors of the economy to build trust (note that there trust serves as a corner stone till now). In current era, deploying block chain solutions is becoming more usual in many applications/ sectors. For example, several countries are trying to use Blockchain concept for storing election results safely and securely. Also, some financial institutions are using Blockchain for International money transfer. As another example, in logistics, Blockchain is used for supply chain management and tracking of goods/ products. There is a lot of long list where this novel concept is being used now days. As its biggest advantages, this technology is shifted to industry (as revolution 4.0), i.e., autonomous driving systems (as cyber physical systems) to track vehicles, storing their information safely and securely (during parking, carpooling or travelling over the road network). Hence, today's Blockchain Technology is becoming a Disruptive and Emerging Technology for future (with providing many opportunities to industries). Based on such tremendous uses, this book is aimed at highlighting the various possibilities inherent in Blockchain for autonomous driving systems/ autonomous applications/ vehicles and the added value Block chain can provide for the future of these different sectors. This book discusses Blockchain technology for building next generation secure decentralized, distributed and trusted automated environment and enhancing the productivity of several autonomous applications (like autonomous vehicles, autonomous machine in nuclear plant etc.). This book on Blockchain technology for autonomous applications provides high interest to readers and serves as a motivator for further exploration. This book tries to include Hot topics and chapters on relevant topics like Blockchain for Industry 4.0, Blockchain with Artificial Intelligence, etc. In summary, this book provides the reader with the most up-to-date knowledge of Blockchain in mainstream areas of security, trust, and privacy in the decentralized domain, which is timely and essential (this is due to the fact that the distributed and P2P applications is increasing day-by-day, and the attackers adopt new mechanisms to threaten the security and privacy of the users in those environments). This book also provides the technical information regarding Blockchain-oriented software. This book will encourage both researchers and practitioners to share and exchange their experiences and recent studies between academia and industry, also will provide useful information to readers (in-depth) on Blockchain based Autonomous Vehicles in various applications.

Hence, the overview of this book can be summarized as:

Chapter 1: A Review to Leverage the Integration of Blockchain and Artificial Intelligence

In Blockchain and AI application the primary requirement is data for executing transactions. This chapter proposed completely unique approach based on Bury Planetary Classification System and Ethereum to alter safer information storing, sharing, computing within the large-scale net atmosphere.

Chapter 2: Comprehensive Study on Incorporation of Blockchain Technology With IoT Enterprises

The internet of things provides exceptional advancement in wireless technology, storage and computing power by making communication possible between object to object. It improves the quality of life of human being. The chapter focus on scalability, reliability, privacy, and security challenges are rising because of the huge numbers of IoT nodes, centralized architecture and complex networks.

Chapter 3: Content-Based Transaction Access From Distributed Ledger of Blockchain Using Average Hash Technique

Blockchain-based technology is applied to variety of critical applications such as financial sector, health care, supply chain management. The primary way of transferring financial value is via Bitcoin. In this chapter, an intelligible system is proposed to detect a similar transaction that can mitigate the redundancy of transaction in a distributed ledger.

Chapter 4: Blockchain-Enabled Decentralization Service for Automated Parking Systems

Due to recent development in technology and increment in smart devices in people's life, their life is becoming easier and safe to live. One of popular example in todays is parking. In this chapter author used the Blockchain technology to avoid privacy issues (raised in parking searching). Blockchain technology makes reservation of parking slot transparent, decentralized and secure (privacy-preserved).

Chapter 5: Blockchain Risk and Uncertainty in Automated Applications

Blockchain technology can be easily applied, to optimize and make the transaction more secure. Blockchain based applications bring controversies and yet, many exceptional, and diverse use-cases have been found for Blockchain in both financial and non-financial sectors. This chapter explains the growing risks and uncertainties which accompany the use of Blockchain in automated systems

Chapter 6: Blockchain-Autonomous Driving Systems

Blockchain is the upcoming new information technology and applied in Data-Driven Intelligent Transportation System for Intelligent Vehicle Communication and Decentralized Autonomous Vehicles (DAV) network. This chapter proposes various challenges of research and Privacy and security of vehicular network.

Chapter 7: Reliable (Secure, Trusted, and Privacy Preserved) Cross-Blockchain Ecosystems for Developing and Non-Developing Countries

Blockchain development has the potential to construct productivity, capability, straight imposition, and disintermediation in shared worth or information exchange. This chapter proposes how the Blockchain will be implemented in developing and non-developing countries. These countries can use the Blockchain for financial services, transportation, healthcare, e-marketplace, etc. And what is the risk and danger are encounter in non-developed countries by using Blockchain is discussed.

Chapter 8: Security, Privacy and Trust Management, and Performance Optimization of Blockchain

Blockchain provides great support for storing information, executing transactions, performing functions, creating trust in an open environment etc. In this chapter, the author presents the security and privacy on the Blockchain. Further focus on uncovering few attacks suffered by Blockchain systems and advanced proposals against such attacks.

Chapter 9: Hybrid Approach for Optimizing Energy of Electric Vehicle in Smart Cities

Electric Vehicle (EV) is the most attractive subject in the last decade. This will be the most used in the word. Driver uses an electric vehicle, to find an optimal method that can optimize the energy battery of its electric vehicle. In this paper, the author propose a new concept of the Smart Electric Vehicle (SEV) that can manage, control and optimize the energy of its battery, in condition to satisfy the drivers' and passengers' comfort using a hybrid approach based on the Multi-Agent System and the Genetic Algorithm (MAS-GA).

Chapter 10: Future Blockchain Technology for Autonomous Applications/Autonomous Vehicle

There are many critical applications are working with blockchain-based technology including the financial sector, health care, and supply chain management. In this chapter, the author addressed two main challenges in blockchain technology firstly, how to minimize the storage size of blockchain distributed ledger and secondly, detecting the similar transaction in the distributed ledger to mitigate the redundancy. To detect similar transaction from the distributed ledger we have applied the average hash technique.

Chapter 11: Blockchain Security Using Secure Multi-Party Computation

Secure Multi-Party Computation (SMC), is a new emerging cryptographic technique used in huge applications such as electronic auction bidding, electronic voting, protecting personal information, secure transaction processing, privacy preserving data mining and privacy preserving cooperative control of connected autonomous vehicles. This chapter presents two model paradigms of SMC viz. ideal model prototype and real model prototype.

Chapter 12: Issues and Challenges (Privacy, Security, and Trust) in Blockchain-Based Applications

The major issue in Blockchain over internet of things is pertaining to security, privacy and usability, if a user wants to keep his data confidentially but the hacker or attacker can inject some public key to steal something from someone. Confidentiality, Integrity, and Authentication are the challenges faced in security issue. Hence, this chapter will discuss challenges and opportunities from the prospective of security and privacy of data in Blockchain.

Chapter 13: Blockchain, Cybersecurity, and Industry 4.0

Industry 4.0 is all about leveraging IOT (Internet of things) devices to facilitate further the process of automation that helps all organisations to rapidly scale by leveraging technology. The amount of data and information generated by the connected things is being harnessed with the help of advanced algorithm empowered analytics to induce intelligence into all the actions undertaken for the functioning of these connected devices. The author explores the very imminent use cases of what we call as the Industry 4.0

including Remmitance, Insurance, Governance, Internet of Things (IoT), and Supply Chain, including the kinds of challenges we currently face.

Chapter 14: Use of Smart Contracts and Distributed Ledger for Automation

Blockchain with the help of Bitcoin cryptocurrency provide immense opportunities for development of several other Blockchain solutions such as Ethereum, which focused more on the unique competencies much beyond just the digital currency. In this chapter author discusses the integration of Ethereum Blockchain with Confidential Consortium Framework (CFF) to overcome the shortcomings of Blockchain in terms of speed and volume.

Chapter 15: Blockchain in Clinical Trials

The Blockchain technology has emerged as one of the possible solution for clinical research. It has a potential to address all the problem associated with patient details. It provides the comfort for building transparent, secure services relying on trusted third party and also enables sharing the control of the data, security and the parameters with a single patient or a group of patients or any other stakeholders of clinical trial. This chapter addresses the use of Blockchain in execution of secure and trusted clinical trials.

Acknowledgment

First of all, we would extend our gratitude to our Family Members, Friends, and Supervisors, which stood with us as an advisor in completing this book. Also, we would like to thank our almighty "God" who makes us to write this book. We also thank IGI Global Staff (who has provided their continuous support during this COVID 19 Pandemic) and our colleagues with whom we have work together inside the college/ university and others outside of the college/university who have provided their support.

Also, we would like to thank our Respected Madam, Prof. G Aghila, and our Respected Sir Prof. N. Sreenath for giving their valuable inputs and helping us in completing this book.

Amit Kumar Tyagi
Vellore Institute of Technology, Chennai, India

Gillala Rekha
K. L. University, India

N. Sreenath
Pondicherry Engineering College, India

Chapter 1
A Review to Leverage the Integration of Blockchain and Artificial Intelligence

rangu manjula

KU College of Engineering and Technology, India

ABSTRACT

Information is the input for several transactions in blockchain technology and AI algorithms. Information in the net is scattered everyplace and controlled by totally different stakeholders. The net is hard to authorize or validate. In this chapter, the authors have a tendency to propose a completely unique approach. Bury Planetary Classification System and Ethereum offer safer information storing, sharing, computing within the large-scale net atmosphere. Here the authors have a tendency to square measure desegregation of two key components: 1) blockchain-based information sharing with possession guarantee and trustworthy information sharing within the large-scale atmosphere to make real huge information and 2) AI-based mostly secured computing technology to supply a lot of intelligent security policies to make a trustworthy net. Bury Planetary classification system makes it attainable to distribute high volumes of knowledge with high potency and no duplication.

INTRODUCTION

Blockchain

An increasing quantity of private information, internet looking out behavior, client calls, user preferences, location data is being mutely collected by sensors within the product from huge firms, that results in high complexness on privacy run of knowledge homeowners (Wang et al., 2019). presently there's no reliable thanks to record however the information is employed and by United Nations agency and has few strategies to trace or penalize the violators United Nations agency abuse the information (Nebula Ai (NBAI), 2018).

DOI: 10.4018/978-1-7998-3295-9.ch001

Blockchain was introduced within the year 2009, by Santoshi Nakamoto for implementing virtual currency Bitcoin. Blockchain technology started new era in decentralization. In Block chain all the transactions associated information square measure recorded in an exceedingly immutable ledger in a verifiable, secure, clear and permanent means. the knowledge is hold on in an exceedingly chain of knowledge blocks permitting entities to retrieve, validate, trace, and verify all the transactions, sequences, associated temporal order of actions taken in an scheme providing transparency, trust, and responsiveness. Blockchain technology has accomplished a fantastic rate in gift and future. Example freelance blockchain specialists saw demand rate as high as 6000% in 2018. By 2025 100% of the GDP are hold on blockchain technology. $176 billion of business are price additional by blockchain by 2025 so surge to exceed $3.1trillion by 2030.

Basically, blockchain may be a chain of blocks that frame the ledger. This ledger holds a permanent record of transactions and interactions. Sensible contracts square measure codes that may be dead by the blockchain nodes. A wise contract may be a self-executing code that may verify the implementation of predefined terms and conditions (Bocek et al., 2017). A wise contract is triggered by consigning a group action to its Ethereum address and capital punishment it betting on the input given for that group action.

Blockchain may be a shared, replicated, and permission ledger with agreement, provenance, fixity, and decisiveness. The shared ledger ensures that participants will decide that assets to share and permits them to grasp the identity of the opposite participants that they're addressing. Blockchain conjointly provides participants with demonstrable endorsement, that comes with confidentiality — data shared solely on a need-to-know basis. It's no secret that blockchain and blockchain applications aren't resistant to cyber-attacks and fraud. Here square measure many examples:

The Decentralized Autonomous Organization (DAO), a risk capital fund operative through a suburbanised blockchain galvanized by bit coin, was robbed of quite $60 million price of Ether digital currency (about simple fraction of its value) through code exploitation. A thieving of nearly $73 million price of customers' bit coins from one in every of the world's largest cryptocurrency exchanges, Hong-Kong-based Bit finer, incontestable that the currency continues to be a giant risk. The possible cause was purloined keys.

When Bithumb, one in every of the most important Ethereum and bitcoin cryptocurrency exchanges within the world, was recently hacked, the information of thirty,000 users were compromised, and $870,000 price of bitcoin was purloined. despite the fact that it absolutely was Associate in Nursing employee's pc that was hacked — not the core servers — this event raised questions on the general security. Addressing and examining the key security issues/risks for blockchain helps make sure the security of blockchain solutions. Security risks related to blockchain-based solutions. Security is regarding risk management, thus it's vital to begin with Associate in Nursing understanding of the risks related to blockchain solutions. the particular risks of a blockchain resolution depend upon the kind of blockchain being employed. Let's take a glance at the varied sorts of blockchains with decreasing levels of risk and increasing levels of security:

Public blockchains square measure public and anyone will be a part of them and validate transactions. they're usually additional risky (for example, cryptocurrencies). This includes risks wherever anyone is a part of the blockchain with none level of management or restrictions. personal blockchains square measure restricted and typically restricted to business networks; membership is controlled by one entity (regulator) or pool. Permission less blockchains haven't any restrictions on processors. Permissioned blockchains enable the ledger to be encrypted in order that solely relevant participants will see it, and solely those that meet a need-to-know criterion will rewrite it. There square measure many alternative risks with blockchain solutions, and that they are generally categorised into 3 areas:

Business and governance: Business risks embrace money implications, reputational factors, and compliance risks. Governance risks emanate primarily from the suburbanised nature of blockchain solutions, and need sturdy controls on call criteria, governing policies, identity, and access management.

Process: These risks square measure related to the varied processes that a blockchain resolution needs in its design and operations.

Technology: The underlying technology want to implement varied processes and business desires might not continually be the simplest alternative, and this may ultimately result in security risks.

AI INTRODUCTION

AI is creating one in every of the most important ideas that has tremendous impact to the digital community and our world. Computer science was initially recognized at Dartmouth College in 1956. AI covers an oversized vary of machine intelligence from easy text to speech to application of autonomous vehicles and craft. Today, AI is showing in our homes, cars, businesses, buildings, mobile phones, and appliances from operator assistants to mapping package to produce the foremost effective routes to your required locations. AI is enjoying a serious role in providing prescriptive analysis and proposals to establishments, governments and researchers on choices and patterns that aren't as apparent on the surface. The trust less relationship among totally different information stake holders considerably prevents the information sharing within the whole net. in order that the information used for computer science analysing is proscribed in quantity and in selection. one in every of the newest rising technologies is computer science, that makes the machine mimic human behaviour. the foremost vital part wants to sight cyber-attacks or malicious activities is that the Intrusion Detection System (IDS&#41. Computer science plays a dynamic role in perceiving intrusions and generally thought-about because the higher method in adapting and building IDS. In modern days, computer science algorithms square measure growing as a novel computing technique which can be applied to actual time problems. In current days, neural network algorithms square measure rising as a brand-new computer science technique that may be applied to time period issues (Kanimozhi & Jacob, 2019).

BLOCKCHAIN AND AI

Blockchain with AI introduced new options to the traditional distributed architectures, that cover decentralization with shared management, immutable audit trails, and native quality exchanges. Combined infrastructure facilitates users with new information models, shared management of coaching information and models, and increased trustiness on information. computer science desires huge information, that is provided by blockchain, for manufacturing higher information models (Salan et al., n.d.). With the idea of blockchain technologies there's a hopeful, economical thanks to modify trust information sharing in distributed and suburbanised atmosphere. this may facilitate computer science create additional correct selections that deals with real immense information collected from varied places within the net. secNet (Wang et al., 2019) used personal information Centre (PDC) to boost the protection of information sharing and for the protection of the total network. every PDC is a secured still as centralized physical house for every secNet user wherever his/her information lives. In paper (Blockchain-Base Structures, 2018) remote-controlled Aerial Vehicles — UAVs, or drones — square measure currently being operated by many military forces and presently, to a additional restricted extent, by non-combatant organizations. These latter operations, however, could eventually expand to exceed, in range and variety, those of the military. additional expected development in battery capability, construction materials and package, particularly concerning machine learning algorithms and drone integration, will certainly increase UAVs' autonomous. distinctive risks related to UAVs like risk of hackers' attacks to intercept the management also are increasing. additional incidents possible can occur once rules square measure finalized that encourage additional use that's widespread. Such incidents may end in multi-million greenback claims against businesses, operators and makers. Blockchain is that the basis technology for cryptocurrencies. However, Blockchain will have so much larger applications within the field of UAVs, as a result of Blockchain is very distributed and brazenly visible system of consecutive connected cryptographically.

As complementary technologies, AI and blockchain will deliver vital blessings across a range of fields, that embrace analytics, health care, money services and plenty of additional. the 2 technologies have still largely been unbroken separate, however initial tries to mix them have seen attention-grabbing applications unfold. one in every of the earliest ideas of AI and blockchain integration revolves around information analysis. very similar to centralized information sets, blockchain offers AI a vast base to gather and analyse from to uncover higher insights and solutions. not like off-chain storage, however, blockchain information remains secure and immutable even within the case of storage failure. Blockchain agreement. conjointly mean that the information being employed is additional clear and fewer susceptible to meddling. Another key issue AI has is access to computing power. additional powerful AI engines need additional process capability, in distinction with hardware and cloud-based solutions that exhibit vital scaling problems. victimisation blockchain would mean that AI will access shared pools of computing power across networks, effectively scaling on demand. On the opposite hand, AI machine learning may considerably scale back the facility consumption and needs for mining coins. Another attention-grabbing application for AI and blockchain lies within the net of Things (IoT). As IoT devices become additional commonplace, blockchain is Associate in Nursing optimum technology to support the infrastructure, and AI may function a perfect manager of huge suburbanised networks.

CHALLENGES OF INTEGRATION AI AND BLOCKCHAIN

Even with huge shared potential, there square measure still some vital challenges that AI and blockchain should resolve to become really viable as a try. Despite blockchain's tremendous potential for information accessibility, privacy remains an oversized concern on public blockchains. whereas the goal is to democratize information, the presence of presumably sensitive information from IoT and alternative devices may raise some privacy problems for people and organizations alike. One resolution would be to use personal blockchains that limits the provision of information to solely those that own the chains. to boot, measurability remains a difficulty on major blockchains, that weren't designed to handle the large demands expected of them presently. Ethereum, one in every of the foremost common blockchains for development, will still solely method roughly 15transactions per second, and although alternative blockchains currently claim to be process thousands of transactions per second, for the foremost half, laborious proof supporting their claims remains absent. Finally, sensible contract technology presents a hurdle, particularly for AI. Security problems stay an oversized challenge, and therefore the settled nature of sensible contract execution may be a drawback for AI engines, that typically need a additional random approach to execution.

ETHEREUM AND IPFS

January 2014: the event of the Ethereum platform was in public proclaimed. the first Ethereum development team consisted of Vitalik Buterin, Mihai Alisie, Anthony Di Iorio, and Charles Hoskinson began work on a next-generation blockchain that had the ambitions to implement a general, totally trust less sensible contract platform. Ethereum may be a blockchain based mostly open supply distributed platform that allows to program sensible contracts (Wood, 2014). Ethereum uses Ether as a coinage for creating payments for the transactions distributed on the Ethereum blockchain. every participant within the Ethereum network is acknowledged identically by Associate in Nursing Ethereum Address. The Ethereum platform is being employed to form applications across a broad vary of services and industries. However, developers square measure in unchartered territory, thus it's laborious to grasp that apps can succeed and which of them can fail. Here square measure many exciting comes. Ethereum may be a spectacular public experiment that's showing the worth of sensible contracts on a public blockchain. it's the results of and therefore the supply of tumultuous innovation of the likes that we tend to haven't seen since the first days of the web.

- Weifund provides Associate in Nursing open platform for crowdfunding campaigns that leverages sensible contracts. It permits contributions to be was contractually backed digital assets that may be used, listed or sold at intervals the Ethereum scheme.
- Uport provides users with a secure and convenient thanks to take complete management of their identity and private data. rather than wishing on government establishments and surrendering their identities to 3rd parties, user's management World Health Organization will access and use their information and private data.
- BlockApps is trying to produce the best method for enterprises to make, manage and deploy blockchain applications. From the proof of idea to full production systems and integration with heritage systems, Blockapps provides all the tools necessary to form personal, semi-private and public industry-specific blockchain applications.
- Provenance is victimisation Ethereum to create opaque provide chains additional clear. By tracing the origins and histories of merchandise, the project aims {to build|to create|to create} Associate in Nursing open & accessible framework of knowledge thus customers will make advised selections after they purchase merchandise.

ETHEREUM VIRTUAL MACHINE

Ethereum may be a programmable blockchain. instead of offer users a group of pre-defined operations (e.g. bitcoin transactions), Ethereum permits users to form their own operations of any quality they want. during this method, it is a platform for several differing types of suburbanised blockchain applications, as well as however not restricted to cryptocurrencies. Ethereum within the slender sense refers to a set of protocols that outline a platform for suburbanised applications. At the guts of it's the Ethereum Virtual Machine, which may execute code of arbitrary algorithmic quality. In computing terms, Ethereum is "Turing complete". Developers will produce applications that run on the EVM victimisation friendly programming languages modelled on existing languages like JavaScript and Python. like all blockchain, Ethereum conjointly includes a node-to-node network protocol. The Ethereum blockchain information is maintained and updated by several nodes connected to the network. every and each node of the network runs the EVM and executes a similar direction. For this reason, Ethereum is usually delineate evocatively as a "world computer". This huge parallelization of computing across the complete Ethereum network isn't done to create computation additional economical. In fact, this method makes computation on Ethereum so much slower and costlier than on a conventional "computer". Rather, each Ethereum node runs the EVM so as to take care of agreement across the blockchain. suburbanised agreement offers Ethereum extreme levels of fault tolerance, ensures zero period, and makes information hold on the blockchain forever constant and censorship-resistant. The Ethereum platform itself is plain or value-agnostic. just like programming languages, it's up to entrepreneurs and developers to come to a decision what it ought to be used for. However, it's clear that bound application varieties profit quite others from Ethereum's capabilities. Specifically, Ethereum is suited to applications that modify direct interaction between peers or facilitate coordinated human action across a network. as an example, applications for coordinative peer-to-peer marketplaces, or the automation of complicated money contracts. Bitcoin permits for people to exchange money while not involving any middlemen like money establishments, banks, or governments. Ethereum's impact could also be additional comprehensive. In theory, money interactions or exchanges of any quality may be distributed mechanically and dependably victimisation code running on Ethereum. on the far side money applications, any environments wherever trust, security, and length square measure vital – for insurance, asset-registries, voting, governance, and therefore the net of things – may be massively compact by the Ethereum platform.

ETHEREUM WORK FLOW

Ethereum incorporates several options and technologies that may be acquainted to users of Bitcoin, whereas conjointly introducing several modifications and innovations of its own. Whereas the Bitcoin blockchain was strictly a listing of transactions, Ethereum is basic unit is that the account. The Ethereum blockchain tracks the state of each account, and every one state transitions on the Ethereum blockchain square measure transfers of import and data between accounts. There square measure 2 sorts of accounts:

- Externally in hand Accounts (EOAs), that square measure controlled by personal keys
- Contract Accounts, that square measure controlled by their contract code and might solely be "activated" by Associate in Nursing EOA

For most users, the fundamental distinction between these is that human user's management EOAs - as a result they'll management the personal keys that offer management over Associate in Nursing EOA. Contract accounts, on the opposite hand, square measure ruled by their internal code. If they're "controlled" by somebody's user, as a result of they are programmed to be controlled by Associate in Nursing EOA with a definite address, that is successively accomplished by whoever holds the personal keys that control that EOA. the popular term "smart contracts" refers to code during a Contract Account

– programs that execute once a group action is shipped to it account. Users will produce new contracts by deploying code to the blockchain. Contract accounts solely perform Associate in Nursing operation once taught {to dolto try to tolto try Associate in Nursingd do} thus by an EOA. So, it's unimaginable for a Contract account to be playing native operations like random range generation or API calls – it will do this stuff on condition that prompted by Associate in Nursing EOA. this is often as a result of Ethereum needs nodes to be able to agree on the result of computation, which needs a guarantee of strictly settled execution. Like in Bitcoin, users should pay tiny group action fees to the network. This protects the Ethereum blockchain from featherbrained or malicious process tasks, like DDoS attacks or infinite loops. The sender of a group action should get every step of the "program" they activated, as well as computation and memory storage. These fees square measure paid in amounts of Ethereum's native value-token, ether.

These group action fees square measure collected by the nodes that validate the network. These "miners" square measure nodes within the Ethereum network that receive, propagate, verify, and execute transactions. The miners then cluster the transactions – that embrace several updates to the "state" of accounts within the Ethereum blockchain – into what square measure known as "blocks", and miners then contend with each other for his or her block to be consecutive one to be another to the blockchain. Miners square measure rewarded with ether for every victorious block they mine. This provides the economic incentive for folks to dedicate hardware and electricity to the Ethereum network.

Just as within the Bitcoin network, miners square measure tasked with determination a posh mathematical drawback so as to with success "mine" a block. this is often called a "Proof of Work". Any process drawback that needs orders of magnitude additional resources to unravel algorithmically than it takes to verify the answer may be a sensible candidate for proof of labour. so as to discourage centralisation because of the employment of specialized hardware (e.g. ASICs), as has occurred within the Bitcoin network, Ethereum selected a memory-hard process drawback. If the matter needs memory still as central processing unit, the perfect hardware is actually the overall pc. This makes Ethereum's Proof of labour ASIC-resistant, permitting a additional suburbanised distribution of security than blockchains whose mining is dominated by specialised hardware, like Bitcoin.

Although normally related to Bitcoin, blockchain technology has several alternative applications that go method on the far side digital currencies. In fact, Bitcoin is merely one in every of many hundred applications that use blockchain technology nowadays. "[Blockchain] is to Bitcoin. a giant electronic system, on prime of that you'll be able to build applications. Currency is simply one.", building blockchain applications has needed a posh background in committal to writing, cryptography, arithmetic still as vital resources. However times have modified. Antecedently incredible applications, from electronic selection & digitally recorded property assets to regulative compliance square measure currently actively being developed and deployed quicker than ever before. By providing developers with the tools to make suburbanised applications, Ethereum is creating all of this potential. Like Bitcoin, Ethereum may be a distributed public blockchain network. Though there square measure some vital technical variations between the 2, the foremost vital distinction to notice is that Bitcoin and Ethereum take issue considerably in purpose and capability. Bitcoin offers one specific application of blockchain technology, a peer to look electronic money system that allows on-line Bitcoin payments. whereas the Bitcoin blockchain is employed to trace possession of digital currency (bitcoins), the Ethereum blockchain focuses on running the programming code of any suburbanised application.

In the Ethereum blockchain, rather than mining for bitcoin, miners work to earn Ether, a sort of crypto token that fuels the network. on the far side a tradeable cryptocurrency, Ether is additionally utilized by application developers to get group action fees and services on the Ethereum network. there's a second form of token that's wont to pay miners fees for as well as transactions in their block, it's known as gas, and each sensible contract execution needs a definite quantity of gas to be sent along side it to stimulate miners to place it within the blockchain. "Bitcoin is initial and foremost a currency; this is often one specific application of a blockchain. However, it's removed from the sole application. to require a past example of an analogous state of affairs, e-mail is one specific use of the web, and evidently helped popularise it, however there square measure several others." Dr Gavin Wood, Ethereum Co-Founder

SMART CONTRACT

Smart contract is simply a phrase want to describe a coding system that may facilitate the exchange of cash, content, property, shares, or something of import. once running on the blockchain a wise contract becomes sort of a self-operating bug that mechanically executes once specific conditions square measure met. as a result of sensible contracts run on the blockchain, they run precisely as programmed with none chance of censorship, downtime, fraud or third-party interference. whereas all blockchains have the power to method code, most square measure severely restricted. Ethereum is totally different. instead of giving a group of restricted operations, Ethereum permits developers to form no matter operations they need. this suggests developers will build thousands of various applications that go method on the far side something we've seen before. " [Ethereum] blockchain has some extraordinary capabilities. one in every of them is that you just will build sensible contracts. It's quite what it appears like. It's a contract that self-executes, and therefore the contract handles the social control, the management, performance, and payment" Don Tapscott

Before the creation of Ethereum, blockchain applications were designed to try and do a really restricted set of operations. Bitcoin and alternative cryptocurrencies, as an example, were developed completely to work as peer-to-peer digital currencies. Developers featured a haul. Either expand the set of functions offered by Bitcoin and alternative sorts of applications, that is incredibly sophisticated and long, or develop a brand new blockchain application and a wholly new platform still. Recognizing this difficulty, Ethereum's creator, Vitalik Buterin developed a brand new approach.

ETHEREUM AND USES

Ethereum permits developers to make and deploy suburbanised applications. A suburbanised application or Dapp serve some specific purpose to its users. Bitcoin, as an example, may be a Dapp that has its users with a peer to look electronic money system that allows on-line Bitcoin payments. as a result of suburbanised applications square measure created of code that runs on a blockchain network, they're not controlled by anyone or central entity. Any services that square measure centralized is suburbanised victimisation Ethereum. rely on all the mediator services that exist across many totally different industries. From obvious services like loans provided by banks to mediator services seldom thought of by the majority like title registries, selection systems, regulative compliance and far additional.

Ethereum also can be wont to build Decentralized Autonomous Organization (DAO). A DAO is totally Decentralized Autonomous Organization with no single leader. DAO's square measure go by programming code, on a set of sensible contracts written on the Ethereum blockchain. The code is meant to exchange the principles and structure of a conventional organization, eliminating the requirement for folks and centralized management. A DAO is in hand by everybody World Health Organization purchases tokens, however rather than every token equalisation to equity shares, tokens act as contributions that offer folks selection rights. "A DAO consists of 1 or additional contracts and will be funded by a bunch of similar people. A DAO operates utterly transparently and utterly severally of any human intervention, as well as its original creators. A DAO can be the network as long because it covers its survival prices and provides a helpful service to its client base".

Ethereum is additionally being employed as a platform to launch alternative crypto currencies. owing to the ERC20 token commonplace outlined by the Ethereum Foundation, alternative developers will issue their own versions of this token and lift funds with Associate in Nursing initial coin giving (ICO). during this fundraising strategy, the issuers of the token set Associate in Nursing quantity they need to lift, supply it during a crowd sale, and receive Ether in exchange. Billions of bucks are raised by ICOs on the Ethereum platform within the last 2 years, and one in every of the foremost valuable cryptocurrencies within the world, EOS, is Associate in Nursing ERC20 token.Ethereum has recently created a brand new commonplace known as the ERC721 token for pursuit distinctive digital assets. one in every of the most important use cases presently for such tokens is digital collectibles, because the infrastructure permits for folks to prove possession of scarce digital merchandise. several games square measure presently being designed victimisation this technology, like the long hit Crypto Kitties, a game wherever you'll be able to collect and breed digital cats.

Benefits of a suburbanised Ethereum Platform -Because suburbanised applications run on the blockchain, they take pleasure in all its properties.

Immutability – a 3rd party cannot create any changes to information.

Corruption & tamper proof – Apps square measure supported a network fashioned round the principle of agreement, creating censorship not possible.

Secure – With no central purpose of failure and secured victimisation cryptography, applications square measure well protected against hacking attacks and fallacious activities.

Despite transportation variety of advantages, suburbanised applications aren't perfect. As a result of sensible contract code is written by humans, sensible contracts square measure solely nearly as good because the folks that write them. Code bugs or oversights will result in accidental adverse actions being taken. If a slip-up within the code gets exploited, there's no economical method within which Associate in nursing attack or exploitation is stopped apart from getting a network agreement and redaction the underlying code. This goes against the essence of the blockchain that is supposed to be immutable. Also, Associate in nursing action taken by a central party raises serious questions on the suburbanised nature of an application.

There square measure many ways you'll be able to plug into the Ethereum network, one in every of the best ways in which is to use its native Mist browser. Mist provides an easy interface & digital notecase for users to trade & store Ether still as write, manage, deploy and use sensible contracts. Like internets browsers offer access and facilitate folks navigate the web, Mist provides a portal into the globe of suburbanised blockchain applications.

There is conjointly the MetaMask browser extension that turns Google Chrome into Associate in Nursing Ethereum browser. MetaMask permits anyone to simply run or develop suburbanised applications from their browser. Though at the start designed as Chrome plug-in, MetaMask supports Firefox and therefore the Brave Browser still.

BLOCKCHAIN / ETHEREUM: FILLING THE GAP

The job market is troubled to stay up with the sharp demand for blockchain developers. Some universities and personal corporations have responded by giving a spread of blockchain connected courses in an endeavour to fulfil the wants of the trade. In step with Bitcoin pioneer Jered Kenna, older blockchain professionals will internet over $200,000 USD in annual financial gain. "The provider of individuals that have in depth blockchain experiences is pretty low," Kenna explained. "And the demand is quickly increasing. Typically, they get 5 job offers on a daily basis." As a frontrunner within the blockchain community, Block geeks have organized our own courses to assist folks gain a bigger understanding of the technology and prime them for glorious opportunities within the job market. These categories aim to bring students up to hurry on blockchain technology, still as offer them sensible skills that may facilitate their careers.

APPS THAT SQUARE MEASURE PRESENTLY BEING DEVELOPED ON ETHEREUM

The Ethereum platform is being employed to form applications across a broad vary of services and industries. However, developer's square measure in unchartered territory, thus it's laborious to grasp that apps can succeed and which of them can fail. Here square measure many exciting come. Weifund provides Associate in Nursing open platform for crowd funding campaigns that leverages sensible contracts. It permits contributions to be was contractually backed digital assets that may be used, listed or sold at intervals the Ethereum eco system. Uport provides users with secure and convenient thanks to take complete management of their identity and private data. Rather than wishing on government establishments and surrendering their identities to 3rd parties, user's management World Health Organization will access and use their information and private data.

Blackcaps are trying to produce the best method for enterprises to make, manage and deploy blockchain applications. From the proof of idea to full production systems and integration with heritage systems, Block apps provides all the tools necessary to form personal, semi-private and public industry-specific blockchain applications.

Provenance is victimisation Ethereum to create opaque provide chains additional clear. By tracing the origins and histories of merchandise, the project aims {to build to create to create} Associate in Nursing open & accessible framework of knowledge thus customers will make advised selections after they purchase merchandise.

Augur is Associate in Nursing ASCII text file prediction market platform that permits anyone to forecast events and find rewarded for predicting them properly. Predictions on future globe events, like World Health Organization can win consecutive North American nation election, square measure distributed by mercantilism virtual shares. If an individual buys shares during a winning prediction, they receive financial rewards.

"Ethereum may be a spectacular public experiment that's showing the worth of sensible contracts on a public blockchain. It's the results of and therefore the supply of tumultuous innovation of the likes that we tend to haven't seen since the first days of the web." – Caleb bird genus London Trust Media.

The DAO was a project developed and programmed by a team behind another start up known as Slock. it. Their aim was to make a human less risk capital firm that might enable investors to create selections through sensible contracts. The DAO was funded through a token sale and over up raising around $150 million bucks from thousands of various folks.

Shortly once the funds were raised, The DAO was hacked by Associate in nursing unknown aggressor World Health Organization Scarf Ether price around $50 million bucks at the time. Whereas the attack was created potential by a technical flaw within the DAO package, not the Ethereum platform itself, the developers and founders of Ethereum were forced to upset the mess.

Ethereum relies on blockchain technology wherever all transactions square measure meant to be irreversible and constant. By capital punishment a tough fork and redaction the principles by that the blockchain executes, Ethereum set a dangerous precedent that goes against the terribly essence of blockchain. If the blockchain is modified on every occasion an oversized enough quantity of cash is concerned or enough folks get negatively compact, the blockchain can lose its main worth proposition – secure, anonymous, tamper proof.

While another less aggressive soft fork resolution was place forth, the Ethereum community and its founders were placed during a precarious position. If they didn't retrieve the purloined capitalist cash, confidence in Ethereum may be lost. On the opposite hand, ill capitalist cash needed actions that went against the core ideas of decentralization and set a dangerous precedent.

In the end, the bulk of the Ethereum community voted to perform a tough fork, and retrieve The DAO investors' cash. However not everybody united with this course of action. This resulted during a split wherever 2 parallel blockchains currently exist. For those members World Health Organization powerfully pain any changes to the blockchain even once hacking happens there's Ethereum classic. For the bulk World Health Organization united to rewrite a tiny part of the blockchain and come the purloined cash to their house owners, there's Ethereum.

Both blockchains have a similar options and square measure identical in each far to a definite block wherever the hard-fork was enforced. This suggests that everything that happened on Ethereum up till the hard-fork continues to be valid on the Ethereum Classic Blockchain. From the block wherever the laborious fork or amendment in code was dead onward, the 2 blockchains act on an individual basis.

A way forward for incredible potentialities. Despite the fallout from The DAO hack, Ethereum is moving forward and searching to a bright future. By providing an easy platform that allows folks to harness the facility of blockchain technology, Ethereum is rushing up the decentralization of the globe economy. Suburbanised applications have the potential to deeply disrupt many industries as well as finance, assets, academia, insurance, care and therefore the public sector amongst several others. "If you're thinking that the web has affected your life, Ethereum can have that very same pervasive influence on our communications, on our entire data infrastructure. It's reaching to impact all aspects of our existence

Building the general public Ethereum ecosystem: As measurability configurable privacy confidentiality grow public Ethereum over consecutive 2 years, customers use their blockchain identity access purpose (uPort) to act with a range of attention-grabbing early stage offerings. As well crowd funding platforms (Weifund), cluster governance tools (Boardroom), music/film/art content registration and utilization platforms (ujo), knowledge markets (Gnosis), and gambling apps (Virtue Poker)". Most important corporations can run business processes on their personal blockchains.

Private Blockchains: at intervals 2 years, major corporations can conduct many business processes on their own personal, permission company blockchains. Employees, customers, vendors, and repair suppliers at every company are going to be able to firmly access that company's personal blockchain via sturdy cryptographically genuine transactions. Consortia blockchains: In 2 years, several corporations can have begun to build bottom-up consortia blockchains with a tiny low range of counterparties in their scheme collaborating on a tiny low range of use cases to share sure source-of-truth infrastructure, provide or worth chains. Business use of public blockchains: Some corporations can use public Ethereum with their use cases that use a similar stack of blockchain parts that they need purchased or designed for his or her personal Ethereum-based implementations. The Ethereum platform is additionally serving to shift the method we tend to use the web. suburbanised applications square measure pushing a basic amendment from an online of knowledge wherever we will instantly read, exchange and communicate data to the web {of worth|useful|valuable|important |of import} wherever folks will exchange immediate value with none intermediaries.

As the trade continues to analyse blockchain platforms, it's apparent that Ethereum is turning into a de facto leader. As an example, many days gone JPMorgan in public open-sourced its gathering platform, architected and developed round the Go Ethereum consumer by Jeff Wilcke and his team. Many alternative major banks square measure victimisation Ethereum, and Microsoft is anchoring its Bletchley platform thereon because the foundational blockchain component. Industry, each in public and confidentially, continues to contribute to Ethereum and work with North American nation et al to assist our promising, toddler-age codebase reach maturity. Keep tuned for news on this front.

It takes a (global) village to lift a blockchain. The live network and therefore the community of open supply developers contribute considerably to the present effort. They ceaselessly refine and harden the Ethereum platform, serving to it get quicker at responding to trade demands for the worth propositions it offers. Whereas it's still youth and there'll little question be additional hurdles to beat, Ethereum appearance to be a very transformational platform. With several of the foremost exciting applications nevertheless to be developed, we will solely begin to marvel regarding the incredible potentialities that expect. The Bury Planetary Classification System (IPFS) may be a protocol and peer-to-peer network for storing and sharing information during a distributed classification system. IPFS uses content-addressing to unambiguously determine every go into a worldwide namespace connecting all computing devices. Content available, implies that the contents of IPFS is accessed victimisation IPFS hash addresses.

During this chapter, the review referring to the combination of the on top of is formed. We tend to supposed to secure information in cloud that is provided by a company or company and has ability to ensure information security by introducing Secure Cloud Knowledge Centre (SCKC) with integration IPFS and Ethereum. The remainder of the chapter is organized as follows: in section II, explains literature review and gap analysis square measure created. Section III provides connected work and section IV offers conclusion and future scope.

REVIEW OF THE LITERATURE AND GAP ANALYSIS

Data Sharing and Secure Computing by Secnet Design

SecNet (Wang et al., 2019) is developed as Associate in Nursing design for integration 3 mechanisms: 1) blockchain based mostly information sharing with possession guarantee; 2) AI-based secure computing platform; 3) trust value-exchange mechanism for getting security services. For information protection, SecNet uses personal information Centre that provides the uniform information access management with 2 aspects. The primary one is uniform information illustration, helps information be delineate during a commonplace format. The second is uniform access management. In figure1, PDC conjointly provides the same information symbol platform for information identification and routing data. With uniform information symbol, PDC will determine the supply, version, possession and plenty of alternatives attributes of information. Each entity contains a PDC to store information. All the information created in Internet associated with Associate in Nursing entity is hold on in corresponding PDC, and might be unified, computed to create a data system to additional improve the information security. Any interaction with the information in net would be recorded by DRB and therefore the credibleness and integrity of information is valid by DRB.

Figure 1. SecNet Architecture

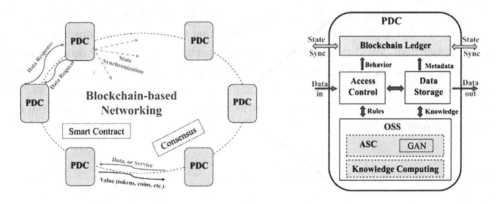

For secure computing SecNet nodes have Associate in Nursing Operation web (OSS) module that allows AI-based Secure Computing (ASC) for generating information and secure rules from information. ASC will embody Generative Adversarial Network that may learn these security rules of PDC. PDC can't handle the info in cloud; here is that the demand for integration of put down planetary classification system and Ethereum.

S or celestial body classification system may be a peer to look classification system (Nebula Ai (NBAI), 2018). It's impressed and designed upon distributed technologies via peer to look systems like scum bag and BitTorrent. It uses hashing and classification system storage for distributing content across the online, basically, it's how to duplicate and address files supported their content rather than their location. IPFS isn't in itself a blockchain, however, it's been tokenized Associate in Nursing Filecoin exists to incentivize persons to work an IPFS node and promote storage on their classification system. Users willing to store IPFS information area unit rewarded with Filecoin. What concerning the priority that the net has become additional centralized Associate in nursing an increasing potential for censorship of content and ideas? Authors have a tendency to area unit seeing limitations on allowed content at intervals bound regions by government's motility down websites or interference sites via ISP's. during a country like Turkey that has blocked sites like Wikipedia, the positioning has been reflected on IPFS, and intrinsically it's possible to still gain access to the content on Wikipedia via P2P networking (it's replicated, not the particular Wiki site). IPFS may be a decentralized and distributed network permitting sharing of files, and content. This prevents management and restriction of content.

Key issues stemming from the implementation of protocol nowadays area unit a result of the huge increase in net traffic and also the ensuing stress points that are amplified. With this implementation of protocol, issues like the subsequent have emerged.

- Inefficient content delivery stemming from downloading files from one server at a time.
- Expensive information measure prices and file duplication resulting in turgid storage.
- Increasing centralization of servers and suppliers resulting in redoubled net censorship.
- Fragile history of data hold on the net and short lifespan of web pages.
- Intermittent affiliations that result in Associate in nursing offline developing world and slow connection speeds.

The list of issues goes on Associate in Nursing it's no surprise that a technology quite twenty years previous is turning into additional perceptibly superannuated in an age of technological innovation. IPFS provides the distributed storage and classification system that the net has to bring home the bacon its true potential. Rather than downloading files from single servers, in IPFS, you raise peers within the network to present you a path to a file instead of it's coming back from a central server. This permits high volume information distribution with high potency, historic versioning, resilient networks, and protracted accessibility of content secured and verified through cryptanalytic hashing and distributed across a network of peers.

Figure 2. Difference between HTTP and IPFS

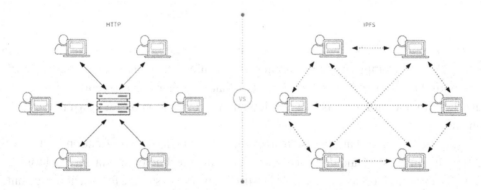

IPFS fixes these problems and helps North American country move toward a secure, economical and cheap internet.

- Information processing's uses a content addressing technique compared to IP addressing technique utilized by communications protocol. Mistreatment content address fetches the information quicker because it can retrieve the information from the highest system that includes a copy of it. Since its content self-addressed you would possibly raise, however will IPFS differentiate the web pages? It will therefore by generating a singular address for every page. The content is known by a cryptographically generated hash that cannot be modified.

- IPFS uses a Distributed Hash Table to store the information on varied systems. AN example of DHT is Chord.

- To have management over the DHT and provides structure thereto, IPFS uses the Merkle DAG protocol impressed by skunk. Skunk uses this protocol for version management whereas IPFS uses it for providing a structure.

- Another advantage of IPFS is that the user will transfer elements of a file from varied supplies right away and mix it at their aspect instead of downloading the entire file from one source.

As in figure3 distributed hash table (DHT) could be a category of a redistributed distributed system that gives an operation service like a hash table: (key, value) pairs are keeping in a very DHT, and any collaborating node will expeditiously retrieve the worth related to a given key. Responsibility for maintaining the mapping from keys to values is distributed among the nodes, in such the way that a modification within the set of participants causes a nominal quantity of disruption. This enables a DHT to scale to very giant numbers of nodes and to handle continual node arrivals, departures, and failures. DHTs type an infrastructure which will be wont to build a lot of advanced services, like any cast, cooperative internet caching, distributed file systems, name services, instant electronic messaging, multicast, and additionally peer-to-peer file sharing and content distribution systems.

Figure 3. Distributed Hash Table

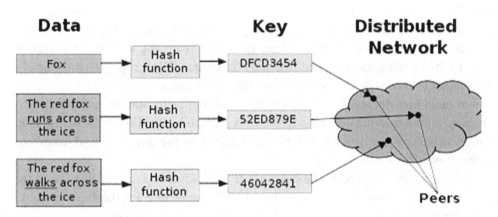

The protocol uses DAG's for controlling the hashed files namespace. DAG's or Directed Acrylic Graphs is a data structure that has been around for a while. If you've ever used git (distributed source control system), then realize it or not, you've been working with DAG data structures. This data structure is similar to a Tree, in that they are directed, have a root node, but the difference is that there can be multiple parent nodes (or paths between the nodes).

FUNCTIONALITY OF IPFS

The design of the protocol provides historic versioning of the Internet like with Git. Each file and all blocks within it are given a unique identifier, which is a cryptographic hash. Duplicates are removed across the network and version history is tracked for every file. This leads to persistently available content where web pages do not disappear because of a failed server or bankrupted web host. Further, the authenticity of content is guaranteed through this mechanism and when looking up files, you are essentially asking the network to find nodes storing the content behind the unique identifying hash associated with that content.

The links between the nodes in IPFS take the form of cryptographic hashes, and this is possible because of its Merkle DAG (Directed Acyclic Graph) data architecture. The benefits of Merkle DAGs to IPFS include the following:

- Content Addressing – Content has a unique identifier that is the cryptographic hash of the file.
- No Duplication – Files with the same content cannot be duplicated and only stored once.
- Tamper Proof – Data is verified with its checksum, so if the hash changes, then IPFS will know the data is tampered with.

IPFS links file structures to each other using Merkle links and every file can be found by human-readable names using a decentralized naming system called IPNS. The implementation of Merkle Directed Acyclic Graphs (DAGS) are important to the underlying functionality of the protocol. Each node only stores the content that it is interested in and indexes the information that allows it to figure out who is storing what. The framework for IPFS fundamentally removes the need for centralized servers to deliver website content to users. Eventually, this concept may entirely push the HTTP protocol into irrelevance and allow users to access content locally, offline. Instead of searching for servers as with the current infrastructure of the Internet, users will be searching for unique ID's (cryptographic hashes), enabling millions of computers to deliver the file to you instead of just one server.

The current main implementation of IPFS is in Go with implementations in both Python and Java script on the way. It is compatible with Linux, MacOSX, Windows, and FreeBSD. Being an open source and community driven project, you can contribute by following the directions and documents on their Git hub page or operate our own IPFS node.

There are already some important use cases for IPFS, and more are sure to arise as the protocol continues to develop. Offering the new, distributed P2P architecture for the Internet comes with its complexities, but the benefits can be seen in everything from massive financial savings in storage and bandwidth to integration with distributed blockchain networks. Obvious advantages that come with the distributed storage model of IPFS apply to vastly more efficient data storage and immutable, permanence along with it. No longer will websites be relegated to cyclical 404 error messages due to downed servers or interrupted chain of HTTP links. Further, significant advantages are available for researchers in terms of efficiency, especially those needing to parse and analyses very large data sets. With the prevalence of Big Data in modern science, the fast performance and distributed archiving of data afforded by IPFS will become pertinent to accelerating advancements. Service providers and content creators can also substantially reduce their costs associated with delivering large amounts of data to customers. Current iterations of this paradigm are hindered by increasing bandwidth costs and data providers getting charged for peering agreements. The costs associated with delivering content through centralized infrastructures of interconnected networks is only increasing and creating an environment of critical inefficiency and further centralization in an attempt to overcome these burdens. Additionally, centralization of servers leads to government snooping, increasing DDoS attack prevalence, ISP censorship, and private sale of data.

As Juan Benet, the creator of IPFS stated "Content on IPFS can move through any untrusted middlemen without giving up control of the data or putting it at risk." Finally, integration of IPFS with blockchain technology seems to be a perfect fit. Using IPFS within a blockchain transaction, you can place immutable, permanent links. Timestamps secure your data without having to actually store it on-chain which leads to reduced blockchain bloating and provides a convenient method for secure off-chain solutions to help blockchains scale. IPFS is being included in a number of cryptocurrency platforms and has the potential to symbiotically help the industry to scale by providing the peer to peer and distributed file system architecture that is needed as a foundation to help support the growth of cryptocurrency platforms. IPFS brings the freedom and independent spirit of the web at full force and at low cost. IPFS can help deliver content in a way which can save you considerable money. Some of the concepts included here.

Content Identifiers

A Content symbol, or CID, could be a label accustomed purpose to material in IPFS. It doesn't indicate wherever the content is hold on, however it forms a form of address supported the content itself. CIDs are short, in spite of the dimensions of their underlying content. CIDs are supported the content's science hash. That means: Any distinction in content can manufacture totally different in special unique distinct} Criminal Investigation Command and also the same piece of content additional to 2 different IPFS nodes victimisation a similar setting can manufacture a similar Criminal Investigation Command

Hashes

Hashes are functions that take some arbitrary input and come back a fixed-length price. The worth depends on the given hash formula in use, like SHA-1 (used by Git), SHA-256, or BLAKE2, however a given hash formula forever returns a similar price for a given input.

Inter-Planetary Name System

Inter-Planetary Name System (IPNS) could be a system for making and change mutable links to IPFS content. Since objects in IPFS are content-addressed, their address changes whenever their content will. That's helpful for a spread of things, however it makes it onerous to urge the newest version of one thing. a reputation in IPNS is that the hash of a public key. it's related to a record containing info concerning the hash it links to it is signed by the corresponding personal key.

Merkle Direct Acyclic Graph (DAG)

A Direct Acyclic Graph (DAG)is a kind of graph during which edges have direction and cycles aren't allowed. as an example, a joined list like A→B→C is associate degree instance of a DAG wherever A references B then on. we are saying that B could be a kid or a descendant of A, which node A encompasses a link to B. Conversely A could be a parent of B. we have a tendency to decision nodes that aren't youngsters to the other node within the DAG root nodes.

Mutable Classification System (MCS)

Because files in IPFS are content-addressed and immutable, they will be difficult to edit. mutable classification system (MCS) could be a tool engineered into IPFS that lets USA treat files such as you would a traditional name-based filesystem — we will add, remove, move, and edit MFS files and have all the work of change links and hashes taken care of for you. MCS is accessed through the file's commands within the IPFS CLI and API.

Pinning

IPFS nodes treat the info they store sort of a cache, which means that there's no guarantee that the info can still be hold on. Promise a Criminal Investigation Command tells associate degree IPFS server that the info is very important and mustn't be thrown away. We must always pin any content you concentrate on necessary, to make sure that content is maintained long. Since knowledge necessary to somebody else might not be necessary to USA, promise lets USA have management over the disc space and knowledge retention we want.

UnixFS

A go into IPFS isn't simply content. It would be too massive to suit during a single block; thus, it wants information to link all its blocks along. it would be a symlink or a directory, thus it wants information to link to alternative files. UNIX system FS is that the information accustomed represent files and everyone their links and information in IPFS and is loosely supported however files add Unix.

The Secure Cloud Knowledge Centre

All the ideas and solutions projected to safeguard knowledge security or by desegregation AI algorithms as a practical element to analyse knowledge security. SecNet made common and general networking design at an outsized scale, which may support dynamic update of all the practical parts on an individual basis, with efficiency and effectively improved the info security for all applications. However SecNet is unable to store and manage the info in cloud. To fill this gap secure cloud knowledge centre uses IPFS and Ethereum to safeguard distributed knowledge and share the info a lot of firmly.

The overall style of Secure Cloud Knowledge Centre may be viewed as 3 tier design. forepart programme is employed for interacting with users. User knowledge is passed as input to the web3 library and IPFS library. Here the web3 library can act with blockchain Ethereum virtual machine for call, sensible contract and fund transfer transactions. IPFS library is employed once user input with image or video that's hold on in IPFS knowledge storage. IPFS storage returns connected IPFS hash back to the user.

The Ethereum Virtual Machine (EVM) is that the element of the Ethereum platform that handles the event, readying and execution of the sensible contract. The EVM could be a complete state machine as all transactions on the EVM concerned limit commands and alter of the state values because of the gas limit given to the contract execution. EVM encompasses a stack-based design, as well as fixed storage, memory and account storage. They're accustomed store the state values further because the contract program bytecode. once a dealing involving state changes from contract functions, associate degree EVM are going to be instant to load the program bytecode and execute the perform and states are going to be updated upon sure-fire execution of the transactions. Ethereum Virtual Machine (EVM) could be a Alan Turing complete computer code that runs on the Ethereum network. It allows anyone to run any program, in spite of the programming language given enough time and memory. The Ethereum Virtual Machine makes the method of making blockchain applications abundant easier and economical than ever before. Rather than having to make a completely original blockchain for every new application, Ethereum allows the event of probably thousands of various applications all on one platform.

Figure 4. Overall view of the secure cloud data storage system.

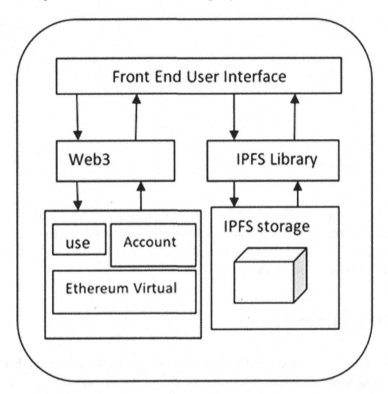

As in figure 4, Account Manager Contract includes a mapping organization from consumer account address to user contract address. This is often to make sure that every consumer account is barely once and to avoid any issues caused. Account manager contains register and retrieve functions specified every user contract is in a position to bind its address and be retrieved for later reusage.

While retrieving the information through internet applications, distributed knowledge storage organization is economical for multi user setting it provides the higher quality of services to users of various geographic regions. Knowledge storage layer within the Secure Cloud Knowledge Centre design are going to be lay to rest joined with varied varieties of storage devices to realize integrated management of huge knowledge. The accessibility of the information has to be monitored as in figure5. So, the standard of service is going to be thus speedy. The usage in varied layers of cloud storage system, offers an integrated approach for the maneuver management, security management, etc. in an exceedingly multi user setting, sharing of data through the storage devices supports for quicker accessibility. Reckoning

Figure 5. Distributed web

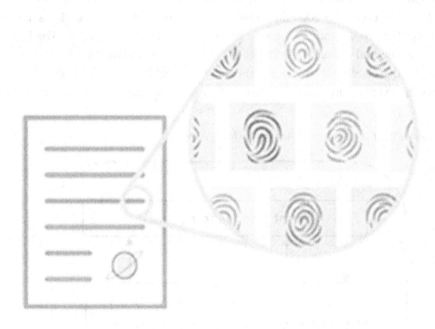

on the user needs the front interface will support for the upkeep of services through the cloud storage system services, public resources services, multi user knowledge sharing services may be achieved. The service may be provided to the users through lay to rest planetary classification system cargo hold that is economical for the standard of services.

CONCLUSION AND FUTURE WORK

As you'll see, IPFS could be a each technically and conceptually advanced protocol that has supercilious ambitions to revolutionize the exchange of knowledge across the net. HTTP was self-made in its title and helped the net to achieve the grand stage that it's at nowadays, however new technologies square measure rising, and therefore the would like for a reformed and distributed infrastructure has created itself apparent. To empower and enhance the technology of AI and blockchain for trustworthy knowledge management in trust-less setting at cloud, we have a tendency to introduced the Secure Cloud Knowledge Centre. knowledge storage layer within the Secure Cloud Knowledge Centre design are going to be lay to rest joined with varied varieties of storage devices to realize integrated management of huge knowledge. because the work of IPFS and Ethereum continues to be underneath the analysis, a lot of analysis is needed to urge completeness of the system. The planned work has established the concept of mistreatment IPFS, sensible contracts at the side of Ethereum blockchain and more work has to analyse the performance and improve the sensible contract supported the important wants of the social media network.

REFERENCES

Benet, J. (n.d.). IPFS - Content self-addressed, Versioned, P2P File System (DRAFT 3).

Blockchain-Base Structures for a Secure and Operate Network of Semi-Autonomous Unmanned Aerial Vehicles. (2018). IEEE.

Bocek, T., Rodrigues, B. B., Strasser, T., & Stiller, B. (2017). Blockchains everywhere—A use-case of blockchains within the pharmaceutical company supply-chain. *Proc. IFIP/IEEE Symp. Integr. Netw. Service Manage.*, 772–777.

Kanimozhi & Jacob. (2019). *Artificial Intelligence primarily based Network Intrusion Detection with Hyper-Parameter improvement standardisation on the Realistic Cyber Dataset CSE-CICIDS2018 mistreatment Cloud Computing.* IEEE.

Nakamoto, S. (2008). *Bitcoin: A peer-to-peer electronic money system.* Tech. Rep. Available: https://archive.is/rMBtV

Nebula Ai (NBAI). (2018). *Decentralized ai Blockchain white paper.* Nebula AI Team.

Salan, Rehman, Nizamuddin, & Al-Fuqaha. (n.d.). Blockchain for AI: Review and Open analysis Challenges. *IEEE Access: Practical Innovations, Open Solutions.* Advance online publication. doi:10.1109/ACCESS.2018.2890507

Understanding Blockchain Technology and the way to urge involved. (2018). In *The ordinal International Scientific Conference eLearning and software system for Education Bucuresti.* . doi:10.12753/2066-026X-18-000

Wang, Dong, & Wang. (2019). Securing knowledge with Blockchain and AI. *IEEE Access.*

Wood, G. (2014, April). Ethereum: A secure decentralized generalized group action ledger. *Ethereum Project Yellow Paper*, *151*, 1–32.

Xu, Song, Goh, & Li. (n.d.). *Building AN Ethereum and IPFS-based decentralized Social Network System.* Academic Press.

Chapter 2
Comprehensive Study on Incorporation of Blockchain Technology With IoT Enterprises

Ashok Kumar Yadav

ⓘD https://orcid.org/0000-0002-7822-5870

School of Computer and Systems Sciences, Jawaharlal Nehru University, New Delhi, India

ABSTRACT

Unprecedented advancement in wireless technology, storage, and computing power of portable devices with the gigabyte speed of internet connectivity enables the possibility of communication among machine to machine. IoT has a different way to connect many nodes simultaneously to store, access, and share the information to improve the quality of life by the elimination of the involvement of human. Irrespective of unlimited benefit, IoT has so many issues that arise to eclipse IoT in reality because of its centralized model. Scalability, reliability, privacy, and security challenges are rising because of the huge numbers of IoT nodes, centralized architecture, and complex networks. Centralized architecture may lead to problems like a single point of failure, single way traffic, huge infrastructure cost, privacy, security, and single source of trust. Therefore, to overcome the issues of the centralized infrastructure of the IoT, the authors diverted to decentralized infrastructure. It may be the best decision in terms of performance, reliability, security, privacy, and trust. Blockchain is an influential latest decentralization technology to decentralize computation, process management, and trust. A combination of blockchain with IoT may have the potential to solve scalability, reliability, privacy, and security issues of IoT. This chapter has an overview of some important consensus algorithms, IoT challenges, integration of the blockchain with IoT, its challenges, and future research issues of a combination of blockchain and IoT are also discussed.

DOI: 10.4018/978-1-7998-3295-9.ch002

INTRODUCTION

The Internet of Things (IoT) is a most recent technology to connect and facilitate to communicate among numerous things simultaneously for providing different benefits to consumers that will change user's interaction with the technology. The concept of IoT is not new. "The Internet of Things has more potential than the internet which changes the world, just as the internet did in the last few years (Hong-Ning Dai, Zibin Zheng, Yan Zhang, 2019). The core concept behind IoT is establishing a system to store all the data on the cloud without having the requirement of human efforts in collecting it. It is believed that the impact of IoT on the world will be immense in the upcoming years. Though the presence of IoT offers a cutting-edge opportunity in fully automated systems, traffic management, and solutions, it comes with certain limitations that we cannot ignore. IoT offers a universal model of sharing information to enhance society, enabling advanced services by interconnecting things based on existing wireless communication technologies. A study confirms approximate 60% of companies are already engaged in developing IoT projects. Recently more than 30% startups are at an early stage of deployment of IoT. More than 69% of these IoT based companies are now focusing problems like, how IoT operational cost can be reduced? Cisco says, 74% of organizations have failed with their IoT startups. It is happening due to the involvement of humans in IoT implementation, beyond the functional elements of sensors and network complexity. Data reliability, security, and privacy are rigorous issues in cloud-based IoT applications.

Heterogeneity, centralization, the complexity of networks, interoperability, privacy vulnerability, and security vulnerability are the root cause of security, privacy and reliability issues in IoT systems. To overcome problems of security, privacy, reliability, and the trust of the IoT system; there is a requirement of the new advanced techniques. The blockchain is one of the best emerging technology. It may ensure the privacy and security issues by using a public ledger, cryptographic and hash algorithms. Blockchain is an incorruptible decentralized digital public ledger of economical transactions that can be programmed to record not just only for financial transactions but also virtually everything which have value to facilitate data decentralization, transparency, tamper-proof, replicated ledger, immutability, and improved trust in peer to peer network. The blockchain has emerged as one of the major technologies that have the potential to transform the way of sharing the huge information. Improving trust in a peer - peer environment without the requirement of a trusted third party is a technological challenge to transform present scenarios of the society and industries. Decentralized and distributed nature, transaction verifiability, transparency and immutability features of blockchain can tackle challenges of IoT. Without considering the heavy computational load, delay, storage, bandwidth overhead of blockchain can lead to a new set of challenges in the integration of the blockchain with IoT (A. Baliga, 2017). Blockchain uses the technique of hash function, Merkle Tree, Nonce (to make the hash function harder to retrace) and others to provide Data Centralization, Transparency, Security and Privacy, Tamper proof replicated ledger, Immutable Ledger Non-Repudiation, irreversibility of records, Automation and Smart Contract, a new way of storing (M. Conoscenti, A. Vetro, and J. C. De Martin, 2016). Figure 1 shows the component of blockchain.

Issues of IoT are like security, privacy, scalability, reliability, maintainability. Blockchain has decentralizations, persistence, anonymity, immutability, identity and access management, resiliency, autonomy, apriority, cost-saving as attractive features.

These features may address challenges of IoT, Big data and machine learning. Blockchain pushes centralized network-based IoT to blockchain-based Distributed Ledger. Blockchain mainly can tackle scalability, privacy, and reliability issue in the IoT system. This chapter proposes a trusted, reliable and flexible architecture for IoT service systems based on blockchain technology, which facilitated self-trust, data integrity, audit, data resilience, and scalability (A. Panarello, N. Tapas, G. Merlino, F. Longo, & A. Puliafito, 2018).

The concept of Hashcash was suggested by Adam Back in 1997 (Z. Zheng, S. Xie, H. N. Dai, X. Chen, H. Wang, 2018). Hashcash is a mining algorithm used as Proof-of-Work Consensus algorithm (Used for Permission less blockchain Technology i.e. Bitcoin). It is used to restrain email and save such a system from Denial of service Attacks. Brute Force method is the only way to implement the Hashcash. The consensus algorithms are the heart of blockchain technology. The consensus algorithms are considered as the pillar of the blockchain network. Many consensus algorithms have been suggested to get system safe from any malicious activity in blockchain technology. Proof-of-Work, Proof-of-Stake, delegated proof of stake, Practical Byzantine Fault Tolerance are some of the popular consensus algorithms (D. Larimer, 2018). Basically, consensus ensures the attainment of logical decisions so, every peer should agree whether a transaction should be committed in the database or not (A. Panarello, N. Tapas, G. Merlino, F. Longo, & A. Puliafito, 2018).

CONSENSUS ALGORITHMS

The concept of PoW is used beyond blockchain. Ideally, the concept is to produce a challenge to a user, the user has to produce a solution which should show some proof of work being done against that challenge. Once it is validated the user accepted. It eliminates the entity that is slow or not capable enough to generate PoW In blockchain PoW is used to generate a value that is difficult to generate and easy to verify. To generate block hash there are n leading zeros. It will help in solution and known as a nonce. In PoW node having high power machine will perform more transaction to be committed and generate a new block. This will lead to higher incentives towards node utilizing more powerful machine in generating new blocks (Bentov, I., Gabizon, & M., 2016). In proof of work, miners are required to give a solution for the complex cryptographic hash problem. Miners compete with each other to become the first to find the nonce. The first miner solves the puzzle gets the reward. Mining in proof of work algorithm requires a lot of computing power and resources. Proof of work uses a huge amount of electricity and encourages mining pools which take the blockchain towards centralization (Z. Zheng, S. Xie, H. N. Dai, X. Chen, H. Wang, 2018). To solve these issues, a new consensus algorithm was proposed called Proof of Stake. A validator is chosen randomly to validate the next block. To become a validator, a node has to deposit a certain amount of coins in the network as a stake. This process is called staking/minting/forging. The chance of becoming the validator is proportional to the stake. The bigger the stake is, the higher the chances validate the block. This algorithm favors the rich stake. When a validator tries to approve an invalid block, he/she loses a part of the stake. When a validator approves a valid block, he/she gets the transaction fees and the stake is returned. Therefore, the amount of the stake should be higher than the total transaction fee to avoid any fraudulent block to be added. A fraud validator loses more coins than he/she gets. If a node does not wish to be a validator anymore, his/her stake as well as transaction fees are released after a certain period of time (not immediately as network needs to punish the node if he/she is involved in fraudulent block). Proof of Stake does not ask for huge amounts of electrical power and it is more decentralized. It is more environmentally friendly than Proof of Work. 51% attack is less likely to happen with Proof of Stake as the validator should have at least 51% of all the coins which is a very huge amount. Proof of Stake is performing for the more protective way and to use less usage of power to execute the transaction. Sometimes a person having the more cryptocurrency (i.e. Bitcoin) will have more probability to mine new block, but again, it was arising the problem of dominance when a person having 50 percent or more then it will have the highest probability to mine the block so the solution has been made in terms of some randomization protocol in which random nodes are selected to mine new block. Since it was also found that nodes are priory starting with PoW and then they move to PoS for better and smoother usage.

Since PoA can be considered as the combination of Proof-of-Stack (PoS) and Proof-of-Work (PoW). PoA modifies the solution for PoS. If any miner wants to commit some transactions in a block as to mine a new block, then if that miner wants to commit that mined block into the database, then most of every node sign the block for validation (D. Larimer, 2018). PoET algorithm suggests some common steps to select the miner that which would mine a new block. Each miner that had mined the prior block had waited for random time quantum to do so. Any miner which is proposing any new block to mine should wait for the random moment of time and it will be easy to determine whether any miner which is proposed for the new block to mine has waited for some time or not by making a determination that a miner has utilized a special CPU instruction set.

PBFT algorithm concerns when one or more node in any network becomes faulty and behave maliciously that results in improper communication among all nodes connected to that network. Such things result in a delay in functioning, whereas time is a very serious concern as we already are working in an asynchronous system where if at least one fault occurs then it would be impossible to solve the consensus problem. I will also generate discrimination in responses of various nodes. PBFT works for the permissions model. In practical Byzantine fault tolerance, state machine replication occurs at multiple nodes and the client will wait for an n+1 response from all nodes where n is the number of faulty nodes, but it isn't giving the proper solution for this because n+1 cannot determine the majority vote for the client. PBFT applies to the asynchronous system (M. Samaniego and R. Deters, 2016).

Generally, PBFT was attained after PAXOS and RAFT that both have maximum fault tolerance of $n/2 - 1$ among all nodes where n seems to be the number of faulty nodes (T. M. FernÃaˍndez-CaramÃl's & P. Fraga-Lamas, 2018). Since PBFT is getting around 3n+1 response among all non-faulty nodes where n is determined as the faulty nodes. As we are discussing the state machine replication, then it is important to understand it. Delegated proof of stake is similar to PoS algorithm. It refers to more decentralized fashion in blockchain network and it also modifies the way by which energy can be utilized often very less in executing the proper manipulation. Now Delegated proof of stake is generally given the chances to stockholders to give their votes to whom they wanted to mine further coming block which should be committed in the database. Cryptocurrency holders will also have the opportunity to select the miner to mine a further block. Stockholders will choose the delegates which will be responsible for the mining of new block and somehow, some witnesses are also selected on an election basis by currency holders to perform proper manipulation like searching of nonce and validation of block etc. And what the delegates need to do is that they will decide how much incentives to be given to witnesses, and they will also decide the factors like block size, power, etc. And final decision will be made by stakeholders to what delegates will have proposed to them. Witnesses will change within some time duration or within a week. Witnesses should perform the transaction allotted within the given time duration. It's all about the reputation of witnesses, more they perform the transaction efficiently within the given time duration, more will be their chance to get selection again in the mining process by selectors (i.e. Cryptocurrency holders). DPoS is also increasing more decentralized fashion as what proposed in PoS was more in a centralized fashion to whom will have the higher amount of currency will have the more dominating effect in the whole network, but in DPoS it has been modified and made a system something distributed that is removing the centralization process (A. Baliga, 2017).

CHALLENGES OF BLOCKCHAIN TECHNOLOGY

Blockchain is an emerging technology that provides a way to record transactions in such a way that it ensures security, transparency, auditability, immutability, anonymity. Decentralization is one of the key features of blockchain technology because it can solve problems like an extra cost, performance limitations, and central point failure. Blockchain allows the validation of transactions through the nodes without authentication, jurisdiction or intervention done by a central agency, reduce the service cost, mitigate the performance limitations and eliminating the central point failure. Instead of transparency,

Table 1. Comparison of Permissioned Network Consensus Algorithms

BFT	RBFT	PBFT	PAXOS	RAFT
A closed network	A closed network	Synchronous	Synchronous	Synchronous
Used for business working based on smart contracts	Used for business working based on smart contracts	Smart contracts dependent	Smart contracts dependent	Smart contracts dependent
State machine replication is used	The proper authorities are handling, proper work	State machine replication is used	Sender, proposer and acceptor jointly work	Collecting selected ledger on some agreement to work
Good transactional throughput	Good transactional throughput	Greater transactional throughput	Greater transactional throughput	Greater transactional throughput
Byzantine faults	Byzantine faults (i.e. Hyperledger body)	Byzantine faults	Crash fault	Crash fault
Based on traditional notions	Based on traditional notions	It can bear f-1 tolerance	PAXOS can bear f/2-1 fault	RAFT can bear f/2-1 fault

Table 2. Comparison of Permissionless Network Consensus Algorithms

Proof of Work (PoW)	Proof of Stake (PoS)	Proof of Burn (PoB)	PoET
Used for industries working on a financial level	Used for industries working on a financial level	Used for industries working on a financial level	Used for industries working on a financial level
Using public key encryption (i.e. Bitcoin)	Using an RSA algorithm for encryption	RSA algorithm for encryption	RSA algorithm for encryption
Miners having higher work done after investing higher power will have higher probability to mine the new block	It is some election type selection of miners for the next block to be mined	PoB acquires some cryptocurrencies (wealth) to mine new block using virtual resource	A person spends some time and power to mine new block who finishes the first priority task will be the next miner
Power inefficient	Power efficient	Power efficient	Power efficient
An open environment	An open environment	An open environment	An open environment
Bitcoin script is used	Mostly Golong is used	Mostly Golong is used	

blockchain can maintain a certain level of privacy by making blockchain addresses anonymous. It must be noted that the blockchain can only maintain pseudonyms. It may not preserve the full privacy. The features of blockchain-like decentralization, immutability, and transparency make it a suitable technology to integrate with IoT to provide a solution to the major challenges of IoT. Despite being a very efficient emerging technology for recording transactions, this technology still faces some challenges like storage and scalability. Long-chain may have a negative impact on the performance of IoT. It may increase the synchronization time for new users. Consensus protocol has a direct impact on the scalability of the blockchain. Besides this, blockchain technology also faces security weaknesses and threats. The most common attack is 51% or majority attack. In this situation, the consensus in the network can be controlled, especially those that centralized the consensus among fewer nodes. Double spending attack, race attack, denial of services and man in the middle attack are also some of the challenges faced by blockchain technology. Blockchain infrastructure is vulnerable to man in the middle kind of attack since they strongly depend on communication. In this attack, the attacker can monopolize the node's connections isolating it from the rest of the network (F. Atlam, A. Alenezi, M. O. Alassafi, G. B. Wills, 2018).

INTERNET OF THING (IoT)

We are entering an era where everything is going to be smart and is connected to each other through a network. All the different things around us is going to interconnect via wireless over the internet. These things are not only the computer and computing devices, but also the things we see and use in our daily life like, table, chair, dustbin, etc. The concept of interconnecting of things through internet, introduce a new buzzword "Internet of Things (IoT)". Now IoT is going to connect human to machine, machine to machine, human to things, things to machine and things to things. It means, things can communicate to things without any physical medium. Internet of Things is comprised of two terms Internet and Things. The Internet is the global system of interconnected computer networks that use the Internet Protocol suit to link the devices worldwide (A. Reyna, C. Martín, J. Chen, E. Soler, M. Díaz, 2018). The things in the internet of Things are not only the computers and computing devices, but also the real-world objects that are going to be transformed into intelligent virtual objects. The scope of this internet is going to expand beyond computers and computing devices, anything and everything in the real world is going to be connected with each other. IoT is going to provide advanced level services to the society and business enterprises. IoT is going to work as the basic building block for smart homes, smart cities, smart campus, smart dust, etc. IoT is a revolution in technical field in which computers, computing devices and real-world things are going to be interconnected, communicate with each other and generate a huge amount of data. Now IoT has considerable attention of researcher from industry and academics, that they must involve in research to overcome the challenges of IoT, to solve real application problems.

Challenges of IoT

Authentication, authorization and encryption are not enough tackling issues of IoT due to resource limited node. Instead of resource limited node, IoT systems are also vulnerable to malicious attacks. It is possible due to the failure of security firmware updates in time. So, major challenges in IoT are compatibility & interoperability of different IoT nodes. It requires nearly 40% to 60% effort. In IoT there are many nodes have very low computing power and their different working mechanism. IoT device uses different types of protocols. Identification & authentication of IoT devices are very difficult because of huge diversity and number of IoT devices. Currently, 20 billion devices are connected in IoT systems. Working with the IoT system is totally depends on the speed of internet connectivity. IoT needs a very high speed for the proper and efficient working of IoT. IoT system is not so applicable because the internet still not available everywhere in a seamless and appropriate speed. So, seamless and appropriate internet connectivity issues may be one of the biggest challenges in IoT deployment (J. Lin, W. Yu, N. Zhang, X. Yang, H. Zhang, and W. Zhao, 2017). Advancement of wireless technology, computing, and processing speed of the CPU, IoT makes human beings' life so easy and flexible but may generate huge amounts of structured, semi structured and structured data at very high speed and variation in a very short time (S. Muralidharan, A. Roy, N. Saxena, 2016). 80% of data generated by IoT system are unstructured data. Handling unstructured data may create a challenge to the deployment of IoT systems for real time applications. Conventional security & privacy approaches not applicable to IoT because of decentralized and resource constraints of the majority of IoT devices. By 2020, 25% of cyber-attacks will target IoT devices. And also 54% IoT device owners, do not use any third party too & 25% out of these do not even change the default password on their device. The device does not know neighbors in advance, no cooperative data exchange, the adversary can compromise device's data, energy-inefficient protocol, data capturing, intelligent analytics, and delivering value may create challenges for deploying the IoT systems. IoT nodes ask blockchain to store their state, manage multiple writers, and prevent from the need of a trusted third party (Hong-Ning Dai, Zibin Zheng, Yan Zhang, 2019).

IoT security and Privacy Solution

The Internet is the global system of interconnected computer networks that use the Internet Protocol suit to link the devices worldwide. Due to the worldwide interconnectivity of IoT device and resource constraint, the security of IoT is crucial issues. There are many solutions to resolve the security and privacy challenges from IoT. Some of the privacy solution is mentioned in the figure.

Integration of Blockchain with IoT

This is the era of peer to peer interaction. Unprecedented growth in IoT explores the new mechanism of storing, accessing and sharing information. This new mechanism of storing, accessing and sharing of information raises the issue of security, privacy and data availability. The centralized architecture of IoT enhanced the evolution of IoT, but creates the issue of single-point failure and also provide the entire control of the system to a few powerful authorized users. Blockchain is one of the latest emerging technology, which has the capabilities of a new way to store, access and share information in a decentralized and distributed system. Blockchain technology can be integrated with IoT to resolve the problem with IoT such as storing, accessing, sharing and central point failure. So, we can say that the use of blockchain may be a complement to the IoT with reliable and secure information. Blockchain may be defined as the key to solving scalability, reliability and privacy problems related to IoT paradigm.

Interaction of IoT with Blockchain can be mainly IoT-IoT, IoT-Blockchain and combination of IoT -IoT and IoT-Blockchain. In IoT-IoT data are stored in blockchain while its interaction takes place with the use of blockchain. It is a useful scenario where reliable IoT interaction with low latency is required. In IoT-Blockchain all interaction and their respective data go through blockchain, to collect an immutable and traceable record of interactions. It is helpful in scenarios like trade and rent to obtain reliability and security. In hybrid platform some interaction and data part are stored in blockchain and the remaining are directly shared between the IoT devices. This approach is a perfect way to leverage and benefit of both Blockchain and real-time IoT interaction. The interaction method can be chosen on a parameter such as a throughput, latency number of writers, a number of interested writers, data media, interactive media, consensus mechanism, security and resource consumption., Blockchain integration with IoT has the potential to overcome the challenges in the control IoT system (A. Reyna, C. Martín, J. Chen, E. Soler, M. Díaz, 2018).

Blockchain can improve the power of IoT by offering a trust, sharing service for reliability and tractability of information. Shifting from a cloud to a peer to peer network will resolve central points of failure. It also prevents few powerful companies to control the processing & storage of the information of a huge number of people also improve fault tolerance & system scalability. Blockchain specially designed for an internet scenario with high processing computer, it was far from the reality of IoT. Blockchain technology can be used to keep a track of connected IoT devices which can enable the process of transaction and coordination between devices. Blockchain technology can also be used to keep an immutable record of the history of smart devices in an IoT network, which will maintain the autonomy of peers without any requirement of the single authority (X. Liang, J. Zhao, S. Shetty, D. Li., 2017).

The fundamental issues of IoT such as security, privacy, scalability, reliability, maintainability can be solved by blockchain because blockchain provides many attractive features such as decentralization, persistence, anonymity, immutability, identity and access management, resiliency, autonomy, apriority, cost-saving. These features may address challenges of IoT, Big data and machine learning. Blockchain pushes network-based IoT to blockchain-based one. IoT system facing challenges such as heterogeneity of IoT system, poor interoperability, resource-limited IoT devices, privacy & security vulnerabilities. Blockchain can support the IoT system with the enhancement of heterogeneity, interoperability, privacy & security vulnerability. Blockchain can also improve the reliability & scalability of the IoT system. We can say blockchain can be integrated with the IoT system.

Advantages of integration of Blockchain with IoT

1. **Enhance interoperability** Heterogeneous type of data can be converted, process, extracted, compressed and finally stored in the blockchain.
2. **Improve security and privacy** IoT data transactions can be encrypted and digitally signed by cryptographic keys. Blockchain support automatic updating of IoT devices firmware to heal vulnerable breaches thereby improving the system security.
3. **Traceability and Reliability** All the historical transactions stored in the blockchain may be traceable because of anywhere, anytime verification. The immutability of blockchain helps in the reliability of IoT data due to the impossibility of temper blockchain stored information.
4. **Decentralization and use of public ledger** After integration of IoT with block chain, the central governing body is eliminated, which will remove the single point failure problem. Further, due to decentralization, the trust issue is also solved since the majority of the nodes in the network agree on the validation of a particular transaction. So, blockchain will provide a secure platform for IoT devices.

Challenges of integration of IoT with Blockchain

The integration of blockchain with IoT is secured around 99% from any attacker who belongs to the outside of the network or system. But when any miner becomes attacker or peers itself create their own virtual blockchain network to communicate and may start malicious activities. Since we update blockchain ledger regularly, and regular updating may lead to the problem of centralization. As time passes incentives are gradually decreasing due to limited available currency to pay the miners for mining. There may be a chance of not getting any incentive. To overcome the deficiency of currency blockchain authority may charge some fee to the node just like to trusted third party. İt will gain the concept of blockchain because one of the primary goals of blockchain is to reduce transaction charges. If we are discussing the permission-less model, then the first cryptocurrency comes in mind is Bitcoin. But a major problem with the permission-less model is one address of one user. A user can directly enter into the network and participate in a transaction that is very difficult to know the sender authentication by the receiver whereas digital signature is applied there to solve this problem. It also has the problem of 'how digital signatures can be identified or validated' whereas it may possibly use public key verification of the sender, but may have the problem of multiple addresses because public and private keys are changeable or dynamic in nature. Another point in a permission-less model is that if nodes are not active for almost 3 hours of time duration in the bitcoin network, then they would be disconnected from the same network.

Blockchain technology implementation has problem of scalability, block size, number of transactions per second, not applicable for high-frequency fraud. There may be a trade-off between block size and security. To improve the selfish mining strategy, miners can hide their mined block for more revenue in the future. There may be privacy leakage when users make transactions with their public key and the private key. A user real IP address could be tracked. The number of blocks is mined per unit time cannot fulfill the requirement of process of millions of transactions in a real-time fashion. What may be the maximum chain length and maximum number of miners? Is there any possibility to go for a centralized system using blockchain? Larger block size could slow down the propagation speed and may lead blockchain branch, small transactions can be delayed because miners give more performance to a high transaction fee technical challenge (T. M. FernÃa ndez-CaramÃl's & P. Fraga-Lamas, 2018).

To ensure the immutability and reliability of the information, blockchain is required to store all the transaction information for verification and validation. Due to storing all the transaction information and the exponential increase of storage limited IoT devices leads to a drastic increase in the size of Blockchain. This is the primary drawback of integration with IoT. Some of the blockchain implementations have the processing of very few transactions per second. But some real-time IoT applications need very high processing transactions per second. This may be also a major bottleneck of integrating IoT with blockchain. To resolve the issues of scalability of storage size, researchers are proposing a new optimized storage blockchain using the concept of removing old transaction records from the blockchain.

The biggest challenges in the integration of the blockchain with IoT are the scalability of the ledger and the rate of transaction execution in the blockchain. Huge number of IoT devices generate exponential transactions at a rate which current blockchain solution cannot handle. Implementing blockchain peers into IoT devices is very difficult because of resource constraints. Integration of IoT is limited by scalability and expensive computation and high transaction cost of public blockchain. Industries will face a lot of challenges after the integration of IoT with Blockchain such as the connection of huge numbers of IoT devices in the coming next five years, control and management of the huge number of IoT devices in a decentralized system. The integration of IoT with blockchain will raise a few questions for industries like how the industry will enable peer to peer communication between globally distributed devices, how the industry will provide compliance and governance for autonomous systems and how industry will address the security complexities of IoT landscape (M. Samaniego and R. Deters, 2016). Integration of blockchain with limited resource IoT devices is not suitable due to the lack of computational resources, limited bandwidth and they need to preserve power (H.N. Dai, Z. Zheng, & Y. Zhang, 2019).

Open Research Issues in Blockchain IoT (BCIoT)

Due to resource constraints of IoT devices, conventional big data analysis scheme may not apply to IoT. So, it is very difficult to conduct big data analysis in IoT blockchain systems. Security vulnerability and privacy mechanism are most important research areas in the fields of integration of the blockchain in IoT (R. Zhang & R. Xue, 2019).

IoT tries to make the system fully automated, but to ensure verifiability, authentication, and immutability of the blockchain requires an efficient incentive mechanism. Designing an efficient incentive mechanism is another area of research in the integration of the blockchain with IoT. The drastic increase in the complexity of the network and the addition of a huge number of IoT devices require an effective, scalable mechanism of integration of the blockchain with IoT. It is also one of the future research areas in the integration of blockchain with IoT.

CONCLUSION

Today, due to the emergence of IoT and Big data, the huge, diverse and critical information is available over the internet. The trust over the information is reduced drastically in IoT systems, causing an increase in security and privacy concern day-by-day of the industry and organizations. The integration of blockchain technology with IoT has the potential to change upcoming scenarios of society, industries, and organizations in the coming future. The Integration of blockchain with IoT is one of the emerging technologies for ensuring privacy and security by using cryptographic algorithms and hashing. In this book, chapter authors have discussed the basic consensus algorithms, comparison, and analysis of important consensus algorithms. This book chapter also have covered the basic concept of IoT, challenges of IoT. This chapter mainly have focused on possibility of Integration of blockchain with IoT, advantage, and challenges. In the future, the author will cover the different implementation platforms of integration of blockchain with IoT.

REFERENCES

Ali, M. S., Vecchio, M., Pincheira, M., Dolui, K., Antonelli, F., & Rehmani, M. H. (2019). Applications of Blockchains in the Internet of Things: A Comprehensive Survey. *IEEE Communications Surveys and Tutorials*, *21*(2), 1676–1717. doi:10.1109/COMST.2018.2886932

Atlam, Alenezi, Alassafi, & Wills. (2018). Blockchain with Internet of Things: Benefits, Challenges, and Future Directions. *International Journal of Intelligent Systems and Applications*.

Baliga. (2017). *Understanding blockchain consensus models*. Persistent Systems Ltd, Tech. Rep.

Bentov & Gabizon. (2016). Cryptocurrencies without proof of work. In *International Conference on Financial Cryptography and Data Security* (pp. 142-157). Springer. 10.1007/978-3-662-53357-4_10

Biswas, S., Sharif, K., Li, F., Nour, B., & Wang, Y. (2019). A Scalable Blockchain Framework for Secure Transactions in IoT. IEEE Internet of Things Journal, 6(3).

Conoscenti, M., Vetro, A., & De Martin, J. C. (2016). Blockchain for the internet of things: A systematic literature review. *3th International Conference of Computer Systems and Applications*, 1–6. 10.1109/AICCSA.2016.7945805

Dai, H.-N., Zheng, Z., & Zhang, Y. (2019). *Blockchain for Internet of Things: A Survey. IEEE Internet of Things Journal.*

Dai, H. N., Zheng, Z., & Zhang, Y. (2019). Blockchain for Internet of Things: A Survey. IEEE Internet of Things Journal, 6(5).

Fernandez-Caramals & Fraga-Lamas. (2018). A review on the use of blockchain for the internet of things. *IEEE Access, 6.*

Larimer. (2018). *Delegated proof-of-stake consensus.* Academic Press.

Larimer, D. (2018). DPOS Consensus Algorithm – The Missing Whitepaper. *Steemit.* Available: https://steemit. com/dpos/dantheman/dpos-consensus-algorithm-this-missingwhite-paper

Liang, X., Zhao, J., Shetty, S., & Li, D. (2017). Towards data assurance and resilience in IoT using blockchain. *IEEE Military Communications Conference (MILCOM).* 10.1109/MILCOM.2017.8170858

Lin, J., Yu, W., Zhang, N., Yang, X., Zhang, H., & Zhao, W. (2017). A survey on internet of things: Architecture, enabling technologies, security and privacy, and applications. *IEEE Internet of Things Journal, 4*(5), 1125–1142. doi:10.1109/JIOT.2017.2683200

Liu, B., Yu, X. L., Chen, S., Xu, X., & Zhu, L. (2017). Blockchain based data integrity service framework for IoT data. In *IEEE International Conference on Web Services (ICWS).* IEEE. 10.1109/ICWS.2017.54

Muralidharan, S., Roy, A., & Saxena, N. (2016). An Exhaustive Review on Internet of Things from Korea's Perspective. *Wireless Personal Communications, 90*(3), 1463–1486. doi:10.100711277-016-3404-8

Panarello, A., Tapas, N., Merlino, G., Longo, F., & Puliafito, A. (2018). Blockchain and IoT integration: A systematic survey. *Sensors (Basel), 18*(8), 2575. doi:10.339018082575 PMID:30082633

Reyna, A., Martín, C., Chen, J., Soler, E., & Díaz, M. (2018). On blockchain and its integration with IoT Challenges and opportunities. *Future Generation Computer Systems, 88*, 173–190. doi:10.1016/j.future.2018.05.046

Samaniego, M., & Deters, R. (2016). Blockchain as a service for IoT. *IEEE International Conference on Internet of Things (iThings) and IEEE Green Computing and Communications (GreenCom) and IEEE Cyber, Physical and Social Computing (CPSCom) and IEEE Smart Data (SmartData)*, 433–436. 10.1109/iThings-GreenCom-CPSCom-SmartData.2016.102

Song, J. C., Demir, M. A., Prevost, J. J., & Rad, P. (2018). Blockchain design for trusted decentralized iot networks. In *13th Annual Conference on System of Systems Engineering (SoSE)*. IEEE. 10.1109/SYSOSE.2018.8428720

Viriyasitavat, W., & Li Da Xu. (2019). Blockchain Technology for Applications in Internet of Things—Mapping from System Design Perspective. IEEE Internet of Things Journal, 6(5).

Zhang, R., & Xue, R. (2019). Security and Privacy on Blockchain. *ACM Computing Surveys*, *1*(1).

Zheng, Z., Xie, S., Dai, H. N., Chen, X., & Wang, H. (2018). Blockchain challenges and opportunities: A survey. *International Journal of Web and Grid Services*, *14*(4), 352. doi:10.1504/IJWGS.2018.095647

Chapter 3
Content–Based Transaction Access From Distributed Ledger of Blockchain Using Average Hash Technique

Randhir Kumar

ⓘ https://orcid.org/0000-0001-9375-2970

National Institute of Technology, Raipur, India

Rakesh Tripathi

National Institute of Technology, Raipur, India

ABSTRACT

There are many critical applications working with blockchain-based technology including the financial sector, healthcare, and supply chain management. The fundamental application of blockchain is Bitcoin, which was primarily designed for the financial value transfer. Owing to the feature of decentralized storage structure, immutability, integrity, availability, and reliability of transactions, the blockchain has become the need of the current industry like VANET. However, presently, not much work has been done in order to mitigate the redundancy in the distributed ledger. Hence, the authors arrive at the intelligible conclusion to detect a similar transaction that can mitigate the redundancy of transaction in a distributed ledger. In this chapter, they are addressing two main challenges in blockchain technology: firstly, how to minimize the storage size of blockchain distributed ledger and, secondly, detecting the similar transaction in the distributed ledger to mitigate the redundancy. To detect similar transaction from the distributed ledger they have applied the average hash technique.

DOI: 10.4018/978-1-7998-3295-9.ch003

INTRODUCTION

The coming era of vehicles will be in needs to connected, and intelligent with the requirements like real-time applications, security, seamless connection, and privacy. The Blockchain provides the secure message dissemination and information sharing in vehicular network. The blockchain framework provides the privacy, integrity, availability, and security of information in vehicular network.

In recent decades, there has been a determined increase in the smart and autonomous vehicle. Today vehicular networks are being used for the accidental avoidance, parking management, traffic control, and critical message dissemination (Technologies, 2010). The recent article (Shrestha, 2018), state that most of the developed country like US, China, Germany are working on self driving vehicles.

The aim of the vehicular network (VANET) is to disseminate the critical information (such as accident report) in a secure and accurate manner in order to ensure the safe driving (Shrestha & Nam, 2017). However, this is still a challenging task to disseminate critical information to the all active nodes (peers) in the vehicular network. Most of the previous work on message dissemination and security in VANETs is working with centralized structure. The main issue with the centralized structure is the single-point-of-failure problem. To overcome this challenge in VANETs, distributed structure of vehicular networks has been proposed (Security, Security, & Security, n.d.). However, the issue with distributed structure system is distributed key management, message trust, privacy of data, consent dissemination, owing to the dynamic nature of the VANETs. The distributed trust in information sharing might not work because of consent mechanism, and at the same time the trust value might be inaccurate owing to insufficient information. These issue of distributed structure of VANETs demands for secure mechanism to share the accidental information or critical information.

The security mechanism is required to mitigate the critical information manipulation like deletion, change, and interface with insecure communication by the malicious VANETs node. The message which is generated by the known vehicle should be stored into the distributed storage (database) in order to provide safety in safe driving. The same information must be shared to all the VANET nodes (peers) in consistent state. This type of security attention can be achieved by using blockchain technology, which is currently gaining attention and great potential in diverse fields (Dorri, Steger, Kanhere, & Jurdak, 2017),(Jaoude & Saade, 2019).

The blockchain is emerging technology that provides decentralized and distributed storage platform which supports security and privacy for the cryptocurrency (Bitcoin) (Nakamoto, 2008). The blockchain can be utilized to maintain a history of traffic and accidental events, which can work as a ground truth for the vehicular networks in essence of information sharing. The main objective to apply the blockchain in a VANET is the robustness of storage structure, where each block is shared and stored among the peers. The peers continuously validate the integrity of the blocks in a network. The recorded information in the block of blockchain cannot be changed and forged easily owing to the feature of immutability

There are various study of blockchain has been proposed in geospatial systems such as logistics and energy micro grids (Mengelkamp, Notheisen, Beer, Dauer, & Weinhardt, 2018),(Min, Li, Liu, & Cui, 2016). In this book chapter, we propose blockchain based vehicular adhoc networks (BVANETs) which provide the peer-to-peer message delivery (content-based transaction access) by using IPFS and blockchain. The proposed model mitigates the redundancy of the information in the VANET by using average hash technique.

BACKGROUND

The VANET privacy and security are the major issue which is identified, where some of the security baseline is encountered but no complete protocol is maintained. The author in (Ostermaier, Florian, & Strassberger, 2007), has applied voting scheme to identify the fraud content delivery in the VANET network. To check the trustworthiness of the message, the voting is disseminated among the peers of the network and decision is taken whether the message is valid or not. However, the authors have provided the simulative analysis using voting scheme, but the privacy issue remains unaddressed and issue of security is not completely resolved. Similarly, The work of (Khelifi, Luo, Nour, Moungla, & Ahmed, 2018) introduces the reputation-based blockchain model, to secure the trust in the VANET by using cache store of the consumer vehicles. The model only caches the trusted data and assigned each cache store a reputation value that gets increased and decreased on the basis of served content into the network.

The Intelligent Transportation System (ITS) is playing major role in the VANET to manage the better traffics on the roads. The ITS is providing an efficient support for traffic management using V2V communications. The authors have integrated the ITS with cloud structure for reliability and scalability (Abuelela & Olariu, 2010). ITS also reduces the delay which is critical in the case of message exchange (critical-event). The major issue with ITS approach is that the malicious peers (vehicle) group together and can perform adversary operations like mutation of the critical event message(Shrestha, 2018).

The authors have proposed the VehiCloud that is based on cloud infrastructure for VANET. In the VehiCloud, the vehicle share their location update and the cloud provides the optimal routing information. The VehiCloud is used as a service-oriented cloud structure. To estimate the optimal route of the vehicle MobiCloud has been used in the routing scheme of VANET (Qin & Huang, 2012). However, the provided approach suffers from various challenges like cost of the service constrained due to high mobility of the vehicle, privacy issue of the message (critical-event), and mutability of the message.

Due to the mobility and intermittent connections between the vehicles in VANET, the VANET cloud is facing many challenges today like update of the critical message, distribution of the message among the peers (vehicular node), security of the message, and resource management in the cloud. In (Salahuddin, Al-fuqaha, Guizani, & Cherkaoui, 2014) proposed the roadside unit(RSU) cloud structure for the VANET, to support the data distribution. The authors have used RSU model in order to minimize the cost of service deployment and routing delay. However, the RSU suffers from the issue of integrity, privacy, and security while V2V communication. The author of (Yang et al., 2019) proposed a decentralized trust management in the VANET using blockchain. In this approach, the vehicles trust the neighboring vehicle and assign a vote for the trust based communication. The roadside unit (RSU) calculates the trust score by adding number of votes. The RSU then transfer data into the blockchain network (Li, Jiang, Chen, Luo, & Wen, n.d.). However, the system does not provide any privacy for the voting in decentralized structure. The authors of (Jiang, Fang, & Wang, 2019) have proposed the internet of vehicle (IoV) to ensure distributed storage in VANET with required security. The validation of data is applied by the smart contract, to avoid the interruption and damage of data caused by attack on single roadside unit (RSU) node. To identify the entity in the network consensus mechanism has been designed (Gervais, Wüst, & Ritzdorf, n.d.). The process of consensus approval removes the malicious attack on the VANET. However, the model does not include privacy of the message in the network.

The authors of (X. Wang et al., 2019), (Lu et al., 2019) have addressed the issue of privacy and vehicle authentication in VANET by using blockchain. The first steps includes in the scheme is to implement the new identity based on key distribution (cryptographic approach) rather than simply checking with the consensus algorithm. There are two verifications are maintained in VANET firstly, to verify the internet of vehicle (IoV) identity to roadside unit (RSU) and secondly, verification of roadside unit to cloud infrastructure. The scheme works efficiently in improvement of quality in authentication and reduced malicious attack on the VANET.

The authors of (Ahmad, Kazim, & Adnane, 2015) have presented study on the vehicular network and cloud environments. The presented study describes that, how cloud infrastructure can be beneficial to the VANET. The cloud storage is applied for storing as a service using traffic simulator. The traffic simulator is designed for tracing the traffic conditions in order to provide roadside service by using cloud infrastructure. However, the presented study suffers from DoS attack by the malicious mobile nodes (peers) in the VANET. The cloud structure becomes more in danger when mobile attacker nodes (peers) block the network for large geographical area.

Traditional VANET (centralized) is not capable to handle the complexity of current ITS system. To overcome the complexity of centralized VANET system, the authors have proposed blockchain based anonymous reputation system (BARS) to avoid the forged message delivery by the authenticated vehicles. The model, maintains the privacy and trust issues (Yahiatene, 2018). However, to manage the authentication of the vehicle certificate blockchain (CerBC) and for the storage verification revoked blockchain (RevBC) has been used (Lu, Wang, Qu, & Liu, 2018).

The authors (Xiaohong Zhang & Chen, 2019) proposed integration of edge computing and blockchain to store huge amount of data. To store the heavy data in VANET consortium blockchain has been used. The purpose to use consortium blockchain in VANET, to address the issue of privacy of message and validation of vehicular node. Moreover the consortium blockchain can be used to tackle the scalability issue in the VANET network. The main objective of the VANET is to distribute critical-message (accidental reports) in secure, timely, and accurately in order to ensure safe driving (Shrestha & Nam, 2017). However, the dissemination of critical-message is still challenging due to dynamic vehicular and untrustworthiness of dishonest vehicle. Most of the work on critical-message privacy and security in VANET uses centralized approach. The consortium blockchain also address the issue of centralized storage of VANET infrastructure like mutability, privacy, reliability, and single point of failure (Guo et al., 2019) (Baldini, 2019).

The offloading computation in mobile edge computing (MEC) has limitation in terms of data security, security of transmitted data, and data privacy (Xiaodong Zhang & Cui, 2018),(Y. Wang, Su, Zhang, & Member, 2019). As the data volume increases continuously in VANET, the security, privacy, and data integrity must be ensured. The traditional approach of data storage includes central authority. The limitation of central storage depends on trust based communication and this becomes serious issue for the MEC due to threat of whole edge computing systems. Moreover, the traditional transportation model improves the communication, resource management, and communication using edge computing. In other hand, intelligent transportation system (ITS) is growing with distributed storage in transport management system to provide resource management in VANET. The ITS is handling wide range of new technologies to address the issue of VANET (Kim, 2019), (Leiding & Vorobev, 2018). The limitations of MEC, demands for decentralized storage including privacy, integrity, data security, and availability of critical message on time (W. Wang & Hoang, 2019).

MOTIVATION

The work in this chapter is motivated by the following observations from the literature. While vehicular nodes (peers) share the critical-message in the VANET then privacy, security, and integrity of the message needs to be maintained which has been widely addressed in the literature (related work). There is no work on privacy, security, and integrity of critical-message has been maintained completely in VANET. The redundancy of similar critical-message needs to be mitigated in vehicular network, sent by the multiple authorized vehicular nodes (peers) at same time. Here, the authors proposed various framework with the objective of centralized storage (cloud), without considering the decentralize storage and the privacy, security, and integrity of critical-message.

ISSUE IN THE EXISTING VANET SYSTEM

1. Single point of failure (Centralized storage model- cloud)
2. Mutability of record (Critical information might be modified by malicious VANET)
3. Third party dependency for access and storage (Critical information might be compromised)
4. Does not provide provenance of record(History of critical information in VANET)

CONTRIBUTION OF THE CHAPTER

The contribution of the chapter is as follows:

1. The BVANET provides dissemination of mined block among the peers.
2. The immutability of the critical event (transactions) of block in the BVANET
3. The privacy of critical information and reduced size of information is stored into the BVANET network by content-addressed hash
4. The average hash technique is applied to mitigate the redundancy of similar critical information(Uploaded by many VANET nodes) in VANET
5. The security of VANET information is maintained by nodes (peers) registration process (only authorized peers can see the critical information).
6. The permissioned blockchain structure has been designed in such a way that, the malicious VANET nodes cannot manipulate the information

PROPOSED MODEL

In this section, we have proposed blockchain based vehicular adhoc network (BVANET) to share the critical-message. The critical-message (accident, heavy traffic, land slide) can be easily shared by the intelligent vehicular node (IVN) in the BVANET model. We have designed graphical BVANET model which is user friendly (web UI) to the vehicular node. The proposed model is divided into four different parts like vehicular nodes, mining process, and roadside unit (RSU) peers. The vehicular nodes can upload (current scenario image) / share the critical information to the RSU units by our BVANET graphical user interface (GUI) model. The list of uploaded transactions which is uploaded by the vehicular nodes gets validated by the miners using mining process. To reduce the size of the blockchain ledger, we have applied content-addressed hash storage for the uploaded transactions rather than storing original size. To mitigate the redundancy in the blockchain ledger with similar upload of the transaction (critical-message), we have applied the average hash technique. The underlying technique can easily detect the similar transactions uploaded by the peers. In BVANET, we have removed the transaction which is already uploaded by the vehicular node earlier by matching similarities of the transaction (critical-event /message). The roadside unit can access the list of transactions from distributed ledger of blockchain after registration into the BVANET model. The proposed model (BVANET) is designed based on the permissioned blockchain model. The permissioned blockchain model (BVANET) can be accessed only by the authorized vehicular nodes or RSU who have already completed registration process. In proposed model, we have applied consensus approach to disseminate the blockchain ledger to authorized peers (vehicular node / RSU).

The following steps are involved in our proposed model:

1. The vehicular node can upload the critical-message by using the BVANET GUI model in order to share the information among the peers of network. The redundancy of the critical-message is checked against the already existing transactions of the blockchain network using average hash technique.
2. The uploaded record (transaction) gets validated by the miners of the BVANET network to create a new block and content-addressed hash of the transaction to reduce the size of original transaction (critical-message) into the blockchain network.
3. The miner disseminates the transactions among the peers of blockchain network to verify the transactions with their local copy of distributed ledger in order to create the block into the BVANET model.
4. The verified transactions get stored into the IPFS distributed file storage system and the generated content-addressed hash by the IPFS included into the distributed ledger of BVANET model.
5. The list of transactions can only be accessed by those peers who have registered into the proposed BVANET model.
6. The list of RSU or vehicular node can be a part of the BVANET model after the registration process into the proposed model and by maintaining the consensus of the network.

IMPLEMENTATION OF PROPOSED MODEL BVANET

The implementation of our proposed BVANET model is carried out in the IPFS distributed file sharing system where each transaction is represented into the blockchain network with their content-addressed hash value against the original size of transaction. The experimental setup consists of python anaconda, python flask. The setup is performed on Intel(R) Xeon(R) W-2175 CPU @ 2.50GHZ running Window x64- based processor with 128 GB of RAM and 1 TB of local storage. In this section, we have categories our model in four different parts like vehicular node, miner section, off-chain storage, and blockchain storage. As shown in Figure 2, the graphical user interface (GUI) is implemented to share the critical-message in the BVANET model. The upload section consists of vehicle number, owner name, owner address, vehicle location and the critical-event (traffic, accident, road land slide) images. We have stored the details of vehicular node in pdf format into the blockchain ledger by using content-addressed hash technique.

Figure 1. BVANET Model for data sharing using Blockchain and IPFS based Decentralized Storage

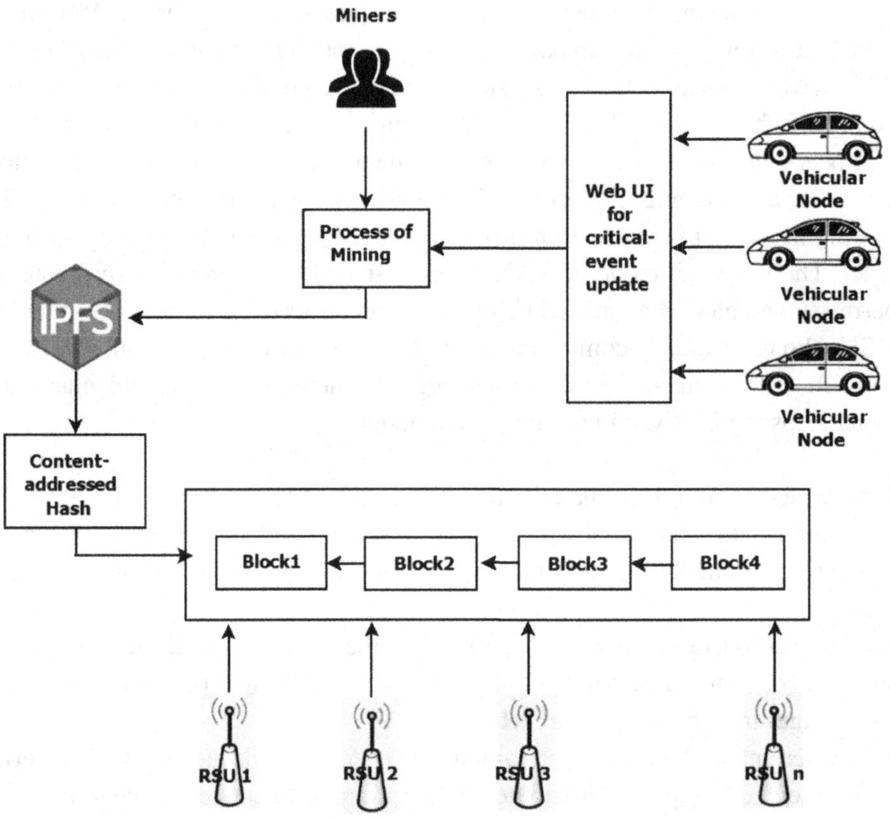

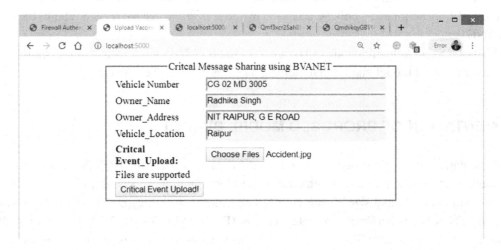

Figure 2. Critical message upload by Vehicle nodes (peers) in BVANET Model

The upload section can only be accessed by the authorized peers (registered vehicular node or RSU) of the network. The roadside unit (RSU) can take different decision based on the shared information by vehicular node.

As shown in Figure 3, Figure 4, and Figure 5, the process of mining is performed in order to ensure the validation of uploaded transactions by the user. To validate the transactions consensus approach (Proof-of-Work) has been used. In the mining process we are creating content addressed hash of the transaction (ipfs), detail of vehicular node (vehicle_detail). The average hash is created to mitigate the redundancy in BVANET for similar transaction (critical-message) uploaded by the multiple vehicular nodes. The average hash finds the similarity of hash by checking the analogous feature in another transaction.

Figure 3. Process of mining to validate the transactions in BVANET Model

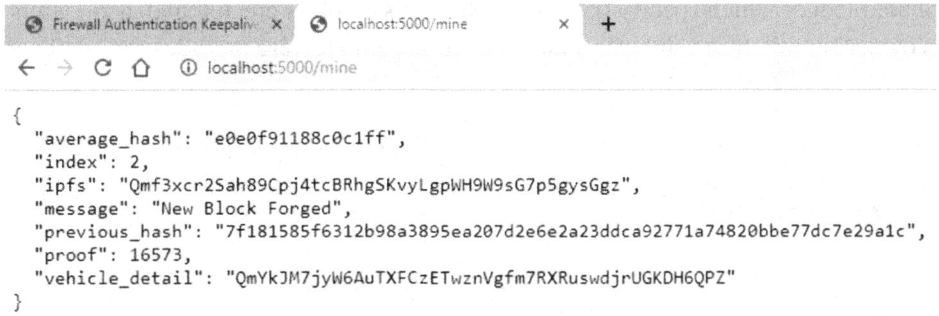
Firewall Authentication Keepaliv
localhost:5000/mine
localhost:5000/mine
{
"average_hash": "e0e0f91188c0c1ff",
"index": 2,
"ipfs": "Qmf3xcr2Sah89Cpj4tcBRhgSKvyLgpWH9W9sG7p5gysGgz",
"message": "New Block Forged",
"previous_hash": "7f181585f6312b98a3895ea207d2e6e2a23ddca92771a74820bbe77dc7e29a1c",
"proof": 16573,
"vehicle_detail": "QmYkJM7jyW6AuTXFCzETwznVgfm7RXRuswdjrUGKDH6QPZ"
}

Figure 4. Process of mining to validate the transactions in BVANET Model

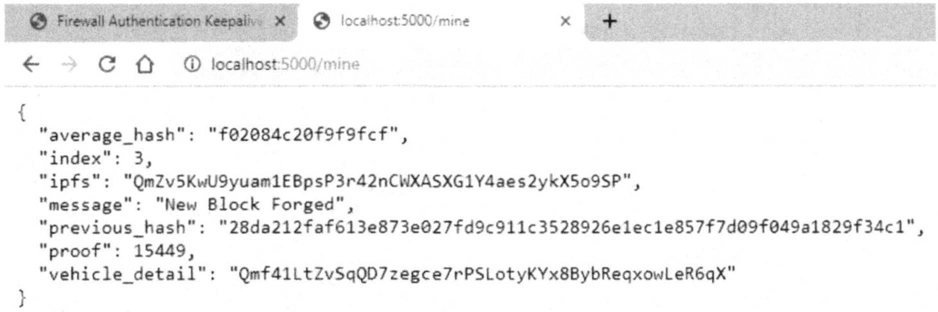
Firewall Authentication Keepaliv
localhost:5000/mine
localhost:5000/mine
{
"average_hash": "f02084c20f9f9fcf",
"index": 3,
"ipfs": "QmZv5KwU9yuam1EBpsP3r42nCWXASXG1Y4aes2ykX5o9SP",
"message": "New Block Forged",
"previous_hash": "28da212faf613e873e027fd9c911c3528926e1ec1e857f7d09f049a1829f34c1",
"proof": 15449,
"vehicle_detail": "Qmf41LtZvSqQD7zegce7rPSLotyKYx8BybReqxowLeR6qX"
}

Figure 5. Process of mining to validate the transactions in BVANET Model

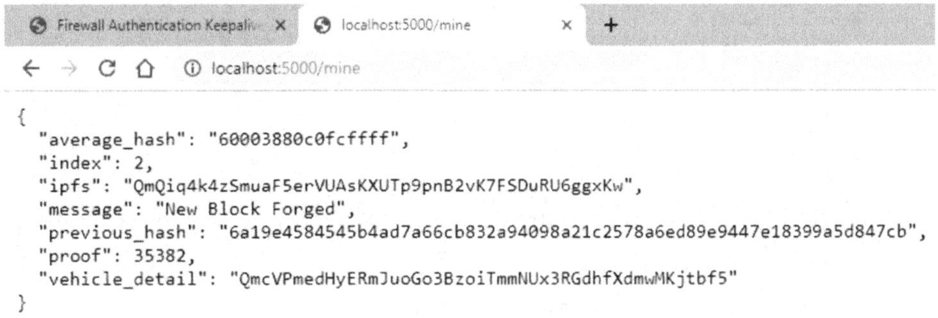
Firewall Authentication Keepaliv
localhost:5000/mine
localhost:5000/mine
{
"average_hash": "60003880c0fcffff",
"index": 2,
"ipfs": "QmQiq4k4zSmuaF5erVUAsKXUTp9pnB2vK7FSDuRU6ggxKw",
"message": "New Block Forged",
"previous_hash": "6a19e4584545b4ad7a66cb832a94098a21c2578a6ed89e9447e18399a5d847cb",
"proof": 35382,
"vehicle_detail": "QmcVPmedHyERmJuoGo3BzoiTmmNUx3RGdhfXdmwMKjtbf5"
}

The Figure 6 shows the list of transactions (critical-message) into the distributed ledger of BVANET model. The first block in the chain is genesis block where random entry has been assigned. The second block onward, we have stored the average hash of transaction (critical-message), ipfs content addressed hash, previous hash, proof-of-work (PoW), timestamp, and vehicle details. The previous hash maintains the integrity of consequent blocks in the distributed ledger. The integrity property of the distributed ledger maintains the immutability of the records from the BVANET model. The PoW ensures the consistency of block with the unique block number. The peers of the blockchain network get same PoW during dissemination of the distributed ledger that ensures the availability of the transactions. The timestamp ensures the provenance (history) of the transactions. The transactions time is recorded into the block of the distributed ledger which specify that, when the transaction is created and also details about the transactions owner (in this case vehicular node). The timestamp feature provides transparency and trust

Figure 6. List of transactions (critical-message) in distributed ledger of BVANET Model

```
{
  "chain": [
    {
      "average_hash": "1",
      "index": 1,
      "ipfsh": "1",
      "previous_hash": "1",
      "proof": 100,
      "timestamp": 1568422962.460897,
      "transactions": [],
      "vehicle_detail": "1"
    },
    {
      "average_hash": "f02084c20f9f9fcf",
      "index": 2,
      "ipfsh": "QmZv5KwU9yuam1EBpsP3r42nCWXASXG1Y4aes2ykX5o9SP",
      "previous_hash": "61378f43979cc6c3a8e37943f306fc59800ea8e2be5f09f408282d2cdcb526b0",
      "proof": 22588,
      "timestamp": 1568423066.9522445,
      "transactions": [],
      "vehicle_detail": "QmfUDbnS55ZvcZkYMWfcKaVmsXoMH8sZ8p1ykwnxcydsoH"
    },
    {
      "average_hash": "60003880c0fcffff",
      "index": 3,
      "ipfsh": "QmQiq4k4zSmuaF5erVUAsKXUTp9pnB2vK7FSDuRU6ggxKw",
      "previous_hash": "8466f87a918c9c73592dce27e1c2dfe8678b1c2af3f471373a2126028f4f892b",
      "proof": 106178,
      "timestamp": 1568423139.5188725,
      "transactions": [],
      "vehicle_detail": "QmV82uru4xzEz7NJqVnUhscmVyDdn8UKhnwRnCZzfxpQ39"
    },
    {
      "average_hash": "e0e0f91188c0c1ff",
      "index": 4,
      "ipfsh": "Qmf3xcr2Sah89Cpj4tcBRhgSKvyLgpWH9W9sG7p5gysGgz",
      "previous_hash": "1360e70ea45fd91f2baa48b2aecc215e2a2044673419579cd4730c5a4156ec19",
      "proof": 51497,
      "timestamp": 1568423205.952914,
      "transactions": [],
      "vehicle_detail": "QmdvkqyGBVt8A84iwA1huf4DfS8CQqszjwvDh2iHNmLK4M"
    }
  ],
  "length": 4
}
```

among the peers in the system (BVANET). The detail of vehicular node is stored into the distributed ledger using content-addressed hash. We have stored content addressed hash rather than original size of the transaction into the distributed ledger of BVANET model. This underlying approach reduces the size of distributed ledger chain.

As shown in Figure 7, the critical-message is accessed by using content-addressed hash which is already stored into the distributed ledger of BVANET. The content-addressed hash can only be accessed by the already registered vehicular node. In Figure 7, the critical-message (traffic) has been shared by the vehicular node to the RSU. The registered RSU can access the vehicular details and critical-message details by using the content addressed hash from the distributed ledger.

Figure 7. Content-addressed hash to access the transaction (critical-message) in BVANET Model

As shown in Figure 8, the detail of vehicle is accessed by using content-addressed hash by the registered RSU in BVANET model. We have created a PDF file during upload of the critical message by vehicular node. The original PDF file is stored into the IPFS off-chain model and the generated hash is stored into the distributed ledger. The underlying scheme minimizes the storage size of the distributed ledger by storing content-addressed hash of the PDF (vehicular detail) file.

As shown in Figure 9, the similar or analogous (nearest similarity) feature of the transaction (critical-message) is matched against the stored average hash of the distributed ledger in BVANET model. The computed average hash of the transaction is matched with log of the average hash (stored in python list). The similar critical-message does not get uploaded to the distributed ledger to reduce the redundancy and congestion in the BVANET model. The original critical-message (image) is stored into the IPFS off-chain storage model and the average hash of the critical-message gets stored into the blockchain ledger.

The underlying technique of finding the average hash not only detects the similar original transactions but also detect the modified transaction. The transaction which is not similar or analogous to the original transaction after matching the existing average hash of distributed ledger gets disseminated among the peers of BVANET model.

Figure 8. Content-addressed hash to access the transaction (vehicle details) in BVANET Model

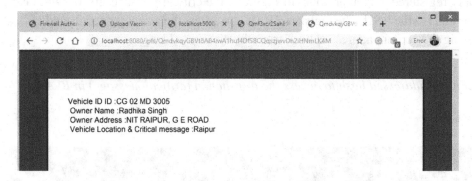

Figure 9. Average hash technique to detect the similar transaction upload in BVANET Model

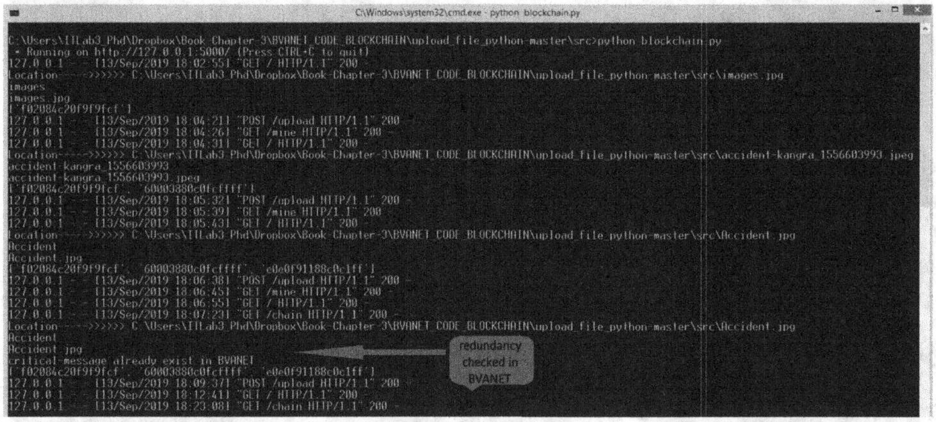

As shown in Figure 10, we have implemented the permissioned blockchain model, to maintain the authentication of the vehicular node. The underlying blockchain model mitigates the malicious attack on the BVANET owing to authorized access of transaction. In our permissioned (Consortium) network, the vehicular node (http://127.0.0.1:9007/nodes/register) is registered on the port 9007 in order to access the list of transactions from distributed ledger. To access the content from the distributed ledger, we have used content-addressed hash approach which ensures privacy of the transaction. The registration process of the vehicular nodes or RSU in the proposed model authenticates the peers in BVANET and also ensures security during transaction access. The malicious nodes cannot access the transactions (critical-message) of the distributed ledger owing to registration process of the peers. The registered vehicular node (http://127.0.0.1:9007/nodes/register) can access the distributed ledger (main chain) which is deployed on (http://127.0.0.1:5000/chain) by agreeing the consensus (PoW) approach of the proposed model on registered port number 9007. To access the similar content-based transaction from the distributed ledger (main chain) consensus resolve is applied (http://localhost:9007/nodes/resolve). In BVANET model, multiple vehicular node or RSU can register to share the critical-message on the distributed ledger (main chain). We have applied the process of registration to ensure the security in model from the malicious attack. We have also disseminated the distributed ledger among the peers of the BVANET to address the issue of centralized storage and single point of failure. The decentralized storage of distributed ledger (main-chain) on various sides of peers (vehicular nodes) ensures availability of the content in BVANET. The dissemination of the distributed ledger among various peers ensures the content recovery, if the distributed chain gets corrupted by the malicious vehicular node attack. Moreover, the BVANET model does not allow access of distributed ledger content to outside the network model owing to feature of permissioned or private infrastructure.

Figure 10. Adding new peer (vehicular node/ RSU) in BVANET Model

As shown in Figure 11, the lists of transactions are disseminated to the registered vehicular node (http://localhost:9007/nodes/resolve) by applying the consensus. As we can see the similar distributed ledger is shared to the peer (9007). The distributed ledger (main chain 5000 port) is replaced to the peer side with same number of block and their contents. The consistency of the block in BVANET is maintained during distributed ledger (main chain) content accessed by the peers owing to feature of consensus (PoW) approach.

RESULT ANALYSIS

In this section, we have evaluated the critical-message upload to detect the similar content upload in the blockchain network, in order to mitigate the redundancy and minimization of the storage size. In our proposed model, we have computed both average hash and content-addressed hash to address the existing challenges in blockchain technology. The computed average hash has been used to minimize redundancy in network and the content-addressed hash to minimize the storage size of distributed ledger.

Figure 11. List of transactions accessed by peers (vehicular node/RSU) on port(9007) after registration in BVANET Model

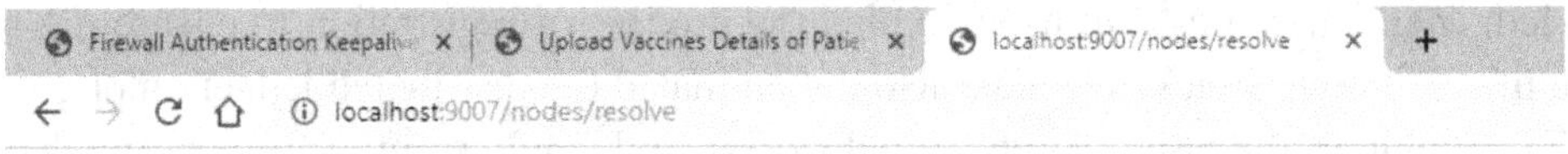


```
{
  "message": "Our chain was replaced",
  "new_chain": [
    {
      "average_hash": "1",
      "index": 1,
      "ipfsh": "1",
      "previous_hash": "1",
      "proof": 100,
      "timestamp": 1568422962.460897,
      "transactions": [],
      "vehicle_detail": "1"
    },
    {
      "average_hash": "f02084c20f9f9fcf",
      "index": 2,
      "ipfsh": "QmZv5KwU9yuam1EBpsP3r42nCWXASXG1Y4aes2ykX5o9SP",
      "previous_hash": "61378f43979cc6c3a8e37943f306fc59800ea8e2be5f09f408282d2cdcb526b0",
      "proof": 22588,
      "timestamp": 1568423066.9522445,
      "transactions": [],
      "vehicle_detail": "QmfUDbnS55ZvcZkYMWfcKaVmsXoMH8sZ8p1ykwnxcydsoH"
    },
    {
      "average_hash": "60003880c0fcffff",
      "index": 3,
      "ipfsh": "QmQiq4k4zSmuaF5erVUAsKXUTp9pnB2vK7FSDuRU6ggxKw",
      "previous_hash": "8466f87a918c9c73592dce27e1c2dfe8678b1c2af3f471373a2126028f4f892b",
      "proof": 106178,
      "timestamp": 1568423139.5188725,
      "transactions": [],
      "vehicle_detail": "QmV82uru4xzEz7NJqVnUhscmVyDdn8UKhnwRnCZzfxpQ39"
    },
    {
      "average_hash": "e0e0f91188c0c1ff",
      "index": 4,
      "ipfsh": "Qmf3xcr2Sah89Cpj4tcBRhgSKvyLgpWH9W9sG7p5gysGgz",
      "previous_hash": "1360e70ea45fd91f2baa48b2aecc215e2a2044673419579cd4730c5a4156ec19",
      "proof": 51497,
      "timestamp": 1568423205.952914,
      "transactions": [],
      "vehicle_detail": "QmdvkqyGBVt8A84iwA1huf4DfS8CQqszjwvDh2iHNmLK4M"
    }
  ]
}
```


As shown in TABLE 1, we have applied various operations on original critical-message which is uploaded by the vehicular network in order to detect the redundancy in the network. To access the content from distributed ledger, we have calculated the content-addressed hash for each transaction. To access the similar transaction from distributed ledger, we have found the average hash of each transaction. The average hash of each transaction is matched against original critical-message which is already stored into the distributed ledger. If the average hash of transaction (critical-event) is matched about 25% then we discard that transaction in order to mitigate the redundancy. We have computed the content-addressed hash to reduce the size of distributed ledger. The content-addressed hash takes only 46 bytes storage of the each transaction in BVANET model irrespective to the original size of transaction (critical-message).

Table 1. Similar transaction access from distributed ledger to detect redundancy in BVANETs

Critical-Message upload by Vehicular Node (Peer)	Types of Operations	Modifications %	Average hash	Content-addressed hash	Redundancy match %
	Original Image	NA	60003880 c0f8ffff	Qmc CTk Laudz3 DaEPkg 4U6t8U mu2WASPs ELTHmh M3ibYs3j	NA
	Blur	10%	60001880 c0f8ffff	QmWYRYu HH42D2 YBFJPHsp EZY1t LtDRH 386oWH4 krEJaThM	93.75%
	Brightness	100%	fec83880 c0f9ffff	Qme f3LAVh LPMMS vrGNByRA zeE6p7tr 3Wv2Cqb Smyda4dvd	68.75%
	Flip	NA	06001 c01031 fffff	Qm ZRfd5 abSSgcb 9gVe3XMQHZQDY uBGV6iU4 WDkMPtFJ8Bf	37.50%
	Gray-scale	NA	60001880 c0f8ffff	Qmec 8NSWNSCMHNe 9smqDq FZHsoksb BMoyt 4EYypSWTpzUF	93.75%
	Noise	100%	60083880 c0f9ffff	QmVx97 qiUBo2 FC4d5f5 feBjkpMhv H7xX8EbB JosPKgqo47	87.50%
	Saturation	100%	60083880 c0f8ffff	Qm RKKbPj L8m5vj1V 7JXBF8WRVMCY y8ZT2FPQPU 2Ja3qi5j	93.75%
	Sharpen	100%	74001880 c0fdffff	QmVeKvw PERbjd881 Cb8EWePva4 Zcv3vbi8 GyNJJPX mr8Ku	75.00%

CONCLUSION

In this chapter, we have implemented blockchain based vehicular adhoc network (BVANET) to share the critical-message among the peers (vehicular node or RSU). There are various applications are working in VANET to share the critical-message among the peers. However, the existing models are using the centralized storage (cloud) that are having various limitations like mutability, integrity, availability, security, and privacy. The existing model of critical-message sharing in VANET also suffers from the single point of failure due to centralized storage. To address these issues we have implemented the model which is based on blockchain (BVANET). The BVANET is based on GUI model which provides facilities to share the critical-message among the peers. In this chapter, we have not only addressed the existing issue but also provided the mitigation of redundancy in the VANET model. To mitigate the redundancy in distributed ledger, we have used average hash technique to find the analogous feature in the uploaded critical-message. We have discarded the transactions (critical-message) if it is matched 25% with original stored transaction in distributed ledger. In addition, we have used content-addressed hash to access the transactions (critical-message) from the distributed ledger. The content-addressed storage minimizes the size of the distributed ledger owing to hash storage of original uploaded transactions. In BVANET, we have stored two types of content-addressed hash namely ipfs and vehicle_detail. The ipfs describe the access of critical-message content from the distributed ledger and vehicle_detail describe the details of vehicular node that have uploaded the critical-message. To store the vehicle_detail we have created the PDF file with the detail of vehicular node. We have stored the generated PDF file into IPFS of-chain storage and their corresponding hash into the distributed ledger of BVANET model. The underlying approach makes better storage model (decentralized) in VANET owing to reduced size and minimized redundancy of transaction.

REFERENCES

Abuelela, M., & Olariu, S. (2010). *Taking VANET to the Clouds*. Academic Press.

Ahmad, F., Kazim, M., & Adnane, A. (2015). Vehicular Cloud Networks : Architecture, Applications and Security Issues. 2015 IEEE/ACM 8th International Conference on Utility and Cloud Computing (UCC), 571–576. 10.1109/UCC.2015.101

Baldini, G. (2019). Zone Keys Trust Management in Vehicular Networks based on Blockchain. 2019 Global IoT Summit (GIoTS), 1–6.

Dorri, A., Steger, M., Kanhere, S. S., & Jurdak, R. (2017). BlockChain : A Distributed Solution to Automotive Security and Privacy. *IEEE Communications Magazine*, *55*(December), 119–125. doi:10.1109/MCOM.2017.1700879

Gervais, A., Wüst, K., & Ritzdorf, H. (n.d.). On the Security and Performance of Proof of Work Blockchains. Academic Press.

Guo, S., Hu, X., Zhou, Z., Wang, X., Qi, F., & Gao, L. (2019). Trust Access Authentication in Vehicular Network Based on Blockchain. *China Communications*, *16*(June), 18–30. doi:10.23919/j.cc.2019.06.002

Jaoude, J. O. E. A., & Saade, R. G. (2019). Blockchain Applications – Usage in Different Domains. *IEEE Access : Practical Innovations, Open Solutions*, *7*, 45360–45381. doi:10.1109/ACCESS.2019.2902501

Jiang, T., Fang, H., & Wang, H. (2019). Blockchain-Based Internet of Vehicles : Distributed Network Architecture and Performance Analysis. IEEE Internet of Things Journal, 6(3), 4640–4649. doi:10.1109/JIOT.2018.2874398

Khelifi, H., Luo, S., Nour, B., Moungla, H., & Ahmed, S. H. (2018). Reputation-based Blockchain for Secure NDN Caching in Vehicular Networks. 2018 IEEE Conference on Standards for Communications and Networking (CSCN), 1–6. doi:10.1109/CSCN.2018.8581849

Kim, S. (2019). Impacts of Mobility on Performance of Blockchain in VANET. *IEEE Access : Practical Innovations, Open Solutions, 7*, 68646–68655. doi:10.1109/ACCESS.2019.2918411

Leiding, B., & Vorobev, W. V. (2018). *Enabling the Vehicle Economy Using a Blockchain-Based Value Transaction Layer Protocol for Vehicular Ad-Hoc Networks*. Academic Press.

Li, X., Jiang, P., Chen, T., Luo, X., & Wen, Q. (n.d.). A Survey on the Security of Blockchain Systems. Academic Press.

Lu, Z., Wang, Q., Qu, G., & Liu, Z. (2018). Article. 2018 17th IEEE International Conference On Trust, Security And Privacy In Computing And Communications/ 12th IEEE International Conference On Big Data Science And Engineering (TrustCom/BigDataSE), 98–103. 10.1109/TrustCom/BigDataSE.2018.00025

Lu, Z., Wang, Q., Qu, G., Member, S., Zhang, H., & Liu, Z. (2019). *A Blockchain-Based Privacy-Preserving Authentication Scheme for VANETs*. Academic Press.

Mengelkamp, E., Notheisen, B., Beer, C., Dauer, D., & Weinhardt, C. (2018). A blockchain-based smart grid : Towards sustainable local energy markets. Computer Science -. *Research for Development, 33*(1), 207–214. doi:10.100700450-017-0360-9

Min, X., Li, Q., Liu, L., & Cui, L. (2016). A Permissioned Blockchain Framework for Supporting Instant Transaction and Dynamic Block Size. 2016 IEEE Trustcom/BigDataSE/ISPA, 90–96. doi:10.1109/TrustCom.2016.0050

Nakamoto, S. (2008). Bitcoin: A Peer-to-Peer Electronic Cash System. www.bitcoin.org

Ostermaier, B., Florian, D., & Strassberger, M. (2007). *Enhancing the Security of Local Danger Warnings in VANETs - A Simulative Analysis of Voting Schemes*. Academic Press.

Qin, Y., & Huang, D. (2012). VehiCloud : Cloud Computing Facilitating Routing In Vehicular Networks. 2012 IEEE 11th International Conference on Trust, Security and Privacy in Computing and Communications, 1438–1445. 10.1109/TrustCom.2012.16

Salahuddin, M. A., Al-fuqaha, A., Guizani, M., & Cherkaoui, S. (2014). RSU Cloud and its Resource Management in support of Enhanced Vehicular Applications. 2014 IEEE Globecom Workshops (GC Wkshps), 127–132. doi:10.1109/GLOCOMW.2014.7063418

Security, D., Security, D., & Security, D. (n.d.). Toward a Distributed Trust Management scheme for VANET. Academic Press.

Shrestha, R. (2018). *Challenges of Future VANET and Cloud-Based Approaches*. Academic Press.

Shrestha, R., & Nam, S. Y. (2017). *Trustworthy Event-Information Dissemination in Vehicular Ad Hoc Networks*. Academic Press.

Technologies, I. (2010). *VANET : Vehicular Applications and Inter-Networking*. Academic Press.

Wang, W., Hoang, D. T., Hu, P., Xiong, Z., Niyato, D., Wang, P., Wen, Y., & Kim, D. I. (2019). A Survey on Consensus Mechanisms and Mining Strategy Management in Blockchain Networks. *IEEE Access : Practical Innovations, Open Solutions*, *7*, 22328–22370. doi:10.1109/ACCESS.2019.2896108

Wang, X., Zeng, P., Patterson, N., Jiang, F., Doss, R., & Member, S. (2019). An Improved Authentication Scheme for Internet of Vehicles Based on Blockchain Technology. *IEEE Access : Practical Innovations, Open Solutions*, *7*, 45061–45072. doi:10.1109/ACCESS.2019.2909004

Wang, Y., Su, Z., Zhang, N., & Member, S. (2019). BSIS : Blockchain-Based Secure Incentive Scheme for Energy Delivery in Vehicular Energy Network. *IEEE Transactions on Industrial Informatics*, *15*(6), 3620–3631. doi:10.1109/TII.2019.2908497

Yahiatene, Y. (2018). Towards a Blockchain and Software-Defined Vehicular Networks approaches to secure Vehicular Social Network. 2018 IEEE Conference on Standards for Communications and Networking (CSCN), 1–7. doi:10.1109/CSCN.2018.8581756

Yang, Z., Yang, K., Lei, L., Member, S., Zheng, K., Member, S., & Leung, V. C. M. (2019). Blockchain-Based Decentralized Trust Management in Vehicular Networks. IEEE Internet of Things Journal, 6(2), 1495–1505. doi:10.1109/JIOT.2018.2836144

Zhang, X., & Chen, X. (2019). Data Security Sharing and Storage Based on a Consortium Blockchain in a Vehicular Ad-hoc Network. *IEEE Access : Practical Innovations, Open Solutions*, *7*, 58241–58254. doi:10.1109/ACCESS.2018.2890736

Zhang, X., Li, R., & Cui, B. (2018, August). A Security architecture of VANET based on blockchain and mobile edge computing. In 2018 1st IEEE International Conference on Hot Information-Centric Networking (HotICN) (pp. 258-259). IEEE. doi:10.1109/HOTICN.2018.8605952

Chapter 4
Blockchain–Enabled Decentralization Service for Automated Parking Systems

Keesara Sravanthi Reddy

iD https://orcid.org/0000-0003-0215-8664

IT Department, Vallurupalli Nageswara Rao Vignana Jyothi Institute of Engineering and Technology, India

ABSTRACT

Due to recent development in technology and smart devices in people's lives, their lives are becoming easier and safer. One of popular examples in todays is parking (i.e., people find free parking space without moving a long distance or consuming more time or fuel over the road network). Today many automated companies are designing vehicles, but we are still unable to get automatic parking system in an area. Finding free parking slot/space has a probability of revealing user's privacy (i.e., either by service provider to third party/attacker or submitted information [user personal information] can be hacked by an attacker [via performing attacks like Man in Middle, Denial of Service, etc.]). Hence, privacy is a main issue in parking. Providing sufficient privacy in parking to vehicle users is a primary concern of this chapter. For that, this chapter used the blockchain technology to avoid privacy issues (raised in parking searching). Blockchain technology makes reservation of parking slot transparent, decentralized, and secure (privacy-preserved).

1. INTRODUCTION

In the modern world, the growth of the industry is rapidly increasing by increase in the number of vehicles on the streets, which raises the parking related issues. In day to day life parking vehicles is becoming a hectic problem. In big cities any place if you want travel first thing, we do is searching for parking lot. If no parking lot is free at our place, we need to search for other parking lot in other location, evenwe cannot park our vehicles road side because government collects fine from us for parking vehicle at road side which is illegal. (parkres, 2018) With the increase of population there is increase in

DOI: 10.4018/978-1-7998-3295-9.ch004

vehicles (for daily needs) on the road than ever before in human history. The more vehicles, more risk to control traffic on the streets. Most of the times people spend more time to find parking lot then doing the main work for which they came out for. Parking lot has become a rare place to find in metropolises, town centers, shopping areas, Imax, railwaystations, busstations, hospitals and sometimes airports also. Getting parking lot at these locations is a luck.In case of emergency hospital visits, people often end up parking in the no-parking zonethe patient still has to suffer more. Ultimately,it causes additional parking problems and adds other patients and ambulances to the traffic woes around hospital. In Current generation the automated vehicles are coming up with new features and many automated companies are competing each other to introduce advanced automated vehicles in the market. Smart driver aid systems play a main role as the automotive industry becomes more automated due to this competition. Smart vehicles are increasing but the parking lot are not sufficient. It is not possible for network companies, because parking providers do not collaborate with the companies, to provide updated data on parking lots over the internet.

A Smart parking system was developed in the creation of traffic management systems to decrease the cost of employing car drivers and optimize the use of resources for owners of parking lots.(Lu et al., 2009) VANET (Vehicular Adhoc Network) is a technology developed to ensure safe and efficient drivingexperience and traffic management. VANET may include wireless sensor networks, vehicle-to-vehicle(V2V) and vehicle-to-infrastructure(V2I) communication. In the existing smart parking system still, it has few major technical issues such as privacy, security and trust. The most promising use cases for blockchain is intersection of blockchain and IoT. Blockchain integrated into IoT can improve the development of IoT application environment. The privacy risks of IoT are increasing day-to-day by the lack of fundamental security concepts in many IoT applications. Blockchain anonymity is well-suited for most IoT applications in which the user's identification must remain confidential.(Zinon et al.,2019) Blockchain with IoT have many benefits. 1.**Trust:** It removes trusted third party and all data correctness and data immutability are done by participants. In IoT applications it is complex task to build trust among various entities while data processing. 2.**Security:** Blockchain uses various security mechanisms like hashing algorithms to secure transaction data. 3. **Transaction:**blockchain by its distributed nature it offers, IoT to process billions of transactions between smart devices by blockchain. 4. **Decentralization:** Blockchain provides decentralized authority, i.e., no centralized system. When IoT applications do nottrust centralized system, it goes for blockchain. Blockchain is a distributed public ledger, it allows users to have secure transactions which are broadcasted into a network and once verified are linked with previous blocks expanding the networks capacity. Blockchain uses peer-to-peer network. Using cryptography, it secures all the transaction. So that no one can temper the data. As, there is a distributed ledger it doesn't require any centralized authority (trusted third party).Before transactions are performed between varies parties, they have to accept the agreement, it is provided by trusted third party. Smart contract is aMemorandum of understanding (MOU) between different parties. In blockchain smart contract plays a vital role. They are saved on a public distributed ledger which cannot be tampered or hacked. Based on smart contract only transactions are implemented. All the transactions are automatically sent on to distributed public ledger without any trusted third party or an intermediator.

Related Work

There are some existing algorithms to improve the smart parking system. Few of the algorithms will be reviewed in this section. (Siemens, 2012)SiPark intelligent parking system was proposed. Which includes easy paying machines, parking guidance system, modern car parking technology. For detecting the status of vehicle in parking lot they used Rader sensors. Which in turn are connected to the network to transmit status of vehicle report. In (Tang et al., 2016) proposed a smart parking system using wireless sensor networks to detect the availability of parking spaces. (Hortin,1995)A prototype model is implemented based on mote products from crossbow.(Caliskan, Graupner& Mauve, 2006) based on wireless-LAN IEEE 205.11 author proposed a parking place availability system using VANET (vehicular ad hoc networks) to broadcast the parking availability status as text packets. In (Benson et al., 2006) proposed car park management system using wireless sensor networks based on Tiny OS 1.1.7. In (Boda, Nasipuri& Howitt, 2006)proposed a parking lots track system at public places using wireless sensor networks, magnetometer signature measurements and this information is communicated to users. It is implemented based on Mica2 Motes. In (Lu et al., 2007) developed a new SPARK (Smart PARKing) model using VANET (Vehicular Ad hoc Network) which provides real-time parking navigation services, security for parked cars and parking guidance services for large parking lots. In (Yan et al., 2011) based on secured wireless networks and sensor communication presented a secure, intelligent and secure Smart parking system. In (Wang &He, 2011) proposed a prototype model for Reservation-based Smart Parking System (RSPS) to provide the reservation for parking cars. It also broadcast the status of parking It is done by registering into a mobile application. In (Bonde, 2014) designed an intelligent car parking system using image processing, using camera captured parking lots on brown rounded image and processed to detect the status of parking lot. Free parking lots will be displayed on 7-segment display. Parking lot images are taken in brown rounded image. Then identify the image boundaries. The noise is deleted from this image and the boundaries of object is identified. This way the free parking lots are found. In (Sebastian et al., 2010) proposed a vision-based car parking system which uses two types of images (negative and positive) to detect free parking lot. Positive images consist of car images from various angles. Negative images contain no cars in the area. To detect the presence of cars in parking area, co-ordinates of parking lots are used. Drawback of this system is types of camera that are located in specific parking areas for selecting as input to co-ordinate system. Limited set of positive and negative images. In (Basharuddin et al., 2012) designed and implemented number plate recognition technique for developing autonomous car parking system using image processing. To process the vehicles number plates. The license number plate images are required. To detect free parking lots ultrasonic sensors are used. Then images of number plates are taken for analysis. Meanwhile the entry timing will be noted to calculate parkin fees. If the parking lots are not available displays FULL sign on LCD screen. Drawback of this system is the background of number plate should be black and white compulsory, Analysis is limited to number plates with just one row. In (Sarkar, Rokoni, Ismail 2012) proposed a smart parking system which is designed as a mechanical model with a facility called image processing. By using lift at multiple levels cars will be parked. Image processing is used to capture number plate and store in database to avoid illegal car entry. It is a fully Automated model with less human involvement. In (Amiri et al., 2019) implemented a privacy- preserving smart parking system using blockchain and private information retrieval. To ensure security, transparency and availability a consortium blockchain is created by different parking lot owners. Consortium blockchain is used to store all parking lots offers on shared ledger. Users can reserve available parking lots and user's private information like identity, location are preserved by private information retrieval system.

2. IMPORTANCE OF PRIVACY PRESERVING PARKING

Drivers feel frustration to find parking lots in the city. It is a time-consuming process to find the parking lots in smart cities or the area where many of shopping malls, Imax exist. Because of unavailable parking lots in busy area there is lot of chance to have traffic congestion. For parking cars, the drivers have to travel large distances from their desired destination. Due to this driver will forget the purpose of coming out. Finding manually parking lots is very difficult.so, many drivers will opt for smart parking system applications. But there is lot of chances to misuse the driver's information by intruder. He will get the drivers private information by compromising the application, to use smart parking services driver has to install the mobile application. (Yang, Portilla, &Riesgo, 2012) It will take the driver`s private information to make him as registered user. Every driver has to register into the application then only he can reserve the parking lots. Driver can check the nearby parking lots; he can also compare the fare for parking car in parking lots. While registering, driver has to supply all his personal information such as his name, ID proof, car type, car license number plate, Type of payment, Credit card details (for paying parking rent). Drivers has to allow the app to track his position so, that it can show you the nearby parking lots. So, that the app can track the driver locations such as what places he is travelling (frequently visiting places). (safi et al., 2018)All his data is stored in cloud. mobile application is a smart application, here driver don't know whether his data is safe or not. Just he is believing the application. But there may be many chances to misuse driver's data by application owners. They can sell this information to intruders. Hackers may take the drivers information by compromising the system and they can track driver's location and he may blackmail or he may do criminal actions. Hackers may steal a driver information and he may book multiple parking lots on his name. so, that there will be congestion in parking areas and other drivers can't avail the parking lots. Hackers may compromise the cloud; he may modify the data which is present in it. Many IoT applications came up with new proposed algorithms, which mainly concentrated on the providing the parking lots, reserving the nearby parking lots and authenticating drivers (checking whether registered driver is availing or not), Recently some IoT applications are introduced to avoid multiple booking by one driver (driver who tries to reserve the parking lot in multiple areas at a time), but not on providing the security to the driver's information. From the above discussion we found who data is replicated and misused by hackers. So, to avoid this we proposed a system using blockchain which protects the driver's information, parking owner's information like this system authenticates the drivers. All the driver's information is protected by cryptography encryption algorithms. Only himself can view his data, drivers without showing their personal information to parking owners they can reserve the parking lots. Blockchain ensures that only one parking lot is reserved by one driver at a time. There are many facilities like they can pay for parking by using app wallet or any online payment method. So, that transactions are permanent they can't be altered. So, everything is transparent to all. There is other most important point is every driver can check there previous parking fairs with location where he parked, time and date. In the automated parking, driver has to operate the car to park itself into the parking lot by smart devices which are located in vehicle, even in the automated parking, driver plays a vital role. Reserving parking lot from mobile application is done by driver/vehicle owner itself. Blockchain stores all transitions for years. By this we can easily trace the people who did criminal activities. For many IoT based smart parking system they used blockchain.

3. ROLE OF BLOCKCHAIN IN PROVIDING DECENTRALIZED PRIVACY/ SERVICES

Unlike the centralized solutions, Blockchain came up with a new advantage of providing decentralized services. In IoT applications blockchain plays a vital role. In centralized system, to make agreement between various parking owners they make use of trusted third party, and for making agreement parking owners has to pay lot of money to trusted third parties. Even we paid we are not sure that the data is secured with trusted third party. So, to overcome the above issue with centralized system we are opting decentralized system in blockchain, it doesn't require any trusted third party for the agreement between various parking owners. Blockchain is a record of transactions which is distributed in nature. It is transparent, immutable (unchangeable) public ledger organized as blocks of chain and managed by set of miners/validators (participant who validates the data correctness). (Amiri et al., 2019) Consortium blockchain technology provides decentralization. Consortium blockchain is created by parking lot owners to send his parking offers into blockchain network, which records all parking lots information on distributed public ledger. Here, the smart parking system will run on blockchain, so every driver/vehicle owner who want to reserve parking lots they have to register onto mobile app and all that information is encrypted and placed on the blockchain, only driver can view his data. blockchain has smart contract which acts as interface between various parking owners, this feature is obtained by decentralization. Here, no need of wasting money for trusted third parties. Smart contracts are immutable (change cannot take place by outsides). Blockchain is list of blocks where each block consists of Vehicle details like vehicle type, vehicle license number, vehicle brand, parking location details like area of parking, time period of parking, payment details like estimated fare for parking, parking offers and hash algorithms are used for encrypting the block data so that only the authorized block people can view the hash values (encrypted key which secure the block information). Blockchain contains a distributed ledger (which contains all the parking lot information) which is transparent (shows all the parking lot reservation information to public). Blockchain doesn't reveal the driver's information to parking owners, because parking owners may send personal e-mails to drivers about parking offers. But it allows drivers to check parking offers on public ledger (Amiri et al., 2019). Blockchain authenticates the drivers by short randomized signatures. So, only registered drivers can access parking offers on blockchain. Blockchain stores the blocks data permanently. So, it is easy to access the information by car owners at any time. For example, for same parking lot if more than one is trying to reserve the parking lot, will go for first request generated driver. So, we can avoid collision.

4. EXISTING METHODS IN PROVIDING PRIVACY PRESERVING PARKING TO VEHICLES/ AUTOMATED VEHICLES

Few of existing techniques for privacy preserving parking vehicles are discussed below.

Table 1.

Authors	Technology	Smart devices used	Features	Achievements	Limitations	Future scope	Reliability
Rongxing Lu, Xiaodong Lin, Haojin Zhu and Xuemin (Sherman) Shen(Lu et al., 2009)	VANET (vehicular ad hoc network) based SPARK (smart parking) scheme	RSUs (road side units), wireless sensor network	1) Real-time parking navigation service used to find quickly the nearest vacant parking lot. 2)intelligent anti-theft protection service which are used to guard the parked vehicle by using parking lot RSUs. 3)parking information broadcasting service to the moving vehicles, it makes drivers more convenient to choose near by parking lots quickly.	Parking navigation system, antitheft protection, fast finding parking lots.	Used only for large parking spaces.		High
Wesam Al Amiri, Mohamed Baza, Karim Banawan, Mohamed Mahmoud, Waleed Alasmary and Kemal Akkaya (Amiri et al., 2019)	Blockchain and information-theoretic PIR technique.	Low cost sensors, wireless sensor network	1)secure system without a trusted third party-decentralization provided by blockchain to avoid trusted third party.it broadcasts all the transaction information on the distributed public ledger. so, no one can temper or hack the data. 2) location privacy-without revealing the driver's information, driver can check parking offers on blockchain by using PIR technique. 3)reservation request unlikability-driver can reserve different parking lots at different times using short randomized signature (encryption method). 4)authentication-authenticate the driver by short randomized signature.	Secure drivers private information and modifications on performed transactions are impossible.	Preserving privacy of drivers with low communication and Computation overhead.	Preserving privacy of drivers with low computation for large parking areas.	High
ZinonZinonos, Panayiotis Christodoulou, Andreas Andreou, and SavvasChatzichristofis (Zinon et al.,2019)	IoT with Blockchain	License based recognition system and Raspberry pi 3 with camera, wireless sensor network	1)blockchain enables secured transactions over p2p network. Smart contracts record all the transactions which are not hacked, altered, tempered. All the recorded vehicle number plates are called authorized vehicles. 2)it allows only authorized vehicles into the parking area-Cameras will capture number plate of vehicle at the entrance of parking area. vehicle authorization is checked by matching number plates of vehicles barrier.		Blockchain provide trusted access with less money and time.		High
Farhad Rad, HadiPazhokhzadeh and Hamid Parvin (Rad et al., 2017)	VANET, Adaptive neuro-fuzzy systems (ANFIS), Multi-objective genetic algorithm.	Low cost sensors, wireless sensor network	1)traffic flow prediction model-to predict the traffic speed by using VANET. 2)multi-objective genetic algorithm -used to process all the requests for parking at a time.it provides nearest parking lots to all drivers who are requested.	Predicting the time to reach nearby parking lots which are reserved by drivers.	Consider the past traffic information	Predict the traffic speed, density and time on each path with the online data and past data.	High
Zhaojunlu, wenchaoliu, qian wang, gang qu, and zhenglinliu (Lu et al., 2018)	blockchain-based anonymous reputation system (BARS), VANET, reputation evaluation algorithm.	RSUs (road side units), wireless sensor network	1)A reputation evaluation algorithm-To prevent broadcasting of forged messages between internal vehicles to expose misbehaviours. 2)certificate blockchain and revoke blockchain – starts transparent authorities, activities for all VANET entities. 3)message blockchain-used to record all the broadcast messages as persistent evidence for evaluating vehicle status	Transparent, anonymity, efficiency, robustness	Mainly focussing on preserving privacy for drivers' profile and vehicle private information.		High
Sabbir Ahmed, Soaibuzzaman, Mohammad Saidur Rahman, Mohammad SaiedurRahaman (Ahmed et al., 2019)	IoT with blockchain.	Smart integrated parking system, smart contracts, wireless sensor network	Smart integrated system provides the platform for all the parking owners to communicate and offer the parking lots to the users by blockchain network. Smart contract is used to record transactions between parties.	Improves performance, trust	scalability	Provides robust implementation with real-time datasets to verify that the integrated smart system is scalable.	High
Thanh Nam Pham, Ming-Fong Tsai, Duc Binh Nguyen, Chyi-Ren Dow, And Der-Jiunn Deng (Pham et al., 2015)	Cloud, IoT	Cloud service, RFID, Arduino module, wireless sensor network	Registered vehicles (cars) can reserve the parking lots. This information is stored in cloud and sent to system. Used Mathematical models reduce the waiting time of every driver for parking car. and while entering into parking lot RFID authenticates the vehicle and it updates the number of parking lots at entry, exit point.	Improves performance, Minimizes the waiting time for parking.	Small parking areas.	Focus on security and implementation of parking system in large scales.	High

5. ISSUES AND CHALLENGES IN USINGBLOCKCHAIN CONCEPT IN AD-HOC NETWORK/ VEHICLES

Finding a free parking lot in an urban area especially, in peak hours, is always time consuming and frustrating to drivers.Several parking guidance systems have been developed over the past decade to mitigate confusion and inconvenience for drivers. The current smart parking systems use sensors to know the available free parking lots and to provide the parking guidance to the drivers. Major of smart parking systems rely on wireless communication to ensure better performance. It would be of great benefit if the driver had up-to-date traffic updates and information on the free parking area near the destination location. (Arif et al., 2019) In industrial and academic levels VANET have received particular attention. With the massive implementation of wireless communication technologies, most of the car manufactories and telecom industries gear up to equip each car with OBU (On Board Unit), it allows variety of cars to communicate with each other as well as RSU (Road Side Unit), in order to improve driving experience and road safety. Thus, it is possible to track the occupancy of the parking lots, guide drivers to the free parking lots in large parking areas and guarding cars in parking lots by means of vehicular communication network (VANET).

Blockchain is list of transactions which are immutable and these transactions are stored on distributed public ledger. Data receivedby peer-to-peer network.Blockchain is gaining rapid popularity for many other applications including smart contracts, decentralized cloud storage and digital assets. Blockchain is also called as transaction chain. In blockchain peer-to-peer network any node can be a miner. Responsibility of an entity is mining blocks to blockchain by solving resource-intensive cryptographic puzzle known as Proof Of Work (POW) and adding new blocks to blockchain. When new transaction occurs, it is kept in distributed public ledger. miner will validate each and every transaction by signatures and appends new transaction block to the Blockchain. (Arushi&sumit, 2018) The robustness is ensured by blockchain by processing a single transaction with multiple miners.Robustness however comes at a cost because several miners have to spend their resources to perform the same operation, which also increases thedelay in operation. In order to address the above-mentioned security and privacy issue in VANET, Blockchain is distinguished by its following outstanding features:

- Decentralization:The lack of central control guarantees the scalability and robustness of the networks of all participating nodes and removes many-to-one traffic flows that in turn reduces delays and overcomes the issue of a single failure point.
- Anonymity:The inherent anonymity is ideal for most VANET use cases, in which the identity of users has to be kept private.
- Trust: blockchain have smart contract, it makes contract among various parking owners without using trusted third party. Smart contracts are immutable, cannot be hacked.
- Privacy: while reserving the parking lots drivers has to provide his private information. To provide privacy for driver's private information, blockchain uses encryption algorithm i.e., hash values.
- Security: Blockchain handles all unknown parties securely on a peer-to-peer network to perform transactions.
- Traffic congestion: by allowing drivers to pre-book the parking lots .it avoids traffic congestion.
- Authentication: every parking lot reserved vehicles will be recorded in smart contract, before entering into the parking area smart devices like RFID authenticates and allows into the area.

There are some issues in using blockchain over Ad hoc networks:

- Device failure: There may be an instance, while travelling to nearest parking lot, suddenly the parking navigation system was failed in automated cars.
- When RSU stored information is compromised by intruder, the parking lots details will be unsecured.
- Mining process is computationally intensive.
- Miners required time for processing the transaction, it delays the time.
- Blockchain scales poorly as there is an increase in number of users in ad hoc network.

Table 2.

constraint's	Distributed Local ledger	Distributed Shared ledger
Blockchain visibility	Secure/private	Secure/private
Transaction chaining	Previous transaction of same user	Previous transaction of same user
Transaction mining	All transactions	All transactions
Transaction verification	No verification	signature
Transaction parameters	Block-number, hash of data, time, output, Public key, policy rules	Block-number, hash of data, time, output, Public key, policy rules
Blockchain controller	owner	owner
How many blocks required to each transaction	One block	One block
Effects of 51% attack	Not possible	Not possible
Encryption method	No need	Public key/private key

6. OPPORTUNITIES FOR FUTURERESEARCHERS IN RESPECTIVE AREA

Now-a-days society gradually relies on internet (computer-based information system) to improve the performance and efficiency, smart parking systems are quickly increasing in number. In day-to-day life smart parking systems become a necessity, especially in smart cities, dense population centers. While designing smart parking systems in user point of view, two main issues are emerged, operational issues and technical challenges. These issues need to be tackled right from the beginning to ensure that the system works efficiently. All the existing techniques are related to traditional smart parking systems in the last era indicates that they do not satisfy drivers requirements.

(Muftah & Mikael, 2016) The operational and technical challenges- it is very clear that majority of smart parking systems only guarantee a free parking lots virtually, but do not mention where it is exactly located; these types of systems mainly focus on counting number of cars that entered into parking area and number of cars that left from parking area, thus continuously updating thenumber of free parking lots. These systems depend on the driver then finding the free parking lot by driving around until they see it. One of the critical issues for smart parking systems when drivers employ these systems is how to provoke trust in the system: what is the guarantee that users trust the system and whether both trust each other when being directed to a reserved parking space? In many of parking lots CCTV is used to monitor the parked cars. But they don't have idea whether the car is parked in their lot or wrong lot. However, these systems are not "smart" enough to identify and then match cars to their reserved parking lot spots, and so relies on users' grievances after the fact. Based on wireless sensor networks, most of the new proposed smart parking systems that have been studied. Which in turn requires a small place (hole) to place the sensor in each parking lot, so to adopt this system involves infrastructure change in addition to many complex requirements regarding circuits, etc. smart parking system operation is unpredictable, as environmental factors such as dust or snow (anything that covers the sensors, include the units being covered purposely)could results the whole system failure. Despite extensive research, Image processing systems are still not accurate. Especially at night or when cars are parked incorrectly.

It is clear from this analysis that a smart parking system solution is urgently needed to worsen the existing problem with the passage of time. The review found that there were no previous studies published in the literature related to the assessment of these systems that also took into account the views of stakeholders.For the aforementioned reasons, there is a general trend among scholars to use WSNs, and there has been a trend over the past five years to use the IoT principle. The study found a number of limitations in the literature. The best technical solution package seems not to be settled on, because there are limitations in any one area.Each system has their own model which uses different techniques to facilitate parking services for the driver. Each system model has pro and cons in terms of following criteria such as cost, reliability, scalability, accuracy, circuit complexity.

Therefore, the above issues require the future investigation by future researchers.

7. AN OPEN DISCUSSION: IMPORTANCE OF BLOCKCHAIN AS DECENTRALIZED APPLICATIONS AND NEED OF (FOR) FUTURE

A blockchain is a continuously growing blocks of chain, each containing a previous block cryptographic hash, a time stamp and the information it holds. The data present in blockchain is immutable because it contains previous block cryptographic hash value. This immutability feature is fundamental to blockchain applications.Maintenance of cryptocurrencies with peer-to-peer (P2P) ledgers has become the first blockchain killer software. Bitcoin is the cryptocurrency which was an ended with bad reputation. Centralized model controls the operations on all individual units from a single point. Centralized systems can be distributed (broadcasts the transaction) as well. Most of the software applications follow centralized model.

So, it is more prone to single-point-of-failure (SPOF).Because of the single point-of-failure (SPOF) problem, centralized systems are criticized for their weakness.The novel form of the blockchain-empowered software system is dApps (decentralized applications).dApp blockchain is completely hosted by P2P blockchain system.No maintenance and governance from the original developers will be expected for the deployed dApp. In other words, without any human intervention, the blockchain is operable, which forms decentralized autonomous organization (DAO). (Cai et al., 2018)dAppsare categorized by four properties given below:

- Open source:Because of the trustworthy nature of blockchain, dApps need to open-source their codes to allow third-party audits.

- Internal Cryptocurrency Support: Internal currency is the mechanism for a specific dApp that runs the ecosystem.With tokens, quantifying all credits and transactions between network participants, including content providers and consumers, is feasible for a dApp.
- Decentralized Consensus: The foundation of transparency is the consensus of decentralized nodes.
- No Central Point of Failure: A completely decentralized system should have no single point of failure as the blockchain would host and execute all components of the applications.

In one website called "state of dApps" summarized that in many industries, blockchain technology has been implemented. Ethereum is the platform for blockchain, where different categories of dApps are hosted, it includes exchange, media,energy,health,insurance,finance,identity etc. majority of state-of-artsdApps are partially decentralized.Blockstack is a decentralized network of computing and an app ecosystem that manages the identity and information of users.OpenBazaar is fully decentralized peer-to-peer network which is used to develop the e-commerce transactions. We will discuss most popular existing dApps.

- **Games:**

The video game industry fits perfectly with the essence of cryptocurrencies ecosystem as it fulfils most game players ' ultimate dream: Actors in the gaming world are the virtual characters, these can be traded and inherited into a new game. The new game emerging trend is blockchain-based game. Most of blockchain-based games are in initial stage because of its limitations of transaction fee and process delay. These games are mainly focussing on virtual assets. This type of games is not much fun, but it still brought a drastic change in gaming industry. Similar gaming mechanisms have been used to build many other blockchain games on different virtual assets such as Etheremon, CryptoCelebrities, CryptoCountries, Etherbots etc.Blockchain-based games benefits non-fungible tokens and system transparency features.

- **User-generated content (UGC) network:**

User-created content (UCC) is known as user-generated content (UGC). User can create and publish any form of content, such as blogs, video, discussion post which can be cited by other users. Reddit, Flickr, Wikipedia are the most popular UGC applications. Existing UGC applications have complex issues regarding privacy and security. Some small creator's original content is easily stolen by other famous websites. Few of social media platforms gathers the user's private information for selling to advertisers, to target users for advertising. To solve the above problems blockchain technology is used, which is decentralized in nature. Steem,Gems,
ONO are the some of blockchain-based UGC platforms.

- **Internet of things:**

Billions of physical devices equipped with sensors are connected to theinternet for sharing and collecting the information among devices through network and controlling the environment is known as internet of things. In order to build a digital world, data is collected and communicated without human involvement. Most of IoT applications are suffering with lack of security issues. To overcome security issues blockchain emerged with IoT. Blockchain-based IoT solutions are well-suited to improve performance in smart applications. Blockchain is intended as a basis for IoT applications which involves transactions and interactions. Most popular blockchain-based IoT applications are smart hardware, supply chain, source tracing.

8. SUMMARY

This chapter provides a state of blockchain network to find and reserve the parking lots across a city. In first section, discussed about how important the parking lots in our daily life and what are problems drivers are facing on roads in peak hours. Such as waiting time for occupying parking lot, time taken to search the parking lot, because of huge number of vehicles on road waiting for parking leads to traffic congestion, wastage of fuel etc. To overcome the above problems, we proposed blockchain decentralization system, each block contains transaction details, by smart contract we record all the parking offers which are immutable, like that we are providing trust without trusted third party. In next sections, discussed the existing models for smart parking systems with different technologies such as IoT, Blockchain emerged with IoT, VANET (Vehicle Ad hoc Network), features in proposed models, limitations of each model, methods and algorithms used in various models, stating the future scope for smart parking systems. Discussing the issues and challenges in VANET-based parking systems and solutions to overcome these challenges using blockchain and IoT.

REFERENCES

Ahmed, S., Soaibuzzaman, Rahman, S. M., & Rahaman, S. M. (2019). A Blockchain-Based Architecture for Integrated Smart Parking Systems. *2019 IEEE International Conference On Pervasive Computing and Communications Workshops (PerCom Workshops)*. 10.1109/PERCOMW.2019.8730772

Amiri, A. I. W., Baza, M., Banawan, K., Mahmoud, M., Alasmary, W., & Akkaya, K. (2019). *Privacy-Preserving Smart Parking System Using Blockchain and Private Information Retrieval*. https://arxiv.org/abs/1904.09703

Arif, M., Wang, G., Bhuiyan, A. Z., Wang, M., Chen, T., & Jianer. (2019). A survey on security attacks in VANETs: Communication, applications and challenges. *Vehicular Communications, 19*, 100-179. www.elsevier.com/locate/vehcom

Arushi, A., & Sumit, Y. (2018). *Block chain Based Security Mechanism for Internet of Vehicles (IoV). In 3rd International Conference on Internet of Things and Connected Technologies, (ICIoTCT)*. Elsevier. https://www.ssrn.com/link/3rd-iciotct-2018

Basharuddin, N., Yusnita, R., & Norbaya, F. (2012). Intelligent Parking space detection system based on image Processing. *International Journal of Innovation, Management and Technology, 3*(3), 232–253.

Benson, J. P., O'Donovan, T., O'sullivan, P., Roedig, U., & Sreenan, C. (2006). Car-Park management using wireless sensor networs. Proceedings of 31 IEEE coif. Local Computer Networks, 588-595.

Boda, V. K., Nasipuri, A., & Howitt, I. (2007). Design Considerations for a Wireless Sensor Network for Locating Parking Spaces. *Proceedings of IEEE Southeastcon*, 698–703. doi:10.1109/SECON.2007.342990

Bonde, D. J., Rohit, S. S., Akshay, S. K., Suresh, K., & Uday, B. (2014). Automated car parking system commanded by mobile application. *International Conference on Computer Communication and Informatics (ICCCI -2014)*. 10.1109/ICCCI.2014.6921729

Cai, W., Wang, Z., Jason B. E., Hong, Z., Feng, C., & Leung, C. M. V. (2018). Decentralized Applications: The Blockchain-Empowered Software System. *IEEE Access*, *6*, 53019-53033. doi: . doi:10.1109/ACCESS.2018.2870644

Caliskan, C., Graupner, D., & Mauve, M. (2006). Decentralized discovery of free parking places. *Proceedings of the 3rd international workshop on Vehicular ad hoc networks*.

Lu, R., Lin, X., Zhu, H., & Shen, X. (2009). SPARK: A New VANET-based Smart Parking Scheme for Large Parking Lots. *IEEE Communications Society subject matter experts for publication in the IEEE INFOCOM 2009 Proceedings*, 1413-1421. doi:. doi:10.1109/ ACCESS.2018.2864189

Mike, A. H. (1995). *Crossbow Technologies*. http://www.xbow.com

Muftah, F., & Mikael, F. (2016). Investigation of Smart Parking Systems and their technologies Completed Research Paper. *Thirty Seventh International Conference on Information Systems*, 1-14.

Parkres. (2018). https://www.parkres.org

Pham, N. T., Ming-Fong, T., Nguyen, B., Chyi-Ren, D., & Der-Jiunn, D. (2015). *A Cloud-Based Smart-Parking System Based on Internet-of-Things Technologies. Emerging Cloud-Based Wireless Communications and Networks, 3, 1581-1591*.

Rad, F., Pazhokhzadeh, H., & Parvin, H. (2017). A Smart Hybrid System for Parking Space Reservation in VANET. *Journal of Advances in Computer Engineering and Technology*, *3*(1).

Safi, Q., Luo, S., Limin, P., Liu, W., Hussain, R., &Bouk, H. S. (2018). SVPS: Cloud-Based Smart Vehicle Parking System Over Ubiquitous VANETs. *Computer Networks*. doi: .2018.03.034 doi:10.1016/j.comnet

Sarkar, M. A. R., Rokoni, A. A., Reza, M. O., & Ismail, M. F. (2012). Smart Parking system with image processing facility. *Intelligent Systems and Applications*, *3*, 41–47.

Sebastian, P., & Hamada, R. H. (2010). Vision based automated parking System. *10th International conference on Information Science, Signal Processing and their Applications (ISSPA 2010)*, *1*, 757-760.

Siemens, A. G. (2012). *Intelligent Traffic Systems*. https://www.siemens.com/traffic

Tang, Y. W. S., Zheng, Y., & Cao, J. (2006). An Intelligent Car Park Management System based on Wireless Sensor Networks. *Proceedings of the 1st international Symposium on Pervasive Computing and Applications*, 65 - 70. 10.1109/SPCA.2006.297498

Wang, H., & He, W. (2011). A Reservation-based Smart Parking System. *The First International Workshop on Cyber-Physical Networking Systems*, 701-706.

Yan, G., Yang, W., Rawat, D. B., &Olariu, S. (2011). SmartParking: A Secure and Intelligent Parking System. *IEEE Intelligent Transportation Systems Magazine, 3*(1), 18-30.

Yang, J., Portilla, J., & Riesgo, T. (2012). Smart parking service based on Wireless Sensor Networks. *IECON Proceedings (Industrial Electronics Conference),* 6029-6034. 10.1109/IECON.2012.6389096

Zinon, Z., Christodoulou, P., Andreou, A., & Chatzichristofis, S. (2019). ParkChain: An IoT Parking Service Based on Blockchain. *15th International Conference on Distributed Computing in Sensor Systems (DCOSS)*, 687-693. doi: 10.1109/dcoss.2019.00123

Chapter 5
Blockchain Risk and Uncertainty in Automated Applications

Devesh Kumar Srivastava
SCIT, Manipal University, Jaipur, India

Saksham Birendra Bhatt
SCIT, Manipal University, Jaipur, India

Divyangana
SCIT, Manipal University, Jaipur, India

ABSTRACT

Blockchain could be called a string of blocks that acts like a ledger that is also distributed. Members in a defined P2P network are given access to the blockchain and can create new blocks. When the data is stored in a blockchain, changing it becomes virtually impossible. The data stored within blocks is time-stamped to avoid tampering. Blockchain has applications in numerous fields like IoT, digital currency, financial services, reputation systems, smart contracts, security services, etc. If any virtual or real asset transaction is happening online, blockchain technology can be easily applied to optimize and secure the transaction better. Blockchain-based applications bring controversies, and yet many exceptional and diverse use-cases have been found for blockchain in both financial and non-financial sectors. Although it holds immense promise, it doesn't come without risks and uncertainties. This chapter elucidates the growing risks and uncertainties which accompany the use of blockchain in automated systems.

INTRODUCTION

The IT industry has been growing at a fast pace since its inception. Many breakthroughs have disrupted our lives in ways not possible before. Especially the internet has been a godsend, for its capability to shelter disruptive technologies which encompass all walks of life. Since the creation of the internet, people were itching to come up with mechanisms to shift traditional methods of payment onto the internet. In 1999, Confinity was the first organization to attempt the same. Although they faced countless challenges, their

DOI: 10.4018/978-1-7998-3295-9.ch005

efforts resulted in PayPal and the world could transfer money on the internet without any hassle. This system, however, still had a long way to go. It still relied on some crutches which decreased the speed of transaction and were significant drags on the efficiency of commerce. Whenever two entities made transactions, they all had to pass through some intermediary parties which functioned as trust holders to ensure the safety and integrity of the bargain. In some rare cases of failures, these intermediaries could be held accountable, but the business would end up losing capital anyway.

Which gives rise to questions like

1. Can trust be placed in these parties
2. What happens if a successful hack or attack occurs?
3. What would happen if the data is not secure?
4. Why not communicate peer-to-peer, when intermediaries slow down the entire process?

The solution to the questions asked above is a new technology called "Blockchain".

Blockchains permit different members to attain agreement on exchange of information, i.e., a single adaptation of the truth, without a trusted central specialist or notary function. The innovation in this technology is that multiple anonymous entities can come together and form a consensus which renders the network and the data within the 'blockchain' (shared digital ledger), virtually tamper-proof. The integrity and secrecy of the information within the advanced records are cryptographically ensured. The hype around Blockchain started and rose to noticeable heights in 2008 (Satoshi, 2008) with the distribution of the interesting white paper 'Bitcoin: A Peer-to-Peer Electronic Cash Framework'. Blockchain-based smart contracts are expected to encourage coordinated, straightforward and irreversible exchange of assets from benefactors to those who need them, removing intermediary costs. The healthcare segment also fits the charge flawlessly for blockchain usage. Through its decentralized design, blockchain seems to supplant obsolete, divided and heterogeneous healthcare systems, bringing down healthcare conveyance costs. Potential blockchain applications are quite wide ranging, however, the blockchain may not be a solution for every given problem. Whenever commerce is carried out online, the electronic transactions are regulated and facilitated by financial institutions that act as the intermediary trusted parties. These third parties play a major role in regulating and safeguarding online transactions, and upon their completion take up commission. Instead of systems used for traditional online transactions, blockchain applications use cryptographic proof. Keys of two kinds, one private and the other public, are utilized in the process. Every user owns this duo of keys. When a transaction takes place, it is signed using the user's confidential private key. After signing the transaction with the sender's private key, the receiver gets the transaction at their public key. The private digital signature, i.e., private key signature, is then verified by the receiver using the public key. Every node gets the transaction for verification through a broadcast. After every node is verified, it is added to the distributed ledger. However, it cannot be ascertained that the order in which the sender sent the transactions would be the same as that of the order received by the receiver. To solve the problem above, transactions are grouped and treated as 'blocks', each of which links itself to others by containing the 'hash value' of the corresponding previous block. This whole system is called Blockchain. This leads us to the next problem, which is to determine which node should be selected and broadcasted, as the creation of numerous blocks can occur at the same time. The solution to this problem is the introduction of a puzzle of sorts called "proof of work". Blockchain uses a mathematical puzzle called "proof of work". It is a consensus algorithm implemented in Bitcoin by a node to generate a new block. Miners get into a competition to solve the puzzle and thus help in completing the transaction through PoW and receive rewards in the form of some currency (transaction fees, block reward). The complexity of PoW depends upon the network users, network load and the current power.

Hence, it becomes virtually impossible to do malignant transactions, as the attacker not only needs to do the proof of work but also must compete against other benign nodes, to get its transaction accepted. And, because the blocks are linked cryptographically, compromising it becomes even more difficult for the attackers. Then, the question arises, which specific types of applications can be made with Blockchain as their integral part? New forms of currency (i.e., cryptocurrency), providing support and shelter to digital identification in IoT, etc. and many more wide-ranging, disruptive applications are possible due to the blockchain application stack. The block chain technology is revolutionizing the entire business perspective from banking to healthcare.

Applications of blockchain in financial areas:

1. Private securities
   ◦ Coin setter - Helps in fast and convenient trading of Bitcoin
   ◦ Augur - Ethereum based, decentralized prediction market platform
   ◦ Bit shares - Facilitates members to trade in cryptocurrencies in exchange for commodities rather than fiat currency
2. Insurance
   Ever ledger - Uses blockchain to improve the efficiency of diamond industry and reduce adulteration by blood diamonds.

Applications of blockchain technology in non-financial areas:

1. Notary Public
   a. Block Notary
   b. Crypto Public Notary
2. Application in music industry
3. Application in OTT (Over-The-Top media services, e g: Netflix) industry
4. Decentralized IoT
5. Blockchain based Anti-Counterfeit solutions (for better managing identity data)
6. Decentralized storage
   a. STORJ
7. Internet applications
   a. Name coin (improves certain components of internet infrastructure)

Even though a wide range of problems are solved using Blockchain-based technology but there are significant risks of adoption, security, and government regulations. This chapter focuses on the current risks that a developer, business leader, and/ or a user must be aware of.

BACKGROUND

The thought which lead to the idea of blockchain was depicted as early as 1991 (Stuart et. al, 1991) when researchers Stuart Haber and W. Scott Stornetta presented a computational arrangement for time-stamping advanced reports to make their alteration impossible. The framework utilized chain of blocks which was secured cryptographically along to retain and store the time-stamped reports and in 1992 Merkle trees became part of the design, increasing the productivity by permitting a few records to be collected into one piece.

In 2004, a scientist and cryptographic activist Hal Finney (Harold Thomas Finney II, 2004) presented a framework called RPoW, Reusable Proof of Work. The framework worked by accepting a non-exchangeable or a non-fungible Hash cash-based proof of work token and in return made an RSA-signed token that might at that point be exchanged from individual to individual. RPoW unraveled the two-fold investing (double spending) issue by keeping the possession of tokens enrolled on a server that was trusted, that was designed to permit clients all over the globe to confirm its accuracy and purity in real time. RPoW can be imagined as fundamental model and a necessary step, which lead to the rise of cryptocurrencies.

It was in 2008 that the history of Blockchain began to gain momentum, much obliged to the efforts of one person named Satoshi Nakamoto is the brain which gave birth to Blockchain. Exceptionally small information on Mr. Nakamoto is available, but people speculate that he may be a single person or a group of multiple individuals that worked on Bitcoin, the primary use-case of this computerized record technology, called Blockchain. Nakamoto implemented, the very first Blockchain in 2008 A.D. from where the technology progressed and found its way into many use-cases. Satoshi Nakamoto published the main white paper roughly in 2008. In that white paper, he provided details about how the new technology was well equipped to improve digital trust because of the decentralization, which implied that a single entity could never control anything. Ever since Satoshi Nakamoto stopped being involved and handed the reigns of Bitcoin to other people, there have been many advancements in computerized records, and they have started appearing in many modern applications which are a part of the history of the Blockchain technology.

A few blockchain-based applications are being implemented in a wide variety and large number of businesses, extending from supply chain to financial services which has only scratched the surface of this monolithic technology. Whereas there's no question that blockchain technology is one of the greatest developments of recent times, it'll likely take a considerable amount of time before the innovation is adapted broadly in real world applications. That's because there are more than just a few challenges related to blockchain adoption. Risks are mainly put into different types, which are standard risks, risks associated with transfer of value and with smart contracts (programmed which execute the transaction when the conditions are met). In this chapter, a few issues that are being faced while implementing blockchain mass adoption (standard risks) are discussed below:

1. Scalability

Blockchain technologies are having inconvenience in successfully supporting a huge user-base of clients on the blockchain network (Crosby et al, 2016). The current leading blockchain systems (Bitcoin and Ethereum), have experienced moderate transaction speeds and higher expenses charged per transaction as a result of a significant increment in clients (Catalini & Gans, 2016). Block size of Bitcoin is restricted to 1 MB currently and in every ten minutes a block is mined. Hence, the Bitcoin network is confined to a rate of 7 transactions per second, which is incapable of managing with high-frequency trading (Zheng et al, 2017). Bigger blocks mean bigger capacity space and slower propagation within the network. This will lead to centralization slowly as fewer users would like to preserve such a huge blockchain. Hence the trade-offs between block size and security (resistance to bad actors), have been an intense challenge. In this manner, scalability concerns must be effectively addressed before the wide-scale adoption of blockchain. The massive requirements in terms of computations for every transaction, put a lid on the number of transactions and there are ~27 million clients with 210,000 exchanges per day. Around December of 2014, the network of Bitcoin handled approximately ninety thousand transactions a day, which is impressive yet quite low compared to 150 million per day done by VISA. So, then the issue remains, if Bitcoin doesn't scale to accommodate large number of transactions, then users will move on and find other solutions to their demands. As Bitcoin is a modern platform, there are not so many transactions being conducted at the moment. When the demand of transactions rises, perhaps security could be compromised, and attacks could also become common. As the research of Kyle C. et al. shows, the cost of each affirmed exchange lies between $1.4 to $ 2.9, majority of this is spent on electricity. However, it also comprises of mining (Proof of work), hardware required to solve complex problems of proof of work, exchange approval, bandwidth and capacity. Mining takes up 98% of the total cost which a single transaction requires. The scalability depends on several factors, these are:

1. Maximum throughput: The maximum possible rate at which a Blockchain application can verify and append transactions
2. Latency: The difference in time of request of a transaction and its approval or confirmation, it is approximately 10 minutes.
3. Bootstrap time: The time required by a new node computer, to download the necessary Blockchain onto its local machine in-order to be able to validate new transactions and to participate in mining.
4. Cost per Confirmed Transaction: Cost of resources which are consumed in order to approve a transaction in USD.

Proof of Work and Byzantine Fault Tolerance both, support thousands of users at once, when all of them are associated together, so that's good in terms of scalability, but is it enough? Although Bitcoin tout's decentralization, it had to form mining pools for node management which in turn improved its scalability. Compared to Bitcoin's Proof of Work, BFT always had to deal with the reputation of it being not scalable enough, due to its protocols and system communities. Bitcoin, in terms of performance is exceptionally restricted, as it can only take on seven transactions a second and there is also a one-hour latency with six block confirmation. Blockchains based on Proof of Work, have to face their inherited performance issues that come with the enhanced security. Scalability in PoW depends on 2 things, the block size and the rate of the block creations, and if the block size is expanded, it also increases the security (resistance to bad actors) risks, such as the latency is expanded and therefore potential trees within the blockchain are created which may lead to double-spend attacks. Even though BFT protocols handle thousands of transactions, they still maintain an organized speed latency. As more and more people come to Bitcoin, the number of transactions increase day by day and the size of Blockchain rises enormously, which is currently 100GB. Hence, the increasing demand can't be met due to the block size and the rate of block creation (rate of transactions). There are several ways to handle the issue of scalability, one of the suggested ideas directs to enhance the capacity of Blockchain. In one of the proposals the ancient stored transactions in the Blockchain are cleared away from the network, and all non-empty trees are stored in a database which then is pushes to all members. In this way, the nodes that are approving the transactions don't need to store the past transactions that are not important to them. To decouple the blocks are making them into leader and micro blocks is suggested in Bitcoin Next Generation. The leaders block then would be competed for by miners, and only these leader blocks would be responsible for creation of micro blocks.

SOLUTIONS TO SCALABILITY PROBLEM

1. Double Spend Attack

Double spend attack is a scheme which helps in overriding the primary chain and reverse transactions which have already been conducted. In this method, an attacker convinces an existing member to join them and subsequently builds a chain which is identical to the primary chain except the transaction which needs to be reversed. When the attacker pushes the chain, they can essentially replace the record which contain the details of the transaction, and that transaction can be either erased or directed somewhere else. To do this, it takes a lot of processing power, and because of that, it was thought to be impossible if honest nodes combined are supposed to have much more power compared to any attacker. However, as it happened, a mining pool, which had over 40% control of the computations in Bitcoin. In such cases wherein, the malignant entity has a lot of computational power, a possibility remains of that entity generating blocks which could potentially replace the honest and the longest primary chain. In situations where the attacker has more processing power than the honest nodes to compromise the honest primary chain, the attack is called the 51% attack. As the Bitcoin network will try to adapt to the increasing demand by scaling, it would become more vulnerable to the double-spend attacks. When it is assumed that the attacker has the capacity to create blocks at a quicker pace than the pace of the honest chain, it is inevitable that the attacker shall be successful, regardless of the size of the chain. Size of the block and the creation rate of the blocks both affect the throughput of the blockchain. In order to increase the speed of creation of blocks, the complexity of the computational puzzles can be reduced. Either by increasing the size of blocks or by increasing the speed of making of blocks, the security threshold is going to be reduced.

2.Block Size Implementation

When the topic of scalability arises, the most discussed topic is the size of blocks. It has been often suggested that the limit be increased to a higher bound many times. One of the proposals which was given at BIP 100 (Bitcoin Improvement Proposals) gave the idea that the existing limit of 1 MB of the block size should be changed to a fresh floating block size, which itself will be dynamically decided by the consensus protocol followed by the miners. One more suggestion was to increase the size of the block by 4.4% every ninety-seven days until the year 2063, amounting to a total of 17.7% increase per year. All of the suggested ideas and proposals need to be passed on using a hard fork in order to be implemented. This entails that the blocks which are currently unused and have a larger capacity of 1 megabyte, will be perceived as virtually invalid by the current version node.

3.Segregated Witness

Segregated witness popularly called as SegWit is a protocol to extend the block capacity and to give protection from transaction flexibility. It incorporates a wide run of features. A few blockchain usages comprise of 64-digit hexadecimal hash transaction identifiers. The transaction identifiers can be changed by the miners in small ways because the way the transaction identifiers are calculated, that will not alter the meaning of the transaction, but it'll alter the transaction id, typically called third-party malleability. The segregated witness approach does not increase the block size limit, but it increases the number of transactions that can be stored in a square. This approach is the best-case situation, which increases the throughput by four times. The segregated witness approach resolves the transaction malleability issue and hence permits unused mechanisms to be executed, which seem to provide powerful tools for the adaptability issues for the scalability issues in blockchain implementations.

4.Greedy Heaviest Observed Sub Tree (Ghost)

Yonatan S. and Aviv Z suggested an implementation in which the policy for determining the main blockchain varies (Yonatan S., et. al., 2016). This approach keeps up the threshold of security against 51% of the attacks if there are any delays. This approach sets higher rates of the creation of blocks and increases the size. This means that there can be higher transactions in the network without having to worry about a 51% attack threshold. This approach thus provides more security in the expansion of block size and its rate of creations. This concept thus provides more security in increasing the size of the block and its rate of creations. A similar concept was used in Ethereum, but it was not tested enough. Further, it was found that Ethereum's throughput was less than 20,000 transactions a day.

SECURITY RISKS

The blockchain technology provides distinctive features of decentralization, transparency, anonymity and the ability to use multiple generated addresses for identifying a user instead of using their general identity and thus it is considered as a reputable and reliable technology. Even though blockchain has many advantages but it does not assure absolute security of the transactions because the balances of transactions stores in public blockchain are publicly visible with the help of the public key. Another research shows that these bitcoin transactions are connected to user information of an individual and are easily accessible. (Guy et. al., 2015)

The main risk in the blockchain is 51% vulnerability. The consensus mechanism used in blockchain ensures the trust of the blocks and the nodes but if an individual has 50% control over the computational power he/she can have control over the entire blockchain. Research says that in January 2014, gash.io, a mining pool took control of over 42% of the computational power of Bitcoin. This leads to a huge issue that if gash.io reaches more than 50 percent of the computational power, it might escapade the situation but later they ensured in a press release that they would bolt the threshold of 50%. By prompting 51% vulnerability. The attackers can have the power of manipulating, altering transactions they may result in double spending, hampering honest miners, impede the process of confirmation from honest miners and excluding transactions. The blockchain system takes necessary measures to ensure the security and privacy of the transactions in the system by associating a private key to each transaction taking place in the blockchain. In an empirical study in Monero blockchain done by Andrew Miller analyzed the weaknesses of mixings (which are chaff coins in Monero, introduced to not let any attacker get involved in any linkage of the coins being spent in transactions). He found that 66% of the transactions don't have any mixings. The concept of 0 mixings might lead to leakage of personal information and exploitation of Monero weakness which can interfere with transactions with 80 percent accuracy. (Andrew et. al., 2017)

A user may technically have multiple addresses that are not linked to his real identity in bitcoin. It indirectly provides a safety web to criminals. Authorities fail to identify the real identity of the user because of anonymity. There have been cases where the attacker may alter the files of the user and demand ransom to let the victim have access to his records. Blockchain provides many benefits of anonymity but this feature also makes it difficult to track back the attacker. In blockchain-based technology bitcoin, the client is provided with an open key which is visible to everyone and a private key possessed by its rightful user. This private key plays a major role in keeping the transactions and personal information of the user confidential. If the private key is weak, it can be easily acquired with the brute force attack. If this private key is lost it cannot be recovered. If the attacker can generate the private key, he may tamper the user's account. The Decentralized Autonomous Organization (DAO) engrossed on the DAO contract. It was built to implement pooled funding. It was deployed in Ethereum and after a few days an attack was cast towards the DAO which had reached around 10 million USD and attackers stole approximately 60 million USD. The attack was set up by publishing smart contracts having withdrawn () work call to DAO in its callback of 25 functions.

Is a Private Blockchain More Secure than a Public One?

A blockchain network in which anyone can come and join the network. They can read, write, and/ or participate with the public blockchain. They have this unique property, which is that they are decentralized, yet there can be other forms of restrictions implemented to safeguard the blockchain from getting compromised.

Contrary to this, a private blockchain is a permissioned blockchain network, in which all participants are assigned specific roles, and one of them is to decide whether to allow someone into the network or not. And if allowed, to what degree can they participate? Just to read or to both read and write, or even to make changes in the Blockchain itself.

Now before getting into the details, the purpose behind these different networks must be understood. Public Blockchain is used when the needs are such that the Blockchain needs a large number of users and needs to perform transactions that are a system of their own rather than related to anything in the real world. Private Blockchains are used when the number of users is relatively less and the network is used to conduct transactions that have some connection to the real world. As such the benchmarks that these networks are tested against also become different.

While discussing the differences between Private and Public Blockchains, it is often missed that, there are not two but four Blockchain types due to another factor, which is Open or Closed networks. This gives rise to Private Open/ Closed and Pubic Open/ Closed Blockchain. Private Closed examples could be the networks for military, international markets, etc. while Private Open examples would be Public Records of property and other things, Corporate statements to shareholders, etc. On the other hand, example for Public Open Blockchain would be Cryptocurrencies and those of Public Closed Blockchain would be Voting or Document Sharing. Open and closed entail whether the participants get to read the data contained within or just to verify the contents without getting the permissions to read them. The benefits of Public Blockchains are:

1.   Permission to read and/ or write

2.   Distributed Ledger
3.   Immutability
4.   Secure because of complex Consensus mechanisms
5.   And some benefits of Private Blockchain are:
6.   Enterprise usable, and permissioned
7.   Increased speed of transactions
8.   Improved ability to scale the networks
9.   Support for all compliance and regulatory demands
10.   Resource optimized efficient, consensus mechanisms

Risks of Public Blockchains
1.   Giant mining pools lead to partial centralization
2.   Increasing risk of compromised exchanges where Cryptocurrencies are exchanged for other currencies
3.   like USD
4.   Undetected bugs in the code
5.   Legal liabilities for the losses incurred

Risks of Private Blockchains
1.   Lack of stringent consensus mechanisms
2.   A limited number of participants means that once a bad actor gets in, it is easy to compromise the entire system
3.   Unfair practices by trusted intermediaries

Hence, all use-cases of Public and Private Blockchain must be suited to their purpose and rise to solve the problems which come out during their runtime quickly and effectively. This leads to the following conclusion in the context of security:

The practice of building a private blockchain to preserve security is a seriously misguided one. A private blockchain indeed permits the screening of participants, whereas a public blockchain is accessible to everybody. However, it is this exposure that allows a public blockchain that makes it immune to hacks. Bitcoin is the original public blockchain, having withstood years of persistent hacking without ever being compromised, getting more resilient with each hack that it withstands. This epitomizes that public blockchains, which are considerably superior to private blockchains.

Solution to Security Risks

Security Enhancement: SmartPool is used to control the mining pool issues. SmartPool gets transactions from client nodes that hold mining tasks based on which the miners execute hashing computation. The completed shares are returned to the clients of SmartPool. When the completed shares amount to some significant value, the SmartPool contract deployed on Ethereum, substantiates and remunerates the clients.

Loi et al. (Loi et. al., 2016) proposed a concept to detect bugs in Ethereum smart contracts that are called Oyente (Loi et. al., 2016). The concept leverages symbolic executions to analyze the bytecode of smart contracts and the execution model it follows is EVM (Ethereum Virtual Machine) (Loi et. al., 2016).

Ethereum stores the bytecode of its smart contracts within the blockchain, subsequently this proposition is applicable to detect the bugs in the deployed smart contracts (Loi et. al., 2016).

Hyper ledger, an open-source collaborative effort introduced by The Linux Foundation in 2015 for cross-industry blockchain technologies. Hyperledger is a permissioned blockchain using a distributed ledger system, allowing the user to look over their transactions. Unlike blockchain, unknown entities can not take part in the Hyperledger blockchain network. The users must enlist through Membership Service Provider (MSP) to participate in this type of blockchain network. To ensure blockchain security, strong authentication is provided to digital identities to gain access to the network.

Gemalto ensure blockchain security by following ways:

Solid Authentication

To ensure security and strong identity, Gemalto provides a certificate to each digital entity that is a part of a permissioned blockchain network like Hyperledger Fabric.

Core Blockchain Security

Crypto keys play a major role in securing transactions in the blockchain network. The same concept is used to sign smart contracts to maintain the confidentiality of transactions. Thus, Gemalto's SafeNet HSMs facilitate server-side security of private keys and certificates of digital entities that are stored in FIPS 1402, Level 3-validated HSM devices to avoid any alteration and unapproved access to the transactions. With the right combination of public and private keys, the attacker cannot perform brute force to gain access to the data. But the only thing that he requires to hack into the system is the pair of right keys. Mobile devices, android, and windows are prone to malware which makes the attacker's job easier. The following steps can be used to protect the blockchain keys from being stolen:

a. Keep the windows and android software up to date and use a good antivirus
b. Do not store keys in text or word document or add it to the body of any email. Use an encrypted application to keep them safe.

HIGH ENERGY REQUIREMENT

The consensus algorithm for creating a new block is the focal point of blockchain technology. The consensus algorithm is known as "Proof of Work (PoW)", is employed in Bitcoin and Ethereum. To create a large chain in Bitcoin, the data size may increase up to 100 gigabytes and electricity requirements more than Ireland. For example, Bitcoin takes 470 kWh to complete a single transaction occurring in a single 24-hour period which is equivalent to the electricity of an American home for two weeks. This not only results in high direct cost but also a high carbon footprint because the primary source of power is fossil fuels. A Bitcoin transaction in a blockchain has an average carbon intensity of about 223250 grams of carbon consumed per kWh which is equivalent to 14 gallons of gasoline in a car.It was estimated that the annual energy consumption of mining in Bitcoin is 3.38 TeraWatt hours, which is equivalent to the total annual consumption of Jamaica in 2014. Mitigation strategies are being developed to build energy-efficient blockchains. For example, Red Belly Blockchain performs tens of thousands of transactions per second without ramping up energy consumption. However, other consensus algorithms like proof of stake (PoS), delegated Byzantine fault tolerance (BFT) based algorithms require less energy but they come with their disadvantages also.

INEFFICIENT TECHNOLOGY DESIGN

A considerable number of smart contracts when deployed on a platform may have some vulnerabilities due to the code. Bitcoin stores a large amount of data with each transaction which also includes information that may not be important. This makes blockchain heavy and slow. Thus, it necessitates the optimization of blockchain design to avoid inefficiency in data storage.

STRATEGIC RISKS

A company needs to decide if they want to be in the front line of this technology or to wait until the technology matures. Both choices have their pros and cons that may affect the business strategy. Blockchain provides peer to peer nature. It is important to decide which network to participate in (as different digital identities participate network) and which platform to choose.

BUSINESS CONTINUITY RISKS

Blockchain technology is prone to operational failures and cyber-attacks. Firms adopting this technology need to have a robust strategy or plan to mitigate such risks. Blockchains are resilient to resulting redundancy from the distributed nature of this technology. Moreover, the Blockchain shortens business cross strategy process durations, and business continuity plans must resolve such incident and recovery time.

INTEROPERABILITY

Incorporating blockchain with legacy IT platforms is a costly operational challenge. The participants need to convert data models, business processes and integrate new communication protocols and authentications.

Considerations:

a. To prevent the disruption of existing processes and technology, blockchain technology should be introduced in a manageable and contained manner.
b. It is important to identify the data elements that are exchanged between the blockchain software and the existing internal system to maintain data interoperability.

AUDITABILITY

The companies should provide necessary data such as legal information, audit purposes and forensic investigations for the transactions stored on the blockchain network.

Considerations:

a. Authorize extraction of corporate data, metadata for detailed analysis of outside the blockchain environment.
b. Ensure the confidentiality of the corporate data
c. Creation of APIs and query software on a blockchain platform for customized business reporting.

CONTROL AND COLLUSION

If a single participant or a group of participate obtain control on the blockchain by resolving consensus, the transactions may get blocked or delayed.

Solutions:

a. Before entering the blockchain, briefly understand the consensus algorithm and risks associated with it.
b. Recognize large parties that are active participants to know where the collision risks occur.

DATA MANAGEMENT RISKS

Blockchain uses a distributed ledger that grows with every transaction and contains a large volume of transactions and corporate data present outside the network have risks similar to cloud computing environments. Transactions having additional metadata (that are not part of the blockchain transaction) must be transferred outside of the process while ensuring the reconciliation with the blockchain.

Considerations:

a. Define classification standards for all types of data elements in the blockchain platform.
b. Provide security certification, attestation ad reports to participants.

CONTRACTUAL RISKS

There are service level agreements between the participating nodes and administrator of the blockchain network along with SLAs with service providers that are required to be observed for compliance.

SUPPLIER RISKS

Firms source most of the technology from external vendors and may become vulnerable to third party risks.

VALUE TRANSFER RISKS

Confidentiality Risks

Not all information on a distributed ledger needs to be available and accessible to others. Whereas technical solutions may resolve this issue for a few, any commerce considering blockchain technology should decide who will have access to the information. Besides, it's doable that hackers may be able to get the keys to retrieve data on the distributed ledger, particularly considering users can have multiple points of access to the DLT (Distributed Ledger Technology). In the blockchain, ownership of keys and ownership of content are synonymous. All the participants in the permission less blockchain network can view the transaction appended to the ledger while transactions in the permissioned blockchain network are present in hashed format but some metadata is always available to the participants. Monitoring this data can reveal the information on the type and volume associated with the activity of any public address on the blockchain framework to any node participating in it.

Key Management Risks

The consensus protocol seals the blockchain ledger and prevents corruption of transactions, but it is still vulnerable to private key theft. The digital data once lost (in case of accidental loss or private key thefts) then it is not easy to recover the data especially if there singly entity controlling the system.

Liquidity Risks

The Bank for International Settlements warned that DLT (Distributed Ledger Technology) adoption can lead to new liquidity risks. Intermediaries take on the counterparty risks and resolve disputes in current business models but resolving disputes in a distributed trust environment is a requirement that will depend on the preordained arrangements.

CHANGE MANAGEMENT RISKS

Any changes made to the blockchain requires approval from all the participants, which may affect the velocity of the system with which new functionality could be introduced. It may be considered -

a.   Define policies communicating responsibilities of the participants for approving changes, transparent change notifications, and consensus algorithms.
b.   Establish a legal agreement that defines the management of changes in the blockchain. This legal agreement must be signed by all the participants in the blockchain network.
c.   To permit development, approval, and software logic changes, provider-specific logical access rights should be created which are separated from the participants.

LEGAL RISKS

Since the release of Bitcoin, the interest in Blockchain and other forms of DLT (Distributed ledger) have increased tremendously. Everyone from regulators, consultants to techies and academics are pushing Blockchain to be implemented to improve multiple financial services like global payment, trading securities and other assets, property ledgers, banking, insurance, issuing letters of credit, etc. are some of the proposed applications of Blockchain. The reasons are simple; the speed and increased security of the transaction, and, complete immutability of the distributed ledger. This, on the surface, seems to render law and regulations futile. However, the law can't simply be ignored just because of some innovation. As the data is spread among many ledgers, the legal risks, remain. Along with the ledger, the legal risks are also distributed to wherever the users are located at. Hence, the administrators will be subject to the law of all those places where the users reside.

Apart from that, since the technology is quite new, having a legal entity for oversight is desirable.

(1) One such thing is investment fraud in cryptocurrencies. Multiple times, ICOs of new cryptocurrencies have been offered and investors have lost their investment in scams like these. There wasn't a way to track down and hold responsible people accountable. However, the SEC (Securities and trade Commission, U.S.) have devised a method to both prevent and resolve issues around investment fraud. For prevention, they have released a fake cryptocurrency called 'Howey coin' which bears all the marks and flags of a crypto scam to educate investors about fraudulent cryptocurrencies. And, they have revised securities laws to deal with investment fraud in cases where cryptocurrencies are considered as tokens (ICOs) and also when they are traded as securities. They have also devised new methods to prevent Blockchain-based applications from facilitating money laundering and terror funding.

(2) Before branching out into further legal issues, it is pertinent to have an understanding of the technology and its purpose, which can then be analyzed from a legal perspective. The crux of Blockchain resides on distributing ledgers among multiple entities and trust along with the ledgers. This results in better access to markets, ease of transaction, replacing one central trust with many, reducing the intermediary cost, increasing the speed of transaction, etc. So, whether the DLT is public or permissioned private, there are going to be entities upon whom trust will be placed and they are expected to carry out their responsibilities. What if they fail? Shall they be liable, to what extent and how exactly can they be sued? Which regions' law apply? It is said that these applications are far more secure than traditional ones, which despite being true, have caused serious financial damage to many people. How will it be decided who bears the losses and who is held accountable?

(3) The risk may also appear from increased ledger transparency, which was designed to be beneficial and it is, to some degree, but bad actors always find ways to manipulate it for their illicit benefits. When the ledger is distributed amongst multiple entities, it becomes possible to extract personal and or private data via analyzing metadata. By either making an informed guess or by using some techniques to do the same. This itself gives rise to the potential risks like Exposure of private data, Market manipulation & Insider trading and Identity theft

(a)   Exposure of private data:

The two properties of DLT and privacy of data are in a constant tug-of-war in any Blockchain application. In the case of Bitcoin, users' profile information is also attached to the unique string IDs assigned to each user, which can then be used to extract the hidden personal information. The same distribution of ledger which increased security and ease of transaction can also violate data privacy laws. Hence, applications based on DLT must be deployed cautiously. The immutability which makes everything to stay on the ledger forever also poses a legal risk. If, any information which should not be on the DLT, by accident comes-up on it, will stay there forever. Improper photos, false news, manipulated data, etc., once put on a DLT can not be erased and can cause damage to lives and communities.

b)   Market manipulation & Insider trading:

With the metadata available to every node, risk of market manipulation and insider trading. The sensitive information which even in encoded form, can be extracted and used to gain an unfair advantage. If there are no proper safeguards, then the data will at some point be used in a bad manner. Even though there are laws in place to punish insider trading and market manipulation, DLT applications will still have to be made with appropriate solutions in mind for such problems.

c)   Identity theft:

It is good to have transparency in a financial system where everyone trusts each other and hence the convenience increases manifold. The same transparency, however, can be manipulated by bad actors to gain access to the private key of a participant. This enables them to pretty much do anything they want to without facing any consequence in the absence of a central authority.

There are no straight solutions to such problems as the technology is quite new and constantly evolving. However, that cannot be used as an excuse to do nothing. Judicial and technical people should work together to see how this technology can have negative effects and come up with ways to prevent and discourage them by making appropriate policies and laws.

SOLUTIONS AND RECOMMENDATIONS

Assessing the needs of the industry before implementing distributed ledger technology is crucial. Identifying the needs of the company beforehand makes it easier to assess whether blockchain will make significant changes in bringing efficiencies. Implementing blockchain is not an easy task. A distributed system is more scalable, but it is more complex and costly because all computers need to be in sync in real-time. It is important to take care of these complexities when planning to build distributed ledgers in industries. A blockchain network cannot work in isolation within an industry. Actors from various industries need to participate and work on the single blockchain network in a shared ledger. Industries should develop standards considering the integrity and security of data. The next step after planning the right task force is whether to keep the distributed ledger technology, public or private i.e permissioned or permission less blockchain. Permissioned ledgers are applicable where there are simpler networks with more control over the network while permission less ledgers are appropriate where the network doesn't shut down. It is better to check the functionality of the blockchain on a small scale first then examining its impacts afterward.

Blockchain Security Threat Model

To build a risk model for the blockchain-based solution, it is necessary to analyze the risks discussed above. Some of the key considerations for blockchain solutions are as follows:

i.   What are the unique features of blockchain?
ii.   What is the governance model for organization members?
iii. What are the necessary regulatory requirements?
iv.   How are identity details managed?
v.   What is the recovery plan for the participants?
vi.   What is the logic for block collisions?

Blockchain guarantees data integrity and confidentiality, however many risks are associated with the blockchain-based application that may lead to loss and compromise. For example, access control, insufficient communication security, and loose key, etc. The key to avoiding such risks is to develop an inclusive threat model to secure the application.

A well-known is Spoofing, Tampering, Repudiation, information disclosure, Denial of service attacks, and Elevation of privilege (STRIDE) model that's accustomed to study relationships between the actors and assets, review threats and weaknesses associated with these relationships, and propose applicable mitigations. Blockchain applications usually incorporate external parts — Identity and access management (IAM) systems, multi-factor authentication (MFA), public key infrastructure (PKI), and restrictive and audit systems — that are owned and managed by actors. These systems must be compelled to be rigorously scrutinized before they become a part of the general resolution as they're developed or controlled by third parties. These ought to be taken into thought for the threat model in a very blockchain resolution.

The threats illustrated in the figure above can be classified into the following categories:

1.   New threat landscape - it refers to blockchain specific threats.
2.   Threats take a new meaning- conventional threats new meaning adding new threats.
3.   Conventional threat management - the business threats that must be addressed for solutions.

New Threat Landscape

The blockchain chain introduces new standards that may not be understood easily. Vulnerabilities can be present in any component. The system includes a large number of actors, each associated with their identity management mechanisms — thus it becomes challenging to determine the mutual trust mechanisms necessary for the correct management of agreement. It is important to have a balance between the information details collected and the need to manage and eliminate data for the satisfaction of privacy legislation. It is important to identify the attacks across a distributed asset landscape. There should be coordination of response, recovery, and detection among all the participants in the network. Analytics help to identify structured attacks across multiple participant networks. The relationship between dif-

Figure 1. Threat model in a blockchain solution(reference)

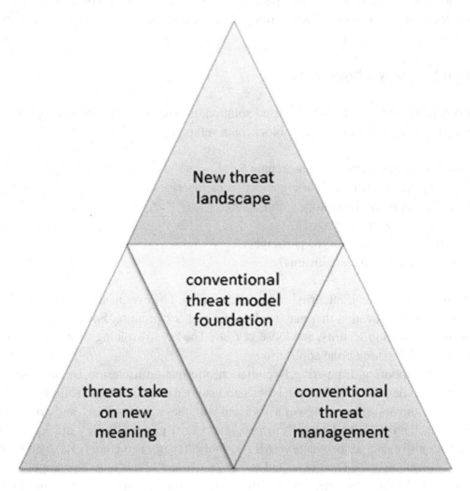

ferent components of the system and the participants should be properly orchestrated. Attackers usually try to attack different components interacting with each other and indirectly attack these relationships between the participants and the system.

Threats Take A New Meaning

New vulnerabilities within the infrastructure and altering with smart contracts will result in new threats. In a localized blockchain resolution, user impersonation and improper elevation of privilege will result in new threats. In a decentralized network like blockchain, new threats may arise due to user impersonation. Any external information can be altered or stolen threatening the overall blockchain solution. Compromised keys, disruption of services, malicious transactions lead to a threat to the overall blockchain network solution.

Conventional Threat Management

Overall scanning of the blockchain solution mitigates a considerable amount of risks. Threat insights, incident response, detection, recovery plans, and correction procedures must be put into a place. Best identity management mechanisms and best disaster recovery and planning must be put into a place.

Individual blockchain-based applications are different that it's not possible to create a universal threat model. However, these apps are often related to a variety of comparable actors, assets, and use cases. In this chapter, we tend to discuss a threat model for common parts that may be used as a model that might function as a starting point for security analysis in specific detailed projects.

Need for Secure Blockchain Solution

For a secure blockchain solution, the starting point should be the development of a risk model that addresses all the business, technological and governance risks.

The next step should be an evaluation of the threats and development of a threat model as shown in fig1. The last step is defining the safety controls to mitigate risks and threats. They can be classified into 3 categories:

1. Enforce security controls that are distinctive to the blockchain.
2. Apply standard security controls.
3. Enforce business controls for blockchain.

Security Control Unique to Blockchain

a   Treat the basic infrastructure of this blockchain solution as essential infrastructure. It ensures that all the important security practices are in one place. Adopt industry-standard certifications.

b.   Partition and adoption of best practices for namespacing to manage access.

The blockchain solution should be separated using channels and namespacing so that it can hold digital assets for all the members. Namespacing allows managing access to digital assets on the platform. The best practice for separation outside the network or an organization is Leverage.

c.   Enforcing endorsement policies that support business contracts.

These endorsement policies outline the standards that should be met to ensure that the transaction being submitted is valid. Examples embody the number of signatures needed from different organizations involved in it. These policies ensure the security of digital assets, data and business networks associated with the contracts. For the best practice, such policies should be defined for the smart contracts(on namespace level) as well as on the ledger key level.

d.   Enforcing access controls to access information and blockchain solution. Defined policies must ensure that there is a right level of access for the right use by the right individual. New members must be on-boarded into the blockchain platform through applicable identity and access mechanisms. The off-boarding method ought to be outlined to prevent any malicious activity through numerous techniques. Audit logs and access processes must be in one place to alert the operations team about any security issues. If any organization is using the in-house IAM system and working as an identity supplier (IDP), applicable tokens like OAUTH, OIDC, and SAML2 need to be utilized for authentication, verification, and authorization. This is applicable to different associated members. Key choices should be made in advance to decide whether these members are IDPs or service suppliers (SPs).

e.   Enforce HSM: To secure the identity keys in blockchain, it is important to use Hardware Security Module (HSM). Each organization has its partition in HSM where their identity keys are stored. Each separate partition has separate admin roles and rights to perform different operations of different organizations.

f.   Use privileged PAM for serious actions: Use Privileged Access Management (PAM) to make sure that the rightful users have the privilege access to the administrative components. It is essential as the blockchain platform has confidential data that includes transaction and payment information of users. This solution should be put along with password rotation. End to end logging configuration is also essential for capturing entry to exit flows.

g.   API security for the safety of API based transactions: APIs are the basic form of communication between various components of the blockchain solution. APIs should be protected from improper use. Three main key controls to protect API need to be enforced: authentication, identification, and authorization.

h.   A secret store for privileged access and application: There are a number of components in the blockchain that interact with both user and API based transactions. Some of them are based on static keys such as tokens, certificates, and passwords that must be stored in encrypted form access to these should be limited.

i.   Data classification approach for data security: Classify data on the basis of business, technical issues and legal so that proper security control can be used.

j.   Privacy-preserving technology for sensitive data: Leverage permissioned ledger technology provides safety to members' private information and hides information related to their transactions such as identity and details of the transactions.

k.   Protection of applications from attacks: Leverage DevOps automate app vulnerabilities scanning during the development lifecycle to ensure data security at different levels.

l.   Enforcing access control: Smart contracts are a major part of the blockchain. Their policies should be well aligned with the objectives of businesses. More focus should be given to the lifecycle management of smart contract access control and applications collaborating with smart contracts.

m.   TPMs for the execution of sensitive codes: Components of a blockchain solution that are more critical than others use Trusted Platform Modules (TPM). TPM helps privacy preservation of chain codes and ensure that execution is not tampered by administrators also.

n.   Communication security: Communication between the components should be highly secured. This can be ensured with the help of Transport Layer Security (TLS) solutions and taking additional security measures like frequent key rotation.

Conventional Security Controls

a.   Corporate standards of security to ensure software development lifecycle security

Corporate standards, policies, and security platforms provide reliability, consistency and operational efficiency.

b.   Enforcing access management for onboarding users

Using identity and access management tools(IAM) for controlling access, authentication and data storage. Necessitate the use of multi-factor authentication (MFA) along with IAM tools for accessing the blockchains.

c.   Use robust certificate management and cryptographic keys
   ◦   Using a robust key management solution for the management of the number of keys employed in the blockchain. These include identity keys, domain certificates, and internal and external TLS certificates.
   ◦   Using efficient internal PKI for managing internal TLS certificates.
   ◦   creating the right certification authority decisions for managing external TLS certificates.
d.   Hardware Security Module (HSM) store key data. Blockchain has multiple members, it is important to analyze the impact of HSM. Store keys in proper partitions.
e.   Application security: Security measures must be taken for all individual components to ensure the security of the overall system.
f.   Infrastructure security: Infrastructure security and data stored in blockchain needs to be secured.
g.   Penetration testing and vulnerability assessment

A penetration test should be done at each level of solution deployment. To ensure the overall security of the system it is important to assess and address the vulnerability at each phase and every individual component level.

Business Controls

a.   Implementation of security governance
   ◦   Define security governance and implement it through different access control mechanisms and policies.
   ◦   Define specific regulating laws for the platform irrespective of location and ensure customer security.
b.   Ensure legal controls

Each organization has its particular requirement controlled by the organization's legal department. It is important to briefly define the responsibilities of each member of the organization and the vendor to avoid any violation. Ensure compliance with application audits and the system to mitigate the risks.

c.   Operational control

Once the blockchain solution is designed and built, all necessary security measures should be followed and executed at each phase after the deployment of the solution. All the actors, instructions and processes should be properly set up to ensure that it functions without any ambiguity.

FUTURE RESEARCH DESCRIPTION

The blockchain technology has the potential that third-party trustees can never match. With blockchain's decentralized infrastructure no one has absolute power or control over it. Even though There have been many developments in different blockchain use cases and their unique features but now the focus should be more on the social inference of this technology and whatever changes it has brought in the use cases. The developers of this technology have been condemned for showing only the positive side of it. Even though this innovation has set us free from high transaction third parties and distributed control over the blockchain network among different digital identities, but it has also resulted in the inability to alter the records according to the user's choice. It is important to elucidate the risks and uncertainties of block-chain that include both short term as well as long term effects and effects on the individuals involved in these markets. Another challenge is to build an energy-efficient system. Power consumption is one of the most important areas where more research needs to be done to make this innovation sustainable. There has been a development that can scale up to a thousand transactions per second. Future developments in the Internet of Things would help to determine speedy confirmations and an increase in the number of transactions per second. When blockchain is used for large scale applications, there are risks of errors and faults in the initial stages because the ecological system of this technology depends on coding new algorithms, a process vulnerable to errors. This results in the detainment of acceptance from the clients. Bitcoin has proved to be flexible but other blockchain platforms like Ethereum have faced many serious issues earlier. Further studies in the security of such attacks are important for the overall infrastructure of blockchain. Another challenge in the blockchain is that when a system is deployed, code needs to be accepted by the other system nodes which leads to the disagreement between multiple forks and nodes. Energy systems adopting blockchain may face fragmentation and mistrust issues. Standards for the blockchain framework should be developed for interoperability between innovation and solutions so that there is no inhibition in the adoption of blockchain. Therefore, we believe that a more critical analysis on block chain is necessary. We also call for further research on the topics mentioned below and communities related to them.

Ø   Disruption in business models caused by blockchain
Ø   Smart contracts platforms
Ø   Change from social currency to cryptocurrency
Ø   Regulatory issues in adoption of blockchain
Ø   Risks in private blockchain
Ø   Blockchain in Internet of Things
Ø   Actors in blockchain
Ø   Development of energy-efficient blockchain
Ø   Blockchain Testing

CONCLUSION

While the benefits of blockchain are clear, there are oodles of risks associated with this aborning technology. The blockchain technology benefits the market and consumers by offering transparent, tamper-proof transactions, and emancipation from third party trustees. However, there is a downside to this technology too. This chapter illuminates the risks imposed by the blockchain that may evolve as the technology matures. Various recommended solutions to overcome various issues like security risks, scalability, vendor risks, legal issues, consensus risks, etc. have been discussed in-depth in this chapter. Security solutions are evaluated based on blockchain threat models. It is important to develop an inclusive threat model to prevent myriad risks and mitigate the weaknesses. The model is categorized into business threats, blockchain specific threats, and conventional threats. Blockchain technology will transform humans form trust into the algorithm-based trust and, therefore it is crucial for the organizations and firms to observe the development of blockchain along with its applications in different use cases. Blockchain might be disruptive for energy companies but with its growth and development, the technology will probably reach its full potential.

REFERENCES

Andrew, M., Malte, M., Kevin, L., & Arvind, N. (2017). *An Empirical Analysis of Linkability in the Monero Blockchain.* arXiv:1704.04299

Catalani & Gans. (2019). *Some Simple Economics of the Blockchain.* Academic Press.

Croman, Decker, Eyal, Gencer, Juels, Kosba, Miller, Saxena, Shi, GunSirer, Song, & Wattenhofe. (n.d.). *On Scaling Decentralized Blockchains.* Academic Press.

Crosby, Nachiappan, Pattanayak, Verma, & Vignesh. (2016). Blockchain Technology: Beyond Bitcoin. *Applied Innovation Review.*

Finney. (2004). *RPOW - Reusable Proofs of Work.* Academic Press.

Guy, Z., Oz, N., & Alex, P. (2015). Decentralized Privacy: Using Blockchain to Protect Personal Data. *IEEE Security and Privacy Workshops (SPW).* Doi:10.1109/SPW.2015.27

Loi, L., Duc-Hiep, C., & Hrishi, O. (2016). Making Smart Contracts Smarter. *Proceedings of the 2016 ACM SIGSAC Conference on Computer and Communications Security,* 254-269. DOI: 10.1145/2976749.2978309

Nakamoto. (2008). *Bitcoin: A Peer-to-Peer Electronic Cash System.* Academic Press.

Sompolinsky & Zohar. (2016). *Bitcoin's Security Model Revisited.* Academic Press.

Stuart, H., & Stornetta, W. S. (1991). Bellcore, How to stamp a digital document. *Journal of Cryptology, 3.*

Zheng, Z., Dai, H., Chen, X., & Wang, H. (2018). Blockchain Challenges and Opportunities: A Survey. *International Journal of Web and Grid Services, 14*(4), 352. doi:10.1504/IJWGS.2018.095647

KEY TERMS AND DEFINITIONS

Bitcoin: A digital independent currency, which has a consensus mechanism and can be securely transferred and verified by receiver over the internet, without relying on any third party.

Blockchain: A ledger that is digital, and decentralized, and distributed on a peer to peer network. Its applications include cryptocurrencies and others.

Consensus Mechanism: Used to ensure that trust is distributed among all concerned parties internally within a network, without relying on external third party.

Cryptography: The practice of deliberately making a message gibberish on surface which can then be understood using a key to receive the original message, to avoid other people from reading the message.

DAO: Decentralized autonomous organization is represented by rules which are encoded as a computer program and it is transparent, shareholders control and cannot be influenced by central government.

Ethereum: Ethereum is an open-source, blockchain-based distributed computing platform and operating system. It also features, smart contracts, and a currency ether which every user gets.

IoT: Various devices are connected to a network in order to facilitate better collection and processing of data to improve business efficiency or consumer satisfaction.

Peer-to-Peer Network: Peer-to-peer (P2P) network is created when two or more peers who access the network through compatible devices, are connected and share resources without involving a separate server to host those resources.

Proof of Work: A type of consensus mechanism, chiefly found in Bitcoin. It utilizes difficult mathematical puzzles that are solved by participants called miners, and they are rewarded when they solve the puzzle. This mechanism is used for verifying transactions, that is, creating new blocks.

Smart Contracts: A computer program which is embedded in a blockchain based system that verifies whether all the conditions necessary for a transaction are being met or not before allowing a transaction.

Chapter 6
Blockchain–Autonomous Driving Systems

P. Lalitha Surya Kumari

iD https://orcid.org/0000-0003-3611-8038

Koneru Lakshmaiah University, Hyderabad, India

ABSTRACT

Blockchain is the upcoming new information technology that could have quite a lot of significant future applications. In this chapter, the communication network for the reliable environment of intelligent vehicle systems is considered along with how the blockchain technology generates trust network among intelligent vehicles. It also discusses different factors that are effecting or motivating automotive industry, data-driven intelligent transportation system (D2ITS), structure of VANET, framework of intelligent vehicle data sharing based on blockchain used for intelligent vehicle communication and decentralized autonomous vehicles (DAV) network. It also talks about the different ways the autonomous vehicles use blockchain. Block-VN distributed architecture is discussed in detail. The different challenges of research and privacy and security of vehicular network are discussed.

I. INTRODUCTION

Blockchain is the upcoming new information technology that could have quite a lot of significant future applications. One is blockchain thinking, formulating thinking as a blockchain process. This could have advantages for both human enhancement and artificial intelligence, and their potential integration. Blockchain thinking is given as an input-processing-output computational system. Its benefits may include the capability to organize digital mind file uploads, supporter for digital intelligences for upcoming timeframes, execute utility functions based on smart-contracts, instantiate thinking as a power law, and make possible to act as friendly AI.

The automotive industry might face numerous comprehensive and interlinked changes in the subsequent decades. The automotive industry has an advantage to improve efficiently through the Internet and technology, but has mainly remained in the same structure in contrast to reorganize its whole ecosystem. Re-conceptualization of core activity must be organized, coordinated, and executed.

DOI: 10.4018/978-1-7998-3295-9.ch006

Many factors like growing aging and urban populations, automotive 3D printing of spare parts, the introduction of self-driving cars, new models for delivery of transportation services and energy innovation could drive the automotive industry into new configurations, possibly towards innovative concepts that are depicted in Fig.1 of an highly developed biopod personal transport system.

Figure 1. The BioThink Advanced Vehicle for Metropolitan Cities (BioThink Futuristic Vehicle for Mega-Cities, 2015, Muhammad ElMahdy, 2015). The different factors that are affecting automotive industry are

a. Demographics: Growing Aging and Urbanized Populations

The world population continues to increase, and is expected to grow up to 9.6 billion in 2050. Not only is the population increasing but also the urbanization; for the past ten years more than half of the world's population has been residing in cities, and this trend may continue and expected more than 5 billion people to live in urban areas in 2030 (United Nations. Urbanization, 2007) The further main worldwide demographic tendency is the aging of populations where we required different types of personalized transportation solutions (United Nations: Current status of the social situation, well-being, participation in development and rights of older persons worldwide. United Nations Department of Economic and Social Affairs, 2012) . Similarly, number of cars and autos on the road is also increasing year by year. Increased urbanization and more cars on the road leads to traffic congestion;

b. Self-Driving Vehicles

Self-driving vehicles are the one of influencing factors to increase autonomy and self-operation capabilities like the ability to sense the environment and navigate with no human inputs. The progression in the development of vehicles is from advanced driver support systems to semi-autonomous systems, to fully autonomous systems. The first vehicle with some self-driving capability is expected to come into the market by 2020. From industry point of view, there must be large and systematic potential factors required for transitioning of self-driving fleets. The regulatory stance of governments will also be crucial, and likewise the corresponding insurance, licensing, regulatory, and financing models.

c. Transportation Service Delivery Ecosystem

A third influencing factor on the future automotive industry is the environment of transportation service delivery. The current transportation models like Uber, Zipcar, Lyft, Getaround, Sidecar, and LaZooz are in progress to shift customer conceptualization of transportation services into an automation system. At the same time, smart city transportation environment is ready to focus on developing various service delivery models. The project on smart city is visualized at Masdar City in Abu Dhabi of the United Arab Emirates. It is designed for a community of a 50,000-person relying on solar and other renewable energy where each element demands personal pod transportation network where any local destination would only be a few minutes away.

Advancement of vehicle technology has continued rapidly to reach ultimate goals of autonomous driverless cars to prevent accidents due to human errors, and to control traffic flow efficiently, emerging electric vehicle charging services and boost the fuel economy. Main features of intelligent vehicles are wireless internet access and the communication elements. The modern intelligent connected car is a computer system like to a Smartphone that is controlled by a complex computer with an internal vehicle network and wireless communication network and these systems are evolving rapidly. However, the introduction of a vehicular cloud network based on wireless internet connectivity means a remarkable increase in the reliance on the networked software. This leads to a cyber-security issue, as well as safety-related function problems in the automotive industry. Based on these aforementioned facts, one of the most important concerns associated with intelligent vehicles is to use a trust network to secure them against malicious cyber attacks. Conventional centralized security system is vulnerable because if a central system is compromised, owing to fraud, cyber attack, or a simple error, the entire network is affected. Conventional security and privacy methods used in personal computers or cloud networks tend to be ineffective in intelligent vehicles owing to their vulnerability in cyber attacks.

Blockchain technology works for the crypto-currency, which has recently been used to build trust and reliability in peer-to-peer networks with similar topologies as networks of intelligent vehicles. Blockchain has shown successful use cases in financial applications, smart contact, and delivering media content with digital copyright protection. Applicable fields have now been extended to secure internet of things (IoT) devices, embedded systems, and to industries other than information-related fields (E.B. Hamida, K.L. Brousmiche, H. Levard, E. Thea, 2017). A superior feature of blockchain is its decentralized, immutable, auditable database for secure transaction with privacy protection (W.-H. Lin and H. Liu, 2010) . In this chapter, we contemplate the trusted environment of intelligent vehicle communication network and how the blockchain technology creates trust network among intelligent vehicles.

II. INTELLIGENT TRANSPORTATION SYSTEM

For the last two decades, Intelligent Transportation Systems (ITS) have promoted to increase the performance of transportation systems, increasing the travel security, and offer additional alternatives to travelers. A major change in ITS in recent years is that large amounts of data are gathered from different sources and can be processed into various structures for different stakeholders. The accessibility of a huge amount of data can possibly lead to a revolution in development of ITS, changing an ITS from a traditional technology-driven system into a more powerful data-driven intelligent transportation system (DITS) to control several functions

a. Data-Driven Intelligent Transportation System (DITS)

It is a system of vision, multisource, and learning algorithm developed to optimize its performance. Besides, DITS has become a privacy based people oriented intelligent system. Although the Intelligent vehicle (IV) has got growth in research and industry it is still suffering from several security vulnerabilities. Conventional security methods are inadequate to provide secured IV data sharing. The main issues in IV data sharing are data accuracy, trust, and reliability of shared data passing through the communication channel. Recently, Blockchain technology is used to build trust and reliability in peer-to-peer networks having similar topologies as IV Data sharing. The blockchain technology is providing the trust environment with the help of proof of driving among the vehicles

Figure 2. Schematic of D²ITS.

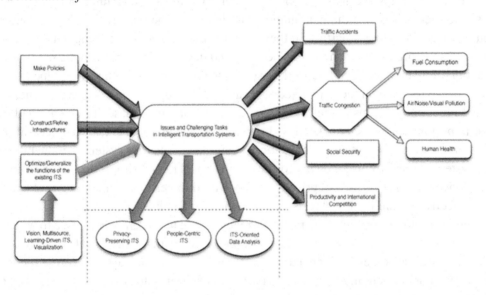

There are six fundamental components in ITS as follows:

1) Advanced transportation management systems;
2) Advanced traveler information systems;
3) Advanced vehicle control systems;
4) Business vehicle management;
5) Advanced public transportation systems;
6) Advanced urban transportation systems.

D²ITS support a huge volumes of data that are collected from various systems that would allow users to interactively utilize or access data resources that are related to transportation systems and utilize data through more suitable and reliable services to increase the performance of transportation systems, and understand and expand the functions of the six fundamental components of ITS. That means the D²ITS interfaces with users or people of transportation systems directly. For D²ITS to widely be accepted, first, it should be privacy aware and people centric. The difference between D²ITS and traditional ITS is that conventional ITS mainly based on human and historical experiences and give less importance to utilization of real-time ITS information or data. The different models are built by different researchers. For example, Lin and Liu (W.-H. Lin and H. Liu, 2010) improved the existing linear-programming based analytical system, an optimal dynamic traffic assignment model to improve practicality in modeling merge junctions (Zhao et al. L. Zhao, X. Peng, L. Li, and Z. Li, 2011) used linear program to achieve fast signal timing for individual oversaturated intersections. Alonso-Ayuso et al. (Alonso-Ayuso, L. F. Escudero, and F. J. Martín-Campo, 2011) used a mixed 0–1 linear optimization model to collision avoidance among an arbitrary numbers of aircrafts in the airspace. Mulder et al. (M. Mulder, D. A. Abbink, M. M. van Paassen, and M. Mulder, 2011) investigated the car-following kinematics to design a haptic feedback algorithm to achieve "safely promoting comfort" in active support systems for drivers. Shieh et al. (W.-Y. Shieh, C.-C. Hsu, S.-L. Tung, P.-W. Lu, T.-H. Wang, and S.-L. Chang, 2011) employed unidirectional cosine functions to approximate the irregular radiation pattern. These models are built based on historical or human experiences. Furthermore, data that are used in conventional ITS are collected from limited sources, e.g., floating cars, inductive loops, and video monitoring and recording. According to the type of data used, the way that data are processed, and the specific D²ITS applications, a full D²ITS can be classified into several major categories.

A.   Vision-Driven ITS
B.   Multisource-Driven ITS
C.   Learning-Driven ITS
D.   Visualization-Driven ITS

b.   VANET

VANET is the encapsulation of Vehicle-to-Vehicle (V-to-V) and Vehicle-to-Infrastructure (V-to-I), for providing notification of any safety critical incident and hazard to the drivers (G. Yan and S. Olariu, 2011). This information is collected through feedbacks of the vehicles which are nearby. This system is prone to security attacks, by marking incorrect feedback, which results in higher congestion and severe hazards (D. Singh, M. Singh, I. Singh and H. J. Lee, 2015).

Security plays a vital role in data sharing of Inter Vehicular network at the time of communication. These networks require trust and privacy (S. Olariu, M. Eltoweissy, and M. Younis, 2011). IV-TP is a crypto number, which is unique and attached to the message format and transmitted during communication time. The cloud storage based on Blockchain manages the IV-TP, and is accessed ubiquitously. This IV-TP mechanism is also based on Blockchain technology, enabled to create the crypto unique ID, self-executing digital contracts and details of IV, controlled over the Blockchain Cloud (C. Wang, Q. Wang, K. Ren, and W. Lou, 2010). A blockchain based trust environment for intelligent vehicle shares information based on blockchain technology.

Figure 3. Depicts Information sharing of Autonomous vehicles like V2I, V2V communication.

Current ITS framework utilizes ad-hoc networks for communication of Vehicles, for example, DSRC, WAVE, and Cell System, which doesn't ensure transmission of data in a secured manner. As of now, security protocols of intelligent vehicles during communication depend on IT and Cellular security standard systems which are not exceptional and reasonable for ITS applications. Still numerous analysts are attempting to produce standard security system to ITS. A straightforward idea of utilizing Blockchain

Figure 3. Intelligent Vehicles Information Environment

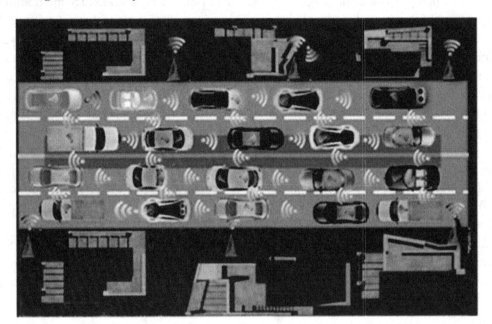

based trust environment for information sharing among smart Vehicles utilizing the IV-TP (Intelligent Vehicle-Trust Point) by exploiting the characteristics of Blockchain for example distributed and open ledger which is encoded with Hash work (SHA-256) and Merkel tree and depend on Consensus Mechanism (Proof of Work Algorithm). Blockchain technology is distributed, open ledger, saved by each node in the network, which is self-maintained by each node. It gives distributed system (peer-to-peer network) without the impedance of the outsider. The integrity of blockchain depends on strong cryptography that authenticate and chain blocks together during data transmission, making it about difficult to alter any individual transaction without being identified (Satoshi Nakomoto, Bitcoin, 2009).

Fig. 4 shows the Blockchain technology features such as shared ledger, Cryptography, Signed blocks of transactions, and digital signatures (Satoshi Nakomoto, Bitcoin, 2009).

Blockchain can utilize numerous different functionalities like communication between vehicles to provide security and peer-to-peer communication without revealing any confidential information.

c. Framework of Intelligent Vehicle Data sharing based on Blockchain

It has three basics technologies including

1. Communication network that enables connected device,
2. Vehicular Cloud Computing (VCC) and
3. Blockchain technology (BT).

Fig.5 has shown the complete data-sharing environment for intelligent vehicles.

1. Network enabled connected device

Figure 4. Blockchain technology

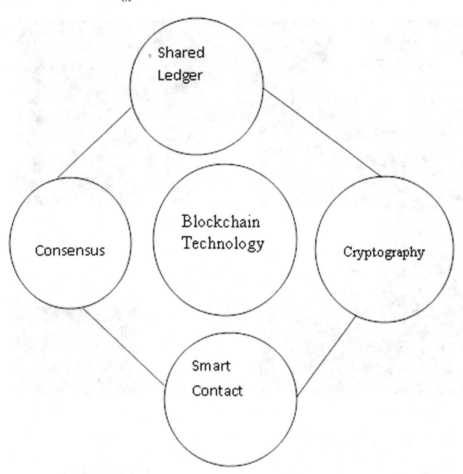

It is an internet-enabled device capable of organizing, interacting in VANET such as PDA, Smart-phone, Intelligent Vehicles, etc.

2.   Vehicular Cloud Computing

VCC is a hybrid system that has a tremendous impact on road safety and traffic management through the direct use of resources of vehicle like data storage, computing, and internet decision-making.

3.   Blockchain supported intelligent vehicles

Blockchain generally contains countless number of blocks which are tied together cryptographically in chronological order. In this, each block comprises of exchanges, which are the concrete information saved in the chain.

In fig. 6 Seven-layer conceptual model for standardizing blockchain architecture for the intelligent communication network.

Figure 5. Blockchain Intelligent Vehicle Communication

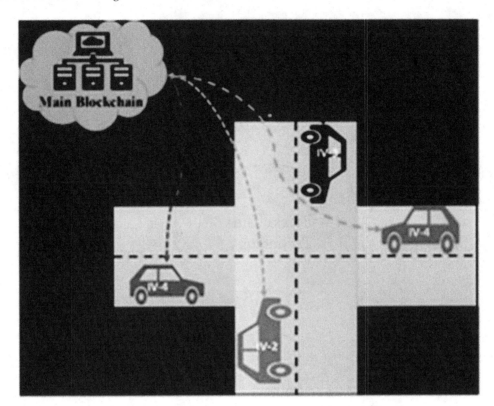

Figure 6. Six Layered Conceptual Model

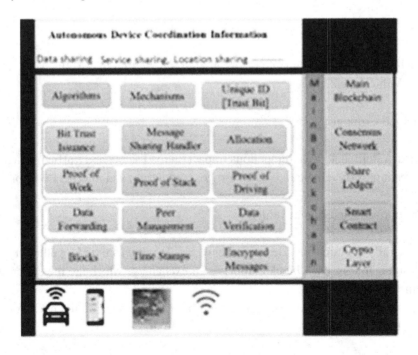

Physical layer: the communication network enabled devices like mobile, IoT devices, camera, intelligent vehicles, PDA, GPS, etc., are present in this lay. They can be used during communication and easily implement the blockchain mechanism.

Data Layer: Processing of data blocks using cryptographic techniques like Merkle tree and hash algorithm to provide security to the blocks is done in this layer.

The structure of block is shown in fig.7, where header contains the previous hash and nonce with current hash (root). Hashing is done by using double SHA 256 algorithm and is not easily tampered (hackable).

Figure 7. The structure of blocks.

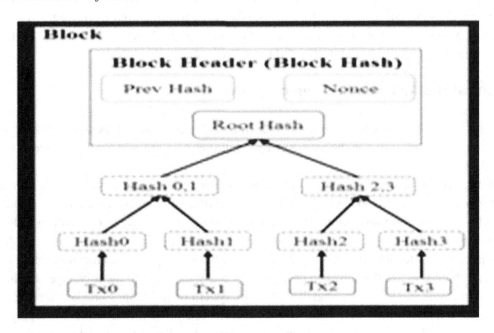

Network Layer: This layer indicates the data forwarding through peer-to-peer communication and also verifies the communication. This layer checks the legality of the message that is broadcasted and monitors the peer connection between two IVs.

Handshake Layer: This layer is called consensus layer in blockchain technology. It presents decentralized communication within network and assists to develop trust among unknown users in the communication environment. More efficient consensus algorithm in intelligent vehicles communication networks is proof of driving (PoD), which validate and verify the vehicles present in the communication networks.

Reward layer: It supplies some crypto data called IV-TP. The IV-TP is assigned to each vehicle and whenever any vehicle wins the consensus competition, its gets some IV-TP from the benefiter IV. The vehicle that has the maximum IV-TP enters into the communication network. IV-TP helps to generate trusted environment among the vehicles during communication.

Presentation Layer: The presentation layer encapsulates multiple scripts, contracts and algorithms, which are provided by the vehicles involved in the network.

Service Layer: This layer indicates the complete picture and use cases of intelligent vehicles communication system.

III. THE RELATIONSHIP BETWEEN AUTONOMOUS VEHICLES AND BLOCKCHAIN

Autonomous vehicles (AVs) are on the edge of absolutely transforming the way how we concern about the transportation of both people and goods. In order to help to do things in this new way, the DAV(Decentralized Autonomous Vehicles) base is used to built a network that not only connect cars to cars or drones to drones, but also can link jointly any and all autonomous vehicles including drones, trucks, cars and rovers, together with the essential infrastructure required to make them work. This comprises of mapping software and services like charging outlets. Blockchain can be used to build a secure, intelligent, autonomous and distributed transport system.

a. Decentralized Autonomous Vehicles(DAV)

The DAV network provides support to communications, discovery, and transactions involving personal vehicles. The charging stations on the network or personal vehicles are paid for the services so that they can provide to their peers

By having grip on this peer-to-peer system, users that are in the network can access infrastructure and an expansive system of DAVs which can transport anything to them or take them anywhere. DAV is laying the base for a transportation infrastructure which is decentralized that will include built-in incentives for all the different consumers, participants: software developers, businesses, hardware makers, insurers, maintenance providers and arbitrators. Industry-specific applications build on top of blockchain technology have the ability to produce new ecosystems where the exchange of value can be done in a immutable and secure manner. This type of system is important to make sure that the players of superior industries like Uber, Tesla, or Alphabet not to end up with a virtual monopoly over the increasing Internet of Transportation. A decentralized network will permit innovators and companies to incorporate their solutions into a greater one, with no level of investment that the tech giants have access to. A decentralized network with many players expanding the best potential solutions for each and every aspect around mobility provides them the finest solutions to rise to prominence without these companies needing to develop parallel infrastructures individually. Blockchain technology is very important to this type of understanding, as it registers and secures the wealth of data of the interactions between dissimilar moving parts that are needs to be created inevitably.

The DAV protocol is a set of interconnected systems that are used to create an open-source transportation infrastructure. The whole network is established on these protocols, so that it can be highly scalable and ensure that it is reliable.

By decentralizing protocols around transactions and communication and open sourcing its technology stack, DAV fosters cooperation in an otherwise severely fragmented industry. Usage of the DAV Network is not permissible; any other player can go through the market and rapidly scale up their participation in the transportation economy. The technology behind this type of DAV network helps in eliminating the barriers that prevent the companies from positively interacting with each other and utilizing the all the innovative solutions otherwise isolated away.

By employing an open-source model DAV is able to push innovation to the edge, giving more participants control over the pace and direction of innovation, and fuelling creativity. Each participant, (be it customer to vehicle) on the network has a unique ID, which allows the system to track the transactions and create smart contracts that stay on that ID's history. The two different ways all members of the decentralized network can communicate are on-blockchain or off-blockchain.

1. On-blockchain communication is where all smart contracts are signed, and where all payments and other transactions happen, taking advantage of the blockchain's strengths when it comes to exchanging, securing and confirming information
2. Off-blockchain communication is where vehicles, infrastructure, and service providers communicate
3. Generally, participants will be providers or consumers (or both), with the latter being the ones who use the services and infrastructure on the network. Consumers mean both vehicles and people themselves when using things like charging services or mapping technology. Providers can split into several categories. For instance, vehicle providers are the companies that provide vehicles for on-demand services, infrastructure providers supply the network with charging station, docking, and parking. Service providers offer the maintenance necessary to the infrastructure and vehicles underpinning much of the wider network
4. Additionally, arbitrators and Insurance providers are the third parties of the system. They are essential for providing on-demand insurance contracts on the blockchain, and for providing independent dispute resolution. Perhaps most fundamental to the network itself are the final category of DAV members, the software and hardware providers who develop the open-source platform of custom services that are accessible to everyone on the network. The DAV Network can be accessed by all these participants using a DAV Token. These tokens are used to purely grant access to the network, and cannot be used in any other way.

IV. DIFFERENT WAYS AUTONOMOUS VEHICLES CAN USE BLOCKCHAIN

For the past few years there is a discussion of cryptocurrencies of Blockchain and is now being used to develop other industries as well. Now it sees a rapidly increasing partnership with automation on the road. The different ways the autonomous vehicles use Blockchain are improved Interconnectivity, easy Roadside Transactions, ride Sharing and E-Transactions etc,.

In forthcoming few years, we assuredly perceive blockchain and its digital economic transactions integrated into our cars. The reason behind is that the blockchain works as a ledger that uses several servers in order to track the networks through which crypto-currencies are shared. It is much protected, and it can screen individual financial interactions depend upon how the code behind blockchain is composed; it can follow whatever its coder decides to be of worth.

a. Improved Interconnectivity

The drive for automated cars working with EV batteries (or their substitutes) has made auto-engineering a more innovative field of late. The significance of the automation also let the Internet of Things (IoT) to find a place in the development of autonomous car. The interconnectivity between phone and the car can already be seen whenever the person uses Bluetooth to play anything through the sound system of the car. Integration of the IoT with blockchain makes these digital possibilities. Smart sensors, like the ones used by Adaptive Cruise Control and, IoT and blockchain the will give you more functionalities so that your car works without you. For example, moving smoothly away from oncoming traffic without need to tap the brakes.

b. Made Roadside Transactions Easy

In terms of profit and remuneration, look attentively the numbers of transactions that take place while you're travelling on the road. For example Toll highways require transactions that can take up significant portions of your time, potentially causing unnecessary traffic. Not merely most of the clever hacker could potentially steal credit card numbers from the toll booths themselves. The assimilation of blockchain technology into your car in the form of Car e-Wallets, for example – will make these transactions smoother and will keep any information of yours more private than it already is. Hacking vehicles still can't seem to wind up basic practice, and regardless of whether it were to, with the increase of self-assisted cars, blockchain is a cyber security wonder with its capacity to spread data over various servers.

c. Ride Sharing and E-Transactions

The blockchain technology has the potential almost everything we can do, whether buying something using a credit card, or traveling by car or by using public transport, involves the creation and movement of data. Consider the rise of the ride-sharing industry. Over the last few years, Lyft and Uber have made waves in the auto industry, not for cars they produce but rather for services they provide.

Presently, a multi-billion-dollar industry and ride-sharing offers blockchain and e-commerce technologies to thrive. Imagine the chance to make payments for a ride without utilizing the credit card or, as a driver, having the option to gather a rider's installment without waiting outside their destination. There is zero chance of getting transient, when a driver utilizes blockchain. With both of the most prevalent ride-sharing organizations investigating self-sufficient driving, maybe getting a ride in the following decade will be altogether interaction free.

d. Individualized Car Insurance

There is additionally the potential for blockchain to be used by insurance organizations. The Mobility Open Blockchain Initiative, for instance, works with Ford and GM so as to establish client based insurance. When set up, can be saved within a blockchain's servers. Installments would then be able to be made when a car's sensors detect a contract violation. In like manner, telematic administrations will have the option to gather information from a driver's street history – anything from area, length of drive, and regular driving velocity – so as to report back to an insurance agency and decide how high or low a premium is set.

e. Security Risks and Rewards

The connected car security model that blockchain put forward in the form of driver monitoring and e-transactions sounds to be perfect. Because bitcoin is foremost example which is open source, we can assume that automotive blockchain would operate similarly. This means that the code can be individualized, but it also means that it is accessible to anyone who wants to be Part of it. The hackability of such a blockchain system remains very difficult because of the spread of blockchain's information across several servers. But the open source nature of such a system still needs to be taken into forethought before it is globally implemented. The assimilation of blockchain in the automotive industry seems inevitable. It provides modern smart services to today's car drivers. Steps have already been taken towards future applications with the improved integration of the IoT into cars. And also provide smart feature of development of mobile e-wallets for all accounts. In future, blockchains seem to have in the average car owner's day-to-day life

V. A DISTRIBUTED BLOCKCHAIN BASED VEHICULAR NETWORK ARCHITECTURE IN SMART CITY

A smart city includes, smart administration for solid waste management, efficient urban mobility and public transport, affordable housing, especially for the poor, robust IT connectivity and digitalization for intelligent life, automatic use of characteristic assets for economics and smart subjects. There are several methods to utilize the current advances applications to construct competent economies and social orders. But there is major task of allocation of application to assets of smart cities. Blockchains have number of tasks newly been drawn in light of a rightful concern for associates on a broad range of businesses applications, medical and hospital services, utilities finance, and the government division.

Blockchain can be used to build an intelligent, smart, authenticated, distributed and autonomous transport system. It allows superior utilization of the infrastructure and resources of intelligent vehicular systems, especially effective for crowd sourcing technology. Block-VN is a reliable and authenticates architecture that operates in a distributed way to design the new distributed transport management system. Internet of Things (IoT) "Things" (IoT devices) which have remote object detection as well as motivating abilities and can interchange information with other connected devices and applications. IoT devices can collect information and process the data either locally or send the data to bring together servers or cloud-based application back-ends for processing. IoT device provide promising modern application and assembling frameworks. Professional expert has to gauge a trillion-dollar effect of IoT devices on the manufacturing and industrial divisions. A recent application on-request model of assembling the utilization of IoT innovations called cloud-based manufacturing (CBM) (D. Wu, D. W. Rosen, L. Wang, and D. Schaefer, 2015). CBM authorize globally for the advantageous of on-request models which arranges access to a common pool of configurable assembling assets. These assembled assets can be easily provisioned and discharged with negligible administration exercises or specialist organization collaboration.

Today, urban brotherhood faces complex challenges in improving the personal satisfaction of their residents. As the 2014 report on the global interpretation for urbanization in the United Nations indicates that the bulk of the world's most population currently lives in urban areas. An additional 2.5 billion people are interpreted to move in urban areas by 2050 (Revision of World Urbanization Prospects .2014). Urban system trying to determine people's living conditions that have been affected by extended parked roads, increase carbon dioxide in atmosphere, nursery oil exits and waste management. The idea of "smart city" is finding the solution to these questions has regained prevalence in recent years. Many urban communities are distinguishing as "smart" when they identified some of their features such as broadband, advancement of incorporation and information workforce. A typical basic certainty is that these acute urban areas take advantage of the innovative use of new variety of data and correspondence innovations (ICTs) to improve mutual sharing. A city cannot be narrated as "smart" by using selected sectoral or constrained changes. However due to the space requirements and the density of the urban population, urban communities are typically meant to pass on savings to use, including access to shared assets in relation to the possession of resources. There are various methods to use the current innovative technique to make competent with respect to economies and social orders. Information sharing in distributed network is one of the main assets of smart cities. Over the past few years, smarter vehicles are more secure and less tiring driving encounters has understood. Currently conventional vehicles have devices, for example GPS, radio handset, small-scale impact radars, cameras, on-board computers, and traffic monitoring and various kinds of detection devices including weather update to warn the driver of a wide range of good and bad conditions being of the street and mechanical breakdowns. The vehicles are more delimit due to their on-board storage density and on-board computing capabilities with respect to significant matching capabilities and fewer power obstacle, which are supported by various sensors, actuators, radar hosts and GPS (M. Walport, 2016, Y. Sung, P. K. Sharma, E. M. Lopez, and J. H. Park, 2016). Most of automotive vehicles can be supported with event data recorder (EDR) and GPS gadgets implanted soon (H. Mousannif, I. Khalil, and H. Al Moatassime, 2011). The EDR is responsible for recording the fundamental attribute of portability, like increasing speed, deceleration, sensor and radar reading, lane changes and comparative information. Once the recorded information is archived appropriately and connected to a GPS. In addition mean while weather reading data and EDR collected data, such as the minimum and maximum remarkable speed with respect to time and position of the best speed/deceleration, as well as the area and target route or the various paths. In addition, most vehicular system will have various sensors which give reading of fuel tank level, tire weight, engine and outdoor temperature and weather condition data. These sensors collected information report is sent to the EDR. As a result, processing of gathered information and detection capabilities by using internet access and power supplies will require smart applications for automotive system which are suitable for computers (PCs). For large storage devices that can be fixed on wheels, for example in-vehicle computing device. However, on highways due to some obstacle, most often we are not warned by notification of route blocking caution for a long time. The ITS discussion arranged separate opinions to diminish the hoof. Among the provisions to predict, the number of lanes on roads and roads should be extended. A late review survey has revealed that this arrangement is ineffective over the long term and may even increase levels of blocking and contamination. By providing appropriate notifications to drivers with satisfied choices taught that would relieve and obstruct improved road safety, save fuel and time. Blockchains technology shows new era for authorized partners on a wide range of businesses application like finance, medical services, and the government division (M. Walport, 2016). The goal and intention behind this explosion is eagerness with a blockchain configuration and applications that might already function just by a delegate put the stock, can now work in a decentralized and distributed manner, without the requirement of administrative specialist, and to accomplish a similar utility with a similar measure of authentication. It was practically unfeasible for some time recently. We can say that the blockchain allows systems without trust since the gatherings can run even though they do not believe. The absence of a trusted representative implies a faster agreement between the performing parties. The immense use of cryptography, a normal key for block chain systems, brings authentication behind each of the connections in the system, intelligent contracts, self-executing scripts that insist on the block chain. Block chain technology integrate these ideas and consider legitimately with scattered and vigorously automated workflows. This should make blocking chains to specialists and engineers working in IoT space.

Benefits of the Blockchain Technique

As a digitalize payment framework, blockchain has some advantages over existing electronic frameworks. These benefits largely consider the beneficiary of a blockchain exchange, but some benefits could be recognized by the exchange of senders as well.

- Transparency: As block chain network is distributed so the information and data exchanges are translucent in the blockchain. which means a totally verifiable and unchanging record of any action exists in block chain network
- No risk of fraud: When some data is sent and deleted over a blockchain network, once exchanged data cannot be canceled by the sender.
- Low or no exchange costs: The administration of the blockchain network is sponsored by the procedure of creation of the treasury, example Ethereum. Thus, exchanges on the blockchain network can be sent for a small or no exchange fee. Although there is no cost to get to the blockchain network.
- Transactions almost instantaneous: Exchanges of data in blockchain networks immediately register in block chain nodes. Affirmation and compensation for these exchanges can occur in minutes to more than 60 minutes. In traditional payment systems, compensation takes much longer. Transaction are faster in blockchain network
- Network security: The blockchain network itself is extraordinarily authenticated. Acknowledge to the use of cryptographic and decentralized blockchain protocol in block chain network. Individuals in general of the private key sets used to provide adequate authorization against the vulnerabilities of a wild restriction to hack or the inadvertent appearance of two clients producing a similar private key. However, there is no single goal to combine with disappointments which limits the vulnerability of the blockchain network to downtime and piracy.
- Financial data assurance: In Blockchain network transactions can be performed without revealing to the beneficiary sensitive and confidential individual and financial data, limiting the potential presentation of such data to database piracy.
- Financial access: In financial access notwithstanding the fact that it cannot give most of the administrations of account management and its specialized complex nature may be too high for some clients. Blockchain can offer incentive storage and payment services for clients who need access traditional financial services.

VI. BLOCK-VN DISTRIBUTED ARCHITECTURE

To encapsulate our observation of the current vehicular network is that, vehicular network applications provide advance feature from basic information purchasers to ones that empower neighborhood coordinated efforts with adequate substance for wealthier client experience. Although the basic systems administration does not appear to bolster the center capacities, the developing applications request effectively. This chapter presents recent research endeavors that address the issues under two classes of networking and computing.

a. Architecture Overview

Block-VN model is blockchain architecture for automotive vehicular network used in the smart city. It develops distributed network of large scale vehicles in more effective and efficient way.

Figure 8. Overview architecture of Block-VN.

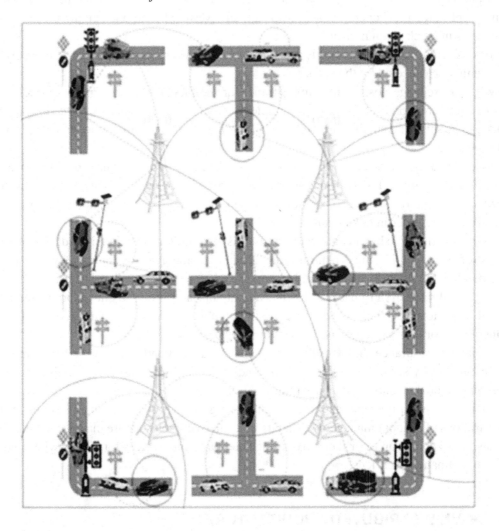

Fig. 8 illustrates the Block-VN architecture of the blockchain vehicle network to meet futures challenges and requirements. In the Block-VN model, the controller nodes are connected in a distributed manner to provide the necessary services on a large scale. The miner node is represented by red circle, which handles responses/ requests. Rest all vehicle nodes are just ordinary nodes. An ordinary node may send a service request message either to minor nodes (vehicle) or controller nodes. By using the minor and controller nodes in a distributed way, we can easily achieve the scalability and high availability of the vehicle network. Block-VN also improves vehicle network architecture by enabling consumer-to-machine and machine-to-machine authenticated intermediary free of cost service and by providing distributed, authenticated, and shared records of all services, assets, and inventories.

b. Block-VN Model Architecture

Each time the registration of a new vehicle issued. The department of motor vehicles (manufacturers) provides full details information to the revocation authority. The revocation authority has the power to decide which vehicle considers being the minor node outside the nodes of the controller. The renouncement authority gives all data of the standard and miner vehicles nodes to the distributed blockchain vehicle system. Each and every controller node fundamentally incorporates a timestamp, a hash, a Merkle root and a nonce to hold all the data required to give the essential services. Every controller works at the personal level to compute and process, offer it to different nodes in a distributed approach. Every

Figure 9. The structure of the Block-VN model.

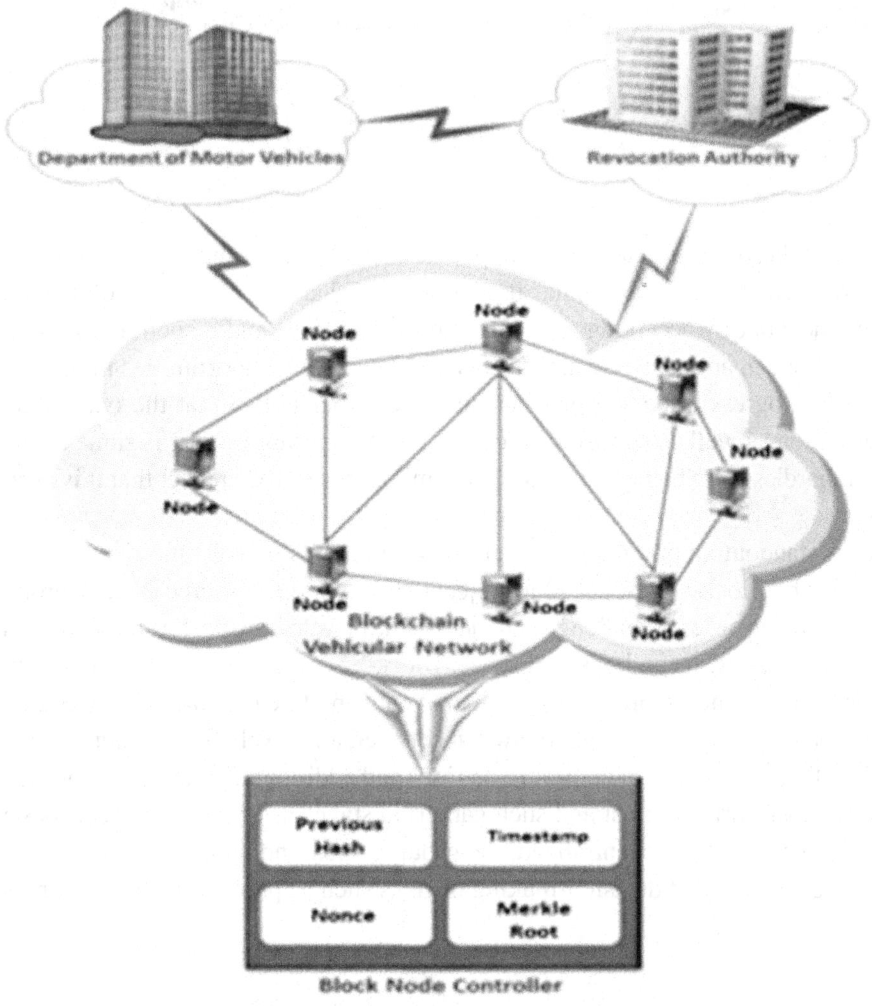

correspondence will be made utilizing the asymmetric key encryption system to verify the security of the customer's information.

The miner node's elements are discriminated from the controller nodes. Each miner node vehicle has three asset classifications: computing, sensors, and data storage, as shown in Fig. 10.

Figure 10. Miner Node's Structural Design

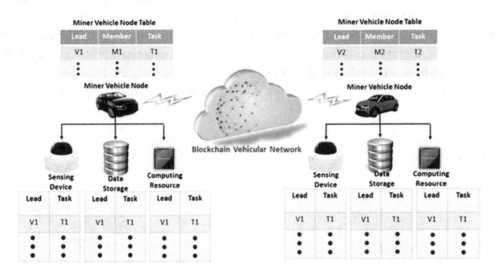

The substance of the vehicle created from applications and sensors are stored in data storage and in addition to records visuals and multimedia. It supports the sharing of information between members of the blockchain network by accepting an external pursuit request and responding with a coordinated substance. The sensor can auto-activate and further distinguish the opportunities in the physical world. With technological progress, each sensor is specifically associated so that the outer frames can read the sensor information as well as control the sensor. The computing benefit is same as the blockchain controller node regardless of whether its capacity is limited in view of the fact that it is an accumulation of portable assets.

SmartShare: A standout among the best application situations is real-time ride-sharing that can be easily accomplished by Block-VN model. Our project to build an open-source system, around the world, circulated ride-sharing, in order to challenge and modify the private transport frameworks built with large quantities of wasted waste seats and payload space. Block-VN model of constant travel sharing allows private car owners to give their empty seats to others venturing to each part of a similar course. It also offers a multi-rebound response for riders to switch between a few vehicles on their approach to goals, focusing on expanding the number of coordination rides and additionally making a more vigorous scope on customer needs transport. Contrast and such gathering stages as Lyft and Uber, Block-VN can take ride-sharing to the next level of decentralized, the group owned-and-supervise transportation arranges without unacceptable embedded decision-making or risks such as privacy leaks and surges pricing.

VII. RESEARCH ISSUES AND CHALLENGES IN VEHICULAR NETWORK

Because of the dynamic environment of registering, conveying, detecting, and sorting out structures authorize self-governance and specialist to become accustomed to the close by surroundings that have a great influence. A vehicular network's physical resource, synchronization, control, and aggregation of a vehicular network are the challenges of research.

- Challenges integrate issues concern about the course of action of the rational structure of the vehicular system and relationship with physical resources. Accordingly, the extraordinary need of managing the adaptability of the host and heterogeneity should be considered for correspondence, figuring, and vehicle affiliations and storerooms, for instance, changes in scheme or zone, resource dissatisfaction, and rejection. As such, we have to think about the going with points.
- Adaptable design of vehicular system: One of the basic characteristics of the vehicular system is the transferable effect of all the nodes that explicitly effects on the open computational limits and resources, for delineation, the amount of halted vehicles in halting isn't predictable. Along these lines, to give fluctuating application requirements and progress of resource accessibility, the significant related design and organization of vehicular system must be made.
- Robust design: The critical development of squares and structures that structure vehicular system should be fabricated and expected to face the fundamental stress of the unpredictable working situation (H. Mousannif, I. Khalil, and H. Al Moatassime, 2011) A solid component engineering for the vehicular system in perspective on Eucalyptus cloud structure and virtualization approach to manage absolute the computational and capable resources. Progressively conspicuous emphasis and more investigates are significant for the development of virtual machines among cars and productive vehicle portrayal.

a. Privacy and Security of Vehicular Network

Protection and security are basic parts of the setting up and keeping up the trust of customers in the vehicular system. Safety efforts are required to ensure the vehicular system correspondence and information in the bound and reliable condition, while security strategies are required to guarantee against framework dangers. Setting up trust associations among individuals is a primary part of dependable count and correspondence. As a part of the vehicles related to the vehicular system may have met already, the proactive task of impelling a basic trust relationship among vehicles is charming and possible. (M. Walport, 2016) A vehicular system as a game plan of vehicles which offer the limit of enlisting power, the Internet get to and ability to outline conventional distributed computing. Along these lines, it is anticipated that vehicular system perseveres through an unclear security issue from distributed computing. The essential security troubles of the vehicular system incorporate:

- Checking the verification of customers and the morality of messages in view of the high motility of components.
- Assurance of security of the sensitive message by using the cryptographic function.
- Assuring the secure territory and limitation in light of the fact that most applications in vehicular systems rely upon region information.
- Giving data withdrawal to guarantee the security of set away data on the cloud.

- Secure data access to guarantee set away data on the cloud against unapproved gets to. The protection ad security challenges of the vehicular system have not yet been tended to record as a hard copy and need more idea.

VIII. A DISTRIBUTED SOLUTION TO AUTOMOTIVE SECURITY AND PRIVACY

Interrelated smart vehicles suggested a variety of sophisticated services that provides assistance for the transport authorities, vehicle owners, car manufacturers, and further service providers. This potentially makes smart vehicles to expose range of privacy and security threats such as remote hijacking or location tracking of the vehicle. Blockchain (BC), a disruptive technology is used to smart contracts and is a possible solution to these challenges.

BC-based architecture is designed to ensure the protection of clients and to build the security of the vehicular biological system. Wireless isolated software updates and other developing administrations, for example, dynamic vehicle protection expenses are utilized to delineate the viability of the recommended security engineering. This architecture also provides the strength against regular security assaults

a. Introduction

Smart vehicles are progressively associated with roadside framework (e.g., traffic the board frameworks), to different vehicles in closeness, and furthermore more by and large to the Internet, in this manner consolidating vehicles into the Internet of Things (IoT). This high scale of availability makes it especially testing to verify smart vehicles. Noxious substances can bargain a vehicle, which imperils the security of the vehicle as well as the wellbeing of the travelers. There is an attack on a Jeep Cherokee utilizing the remote interface of the infotainment framework whereby they had the option to remotely control the center elements of the vehicle. The information traded by the vehicle incorporates susceptible information (e.g., area) and would thus be able to open up new protection challenges.

IX. BLOCKCHAIN BASED EVENT RECORDING SYSTEM FOR AUTONOMOUS VEHICLES

Autonomous vehicles are able to sense their environment and navigating with no human inputs. However, while autonomous vehicles are involved in accidents among themselves or with human subjects, legal responsibility must be unquestionably decided depending on the accident forensics. This chapter discusses a Blockchain based recording system of events for autonomous vehicles. This chapter discusses design of "proof of event" mechanism to achieve indubitable accident forensics by making sure that event information is verifiable and trustable.

a. Introduction

A self-sufficient vehicle (otherwise called driverless vehicle or self-driving vehicle) is equipped for detecting its condition and exploring with no human information. To encourage self-driving, self-governing vehicles embrace an assortment of tangible innovations, for example, camera, lidar, and ultrasound, to identify their environment, and utilize a control framework to decipher tactile data to recognize proper route ways, just as maintain a strategic distance from snags and pursue significant traffic signs. In view of an ongoing review, around 66% of Americans anticipate that vehicles should be absolutely independent in the following 50 years (Pew Research Center)

In any case, self-governance comes with responsibility. When self-sufficient vehicles are associated with mishaps (crashes between themselves, or impacts with customary vehicles, people on foot or different articles), how could such occasions be recorded for measurable purposes to decide obligation? Also, how could such recorded occasions be checked, trusted, and not altered? These are the most important issues when there are motivating forces for various gatherings required to mess with the recorded occasions to keep away from punitive punishments. The blockchain inspired event recording architecture enables self-sufficient vehicles to accomplish a carefully designed evident- proof, event recording and forensics framework. A blockchain comprises of a sequence of blocks, every block is made out of sets of timestamped operations and previous blocks' hash. The first blockchain was intended for Bitcoin, a digital cryptocurrency, to take care of the twofold spending issue by utilizing the Proof of Work (PoW) system. In PoW, excavators contend with each other to turn into the first to crack hash bewilder in order to get the privilege to create the next followed block and to get incentive. Generally PoW takes not more than 10 minutes to solve any problem and produce another new block. In this recording framework, mishaps are recorded as time-stamped exchanged among transactions which are to be stored into another block in real time systems continuously. Even though self-ruling vehicles might be furnished with sensible registering limit, directing PoW to store the incidents of accident continuously is not possible because of the hash puzzle cannot be solved easily. To address this basic issue, Proof of Event with Dynamic Federation Consensus record mishap occasions in another block.

At the point when ever an accident takes place, vehicles directly associated with the accident broadcast 'event generation' demands, which just those vehicles inside the corresponding range will get and react. At that point, both the vehicles straightforwardly associated with the accident and those vehicles getting the request will produce and communicate the occasion into a 'vehicular system' which is characterized on the present cellular network foundation. Inside the vehicular system, an arbitrary group is outlined to confirm and store the data events occurred in another block by utilizing a multi-signature system.

The new block created will be sent and stored in Department of Motor Vehicles (DMV) for the perpetual records. The method of Proof of Event with Dynamic Federation Consensus records instances of undeniable accident forensics and provides reliability and data integrity by using events information from numerous sources and the produces hash digest. The recorded instances additionally give discernible proof. In particular, the Dynamic Federation Consensus system replaces the job of PoW in the first blockchain to affirm and store another block in a quick and viable manner without acquiring extensive computation. As an alliance is progressively conformed to every mishap over a vehicular system, the agreement on the genuineness of the produced instances of accident can be recorded in an adaptable and strong way.

a. Event Data Recorders

An Event Data Recorder (EDR) is a vehicle like a plane's flight recorder or "black box," is introduced in vehicles to record data identified with accidents or mishaps (Event data recorder, 2017). Some EDRs constantly record information until an accident or mishap stops them, and others are enacted by accident like occasions, (for example, an unexpected decline in speed) and may keep on account until the mishap is finished, or until the chronicle time terminates (Event data recorder, 2017). Because of its individual and free establishment, when an EDR is harmed or breakdowns, there is no possibility to reestablish or check the data put away.

A distributed ledger gives responsibility to both bad conduct specialists and vehicles. The objective is to diminish the necessities of trust on clients of vehicular correspondence frameworks and to make responsibility for trouble making specialists by means of hierarchical consensus and worldwide renouncement. By utilizing the method of Proof of Event with Dynamic Federation Consensus, instances of accidents are stored in a verifiable, trustable and tamperproof manner.

b. Blockchain-based Vehicular Systems

By utilizing Ethereums smart contract framework (Y. Yuan and F.-Y. Wang, 2016) a self-guided and decentralized framework is set up and run any sort of application based on vehicular ad-hoc systems without a focal overseeing authority. By utilizing a blockchain-based open key framework, there is an establishment of inter-vehicle session key to verify vehicle-to-vehicle correspondences through observable light and acoustic side-channels.

c. Consensus Methods

1. As Consensus is the basis to the decentralized idea of blockchain. The different existing consensus models are state-of-the-art, PoW, Proof of Stake (PoS), and Proof of Authority (PoA) and a few other Proof of 'X'. They all depend on choosing one single peer to create the new block. Nonetheless, these consensus models slowly move away from the main objectives of democratization and decentralization. For example, only one peer is chosen by nonce lottery by means of mining similarly as with PoW, by arbitrary selection amongst the biggest partners likewise with PoS, and by arbitrary determination of nodes by means of single central unified authority similarly as with PoA. Subsequently, huge mining pools integrated systems of PoS, Bitcoin gives control to central authority to make decision of generating new block (http://www.ubiquicoin.com/assets/proof.pdf). Subsequently, these models have been missing the mark concerning their underlying objectives. Conversely, the system of Proof of Event with Dynamic Federation Consensus leads to the independent and dynamic nature of self-sufficient vehicles so the accident forensic data could be approved by a league than one single person.

d. Architecture of Recording System

i. Cellular Network-based Vehicular Network

A cellular network based framework is used to characterize a 'vehicular system' for every instance of accident, where each and every vehicle is controlled by a one single base station (i.e., inside a similar cell) of the vehicles involved directly form a 'vehicle organize'. All the self-ruling vehicles register with an organization, for example, Department of Motor Vehicles (DMV), using license plate and VIN number. Vehicles utilize the IEEE 802.11p standard of Dedicated Short-Range Communications (DSRC) to send and accept events on demand. In the mean time, vehicles are associated with a cellular network system to communicate and affirm event's information inside the subsequent vehicular system to make new blocks.

Figure 11. Cellular Network-based Vehicular Network

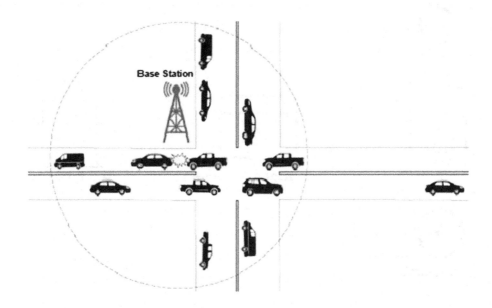

ii. Verification of Event with Dynamic Federation Consensus

To encourage forensic examination after an occurrence of an accident, one issue is the accuracy and dependability of the recorded information, as vehicles included, both straightforwardly and as onlookers, may have motivating forces to adjust mishap related data to keep away from reformatory punishments. In this manner, it is primary to record validated event's information at the particular time and area of the mishap. The recorded data about the mishap could later be recovered and questioned to decide risk. It can give the consensus on whether an incident is provable and dependable at the specific geographic area and time.

The two different stages to accomplish task are

1. Accumulation of trustable event information from the two vehicles legitimately engaged with the mishap and neighboring vehicles,
2. Confirm and store event information with the assistance of a progressively produced alliance of vehicles inside the equivalent vehicular system.

1) Gathering event information: Vehicles straightforwardly associated with a mishap are named "mishap" vehicles, vehicles within the transmission range of DSRC from the mishap scene are named as "witness" vehicles, and vehicles inside a similar cell however outside the transmission range of DSRC from the mishap scene are named "network" vehicles. To record an instance of a mishap, upon the event of a mishap, "mishap" vehicles send 'event generation to "witness" vehicles.

At that point, both "mishap" and "witness" vehicles create their own individual event information from their own positions, EDR records timestamps and the equivalent hash digests, and communicate their event information by means of cellular network inside the vehicular system of the identical cell.

Figure 12. Hash digest of event data.

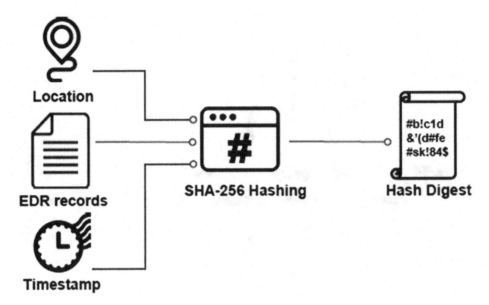

All the communicated event information from both "mishap" and "witness" vehicles will be confirmed and stored in another block by an organization to be portrayed straightaway.

2) Verifying and making new block of mishap instance: Upon the event of a mishap, "mishap" vehicles additionally communicate, through cellular networks, 'alliance development' made a request to the "network" vehicles in the vehicular system to begin the choice of a subset of "network" vehicles as "verifier" vehicles to produce an organization. This selection procedure can be dependent on the reputation score which might be resolved depending on the vehicle's driving and records that are reported. Likewise the "verifier" vehicle with the maximum reputation score is assigned as the lead verifier by means of a distributed leader election algorithm, who is in charge of creating another block for the mishap. From that point, a new block produced by lead verifier vehicle will be send to DMV and reserved for the lasting records.

As delineated in the Fig. 13, after the "mishap" and "witness" vehicles produce and communicate event information into the vehicular system, "verifier" vehicles are responsible for the liability of obtained event information against the accepted hash digests, and affirm with the lead "verifier" vehicle (I in Fig. 4). The lead "verifier" vehicle implements the n-of-m multi-signature plot to accomplish organizational consensus when n out of m "verifier" vehicles prove, and produces another block of mishap instance. The lead "verifier" vehicle may then communicate the new block to all the "network" vehicles. All new blocks have their hash header and connected with the hash header of preceding block. For example, as delineated in Fig. 5, block I is confirmed by 3 out of 4 verifier vehicles from league, while the block I+1 is 3 out of 5 cases.

Fig. 14: Each block contains event information and hash digest of preceding block, and all validated by the verifier vehicles from the alliance. Vehicles "witness" (C, D, and E) perform task uniquely in contrast to "verifier" vehicles (H, I, and J). The activity of the previous is to produce event information, while that of the last is to confirm event information and create another block of mishap instance.

Figure 13. Represents a sequence of accident, witness, verifier vehicles and community

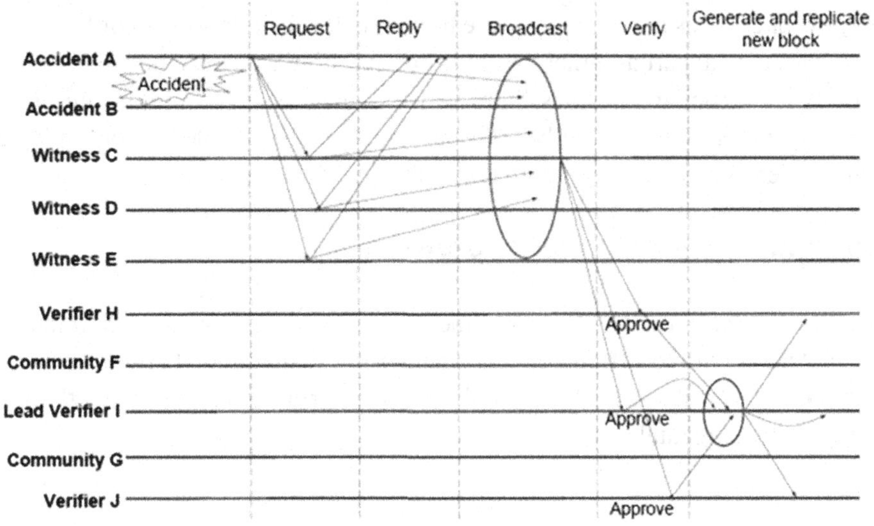

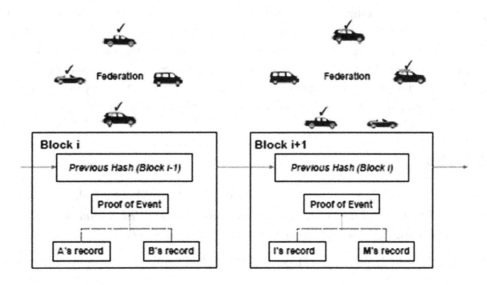

Figure 14. Represents two consecutive blocks.

The vehicles "witness" that are nearer to the mishap scene, whose EDR records may contain tactile readings associated with the "mishap" vehicles. Interestingly, "verifier" vehicles are dynamically selected which are situated indiscriminately geological areas of same cell, even away from the mishap scene, which makes them to be increasingly nonpartisan and autonomous. The decoupling of generation of event information from their validation procedure alleviates the probability of any noxious activities, for example, altering of event information and conspiracy among vehicles.

a. Impetuses for Cooperation and Genuineness

Bitcoin supplies new bitcoins as a motivating force to miners for their endeavors of PoW. To encourage self-sufficient vehicles to take part as either "witness" or "verifier", various incentives (or prizes) must be identified. For example, being a "witness" or "verifier" may increase credit score of a vehicle and alleviate its insurance premium. Additionally, "mishap" vehicles are reliable in Proof of Event and assist completely in an accident forensics may obtain less risk.

b. Investigating Blocks for Accident Forensics.

Afterward, individuals (police or judge) can audit the mishap event information saved in the blockchain from the record of DMV. On the off chance that there is no disturbance between event information produced by "mishap" and "witness" vehicles, risk can be determined clearly. Something else, further examination winds up fundamental.

X. CONCLUSION

In this chapter, we have presented a reward based intelligent vehicle communication based on Blockchain technology. Overall, the automotive industry could be facing a situation of profound change and opportunity, including how it might interrelate with the connected world of ubiquitous computing. Due to its distributed nature, the architecture eliminates the need for a centralized control and allows novel automotive services. The privacy of the users is ensured by using changeable Public Keys (PK). The security is mainly inherited from the potential security properties of the fundamental BC technology. The Blockchain technology is able to support emerging automotive services by providing a secure and trustworthy way to exchange data while protecting the security of the end user.

REFERENCES

Alonso-Ayuso, A., Escudero, L. F., & Martín-Campo, F. J. (2011, March). Collision avoidance in air traffic management: A mixed-integer linear optimization approach. *IEEE Transactions on Intelligent Transportation Systems*, *12*(1), 47–57. doi:10.1109/TITS.2010.2061971

BioThink Futuristic Vehicle for Mega-Cities. (2015) Available online: www.mohammadghezel.com

ElMahdy. (2015). Available online: ww.behance.net/

Event data recorder. (2017). Available: https://en.wikipedia. org/wiki/Eventdatarecorder

Lin, W.-H., & Liu, H. (2010, December). Enhancing realism in modeling merge junctions in analytical models for system-optimal dynamic traffic assignment. *IEEE Transactions on Intelligent Transportation Systems*, *11*(4), 838–845. doi:10.1109/TITS.2010.2050880

Mousannif, H., Khalil, I., & Al Moatassime, H. (2011). (20110 "Cooperation as a service in VANETs,". *Journal of Universal Computer Science*, *17*(8), 1202–1218.

Mulder, M., Abbink, D. A., van Paassen, M. M., & Mulder, M. (2011, March). Design of a haptic gas pedal for active car-following support. *IEEE Transactions on Intelligent Transportation Systems*, *12*(1), 268–279. doi:10.1109/TITS.2010.2091407

Nakomoto. (2009). *Bitcoin: A Peer-to-Peer Electronic Cash System*. bitcoin.org.

Olariu, S., Eltoweissy, M., & Younis, M. (2011, July–September). Toward autonomous vehicular clouds. *ICST Trans. Mobile Commun. Comput.*, *11*(7–9), 1–11.

Pew Research Center. (n.d.). http://www.pewinternet.org/2017/10/04/americansattitudes- toward-driverless-vehicles/

2014 . Revision of World Urbanization Prospects. (n.d.). Available: https://esa.un.org/unpd/wup/

Shieh, W.-Y., Hsu, C.-C., Tung, S.-L., Lu, P.-W., Wang, T.-H., & Chang, S.-L. (2011, March). (20110 "Design of infrared electronic-toll-collection systems with extended communication areas and performance of data transmission,". *IEEE Transactions on Intelligent Transportation Systems*, *12*(1), 25–35. doi:10.1109/TITS.2010.2057508

Singh, D., Singh, M., Singh, I., & Lee, H. J. (2015). Secure and reliable cloud networks for smart transportation services. *2015 17th International Conference on Advanced Communication Technology (ICACT)*, 358-362. 10.1109/ICACT.2015.7224819

Sung, Y., Sharma, P. K., Lopez, E. M., & Park, J. H. (2016). FS-OpenSecurity: A taxonomic modeling of security threats in SDN for future sustainable computing. *Sustainability*, *8*(9), 919–944. doi:10.3390u8090919

Sussman, J. M. (2005). *Perspectives on Intelligent Transportation Systems (ITS)*. Springer-Verlag.

United Nations. (2007). *Urbanization: A Majority in Cities*. United Nations Population Fund. Available online: https://www.unfpa.org/pds/urbanization.htm

United Nations. (2012). *Current status of the social situation, well-being, participation in development and rights of older persons worldwide*. United Nations Department of Economic and Social Affairs 2012. Available online: https://www.un.org/esa/socdev/ageing/whatsnew%20PDF/Ageing% 20Comprehensive%20report%202010%202%20September.pdf

Walport, M. (2016). *Distributed ledger technology: beyond block chain*. Available: https://www.gov.uk/government/publications/distributed-ledger-technology-blackett-review

Walport, M. (2106). *Distributed ledger technology: beyond block chain*. Available: https://www.gov.uk/government/publications/distributed-ledger-technology-blackett-review

Wang, C., Wang, Q., Ren, K., & Lou, W. (2010). Privacy-preserving public auditing for data storage security in cloud computing. *Proc. IEEE INFOCOM*, 1–9. 10.1109/INFCOM.2010.5462173

Wu, D., Rosen, D. W., Wang, L., & Schaefer, D. (2015). Cloud-based design and manufacturing: A new paradigm in digital manufacturing and design innovation. *Computer Aided Design*, *59*, 1–14. doi:10.1016/j.cad.2014.07.006

Yan, G., & Olariu, S. (2011, December). A probabilistic analysis of link duration in vehicular ad hoc networks. *IEEE Transactions on Intelligent Transportation Systems, 12*(4), 1227–1236. doi:10.1109/TITS.2011.2156406

Yuan, Y., & Wang, F.-Y. (2016). Towards blockchain-based intelligent transportation systems. *Intelligent Transportation Systems (ITSC), 2016 IEEE 19th International Conference on*, 2663–2668.

Zhao, L., Peng, X., Li, L., & Li, Z. (2011, March). A fast signal timing algorithm for individual over-saturated intersections. *IEEE Transactions on Intelligent Transportation Systems, 12*(1), 280–283. doi:10.1109/TITS.2010.2076808

Chapter 7

Reliable (Secure, Trusted, and Privacy Preserved) Cross-Blockchain Ecosystems for Developing and Non-Developing Countries

Shubham Kumar Keshri
Banaras Hindu University, India

Achintya Singhal
iD https://orcid.org/0000-0003-0242-2031
Banaras Hindu University, India

Abhishek Kumar
Banaras Hindu University, India

K. Vengatesan
Sanjivani College of Engineering, Savitribai Phule University, India

Rakesh S.
Galgotias University, India

ABSTRACT

The chapter suggests an iterative social system in which individuals and totals use a development, watch its arranged and unintended outcomes, and after that, build new improvements. Blockchain development has the potential to construct productivity, capability, straight imposition, and disintermediation in shared worth or information exchange. This chapter proposes how the blockchain will be implemented in developing and non-developing countries. These countries can use the blockchain for financial services, transportation, healthcare, e-marketplace, etc. And what is the risk and danger of using blockchain in non-developed countries?

DOI: 10.4018/978-1-7998-3295-9.ch007

INTRODUCTION

Every once in a while an innovation goes along that makes a huge difference. To most observers, the most recent to pursue that trend is blockchain. It can possibly revolutionize everything from money to supply chains. Also, blockchain can possibly cross over any barrier between the developed countries and undeveloped countries.

Many people consider of blockchain as the innovation that forces Bitcoin. While this was its unique reason, blockchain is prepared to do a lot more. Despite the sound of the word, there's not only one blockchain. Blockchain is shorthand for an entire suite of distributed record advancements that can be modified to record and track anything of significant worth, from money related transactions, to medical records or even land tiles. What's so unique about blockchain? How about we separate the reasons why blockchain technology stands to revolutionize the way in which we cooperate with one another.

First reason is; the way blockchain tracks and store data, blockchain stores information in batches, called blocks, that are linked to each other in a chronological manner to form a continuous line, a chain of blocks.

Figure 1. Blockchain

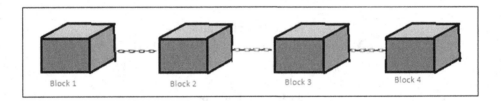

If any person wants to change the existing data of any block, they can't change or rewrite it. Instead the rewritten data is stored in a new block, showing that a changed to b at a particular time and date. It's a non-destructive way to track data changes over time. Presently, here's where things get really interesting. Unlike the traditional record technique initially a book, at that point a database document put away on a network, blockchain was intended to be decentralized and distributed across a large network of computers.

This decentralizing of data minimizes the ability of information tempering and carries us to the *second* factor that makes blockchain one of a kind: it makes trust in the information. Before a block can be added to the chain, few of things need to occur. Initial, a cryptographic puzzle must to be solved, accordingly making the block. Second, the computer that solves the puzzle shares the solution to all the different computers. On the network, this is called proof-of-work (POW). Third, the network will at that point verify and validate this proof-of-work, and if right, the block will be added to the chain. This work will guarantee that we can confide in every single block on the chain. Since the network does the trust working, presently have the chance to interface directly with information in real-time. What's more, that carries us to the *third* reason blockchain innovation is such a distinct advantage: no more mid people (intermediaries). At present, when working with each other, we don't demonstrate the other individual, our money related record or business records. Rather, we depend on trusted intermediaries, for example, a bank or a lawyer, to see our records, and keep that data secret. These intermediaries built trust between the parties and can confirm. This methodology limits risk and hazard, yet additionally adds another progression to the trade, which means additional time and cash spend. As we presently know, all blocks added to the chain have been confirmed to be valid and can't be tempered with. This sort of trusted peer-to-peer cooperation with information can revolutionize the manner in which data can be access, check and execute with each other.

Also, on the grounds that blockchain is a kind of technology, not a network. It tends to be executed from numerous points of view. Some blockchain can be totally open and open to everybody to view and access. Others can be closed to a select group of authorized users, for example, an organization, a banks, or government offices. And there are hybrid public-private blockchain as well. In some, those with private access can see all the data, while the public can see just selected. In others, everybody can see every information, however just a few people have access to new information. An administration, for instance, could utilize a hybrid framework to record the limits of anybody's property, while keeping their own data private or, it could enable everybody to see property records however reserve itself the exclusive authority to update them. It is the combination of all these elements de-centralizing of the information, building trust in the information and enabling us to communicate directly with each other and the information that gives the blockchain technology the possibility to support a large number of the manners in which we connect with each other. In any case, much like the ascent of the internet, this technology will carry with it a wide range of complex strategy questions about administration, international law, security, and financial matters. Here at the centre for International Governance Development, try to bring trusted research that will equip strategy makers with the data they have to progress blockchain advancement, empowering financial matters to prosper in this new computerized economy.

A developed country has all types of resources. The sufficient availability of resources gives strength to the administration of developed countries. These countries are now able to utilize their resources in some other field, like advancement of blockchain, robotics, autonomous industry, IoT based platform. The developed countries can use the blockchain technology in their ecosystem. These countries can use the blockchain in the field of Autonomous Vehicle, Electronic Medical Record, Security and Privacy, Crowd Sensing System, E-Marketplace, Property Rights, Controlling Corruption, and so on.

The undeveloped countries can also use the blockchain technology in their ecosystem. Undeveloped countries basically incorporate those countries that are moderately and comparatively poor socially and financially. These types of countries have no sufficient resources for better advancement of the country. These types of countries may depend on some other developed countries. But the blockchain technology can also be used in undeveloped countries. These countries can initially use the concept of blockchain in the field of education, utilities, finance, government, commerce, and so on.

This report explains about the utility of blockchain in the developed countries as well as undeveloped countries. Also, discuss about the risk arise by using blockchain in undeveloped countries.

Blockchain, the underlying generation at the back of Bitcoin is a unique new way of reaching consensus in a distributed style. At its middle, a Blockchain is only a database that runs on millions of devices simultaneously. The enormous resource pool of devices securing the network prevents malicious actors from enhancing the recorded facts in any way. This gives Blockchain their maximum essential advantage – being absolutely tampered resistant. That is to say, a fact recorded on the Blockchain is everlasting. This makes Blockchain a candidate for a great deal more than simply payments. Information like Land Titles and different asset certificate can also be saved on Blockchain to assist make the statistics tamper-proof.

BLOCKCHAIN TECHNOLOGY IN DEVELOPED COUNTRIES

A large number of the population in the developing world will like to benefit from new blockchain technologies. According to the report of ICT Facts and Figures 2017, 42.9% of households in developing countries use the Internet for different purposes. This percentage of using the internet is growing very rapidly due to the highly demand and use of the smartphones. It can be argued that from multiple points of view, blockchain has a lot of higher offer for the developing world than the developed world. Why? Since blockchain can possibly compensate for an absence of compelling formal foundations—rules, laws, guidelines, and their authorization (Kshetri & Voas, 2018).

How Can Developing Countries Benefit?

The lack of existing infrastructure in developing countries is, in fact, a good thing when it comes to further development. It permits developing countries to skip a couple of cycles of mechanical advancement to bounce to the most developed iteration directly. For instance, nations like Kenya and Tanzania have practically universal telephone get to gratitude to 3G systems. These nations didn't set down copper wires and gave internet access directly via the smartphones. In doing as such, they saved money on the gigantic expenses of setting down copper wires and furthermore had the option to furnish their residents with a vastly superior technology standard. This is called Leapfrogging and has been demonstrated to be enormously effective in developing countries over the most recent couple of years.

In a similar vein, the remote regions of developing countries, which do approach formal banking administrations could jump directly to Blockchain put together arrangements and spare with respect to the enormous expenses of setting up new foundation. Developing countries as of now have a massive system of active smart phones clients on account of the minimal effort information benefits in these nations. Because of the Android cell phone transformation of the previous decade, the measure of cell phone clients in developing countries has skyrocketed, and this gives a novel chance to Blockchains.

CAN BLOCKCHAIN HELP IN DEVELOPING COUNTRIES?

There isn't any doubt about the fact. Blockchains are right here to stay. Blockchains are already allowing us to improve the financial services industry through offering rapid, trust-less payments among peers. But Blockchains are not only for developed countries. In fact, Blockchains might have even extra to make a contribution to emerging markets. Here's a observe how developing countries can more gain even from Blockchain Technology. The developed countries may use the blockchain technology in the field of:

- Autonomous Vehicle
- Electronic Medical Record
- Security and Privacy
- Blockchain based Crowd Sensing System
- E-Marketplace
- Property Rights
- Controlling Corruption etc.

BLOCKCHAIN IN AUTONOMOUS VEHICLE

As per an investigation of the top worldwide automakers, we will see countless vehicles with some self-driving capacity by the mid of 2020s, with the primary vehicles generally being extravagance autos or part of business fleets (Miller, 2018).

What if a vehicle was completely autonomous in every sense of the word? A vehicle could drive itself to refuel or to an electric charging station. Connected vehicle arrangements would advantage from a blockchain and IoT arrangement because of all the more convenient and obvious information caught in the blockchain from vehicle sensors. If the sensors of vehicle feel that any repairing is required then the vehicle, itself derive to the repairing facility. Autonomous vehicle producers would have auspicious access to motor or power train failure data caught on the blockchain and could utilize this data to decide whether failure patterns are happening for the segment (Miller, 2018).

Customers profit by the expanded degree of consideration from the producers of the autonomous vehicle and expanded customer confidence. Producers, designers, controllers, and providers would have suitable perceivability into segment failure on the blockchain and could proactively respond to disappointment inclines all the more rapidly to guarantee buyer safety and fulfilment. The vehicle would safely pay for re-fuelling or fixes quickly without direct human interaction. A permanent record of the refuelling, fixes, and instalments would be recorded on the blockchain and shared by members including vehicle proprietors, makers, fix offices, and financing firms (Miller, 2018).

The IoT stage conjures the fitting blockchain exchange dependent on guidelines attached to the type of received information from the sensors. An open Programming interface combination layer is utilized by the refuelling, charging, parking, or fix facility to summon an exchange on the blockchain when the activity is finished (Miller, 2018).

ELECTRONIC MEDICAL RECORD

Diseases spread and suffered more in developing countries than in developed world. Developing nations today are going to innovation as the silver shot or cure. There arises a lot of advancement in the healthcare management in terms of Information as well as Communication technology. The electronics health records or electronic medical records (EMR), a key component of medical informatics gives potential solutions for advanced health care (Kamau et al., 2018).

The Electronic Medical Record (EMR) as a key component of medical informatics gives potential solutions for enhanced healthcare. In the world of digitalization, EMR is also a digital version of the record of a patient's paper chart (Crosby et al., 2016). EMR is a very safe system to keep critical and highly sensitive private data and information about patient for diagnosis and treatment the health in the healthcare industry, which need to be frequently distributed and shared among peers such as healthcare providers, insurance companies, pharmacies, researchers,, patient families, among others (Wood et al., 2016).

Patient should not access their own medical data in most of the health care institution. Patients are getting worry with this type of privacy of their own medical report. This problem can be resolve by using the blockchain technology (Stephen & Alex, 2018).

Figure 2. Blockchain and IoT autonomous vehicle solution.

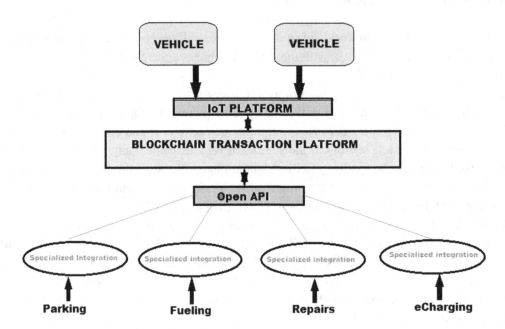

Confidentiality is virtually indisputable in blockchain. With the help of blockchain, data can be completely accessed by the patient as well as patient's can keep eye or track that how the data about his/her health is shared and maintains to fulfil patient's privacy and security of data (Miller, 2018).

The Electronic Medical Report (EMR) should face some challenges and limitations. This system will handle some important challenges at the time of implementing personally control system. It means this personally control information would take the place of hospital record. Some part of this type of personally control record would be downloaded in to the health care institutional record to tribute the previously existing data (Stephen & Alex, 2018).

Because of the encrypted security of the blockchain information, the privacy of the patient is preserved and it is only accessed by the authorized person who has the correct key for decrypt the data (Kamau et al., 2018).

BLOCKCHAIN SECURITY AND PRIVACY

Since blockchain has a feature of decentralization, it provides more privacy and security than any other centralization application. In the blockchain technology, every new created block keeps the track of its previous block. It will give an authentication mechanism during the period of any transaction. Also, there is no any need of any third party to record the information about the transaction in the ledger. By using blockchain technology, all the transactions will be automatically recorded in the ledger without any interference of third party. The data or information stored in the blockchain's ledger is transparent and also immutable (unchangeable), this is the one reason of trustworthy of blockchain. Also, blockchain is free from MITM. MITM means Man in The Middle Attack. Since blockchain doesn't allow any access to any third party (a middle man), so it is protected from MITM (Stephen & Alex, 2018).

Figure 3. Blockchain in Electronic Medical Report, EMR

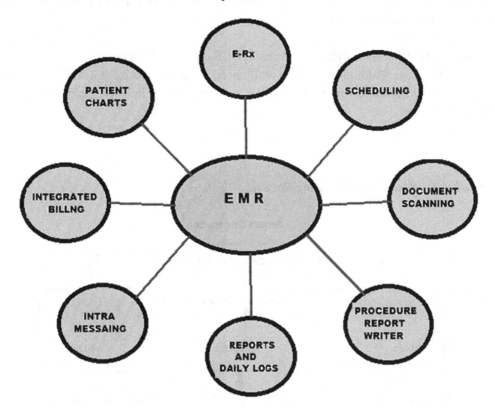

BLOCKCHAIN BASED CROWD SENSING SYSTEM

Blockchain is totally disparate from the traditional architecture, blockchain uses decentralized system, and it has no centralized platform in crowd-sensing process. Instead, by using blockchain technique, the crowd-sensing system is managed by a decentralized system (Huang et al., 2019).

The crowd-sensing process of BCS can be classified into following four steps (Huang et al., 2019):

1) Requesters post task, at that point verify the rules and send them to correspondence stage, i.e., distribute a brilliant contract that comprises of a few predefined functions.

2) Users inquiry distributed smart contracts from blockchain and acquire useful detecting task. After the completion of the task, they present the information on correspondence stage, i.e., call explicit function in smart contracts.

3) By questioning blockchain and tuning in to the correspondence stage, miners get unconfirmed sensing information, and after that look at the quality of information as indicated by guidelines the requester makes. After miners substantiate the quality of detecting information, miners and users will get the rewarded in the wake of pushing handled detecting information into blocks. In general, miners acquire remunerates by contributing figuring power for running smart contracts.

4) Requesters interfere to the blockchain occasionally. When they choose not to keep gathering information, they can send message to the framework to close this work and get the remained hold

cash from smart contract. As this message will be communicated in the framework, miners and users will at that point stop to work.

As a result of decentralized design of blockchain, BCS doesn't rely upon any third party; there is no single step of failure issue. Additionally, users really need to make security stores, i.e., pay transaction charges to miners, before interest in crowd-sensing task, which proficiently avoids different assaults (Huang et al., 2019).

Figure 4. Blockchain Based Crowd Sensing System

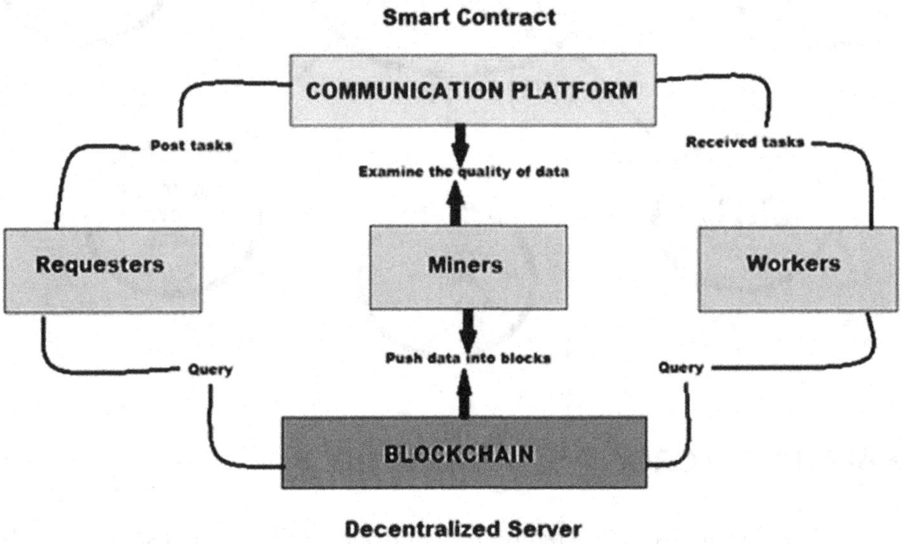

BLOCKHAIN TECHNOLOGY FOR E-MARKETPLACE

The present e-commercial centre environment advanced from internet innovations. It assumes a significant job in the worldwide economy. According to the present condition and circumstance of the e-commercial centre, this part discuss around the accompanying exploration issue (Chang, 2019):

1)   Pervasive computing:

The popularity of cell phones has significantly changed the customer conduct of the present internet based business. From the ad of a game to the buy and conveyance of game tickets and the entering to the stadium should all be possible on a cell phone. Pervasive computing gives access to the context related data for making moment adoptions to the quickly changing versatile online business.

2)   Imposing business model:

There is a great deal of cost based data asymmetry in customary organizations. Significant internet based business stages have caused imposing business model, bringing about high commissions, rate control, and divulgence control. Moreover, user buying conduct is gathered to induce user data, causing security concerns.

3)   Cross-border web based business:

The instalment is ineffective, slow, and expensive for banks and other organizations in cross-border online business transactions. The decentralized blockchain-based electronic commercial centre can offer numerous points of interest for e-commercial centre members, including privacy, trust, minimum transaction expenses, security, and transaction integrity (Chang, 2019).

By utilizing blockchain innovation in e-commercial centre, we can easily resolve the problem discussed above.

PROPERTY RIGHTS

As indicated by a 2011 UN report, weak governance prompted corruption in land inhabitancy and organization in excess of 61 nations. Corruption spread from small scale bribes to the government control at the local levels, state, and national levels (Kshetri & Voas, 2018).

Around 90 per cent of land is undocumented or unregistered in rural Africa. In like manner, an absence of land proprietorship stays among the boundaries to business enterprise and financial advancement in India (Kshetri & Voas, 2018).

As per the report, in excess of 20 million provincial families in India have no land of their own and there are millions of families have no proper document of land where they built house or do work. Lack of land is one of the primary explanations of poverty in any nation (Kshetri & Voas, 2018).

Blockchain can decrease friction and erosion, as well as the expenses related with property registration. It is conceivable to do all or the greater part of the preparing utilizing cell phones. Given this, it is empowering that different activities have been attempted. The US-based stage for land registration, Bitland, reported the presentation of a blockchain-based land vault framework in Ghana, where 78 per cent of land is unregistered. There is a long excess of land-contest cases in Ghanaian courts. Bitland records exchange safely, with GPS facilitates composed portrayals, and satellite photographs. This and comparable procedures are relied upon to ensure property rights and minimise corrupt practices. As of mid-2016, 24 communities in Ghana had expressed interest in the project. Bitland is planning to extend to Nigeria as a team with the OPEC Fund for International Development (Kshetri & Voas, 2018).

In 2017, India's two states, Telangana and Andhra Pradesh states reported designs to utilize blockchain for land registration. Telangana began the registration of land project in the capital city of Hyderabad. In September 2017, it was reported that a total rollout of the program in Hyderabad and close by territories would occur inside a year. In October 2017, the Andhra Pradesh government teamed up with a Swedish start-up, ChromaWay, to make a blockchain-based land registry framework for the arranged city of Amravati (Kshetri & Voas, 2018).

CONTROLLING CORRUPTION

Blockchain makes a carefully designed computerized record of exchanges and offers the record, thus offering straightforwardness. Cryptography takes into consideration access to add to the record safely. It is very troublesome—if certainly feasible—to change or delete information recorded on a ledger. With this component, blockchain makes it conceivable to diminish or dispose of integrity violations, for example, misrepresentation and corruptions while likewise decreasing exchange costs (Kshetri & Voas, 2018).

Blockchain additionally makes it conceivable to create smart ("tagged") property and control it with brilliant contracts. Instances of such properties incorporate physical property (vehicle, house, compartment of metal) and also nonphysical property (shares in an organization). Blockchain-based smart properties just experience activities dependent on the data distributed in a smart contract. On the off chance that property is being utilized as guarantee, the contract probably won't enable the proprietor to expand the same property as a guarantee or security to another bank. Along these lines, the way toward confirming insurance before the credit being made is incredibly streamlined for overseers. Here, a believed exchanging framework is made for smart properties, making credit all the more promptly accessible and less expensive (Kshetri & Voas, 2018).

Since blockchain uses chain of blocks to store any information, it will also store the information about the any priced-based things transparently, which can help us to control corruption.

Blockchain Uses in Developing Countries

Because of the intensely associated nature of the present reality, Blockchain as an innovation can possibly have extensive effects in a moderately short measure of time. This implies developing countries may receive the rewards of the innovation quicker than with past ground-breaking technologies.

Since Blockchains are a type of decentralized, distributed, immutable(changeless) and transparent record, they have the potential to disrupt businesses all through the economy — even in developing markets.

A few instances of such applications are illustrated below (Medium, n.d.):

Figure 5. Applications of Blockchain

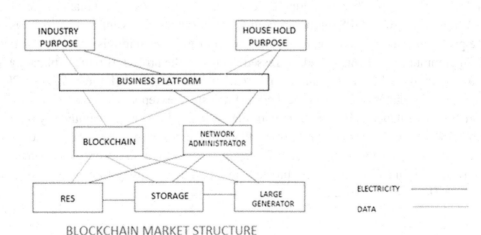

Currency

This is where Blockchain began in. Crypto currencies like Bitcoin and Ethereum have shown the protected utilization of decentralized innovation as a store and move of significant worth.

Developing countries can pilot such currencies in closed, token based frameworks to build transparency in sectors like customs, administration and law.

Goods

Tracking physical goods through the production network is one of the most touted utilizations of blockchain innovation. Firms like Everledger are attempting to implement this by following high worth things like diamonds all through their lifecycle on a worldwide scale. Also, even traditional giants like Walmart are getting into the activity. The organization is trying different things with Blockchains to guarantee food safety all through their inventory network.

Since products provenance is a significant issue in developing countries, this might be a key region of centre as far as executing Blockchain. Parts like nourishment inventory network, government open market deal and customs exchange tracking of import export might be key zones to keep an eye out for.

What's more, Blockchain have likewise been utilized for innovative applications like delivering development aid to that need over the world. A prominent case of this is the way the World Food Program (WFP) utilized blockchain innovation to dispense help to Syrian displaced people living in Jordan.

In the event that International Development Organization like the World Bank and ADB implement token based frameworks to dispense improvement help to nations, at that point it will realize a huge change in transparency in the sector, where as much as 50% of donations may go unaccounted for because of misappropriation and corruption.

Services

Blockchain can possibly change how benefits businesses going from budgetary foundations to lawful foundations work. The mix of Blockchains, smart contracts and Decentralized Autonomous Organizations (DAO) can possibly empower services transactions to happen seamlessly in a decentralized, secure and quick way.

In the event that this is executed appropriately, developing countries can leapfrog counterparts in institutional advancement via computerized legitimate systems, customs instalments, business transactions and allowing widespread disintermediation across enterprises.

Records

Right up 'til today, records of possession, citizenship and different types of personality are put away in incorporated databases to keep them secure. However, this represents issues of altering due to the middle people included. Blockchain open up a chance of decentralized, public, immutable and consensus driven ledger of records that may one day invalidate the requirement for mediators.

These applications become more relevant for developing countries as it exhibits a scope for bringing the whole populace under one stage. It will make giving citizen services like ownership transfers, voter enrolment and sponsorship/tax transfers a lot simpler and progressively transparent.

This can likewise be extended out to organization information, whereby the identity of an organization will be accessible on a blockchain for reference by any stockholder working with the entity. This will permit extraordinary transparency and speed in business exercises and transactions ranging from vendor payments to tax filings.

Possible Advantages of Blockchain Technology for Developing Countries (Energypedia, n.d.)

Compared to developed countries, developing countries are far more likely to be impacted by blockchain technologies. Some of the advantages are listed below:

- Blockchain innovation serves to (re) construct trust among the society (even in reality of weak legislative foundations)
- While many developed countries face the trouble to incorporate blockchain innovation into the legacy infrastructure, this isn't the situation in many developing countries (without a set up framework). Hence, it is a lot simpler to coordinate blockchain innovation.
- Leap frogging the financial area: not having a bank account at a traditional, physical bank but having access to mobile financing options
- Public claimed and shared framework (not to be affected by corrupt politicians and so on.)
- Collaboration is required: This (e) limits manipulation, corruption and fraud.
- There are numerous similitude between the appropriated idea of blockchain and decentralized vitality frameworks like a smaller than expected lattice: prosumers, numerous producers, numerous customers associate and must be synchronised (Runyon, 2017).
- Money remains inside the network: energy producers and consumers don't need to pay a brought together, outside organization. Transactions association charge expenses of 10% or more; blockchain innovation can bring those down to 3%. As per the World Bank, overall settlements are 700 billion USD in 2016 (Rutkin, 2016).
- However, contacting the individuals in remote regions despite everything stays a test. So as to defeat the "last mile", blockchain innovation faces indistinguishable obstacles from in different markets.
- ADB distinguished 4 different ways blockchain innovation can upset the advancement participation area: 1. Limit building and institutional fortifying. 2. Modernizing vitality networks. Blockchain can really assist utilities with staying aware of rising force request in littler, lower-esteem squares. Improve existing vitality industry forms. Respond quicker after disasters (forestalling power outages). 3. Sustainable power source smaller than normal and micro grids. Shared transactions; "prosumers". 4. Green fund and carbon exchanging frameworks. Blockchain can be conveyed to the two plans, which are essential to help the execution of creating part nations' Nationally Determined Contributions under the 2015 Paris Agreement against atmosphere change (Zhai, 2017).

Challenges in Developing Countries

The ultimate numerous many years have shown that the direction to economic prosperity in developing countries depends on having financial services accessible to the poorest people in the society. Micro

Financing is the availability of small loans to terrible marketers and small corporations who've no get right of entry to proper banking offerings. The most deprived sections of the developing countries rely closely on microfinance to growth their economic wealth. Several researches have shown that casual change additionally advantages from the influx of funding similar to in the formal sector. So its miles clean that terrible humans in growing countries want to be supplied avenues to at ease small loans where traditional banking structures may not be willing to installation shop.

Blockchains offer a completely unique possibility here as putting in place Bitcoin wallets does no longer require the same infrastructure as putting in a new physical financial institution store. Since Blockchains run on a allotted network, there's no need for pricey branches to open more workplaces. This saves on expenses for banking that are otherwise passed on to customers inside the shape of fees and switch charges (Medium, n.d.).

BLOCKCHAIN TECHNOLOGY OPPORTUNITIES IN UNDEVELOPED COUNTRIES

Undeveloped countries basically incorporate those countries that are moderately and comparatively poor socially and financially. These countries can possibly advance; however don't have satisfactory access to exhibit day innovation, fundamentally because of absence of infrastructure. On a very basic level, these countries need straightforwardness, security, and responsibility in their procedures, which are all foundations of Blockchain innovation (Ahishakiye et al., 2018).

Blockchain innovation is decentralized and hence eliminates the custodian restraints of any private entity. Every information in the framework are carefully crypt for special distinguishing proof and once posted, a record can never be changed or erased, prompting security. Also, Blockchain idea takes a shot at smart contracts?, wherein transaction happen just if certain pre-set requirements are met, so there will be responsibility of every transactions (Ahishakiye et al., 2018).

Absence of transparency, corruption, and misuse of assets are among the difficulties that international associations face when they provide funds to undeveloped nations. Blockchain offers transparency and unchanging nature. The World Food Program (WFP) tried this innovation in an undertaking called "Building Blocks", in Pakistan and Jordan where weak families got sustenance and money help from the WFP, which was verified and recorded on an open Blockchain through a cell phone interface. Utilizing this strategy, payment was responsible and coordinated with the privileges and the procedure was quicker and progressively precise. Therefore, once Blockchain based technology is copied in other developing nations, the WFP will have straightforwardness and responsibility (Ahishakiye et al., 2018).

The corruption and bribery of authorities happens more oftentimes in undeveloped countries than in developed ones. The use of blockchain on developing and un-developing countries not only can find and resolve the problem of corruption yet in addition lift those nations out of poverty. In spite of the fact that the information governance and security issues stay bigger difficulties, its application to undeveloped nations won't be acknowledged on a huge scale at any point in the near future basically because of two factors: the obstruction of the current authority and absence of framework (Harris, 2018).

DANGERS AND RISKS

In addition to the guarantee that blockchain technology may offer, a comprehension of the orderly dangers and risks is vital. Like any important resources, Bitcoin and blockchain resources can be destroyed, damaged, taken and stolen. The way this can't be confirmed shows the dangers of depending on blockchain innovation as foolproof. Beneath, eight different dangers and risks that blockchain advancements present in the undeveloped nations are portrayed (Harris, 2018):

Manipulation of the Majority Consensus

Blockchain technology creates some potential security issues in undeveloped countries. The most troubling is the probability of a 51percent assault, in which one mining element could snatch control of the blockchain and double-spend recently transacted coins into own account. The issue is the centralization propensity in mining where the challenge to record new exchange blocks in the blockchain has implied that solitary a couple of enormous mining pools control most of the transaction record. Double-spending may likewise still be conceivable in different ways. Another issue is distributed denial of service (DDoS) assaults, which can altogether restrict the chances of mining pools not aligned with an entry that desires to game the framework (Harris, 2018).

In undeveloped nations, especially where the legislature has some incentive to control transaction, the government can present delays in the approval step, permitting government-backed mining elements to give earlier timestamps or to control the majority consensus rule agreement standard utilizing DDoS assaults, making the 51percent assault undeniably bound to happen. This is especially true when the government just permits private and semiprivate blockchains to be executed restricting the adequacy of blockchain transparency (Harris, 2018).

Constraining the Entrance of Miners

Content validation and verification of the transaction is led by clients, this procedure is known as miners who utilize the intensity of their PCs or extraordinarily structured devices to solve numerical equations. This is required for affirming transactions. Thusly, they gain a reward as any digital currency, an amount which is resolved ahead of time. The trouble of equations is extended with the development of mining computational power, with an end goal to keep the time expected to compose the information into a cryptographically-sealed block consistent.

Restricting access of miners to solve this numerical equation is one manner by which a few governments can make validation and verification of transactions far less engaging. Since miners require significant resources, especially electricity, to explain these equations, this effort can draw government consideration rather rapidly (Harris, 2018).

Privacy, Obscurity, and Pseudo-secrecy

Privacy is also an issue. Not all information should be appeared on an open record, accessible for the world to see. Indeed, even in developed nations with solid legal enforcement, one organization may not want its rivals to know the details of its day by day exchanges. This issue is significantly increasingly intense when government transactions are summoned that the government wouldn't like to be transparent.

Second, although private blockchains can improve security issues, transactions between parties in semi-private and open or public blockchains are pseudo-secrecy and not unknown. With enough information, pseudo-secrecy clients can be recognized, and government elements with worries about outside obstruction, which happens in the developing world, can distinguish and follow these clients. This is especially troubling in light of the fact that numerous blockchain clients accept they are anonymous (Harris, 2018).

Issues with Contract Law

Blockchain technology can possibly roll out noteworthy improvements to contract law utilizing self-upholding computerized contracts. These have the advantage of being executed without expecting middle third party to check that the conditions have effectively been met. In this way, in any economy, the legitimate and specialized implications of smart contracts should be considered, especially when disjointed qualities may emerge between genuine contracts and their computerized partners (Harris, 2018).

Guideline

Another test is the uncertain legal structure and government guidelines. Initially, since blockchain arrangements expect crytocurrency to work, it is important to alter the administrative system to perceive Bitcoin and different digital forms of money as a legitimate method for trade. Second, as officially expressed, the courts and different associations need to perceive the administrative parts of smart contracts, which numerous undeveloped nations are reluctant to do (Harris, 2018).

Tax Collection

Another issue is the alteration of tax assessment practice to incorporate the money related exchanges which happen on the blockchain. It is challenging for the most developed countries to follow money related exchanges made between pseudo-anonymous clients and for tax specialists to accurately tax organizations in the sharing economy. Although a move from pay based tax assessment to utilization based tax collection would make these exchanges simpler to pursue, couple of undeveloped government are set up to track such exchanges. These will require a major upgrade of the present tax assessment framework, which not many undeveloped countries are eager to execute rapidly (Harris, 2018).

Scalability and Storage Problem

There are numerous technology issues that presently can't seem to be settled regardless of the advancement of a nation's economy. One issue is identified with the size of blockchain records. Blockchains develop after some time and require proper record management. Indeed, even with open or public blockchains, quickly expanding size issues may prompt record centralization, which focuses to government guideline. This is probably going to influence the future of blockchain technology.

Storage will likewise be an obstacle. Although a blockchain dispenses with the requirement for a central server to store transaction and gadget IDs, the record must be put away on the hubs themselves. In numerous undeveloped nations, the government has a controlling stake in the web. Constraining access to these hubs should be possible through government inclusion, influencing the utility and unwavering quality of a blockchain in those nations (Harris, 2018).

Speed and Veracity of Transaction

Individual blockchain exchanges are delayed in contrast with typical customer instalment norms. The blockchain can't be finished until the new chain and its hash value have been determined and consented to by a majority consensus of clients (Harris, 2018).

Areas where Blockchain will assume a significant job in undeveloped nations incorporate the accompanying as extracted (Ahishakiye et al., 2018):

- *Ease paperwork preparing.* Worldwide compartment dispatching still includes a ton of desk work, costing time and cash. Likewise, paper-based freight documents like the bills are prone to loss, altering and misrepresentation.
- *Identify fake items.* Fake drug is a growing issue for drug store supply chains. This particularly relates to costly, inventive medication like cancer drugs. Drug stores need to make a point to sell "the correct thing" to the customers.
- *Facilitate source tracking.* In the food store network, foodborne episodes are a challenge for retailers. They need to get a speedy review of where the nourishment originated from and which different items are likewise influenced and must be removed from stores.
- *Operate the Internet of Things.* An ever increasing number of strategic items are outfitted with sensors that produce information along the production network e.g., the status of a shipment. This information must be put away in an immutable, available way.
- *Utilities.* Blockchain can enable utilities to stay aware of rising power request in little, lower-value blocks. Improve existing vitality industry forms. Respond quicker after debacles (avoiding power outages).
- *Government.* To record in a transparent manner residents? Votes or legislators? Programs (for checking if guarantees have been kept) or to empower self-governing administration frameworks.
- *Intellectual property.* To confirm the evidence of presence and initiation of a report.
- *Internet.* To decrease oversight, by abusing the changelessness of information put away in the Blockchain.
- *Finance.* To move/ transfer money between two parties without relying upon any outsider like bank.
- *Commerce.* To record goods? Attributes just as their possession, particularly for extravagance products, thus reducing the market of fake/ taken things.
- *Internet of Things.* For instance, by exploiting smart contracts to consequently process information originating from sensors, to give intelligent machines, a chance to interact with one another and independently take activities when explicit circumstances happen.
- *Education.* To store data on qualifications got by students. To diminish employment form fakes; in this specific situation, different entertainers (e.g., colleges, institute, and so forth.) could compose capabilities accomplished by an individual on the Blockchain; HR staff could then effectively get data about when and where a given competency was obtained.

Blockchain technology can solve development problems as it improves existing instruments and enables the development of new ones. Blockchain-based applications particularly address institutional weaknesses and financial inclusion because they restrict deception, corruption and uncertainties. In the future, the blockchain can also be a development vehicle empowering people directly and mitigating power asymmetries.

Poverty and Economic Disparities in Undeveloped Countries

In its "Poverty and Shared Prosperity Report 2016" the World Bank announced that "poverty remains inadmissibly high" with an expected populace of 766 million individuals living on under $1.90 every day in 2013. Numerous nations situated in Sub-Saharan Africa (388.7 million) or South-East Asia (256.2 million) are classified as undeveloped countries. Nevertheless, noteworthy advancement has been made in the previous year's (Luoto et al., 2007). These days, particularly in urban areas, a little accomplished middle class exists which can be a significant fundament for mechanical advancements. Advancement has been distinguished as a way to help improvement in developed and developing countries. All in all, new innovations can carry significant changes to these nations and improve their living conditions. Specifically, blockchain advancements have been proposed as another mechanical answer for some issues in undeveloped countries but has been held to be to somewhat undefined (Ravallion & Chen, 2005).

Weak Institutions

One significant issue of undeveloped countries, and one reason behind why improvement programs regularly don't convey the desired results, is weak institutions. Corruption, for example, is bound to happen in poor areas where an absence of law implementation is watched found that corruption is brought together, with a little gathering of individuals causing an impressive offer and that country zones are especially inclined to corruption. Another issue in undeveloped regions are the low degree of social trust. Key determinants of social trust are characterized as the unwavering quality of lawful foundations and social heterogeneity (Uslaner, 2002). Social trust underpins financial development and improves living conditions for needy individuals through advanced education endeavours, speculation rates and improved administration. Furthermore, training levels ought to be improved. Individuals frequently can't stand to send their kids to class since they come up short on the fundamental monetary capacities which bring about a neediness training trap. In addition, power concentration limits economic improvement on both local and national levels. Local chiefs have incentives for self-centred ruling and frequently catch legislative activities to strengthen social capital and education levels (AbouZahr et al., 2007).

CONCLUSION

Blockchain technology contains three main advantages, namely transparency, distributed architecture and immutability. These all properties of blockchain can help to reduce the fraud and corruption occurring in the developed countries and undeveloped countries. Blockchain can likewise enable financial transaction to occur all the more rapidly and guarantee that aid is distributed with a small chance of robbery and extortion.

These countries can also use the technology of blockchain in various ways, like autonomous vehicle and so on. Blockchain can also use to track and monitor the funds which are transacted for criminal activities like kidnapping. Using this technology all transaction is properly recorded from start to end in immutable fashion.

Even though there are certain limitations of blockchains at present, these are being taken a shot at by a worldwide network and can possibly be explained soon. This will permit the innovation to be executed in frameworks where there is an absence of trust and a requirement for disintermediation.

As a foundational technology that will certainly power new applications in both developed and undeveloped economies, blockchain offers various advantages to economies that can predict and exploit its merit. Undeveloped nations that are impervious to the merits of the blockchain will benefit far not exactly those embrace its advantages.

At last, one of the most energizing viewpoints is that this innovation might be available to developing countries around a similar time as more developed countries adopt them. This has the potential to level the playing field of development to a large extent across countries — both large and small.

REFERENCES

AbouZahr, C., Jha, P., Macfarlane, S. B., Mikkelsen, L., Setel, P. W., Szreter, S., & Stout, S. (2007). A scandal of invisibility: Making everyone count by counting everyone. *Lancet*, *370*(9598), 1569–1577. doi:10.1016/S0140-6736(07)61307-5 PubMed

Ahishakiye, E., Wario, R., & Niyonzima, I. (2018). Developing Countries and Blockchain Technology : Uganda ' s Perspective. *International Journal of Latest Research in Engineering and Technology*, *4*(August), 94–99.

Chang, Y. (2019). Blockchain Technology for e-Marketplace. 2019 IEEE International Conference on Pervasive Computing and Communications Workshops (PerCom Workshops), 429–430. doi:10.1109/PERCOMW.2019.8730733

Crosby, M., Pattanayak, P., Verma, S., & Kalyanaraman, V. (2016). Blockchain technology: Beyond bitcoin. *Appl. Innov.*, *2*, 6–10.

Energypedia. (n.d.). https://energypedia.info/ wiki/Blockchain_Opportunities_for_Social_Impact_in_Developing _Countries#Possible_Advantages _of_Blockchain_Technology_for_Developing_Countries

Harris, C. G. (2018). The risks and dangers of relying on blockchain technology in underdeveloped countries. IEEE/IFIP Network Operations and Management Symposium: Cognitive Management in a Cyber World, NOMS 2018, 1–4. doi:10.1109/NOMS.2018.8406330

Huang, J., Kong, L., Kong, L., Liu, Z., Liu, Z., & Chen, G. (2019). Blockchain-based Crowd-sensing System. *Proceedings of 2018 1st IEEE International Conference on Hot Information-Centric Networking, HotICN 2018*, 234–235. 10.1109/HOTICN.2018.8605960

INC42. (n.d.). https://inc42.com/resources/how-will-blockchain-technology-help-developing-countries/

Kamau, G., Boore, C., Maina, E., & Njenga, S. (2018). Blockchain technology: Is this the solution to EMR interoperability and security issues in developing countries? 2018 IST-Africa Week Conference, IST-Africa 2018.

Kshetri, N., & Voas, J. (2018). Blockchain in Developing Countries. *IT Professional*, *20*(2), 11–14. doi:10.1109/MITP.2018.021921645

Luoto, J., McIntosh, C., & Wydick, B. (2007). *Credit Information Systems in Less Developed Countries: A Test with Microfinance in Guatemala*. University of San Francisco.

Medium. (n.d.). https://medium.com/swlh/what-blockchain-means-for-developing-countries1e-c25a416a4b

Miller, D. (2018). Blockchain and the internet of things in the industrial sector. *IT Professional, 20*(3), 15–18. doi:10.1109/MITP.2018.032501742

Ravallion, M., & Chen, S. (2005). Hidden impact? Household saving in response to a poor-area development project. *Journal of Public Economics, 89*(11-12), 2183–2204. doi:10.1016/j.jpubeco.2004.12.003

Runyon, J. (2017, May 15). How Smart Contracts [Could] Simplify Clean Energy Distribution. Retrieved 10 July 2017, from https://www.renewableenergyworld.com/articles/2017/05/how-smart-contracts-could-simplify-clean-energy-distribution.html

Rutkin, A. (2016, March 2). Blockchain-based microgrid gives power to consumers in New York. Retrieved 10 July 2017, from https://www.newscientist.com/article/2079334-blockchain-based-microgrid-gives-power-to-consumers-in-new-york/

Stephen, R., & Alex, A. (2018). A Review on BlockChain Security. *IOP Conference Series. Materials Science and Engineering, 396*(1). Advance online publication. doi:10.1088/1757-899X/396/1/012030

Uslaner, E. M. (2002). *The Moral Foundations of Trust*. Cambridge University Press.

Wood, W., & Carter, B. Dodd, & Bradley. (2016). How Blockchain technology Can Enhance HER operability. Academic Press.

Zhai, Y. (2017). 4 Ways Blockchain Will Disrupt the Energy Sector. https://blogs.adb.org/blog/4-ways-blockchain-will-disrupt-energy-sector.fckLR

Chapter 8
Security, Privacy, and Trust Management and Performance Optimization of Blockchain

Priti Gupta
Banaras Hindu University, India

Abhishek Kumar
Banaras Hindu University, India

Achintya Singhal
iD https://orcid.org/0000-0003-0242-2031
Banaras Hindu University, India

Shantanu Saurabh
The Maharaja Sayajirao University of Baroda, India

V. D. Ambeth Kumar
Department of Computer Science and Engineering, Panimalar Engineering College, Anna University, Chennai, India

ABSTRACT

Blockchain provides innovative ideas for storing information, executing transactions, performing functions, creating trust in an open environment, etc. Even though cryptographers, mathematicians, and coders have been trying to bring the most trustable protocols to get authentication guarantee over various systems, blockchain technology is secure with no central authority in an open network system because of a large distributed network of independent users. If anyone tries to change the blockchain database, the current hash will also change, which does not match with the previous hash. In this way, blockchain creates privacy and trust in digital data by removing malleability attacks. In this chapter, security and privacy on the blockchain has been focused. The safety and privacy of blockchain are mainly engrossed on two things: firstly, uncovering few attacks suffered by blockchain systems and, secondly, putting specific and advanced proposals against such attacks.

DOI: 10.4018/978-1-7998-3295-9.ch008

INTRODUCTION

Why Blockchain – does it secure? Can we trust on it?

Blockchain technology has been called the one of the greatest innovations since the internet. Blockchain is a peer-to-peer distributed ledger or public registry that permanently records transactions in a way that cannot be erase or update. Blockchain is designed to use a cryptographic hash and timestamps so that record cannot be change once they are created. This makes easier for the blockchain experts to inspect record ledger or registry to determine the facts of any given transactions or to detect attempts to tamper with the ledger.

Blockchain is secure. 'Secure' doesn't means to hide information but it simply means that nobody going to tamper records on the blockchain. Even if somebody does attempt to fraudulently alter records, original records will still exist on the valid ledger and can be pinned down by comparing information on duplicate records.

Billions of people in the world who can't trust intermediaries such as banks, and other legal system for transactions or accurate record keeping. Particularly, Blockchain are useful in these cases to provide trust and assurance to people when transacting with one another. Centralized databases and institutions work when there is trust in the system of regulations, laws, government and people. Even sometimes, this trust is betrayed, causing people to lose money and assets. Blockchain is a decentralized database which remove the need of centralized institutions and databases. With all people connected to the blockchain network having access to the blockchain ledger in a way they can view and validate transactions which create transparency and trust. Although blockchain removed intermediaries to maintain the trust between the people involved in the transactions. The removal of intermediaries improved transparency and decentralized structure of the blockchain (Mark Gates, 2017).

Figure 1. Blockchain architecture diagram

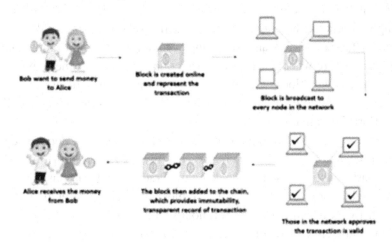

WHY BLOCKCHAIN?

There are many problems faces by the current system like:

- Banks and other third parties charge fees for transferring money.
- Mediating cost increases transaction costs.
- System is lacking transparency.
- System is lacking fairness.
- Financial exchanges are slow so checking and low-cost wire services take many days to complete it.
- Central authority can misuse their power and can create money as per their own will.

We need a system which solve the above problems:

- System which eliminate the need of intermediaries for making transaction cost nil or negligible.
- System which is transparent in order to avoid manipulation.
- System which is tamper resistant in order to avoid misuse.
- System which enhances transaction execution speed and can facilitate instant reconciliation.
- System in which creation of currency is not in control of any central authority.
- System which is regulated to maintain the value of the currency.

STRUCTURE OF BLOCKCHAIN

Blockchains are composed of three core components. They are:

1. Block: A block is like a page of a ledger in which listing of transactions is done periodically. A block is composed of a header and a list of transactions. First block is called Genesis block. For every blockchain the size, period, and triggering event for blocks is different. Chain of blocks is an immutable data structure where each next block contains a hash of the previous block. Result of this hashing is the chain of blocks is immutable. We cannot alter or delete a block from the middle of the chain without rebuilding all the blocks above, because a minor change will require a rebuild of all blocks (Hori K. et al., n.d.).
2. Chain: A hash act as glues for linking one block to another. The hash depends upon the data in the block, as data is change hash will also change. The Secure Hash Algorithm (SHA) is one of the cryptographic hash functions used in blockchains. Practically, think hash as a digital fingerprint of data that is used to lock it in place within the blockchain (Hori K. et al., n.d.).
3. Network: The network is composed of "full nodes". Each node contains a complete record of all the transactions that were ever recorded in that blockchain (Hori K. et al., n.d.).

PERMISSIONED VS. PERMISSIONLESS BLOCKCHAIN

Based on the access control layer built into the blockchain nodes, properly permissioned blockchain networks differ from permission less blockchain networks. Permissioned blockchain are secure because it restricts those actors one who contribute to the consensus of the system state where in permission less blockchain, since the network is open, anyone can participate and contribute in the consensus. In context of privacy, permissioned blockchain allows only actors who have rights to view the transactions. A permission less blockchain is a shared database where everyone can read everything, but no single user has control to write.

VARIOUS PLATFORMS FOR IMPLEMENTING BLOCKCHAIN

§   Ethereum: An open blockchain platform proposed in 2013 by Vitalik Buterin. It provides public blockchain to develop smart contracts and decentralized applications. Ethers are currency tokens in Ethereum.

§   Multichain: A platform that helps users to establish a private blockchains that can be used by the organizations for financial transactions.

§   Hydra chain: It is an open source platform which is joint development effort of Brainbot technologies and the Ethereum project that supports the creation of scalable blockchain based applications and private blockchain networks. The supporting language for Hydrachain is python.

§   Hyperledger: It is a cooperative open source effort designed to promote cross-industry blockchain technologies.

§   Openchain: It is an open source distributed ledger technology which suited for organizations wishing to issue and manage digital assets in secure, robust and scalable way.

§   IBM Bluemix: It is built on top of the Hyperledger project and offers additional security and infrastructure facilities for enterprises.

§   Chain: It is a blockchain platform that runs on the open-source chain protocol. It is used to issue and transfer financial assets on a permissioned blockchain infrastructure.

§   IOTA: Blockless distributed ledger which is scalable, lightweight and for the first time ever makes it possible to translate value without any fees.

FEATURES OF A BLOCKCHAIN PLATFORM

To evaluate a given blockchain platform the following features are important:

1.   Programmability: What are the particular languages for programming?
2.   Scalability: How many nodes can blockchain produce? Is there any upper limit?
3.   Upgradability. What is the developer's track record for improving and upgrading the blockchain?
4.   Transactions manageability: Is all transactions transparent in real time?
5.   Visibility. Do you have a complete perspective on the blockchain activity?
6.   Affordability. What is the cost of transmitting this technology?
7.   Security. What is the documented standard of trust in the safety of the blockchain?

8. Speed/Performance. What are the upper limits for speed in validating transactions?
9. High Availability. What is the uptime's track record?
10. Extensibility. Would you be able to expand the fundamental blockchain functionality with a variety of add-ons?
11. Interoperability. Does it inter-operate well with other blockchains or related technologies?
12. Open Source. Is the code open source? What is the level of collaboration level and contributions from a variety of developers?

PRIVACY OF THE BLOCKCHAIN

Privacy is of utmost significance on the Blockchain organization of agencies. Blockchain use asymmetric cryptography to maintain privacy between transactions.

- Public and private keys

A key component of privacy in blockchains is using private and public keys. Both keys are random strings of number and related cryptographically. It is impossible for the user to know the other user's private key. This results in privacy and protection from the hackers. Each user has an address to send and receive assets on the blockchain. These addresses are derived from the public key using hash function. Users can see earlier transactions and activity that has occurred on the blockchain because networks are shared to all participants. Past transactions of senders and receivers are represented by their addresses. Public addresses do not disclose the personal information rather it suggested that public address is not use by the user more than once. This approach neglects the chances of hacking by tracing a particular address' past transaction to avoid the leak of information (Hasib Anwar, 2018).

Suppose Alice send cryptocoins to Bob on the blockchain. Actually, Alice is sending the hash version of public key. Bob knows their private key, and every user of blockchain knows their private key. Bob should not share their private key with other user otherwise cryptocurrencies will be stolen by that particular user. Public and private key are large integer numbers therefore it is represented by separate Wallet Import Format (WIF). Private key is used to derive the public key by complicated mathematical algorithm. Public key is then transformed with a hash function to produce the address that other people can see. Then Bob receive cryptocoins that Alice sends to his address.

We can derive public key from private key using mathematical algorithm. But we can't derive private key from public key by reverse key generator. The process of reversing the process is even more complex that the world's most powerful computer would need more than 40000000000000000000000000000000 0(31 zeros) years to complete the calculations.

- Peer-to-peer(P2P) network

The Blockchain technology depends on a peer-to-peer computer network comprised of its clients' computer. Blockchain's peer-to-peer infrastructure combined with its immutability (unchangeable of data), transparency, and removal of "mid men" make it a best platform for the business and exchange of any worthy asset.

Figure 2. Transformation of private key to public key

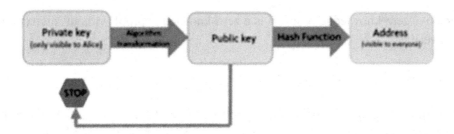

In the blockchain architecture, user's computer work as nodes; they share a record that gets updated or, altered through peer-to-peer replication. Whenever a transaction happens, each node gets the information about transactions from other nodes. Because nodes act as both sender and receiver, nodes can send transactions as well. The data which is transacted synchronized across the network of blockchain as it is transferred.

- Zero-knowledge proofs (ZKP)

Zero knowledge is a technique by which prover proofs to verifier that he knows the key or secret without saying anything about the secret. It means that one party proofs to other party that information is true without revealing the exact information.

Zero knowledge encryption is of two types –

Figure 3. Peer-to-peer

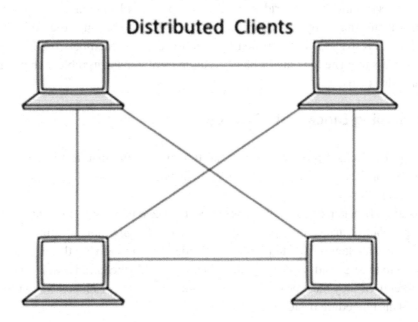

1. Interactive zero knowledge proof: It is a zero-knowledge proof with interaction between prover and verifier.
2. Non-interactive zero knowledge proof: It is a zero-knowledge proof without interaction between prover and verifier.

Where can Zero-knowledge proofs be use?

- Messaging: In messaging end-to-end encryption is required for securing the private messages. With the help of ZKP, no one could hack the message because it provides end-to-end trust without leaking any personal information.
- Authentication: ZKP does not allow any user to access any complex document.
- Complex documentation: It help to convey sensitive information like validation data with additional security.
- Sharing data: ZKP helps in sharing data without any intermediaries.
- Security for sensitive information: ZKP provide high security to the sensitive information like banks statements, or credit card.
- Storage Privacy: ZKP provide highly protection to the stored data which help from the theft.

Comparison of Blockchain Privacy Systems

- Private Blockchain: Private Blockchain is different from public blockchain. In Public blockchain, all transactions and records are publicly accessible. Public blockchains offer full decentralisation. Examples of public blockchain are: Bitcoin, Ethereum, Dash, Factom. A private blockchain is also known as permissioned blockchain. It has restrictions on one who can access it and participate in transactions. So private blockchain network requires an invitation and can be validated by either the network starter or by a set of rules put in place by the network starter. Examples of private blockchain are: Multichain, Blockstack ("IntelliPaat Blogs", n.d.).
- Consortium Blockchain: It is hybrid of public and private blockchain. It is public because the blockchain is being shared by different nodes and it is private because the nodes that can access the blockchain is restricted. It controlled by a consortium of members. Only predefined set of nodes have access to write the data or block. Examples of consortium blockchain are: Ripple, R3 ("IntelliPaat Blogs", n.d.).

Concerns Regarding Blockchain Privacy

1. Transparency: Blockchain provide secured and transparent platform to the users. The allowance of users to control their own data and absence of third parties is the reason behind the adoption of blockchain technology.
2. Decentralization: Blockchain technology is of decentralized nature i.e., no central point of control. Lack of single control makes the system fairer and considerably more secure.
3. Private Keys: Private key is used to protect user's identity and security through digital signatures. It is also used to access funds and personal wallets on the blockchain. Like, if any individual send money to other user, they must provide a digital signature that is produced when provided with the private key. This procedure protects against theft.

How the System Protects Against the Following Privacy Issues

The privacy concerns face by the users while using third party services like mobile applications, application constantly collect personal data of user, of which user has no specific control or knowledge. Like this there are many such examples about which user is unaware about their information wherever it uses. To protect against such privacy issues the following point given below:

- Data Ownership: The main focus is that user has allowance to control their data. User must have the knowledge and control over their personal data.
- Data Transparency and Accessibility: The user must have complete transparency and accessibility over their own personal data.
- Fine-grained Access Control: A major concern with mobile applications is that when signing up, users are needed to grant a set of permissions. These permissions are granted on an indefinite basis and opting-out is the only way to change the agreement. Instead, the user can change the set of permissions at any given time in the framework and cancel access to previously collected data.

One application of this mechanism would be to enhance the existingpermissions dialog in mobile applications. While the user interface is likely to remain the same, the accesscontrol policies would be stored securely on a blockchain, where only the user can modify them.

Cases of Privacy Failure

- *Mt. Gox*

Mt. Gox, world's largest Bitcoin exchange during 2014 was holding around 70% of worldwide cryptocurrency. Mt. Gox suffered a huge theft of more than 450 million-dollar, initial reasons of which were unknown. This security breach was the first major hack of cryptocurrency. However, the public address of the perpetrators was identified by tracking the transactions details.

- *DAO Hack*

DAO, a digital autonomous organisation with an objective to prevent or solve data security breaching, tampering. The DAO system was hacked in 2016, while its funding window was active for a project. The loss was expected to be around $US 3.6 million.

- Coinbase

Coinbase is world's biggest digital currency exchange founded in 2012. It allows its users for storage and transactions of cryptocurrency. It was reported that the personal data of users like Telephone numbers and email address of famous individuals were used by hackers to change their account verification numbers, consequently resulting into theft of thousands of dollars from Coinbase wallets.

SECURITY OF THE BLOCKCHAIN

Security in blockchain refers to protection of transactions information and data in a block against internal, outskirts, malicious, and unexpected threat. Protection involves detection and prevention of threats, response to threat using security policies. Some important methodology related to security are given below (Prashant J. et al., 2018):

1. Defence in penetration: -This methodology uses various remedial measures to ensure the data.
2. Least authority: - In this methodology the access to data is diminished to the most minimal level to raised degree of security.
3. Manage vulnerabilities. In this methodology, manage vulnerabilities by distinguishing, authenticating, altering and fixing.
4. Manage risks: - In this methodology, manage the risks by recognizing, evaluating and controlling.
5. Oversee patches. In this methodology, patch the imperfect part like code, application, operating system, firmware and so forth by securing, testing and installing patches.

Security and Privacy Challenges and Solutions for Blockchain Applications

1. Blockchain in finance: Many Currencies such as Alter coin, Peer coin, Ethereum, Karma, Hashcash, and Binary Coin uses blockchain all across the globe. Most currency uses blockchain structure as the base while they are using use different types consensus algorithms for verification and validation of blocks. Smart contacts require the use of blockchain in the finance sector. Many organizations use blockchain to overcome from security problems, hence, blockchain are ensuring authorized parties to access correct and appropriate data. Blockchain provide the warranty of security of data and data access.
2. Blockchain in IOT: IOT is a technology that interconnects computing devices, mechanical and digital machines, objects, animals or people in order to transfer data across a network without requiring human-to-human or human-to-computer interaction. IoT is used in blockchain as to store data. So, that the user has the access to the data from any place across the world ensuring security and privacy. This can be achieved by creating an account and setting password. Then, permissions are checked and then the process of extraction of previous block number and hash value takes place, consecutively, the user creates a random unique id and sends data to storage by using this id. The life of transaction is checked and the storage availability is confirmed. In this way, IOT uses blockchain.
3. Blockchain in mobile applications: Smartphones also uses blockchain in its software applications which supports peer-to-peer data service, peer-to-peer file transfer and direct payment. Blockchain provide an immense value to the security strategies regarding mobile applications. Blockchain is more secure that it is used in different applications that deal with sensitive data, since blockchain does not have any single point of failure. Blockchain is used for authentication to protect data. One more use of blockchain is that its mobile applications enables to access digital wallets.
4. Blockchain in Defence: defence also uses blockchain technology. In the upcoming era, defense will use cyber-enabled systems and the data they contain. Blockchain technology overturns the cyber security paradigm due to its trust less, transparent and fault tolerant thereby decreasing the chance of data compromise.

Blockchain can be used in defence application by providing the operational or support roles as follows:

a) Cyber defence- This consumes low-cost, high payoff application of blockchain. At first, blockchain helps to ensure that all digital events are widely perceived by transferring to all other nodes in the network and thereafter uses different consensus algorithms to validate and verify. Once the data is secured then it is timestamped and stored, then it cannot be manipulated. If the data is altered or updated, it is again timestamped and the log is maintained. In this way, the advanced weapon and component details can be imaged, hashed and secured in the database and continuously monitored using blockchains.

b) Supply chain management. The day to day increment in concern regarding supply chain management in defence leads to the need of a technology to establish the origin and owner traceability

5. Blockchain in automobile industry: technology in Modern vehicles is increasing results in connecting to online or network-based applications and which in return provide an excellent base for the use of blockchain technology. Automobiles use security architectures which help to address a few requirements to placate the future requirements for smart vehicles.

Automotive security architectures along with several advantages of smart vehicles needs to tackle some challenges to satisfy the needs of future services of smart vehicles from the perspectives listed as follows:

a) Safety. Along with several uses of smart vehicles, there arises the need to secure the data from threats involving security breaches occurring due to malfunction as well as due to numerous autonomous driving functions.

b) Centralization- The security of the system should be concentrated at a single point of failure. So, decentralized architecture is more appreciable due to the low scale ability of the centralized architecture.

c) Maintainability. The automotive architecture has the property to maintain hardware and software for a long-fixed period of time along with the extend-ability option for maintainability of a vehicle.

TRUST IN BLOCKCHAIN

Blockchain technology solves the fundamental and most regular issue trust during transfers, transactions, storing and managing data. A lot of industries like healthcare, education, security, banking, real estate, voting is using blockchain technology because it is trusted (Prashant J. et al., 2018).

The reasons why blockchain technology is trusted given below ("Quora blockchain", 2017):

- Immutability of data: - Immutability means unable to change i.e., once data written in ledger nobody, not even system administrator can update or delete it. It implies once information has been kept in touch with a blockchain then no one including system administrator can transform it. This attempt disallows the fraudulent tampering.
- Verification: - Records and Tracking verified through cryptography. Blockchain verify each transaction through strong encryption.
- Unique Tokens

- Decentralized network: -There is no central authority that guarantees or validations for transactions. No one on a Blockchain network owns the ledger. Because of its decentralized nature, everyone on the network has a copy of the ledger ("Quora blockchain", 2017).
- Consensus: - The blockchain technology has consensus algorithms. The architecture or to say infrastructure has designed which has those consensus base which makes it relevant as well as a trusted approach for the businesses ("Quora blockchain", 2017).
- Distributed Ledger: - A public ledger will provide every information about a transaction and the participant. It's all out in the open, nowhere to hide.

Figure 4. Features of Trust Boundary

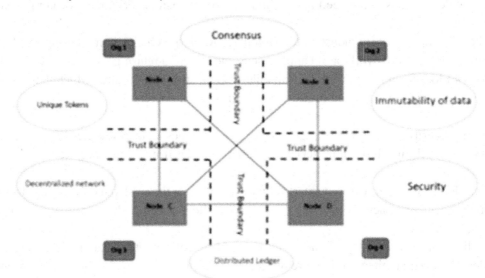

PERFORMANCE ANALYSIS AND OPTIMIZATION OF THE BLOCKCHAIN TECHNOLOGY

Blockchain technology has drawn significant attention of society in the ongoing past, as from previous of years' digital money is consistently in the news with respect to the benefits and demerits and issues identified with security. Another notable name of the Blockchain technology is Distributed Ledger Technology or DLT, which exhibit to save a lot of time and effort of the association. The Blockchain technology is utilized to produce a decentralized record system, which is responsible for the verifying the private data of the network on the channel.

In nowadays, blockchain technology isn't just utilized by different organizations in order to manage financial statement, yet additionally to ideally deal with the standardization of coordination and other supply chain programs. Therefore, broad research on the technology uncovered that achieving the throughput and inertness of the Blockchain technology is the most troublesome challenge, with the end goal that yield of the system channel can be optimal managed.

After the advancement of initial applications, it has been outputted that improvement for the blockchain framework degraded in giving optimal inertness to the system and thus, it makes its measure to solve the difficulties preceding the improvement of technology. Therefore, there are different procedures which can be utilized so as to check the presentation and improve the blockchain technology further for the advancement of society.

Above all else, parameter can be blockchain platforms and foundation arrangement which guarantee the improvement model picked for the advancement is appropriate for it or not. To exemplify, a study was led for the two blockchain technology, for example, Hyperledger Fabric and Ethereum that mirrors the advancement model and installation of essential software is a significant to rely upon the latency and transfer speed of the framework. The pre setup module plays a major role, however after the improvement the assessment depends on the workload dispatcher and execution information gathering module of the blockchain technology. These previously mentioned parameters will make the technology particular regarding the execution time, latency and throughput of blockchain applications. The difference in execution time of the transaction on various stages can be considered as the native functionalities and custom function to check the difference in information access and information management of the framework applications. From that point onward, comparing average latency can be utilized also plot to gauge the exchanges of involvement in securing the trials and stages increment for the rapid action's management. Insurance and transfer value will be responsible for the average latency assumption calculation for the optimal areas to focus for the better administration of the varying functions. Moreover, greatest simultaneous transactions are conveyed for the report management for appropriating the present version of the platform to the CPU used resources of blockchain technology.

Accordingly, suffice to say that performance analysis and optimization are fundamental thought which could effectively guarantee the present adaptation of the platforms as well as finding the present loopholes in the knowledge of the Blockchain technology. Moreover, private blockchain frameworks will be considered as effective platform for communication.

CONCLUSION

The first and foremost reason behind using any technology is that it provides secure and trustworthy result. Thanks to the advent of the blockchain, data is now being recorded, disclosed, transparent, and secured. Blockchain can be considered as sustainable and secure solution for future generations to come.

REFERENCES

Andreas, M. (2014). *Mastering Bitcoin: Programming the Open Blockchain.* Academic Press.

Hasib Anwar. (2018). *What is ZKP? A Complete Guide to Zero Knowledge Proof.* https://101blockchains.com/zero-knowledge-proof/

IntelliPaat Blogs. (n.d.). *What is Blockchain Technology?* https://intellipaat.com/blog/tutorial/blockchain-tutorial/what-is-blockchain/

Mark Gates. (2017). *Blockchain: Ultimate Guide to Understanding Blockchain*. Bitcoin, Cryptocurrencies, Smart Contracts and the Future of Money.

Pathak, N., & Bhandari, A. (2018). *IoT, AI, and Blockchain for. NET : Building a next-generation application from the ground up.* doi:10.1007/978-1-4842-3709-0

Performance Analysis and Optimization of the Blockchain Technology. (n.d.). https://assignmenthelp4me.com/article-performance-analysis-and-optimization-of-the-blockchain-technology-869.html

Prashanth Joshi, A., Han, M., & Wang, Y. (2018). *A survey on security and privacy issues of blockchain technology*. Mathematical Foundations of Computing., doi:10.3934/mfc.2018007

Quora. (2017). *What makes blockchain trusted?* https://www.quora.com/What-makes-blockchain-trusted

Wikipedia. (n.d.). *Privacy and blockchain.* https://en.wikipedia.org/wiki/Privacy_and_blockchain

Zero Knowledge Proof. (2018). *An Introduction to Zero Knowledge Proof.* https://101blockchains.com/wp-content/uploads/2018/11/Zero_knowledge_Proof_ZKP.png

Zyskind, Nathan, & Pentland. (2015). Decentralizing Privacy: Using Blockchain to Protect Personal Data. *2015 IEEE CS Security and Privacy Workshops*.

Chapter 9
Optimizing Energy of Electric Vehicles in Smart Cities

Brahim Lejdel

(iD) https://orcid.org/0000-0002-7193-5204

Univeristy of El Oued, El Oued, Algeria

ABSTRACT

In the near future, the electric vehicle (EV) will be the most used in the word. Thus, the energy management of its battery is the most attractive subject specialty in the last decade. Thus, if a driver uses an electric vehicle, he wants to find an optimal method that can optimize the energy battery of its electric vehicle. In this chapter, the authors propose a new concept of the smart electric vehicle (SEV) that can manage, control, and optimize the energy of its battery, in condition to satisfy the drivers' and passengers' comfort. Thus, they use a hybrid approach based on the multi-agent system and the genetic algorithm (MAS-GA).

1. INTRODUCTION

The Smart City (SC) is a concept which is appeared to have made a city more alive and more liveable. Thus, SC is an urban area that is a means to enhance the life quality of the citizens. This new concept has gained increasing importance in the agendas of policy makers (Paolo et al. 2014). The policy maker should introduce Electric Vehicles in smart city to replace traditional vehicles to reduce air pollution, improve energy efficiency and avoid the congestion in road traffic. We will treat in this paper, two main questions. The one is what is the optimal method to manage, reduce and control the energy consumption of the battery? The second is what is the optimal strategy which permits, finding the charging station?

In this paper, we propose to use a multi-agent system which allows to distribute the different tasks between the agents when each agent can perform Genetic Algorithms to optimize energy consumption of electric vehicle battery in real-time, thus adapting rapidly to battery consumption. Thus, all agents can cooperate and negotiate to find the best solution which can regulate the energy consumption battery in electric vehicle. Then, we develop a GIS system which allows knowing the position of electric vehicle and all data associated with it as electric vehicle-id, energy consumption, charging station, etc.

DOI: 10.4018/978-1-7998-3295-9.ch009

After a deep study of the subject, we have found that we have four factors that can affect the energy consumption of battery in electric vehicle, as the time of system peak, energy costs, peak energy demand and the quantity of energy per hours, etc. Also, we find two mainly energy equipment such as HVAC system and lighting systems, we can use HVAC-L system to designate these two systems.

This paper is organized as the following. Firstly, we will present a state of the art review for optimization of energy consumption of battery in electric vehicle and a state of the art review for the localization of the optimal charging station for electric vehicle. Then, we describe our proposed approach which is based on two approaches, the Multi Agent System and Genetic Agent (MAS-GA). Finally, we add a conclusion.

2. ENERGY MANAGEMENT OF BATTERY ELECTRIC VEHICLES

2.1. Overview

The electric vehicles are quickly merged in the smart city, but many problems are appearing as the high consumption cost, the limited capacities, and the long recharge time of their batteries. To increase of these batteries, multi-battery systems that combine a standard battery with super-capacitors are currently one of the most promising ways to increase battery life's and reduce consumption costs. However, their performance essentially depends on how they are designed. In this paper, we focus on a complementary aspect of the problem that is optimizing the energy consumption of batteries in electric vehicles.

2.2. State of the art for Energy Management

Several works are introduced to address the different aspects of this problem. In particular, there are many researches that aim to improve the navigation systems with novel routing algorithms by taking into account the capacity of electric vehicles' battery, and the real-time data of traffic lights in all the road conditions.

Laroui M et al. (2019) propose a solution for Electric Vehicles (EVs) energy management in smart cities, where a deep learning approach is used to enhance the energy consumption of electric vehicles by trajectory and delay predictions. In this work, two Recurrent Neural Networks are adapted and trained on 60 days of urban traffic. The trained networks show precise prediction of trajectory and delay, even for long prediction intervals. An algorithm is designed and applied on well-known energy models for traction and air conditioning.

Masjosthusmann et al. (2012) take into account of the advantage of the heating Vehicle system's power control to develop a vehicle energy management for a single source Battery Electric Vehicle. Roscher et al. (2012) also used the cooling system's power control to reduce the overall energy consumption and increase the battery health of Battery through an adaptive control of the heating, ventilation and air conditioning of the vehicle (HVAC system), depending on the driving situation.

Kachroudi et al. 2012 propose to use online particle swarm optimization (PSO) method to optimally control the energy flow between the power train and the other vehicle's auxiliaries for a given Battery. Thus, using a PSO algorithm to search for a global optimum relative to specific objective functions, which take into account battery autonomy, driving comfort indexes, and travel time. According to them decrease the vehicle's energy consumption, and at the same time maintain the comfort of the passengers, by providing some suggestions to the driver.

3. LOCALISATION OF CHARGING STATION FOR ELECTRIC VEHICLE

3.1. Overview

If a driver wants to use an electric vehicle, he wants to find an optimal method which allows knowing where to find the optimal station charging according to its position in the road, amount energy of the battery and the charging time. On the other hand, we know that Battery charging depends on the vehicle characteristics and charging system type. Or, we are different charging systems.

- Fast charge which can take between 20 to 30 minutes,
- Normal (or slow) charge, it can take between 6 to 8 hours.
- Or replacement the Battery.

In this paper, we propose a smart model that permits, finding the optimal charging station.

3.2. State of the art for Localisation of Charging Station

Dong et al. (2020) develop a simulation model that determines the optimal design of the energy storage system (ESS) for a given network of charging stations. The model is made novel by integrating the charging station network and energy storage system as a whole. The optimal ESS design informs the configuration and distribution of battery type, size, amount, and location.

To find the available charging station, many works have been proposed. Wang et al. (2010) created a numerical method for the layout of charging stations using a multi-objective planning model taking into account factors including electric vehicles, sustainable development, characters of the charging station, and characters of charging consumers, distribution of the charging demand, the power grid and factors of municipal planning. Then a solution algorithm is designed based on demand priority and the usage of the existing gas station. Then, li et al. (2011) propose to use a genetic algorithm to find the optimal charging station location. Thus, this signifies that the genetic algorithm can identify the candidate charging station locations. Their method is based on conservation theory of regional traffic flows, taking Electric Vehicles within each district as fixed load points for charging stations. The number and distribution of electric vehicle are forecasted, and the cost-minimizing charging station problem is heuristically solved using genetic algorithms.

Sweda and Klabjan (2011) propose to use an agent-based decision support system to identify patterns of residential Electric Vehicle ownership and driving activities to determine strategic locations for new charging infrastructure. Driver agents consider their own driving activities within the simulated environment, in addition to the presence of charging stations and the vehicle ownership of others in their social network, when purchasing a new vehicle.

Kameda and Mukai (2011) developed an optimization model for locating charging stations, in thr service area by using taxi probe data and focusing on stations for Japan's recently introduced on-demand bus system.

Worley et al. (2012) formulate the problem of locating charging stations and also designing Electric Vehicle routes as a discrete integer programming optimization problem, based on the classic Vehicle Routing Problem (VRP). The objective of this model consists to minimize the cost of locating a charging station and traveling.

Baouche et al. (2014) develop an integer linear programming algorithm mixed with a dynamic consumption demand model, for the City of Lyon. The model minimizes the fixed charge of charging station and the vehicle travel cost. Thus, they focus on the facility location models which consist of defining the best candidate site, the type and the size (number of terminals) of the CS to be assigned to the network in order to satisfy a given mobility demand.

Dong et al. (2014) proposed a genetic algorithmic framework to minimize range anxiety, defined as the total number of missed trips in the network, employing GPS data from conventional vehicles and a household travel choice survey. The main problem of these approaches that is not guaranteed to find the optimum energy distributions between the different system of electric vehicles in different conditions, to satisfy the passengers' comfort level and reduce the energy consumption. Also, these models cannot be regulated by the driver to choose different operating modes, such as the comfort or fuel economy.

4. THE PROPOSED APPROACH

In this paper, we will propose an approach based on multi-agent system and genetic algorithm (MAS-GA).

4.1. Multi-agent System

An agent is a software system that is situated in some environment, and that is capable of autonomous action in order to meet its design objectives (Wooldridge and Jennings, 1995). In this work, we use the multi-agent system because it provides numerous advantages in the domain of energy consumption and passengers' and drivers' comfort level. The proprieties of multi-agent systems that offer autonomy to solve energy consumption problems and satisfy the occupants' demand comfort. Thus, it provides a suitable framework for theses systems. Also, they provide a number of important characteristics as the cooperation, negotiation, adaptation and the mobility. That is, on the one hand, this autonomous agent perceives its environment and on the other hand the agent modifies its environment by its actions. Hence, an agent can dynamically adapt to a changing of environment in real time.

4.2. Genetic Algorithms

Genetic algorithms are developed in (Holland, 1975) to imitate the phenomena adaptation of living beings. They are an optimisation technique based on the concepts of natural selection and genetics. It searches an optimal solution among a large number of candidate solutions within a reasonable time (the process of evolution takes place in parallel). Each of these solutions contains a set of parameters that completely describe the solution. This set of parameters can then be considered as the "genome" of the individual, with each parameter comprising of one or more "chromosomes". They allow a population of solutions to converge step by step toward the optimal solution. To do this, they will use a selection mechanism of the population of individuals (potential solutions). The selected individuals will be crossed with each other (crossover), and some will be mutating by avoiding, whenever possible, local optima. The Genetic Algorithms are used primarily to treat both problems (DeJong and Sarma, 1993).

1. The search space is large or the problem has a lot of parameters to be optimized simultaneously.
2. The problem cannot be easily described by a precise mathematical model.

We will combine Multi-Agent Systems with Genetic Algorithms (MAS-GA), for permitting the agent to choose the optimal actions. Therefore, our proposal model is based on the three following points.

1. Vehicle Agent is a software agent which can manage, control the local optimization process and exchange relevant information with neighboring Agents.
2. Genetic patrimony which transformed between agents, are used as inputs to the genetic algorithm. This genetic patrimony represents values of energy consumption of HVAC-L system that are collected by sensor system.
3. Genetic Algorithms are used to find the optimal solution for the current configuration; this is composed of the two objective functions, the energy consumption and the passengers' comfort level.

5. SYSTEM ARCHITECTURE

The objective of our proposed system is on one hand to optimize the energy consumption of the battery and increase the battery live through an optimal distribution of energy on the different systems of electric vehicles as the heating, ventilation and air conditioning (HVAC) system and lighting system. And in the other hand, find the available station charging. The proposed system determines the optimal energy distribution for the different components of electric vehicle to achieve the drivers comfort level, as the reference speed, the values of temperature, illumination, air conditioning and ventilation system. Thus, our system considers two mainly parameters, the driver demand satisfaction and vehicle environment data. The result of a system can be suggested to the driver or can be applied automatically as a part of a control system. In figure 1, we present the architecture of our system. In this system, we are principally three agents, profile agent, vehicle agent and station agent that can find the optimal charging station placement according to vehicle position and energy cost.

6. VEHICLE AGENT

As we tell previously, a vehicle agent is able to manage, control and regulate its cabin environment of electric vehicle to optimize energy consumption, satisfy the occupants' comfort, saving battery and increase the efficiency and productivity of systems. Therefore, the main objective of a vehicle agent is to solve the conflicts which can be occurred during energy consumption and satisfaction of passengers' and drivers' comfort. Passengers' and drivers' comfort satisfaction is related to both the conditions of the environment and passengers' or drivers' preferences over the environment. In order to evaluate the passengers' comfort level in the electric vehicle, environmental parameters can be used as indices to form the function of passenger's comfort by using the actual value of the environmental parameters and passengers preferences of these parameters. Therefore, the vehicle agent has been designed with three

Figure 1. Architecture of our system.

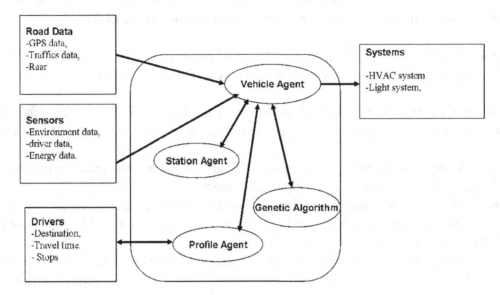

components for controlling and regulates its cabin environment that can optimize energy consumption. These components are an optimizer, simulator and comfort model.

6.1. An Optimiser

It runs a genetic algorithm. Since heuristic algorithms have no guarantee to find the globally optimal solution within the limited iterations, in this research GA runs 100 times in each time step to increase the possibility of achieving the global optimization, saving battery and meet passengers preferences. In principle, more runs of the optimization algorithm will lead to higher probability of achieving better results, but it will inevitably take more computation time. After many trials, it was found that 100 is a reasonable number of runs for balancing the solution quality and computational time cost.

6.1.1. Simulator

Each vehicle agent has a simulator that is used together to discover the passengers' comfort level and optimized energy consumption in the prevailing conditions. The results of simulator could be optimized to achieve a satisfactory balance between discovery time and system performance. The optimizer repeatedly runs the energy flow simulations for every time and calculates the satisfaction of passengers' comfort level. The best passengers' comfort level are then used to generate the subsequent generation of general passengers' comfort level, and over a number of generations, the best candidates' comfort level is identified.

6.1.2. Comfort Model

The passengers' comfort model permits to control the cabin environment in electric vehicle via computer techniques to optimize energy consumption and satisfy passengers' comfort, saving battery and increase the efficiency and productivity of the system. In order to meet the compromise between energy efficiency and passengers' comfort level, vehicle agent needs to evaluate the energy consumption and passengers' comfort level in electric vehicle in response to changes of the cabin environment. However, energy consumption and passengers' comfort level usually affect each other in an opposite way. Therefore, the main goal of a vehicle agent is to solve the conflicts between reducing energy consumption and increasing passengers' comfort level. The passengers' comfort level is related to both the condition of the environment and passengers' preferences over the environment. In order to evaluate the passengers' comfort in the electric vehicle, environmental parameters can be used as indices to form the function of passengers' comfort by using the actual value of the corresponding environmental parameters and passengers' preferences of these parameters. Generally, the cabin temperature, the illumination level, the air conditioning and ventilation inside the electric vehicle are used as parameters to evaluate the passengers' comfort level.

7. OPTIMIZATION PROCESS OF ELECTRIC VEHICLE

As we say previously, the vehicle Agent has an optimizer and simulator that are used together to discover the values of HVAC-L system that they can optimize the energy consumption in the prevailing conditions and also satisfy the comfort level of drivers and passengers. The use of genetic algorithm has a major advantage over systems that rely on predefined values, as each vehicle agent enables a genetic algorithm to discover the values of HVAC-L system that they may not resemble any predefined values, but they may be optimal values for the current cabin conditions of electric vehicle. The optimizers should achieve a satisfactory balance between discovery time of solutions and consumption of energy. Thus, each vehicle agent executes a genetic algorithm to find the optimal values of HVAC-L systems that can be attributed to each system to perform optimal energy consumption and increasing the passengers' or drivers' comfort level.

7.1. Chromosomes' Structure

To apply the genetic algorithm, we should define the genes. The gene can be characterized by its identifier, and a set of values of HVAC-L systems that can be applied to perform the optimal energy consumption and satisfy the passengers' or drivers' comfort level. We use multiple forms to coding the genes. Firstly, we use the stings to coding the identifiers, and then we use real number for encoding the values of temperatures, the ventilation, the air conditioning and lighting system. Figure 2 presents the structure of the gene.

To identify the best chromosome from the population, the optimizer runs a genetic algorithm with its different classic steps, as selection, crossover and mutation. The electric vehicle agent has a simulator, which permits it to identify the best available solution from the population; the optimizer repeatedly runs the energy consumption simulator for each HVAC-L system in a given generation. After a number of generations, the best candidate values of HVAC-L system are identified.

Figure 2. Gene structure's.

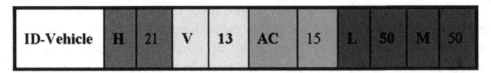

ID-Vehicle : electric vehicle identify,

H: heating system,

V : ventilation system,

AC: Air Conditioning system,

L: light System.

M: Motor consumption.

7.2. Initialisation, Crossover and Mutation

Firstly, the initialization operator determines how each chromosome is initialized for participate in the population of genetic algorithm. Here, the chromosome is filled with the genetic material from which all new solutions will evolve. In this work, we will use the Steady State to initial the generation process and select the population of genetic algorithm for the next generation. First, Steady State creates a population of individuals by cloning the initial chromosomes. Then, at each generation during evolution, it creates a temporary population of individuals, adds these to the previous population and then removes the worst individuals in order that the current population is returned to its original size. This strategy means that the newly generated offspring may or may not remain within the new population, dependent upon how they measure up against the existing members of the population.

Then, the crossover operator defines the procedure for generating a child from two parent chromosomes. The crossover operator produces new individuals as offspring, which share some features taken from each parent. The probability of crossover determines how often crossover will occur in each generation. In this approach, we will use the single point crossover strategy was adopted for all experiments. In this paper,

Figure 3. The crossover operator.

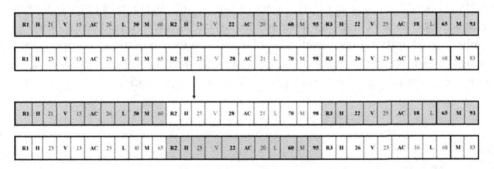

the results for all experiments presented were generated using a crossover percentage of 50%, which is to say that at each generation, 50% of the new population were generated by splicing two parts of each chromosome's parents together to make another chromosome. Figure 3 presents the crossover operator.

Finally, the mutation operator will be applied. It defines the procedure for mutating the chromosome. Mutation, when applied to a child, randomly alters a gene with a small probability. It provides a small amount of random search that facilitates convergence at the global optimum. The probability of mutation determines how much of an each genome's genetic material is altered, or mutated. If mutation is performed, part of a chromosome is changed. The mutation should not occur too often as this would be detrimental to the search exercise. In this work, the results presented here were generated using a 1% mutation probability, which was determined experimentally, utilizing a single case of vector HVAC-L system of electric vehicle. Figure presents the operator of mutation. Figure 4 presents the operator of mutation.

Figure 4. The operator of mutation.

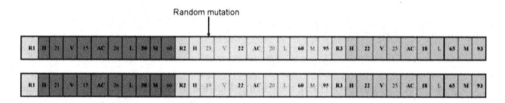

a)   Evaluation of solutions

The purpose of evaluation system is to provide a measure for any given solution that represents its relative quality. In our resolution method of energy consumption problem in electric vehicle, the objective function used here works by calculating and summing the penalties associated with the temperature, the illumination, the air quality and ventilation in electric vehicle. Thus, we will use the objective functions to evaluate solutions of the energy consumption problem in electric vehicle and examines the weighted relationship between the actual measured values of the temperature, the ventilation, the cabin air quality, illumination level and values of drivers' and passengers' comfort level according to these four parameters. The objective functions used to evaluate solutions require a number of definitions that model the problem underlying structure, specifically.

- $EV = \{EV_1, EV_2, EV_3, \ldots\ldots EV_n\}$ is the set of all electric vehicle in the road,
- $H = \{H_1, H_2, H_3, \ldots\ldots H_n\}$ is the set of all heating systems in the electric vehicle,
- $L = \{L_1, L_2, L_3, \ldots\ldots L_n\}$ is the set of all illumination systems in the electric vehicle,
- $A = \{A_1, A_2, A_3, \ldots\ldots A_n\}$ is the set of all air conditions in the electric vehicle,
- $V = \{V_1, V_2, V_3, \ldots\ldots V_n\}$ is the set of all ventilation system in the electric vehicle,
- $CS = \{CS_1, CS_2, CS_3, \ldots\ldots CS_n\}$ is the set of all charging station in city,
- *N1, N2* is a number of all charging station in the city and all electric vehicle, respectively,

- H_m, L_m, A_m, V_m are the measured values of the temperature, the illumination, and the cabin air quality and ventilation, respectively.
- H_c, L_c, A_c, V_c are the comfort values of the temperature, the illumination, and the cabin air quality, respectively.
- $[C_{min}, C_{max}]$ represents the comfort range. This range can be defined by customers.
- $[E_{min}, E_{max}]$ represents the consumption energy range.

Two important parameters are in our MAS-GA, the assigned energy to the HVAC system E_H and the assigned energy, to the lighting system E_L.

In this context, we have mainly two important functions $f(C)$ and $f(E)$ which permits evaluating the performance and efficiency of the proposed approach. These two functions are calculated by building agent.

The objective of this optimization mechanism is to maximize passengers' and drivers' comfort $f(C)$ and to minimize the total energy consumption of battery $f(E)$ for evaluating the performance and the efficiency of our system. Firstly, we have.

$$f(C) = C_1 * \frac{H_c}{H_m} + C_2 * \frac{L_c}{L_m} + C_3 * \frac{A_c}{A_m} + C_4 * \frac{V_c}{V_m} \tag{1}$$

C1, C2, C3 and *C4* are the user-defined weighting factors, which indicate the importance of three comfort factors and resolve the possible equipment conflicts. These factors take values in the range of [0, 1]. The passengers or drivers can set their own preferred values in different situations according to the season or the travel period. As we say previously, since the travel period has a profound influence on energy savings, it should be taken into account in the control strategy design. Generally speaking, in the occupied hours, the vehicle agent activates the optimizer to tune the set point in order to obtain the acceptable cabin visual comfort with minimized energy. Otherwise, the vehicle agent turns off all the resource lights and keeps the blind position to save energy if there are no passengers in the electric vehicle. The objective function is defined in equation (1), and the optimization goal is to maximize these objective functions. Since the ratio between the measured value and comfort value determined by passengers play via graphic interface, it has an important role in achieving the control goal. Thus, it permits increasing the passengers' comfort level and optimize the energy consumption.

The second objective function permits controlling the energy consumption in electric vehicle. The objective of this function consists to minimize the total energy consumption of HVAC-L system. Thus, we can define this objective function as the following.

$$f(E) = E_{HVAC} + E_L + E_M \tag{2}$$

E_{HVAC}, E_L and E_M represent the energy consumption of HVAC system and the lighting system and of the motor, respectively.

8. STATION AGENT

When the electric vehicle needs to use charging station, vehicles agents change their behaviour and try to find a charging station. This behaviour of vehicle agent is triggered by a lower threshold E_1. The electric vehicle finds a charging station; three parameters have to take into account, the distance between the electric vehicle and charging station, availability of plug in the charging station and the charging time. The proposed model should find the closest distance and minimized the charging time.

Firstly, each electric vehicle that needs to charge its battery, it sends a request of charging to all the charging station. Then, the station charging treats this request and sends response to electric vehicle. Finally, the electric vehicle drivers are assumed to charging its vehicle in the optimal charging station. Figure 5 presents a charging station in smart city.

Figure 5. Charging station in smart city.

9. NEGOTIATION AND COOPERATION

To model an optimal energy consumption using the multi agent system and genetic algorithm (MAS-GA), we have to propose an efficient mechanism of negotiation, cooperation and coordination between different agents. We know that a single agent is unable to achieve some complex tasks, as the energy problems because its capability is individually limited or although can complete, but its performance and efficiency are far lower than the performance and the efficiency with the cooperation and the coordination of many agents (Ferber, 1995). In order to solve charging station location conflict, the vehicle agents negotiate, each trying to available charging station. Therefore, when conflicts occur between two or many vehicle agents, it is important to limit their effects. In such case, negotiation techniques enable the involved vehicle agents to resolve their different conflicts by reaching compromises between the three parameters as the distance between the actual position of electric vehicle and charging station, the time of charging and the availability of plug in. This negotiation allows the vehicle agents to solve various conflicts at once, and prevents new conflicts to appear. The vehicle agents negotiate with each other in order to decide whether the optimal plan which can be applied to satisfy the need of electric vehicles' battery in energy and in the same time, reduce the waiting time in the charging station. Thus, in our proposed approach, the vehicle agents negotiate with each other in order to determine the best possible arrangement. This negotiation enables them to solve various conflicts simultaneously and avoids new conflicts from appearing. In figure 6, we present an example of negotiation between two vehicle agents; vehicle Agent 1 and vehicle Agent 2. Thus, these two agents negotiate by proposing a plan of actions which can arrange the two agents. In each cycle, one vehicle agent makes a plan proposal to the other vehicle agents, which they can accept or reject the proposal. If they accept, negotiation ends, otherwise, the other vehicle agent makes a proposal at the next cycle.

Figure 6. Negotiation between two agents.

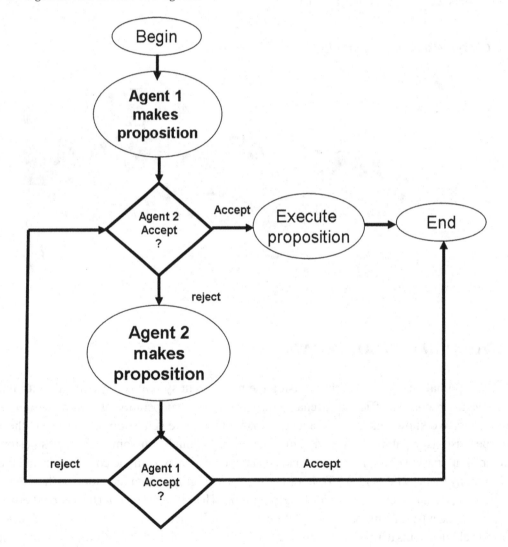

Also, the cooperation is defined as the collaboration between vehicle agents or station agents to find the optimal action to solve conflicts in the research station problem. In this paper, we use cooperation in order to solve conflicts which occur between the different electric vehicles. Each vehicle agent co-operates with the other vehicle agents in order to find the optimal solution which permit reducing the charging time and find the closed charging station. Each vehicle agent sends to the station agent some data as the distance, the amount of energy needed and charging time to permit the station agent analysis this data and performs its genetic algorithm. Then, each building agent sends to the other agents, some requests which composed of the sequence of the distance, the energy amount and the charging time. Next, each agent checks its list of requests to treat them and try to find the final optimal sequence of values of distance, the energy amount and the charging time that permit it to solve the conflict and avoid other conflicts to occur. The vehicle agents can accept or refuse the request of other agents according to their current situations. Thus, station agent sends the demand of the solution founded by its neighbours and it waits to receive the responses of them, it analyzes these responses and determines whether the solution is possible or not. If a solution is feasible, it sends a confirmation to those of its neighbours that accepted this solution. Figure 7 presents a simple configuration of cooperation between three agents.

Figure 7. Cooperation between Agents.

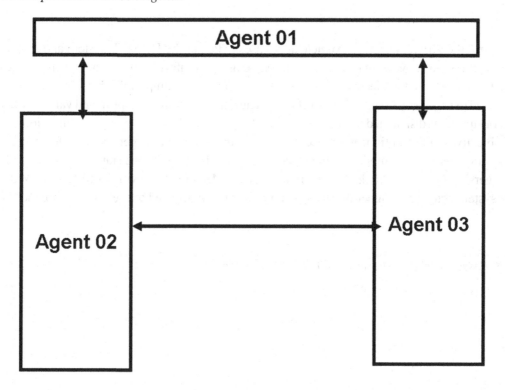

10. EXPERIMENTS AND RESULTS

In this section, we present a two case studies that illustrate how to design the different agents of our system and show collaboration between them. We use Jade to implement the different agents, vehicle agent, profile agent and station agent. Also, we use Java to implement the different steps of genetic algorithm as crossover operator, mutation operator and the evaluation function.

10.1. Management of Battery Energy

Firstly, the vehicle agent uses the sensor to learn the HVAC-L data and motor energy consumption, which can use as input in the genetic algorithms. The passengers and drivers can introduce their preferences in the profile agent via a graphic interface. The vehicle agent runs a genetic algorithm that can find the optimal values of HVAC-L system and Motor energy consumption, which permit optimizing the energy consumption and increase the passengers' or drivers' comfort level. In the table 1, we introduce the different intervals of passengers' satisfaction and the energy consumption.

Table 1. Intervals of passengers' satisfaction.

Evaluation Parameters	Unacceptable	Less satisfaction	Highly satisfaction
passengers' satisfaction	[0,2]	[2.25,3.5]	[3.75, 5]
Battery Energy Consumption (v)	[2.5,4.0]	[2.0,2.5]	[1.5,2.0]

To control the different systems, vehicle agent uses a data of the HVAC-L system and motor energy consumption. As we know, to maintain a higher passengers' comfort level, we must increase the energy consumption. Whereas, the electric vehicle agent tries finding a compromise between the energy consumption and the higher passengers' comfort level. Thus, it should find the optimized values to determine energy consumption dispatched to both the HVAC-L system and motor energy consumption.

The objectives of this optimization mechanism is to maximize passengers comfort level and to minimize the total energy consumption of the electric vehicle . In figure 8, we state that there is difference in passengers' comfort level in the two approaches, with MAS-GA and without MAS-GA. With MAS-GA, the system achieves a higher passengers' comfort level compared to the second approach, without

Figure 8. Passengers' comfort level with and without MAS-GA.

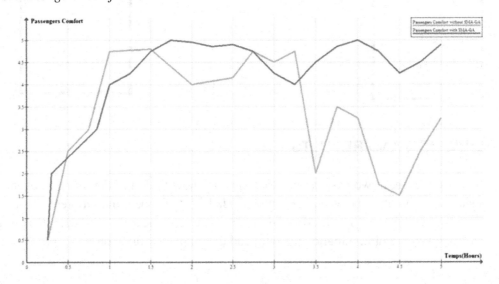

MAS-GA. Thus, the passengers' comfort level in the MAS-GA has been improved rapidly compared to the second approach.

Figure 9 shows that when we use our proposed approach, the energy consumption has been improved compared to classic approach which can be used to decrease the consumption energy. Thus, when we use MAS-GA approach, we can higher minimize the energy consumption, thus, the MAS-GA approach permits optimizing the energy consumption compared to the classic approach, without MAS-GA.

Figure 9. Energy consumption with MAS-GA and without MAS-GA.

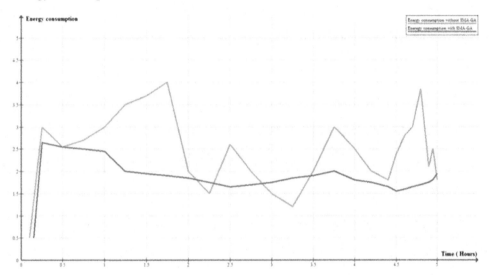

The MAS–GA is designed to enable the interactions between the occupants and the environment by learning the occupants' behaviours. According to the case studies and simulation results, the proposed MAS-GA is capable of managing, regulate and controlling the building effectively to satisfy occupants' comfort and optimize energy consumption.

10.2. Management of Charging Station Location

During each simulation process, the optimizer of station agent can run a genetic algorithm. The optimizer computes the corresponding fitness value of each proposed charging station according to account the energy capacity of a battery, the distance and time charging. In this experiment, the total number of charging plugs that can be served is set to 10.

When the vehicle agent sends a request to all station agents which neighbours with it, each station agent can execute its genetic agent to define the optimal response, according to the parameters of vehicle agent as the distance, the amount of energy demanded and the charging time. This data is sent by vehicle agent. It had the possible charging station configurations distributed in the city. In this work, we use the Euclidean distance to measure the distance between the actual position of electric vehicle and the demanded charging station. Also, the station agent can be cooperate and negotiate to define the final solution.

Figure 10. The waiting time of vehicle without MAS-GA.

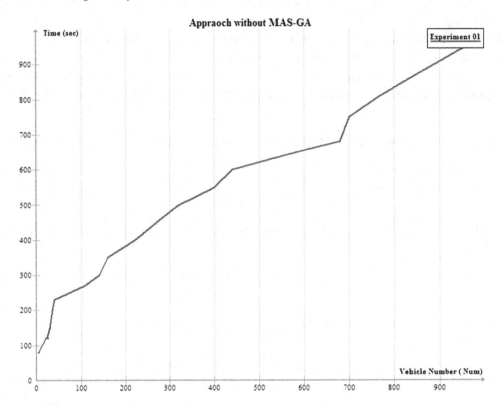

In Figure 10, we present the waiting time of vehicles when we use the MAS approach without GA. We observe that the waiting time increases, according to the number of vehicles which demand charging station.

When we use the approach of optimisation with MAS-GA, each station agent can interact with the other station agents and also it can perform its genetic algorithm to discover the optimal solution and. We observe that the waiting time of vehicle decreases over the generation number. Figure 11 shows the experiment results.

What is clear from figure 11 is that by using Multi-Agents System and genetic algorithm, the waiting time of vehicles is decreased in a few generations, and in significantly less time than the approach without MAS-GA. For the MAS–GA approach, After 600 generations, the maximum expected waiting time achieved by Experiment 02 is less than 85 seconds, whereas the maximum expected waiting time achieved by Experiment 01 was rapidly augmented. Thus, the MAS-GA approach used in Experiment 2 converges to their optimal solution at a significantly faster than the other solution presented Experiment 01.

CONCLUSION

In this paper, we present a hybrid approach to control, manage and regulate the energy consumption in an electric vehicle in a way that a reduction of electrical losses within the HVAC-L system in condition to satisfy the passengers and drivers' comfort level. To save the energy in the electric vehicle, we have

Figure 11. The waiting time of vehicle with MAS-GA

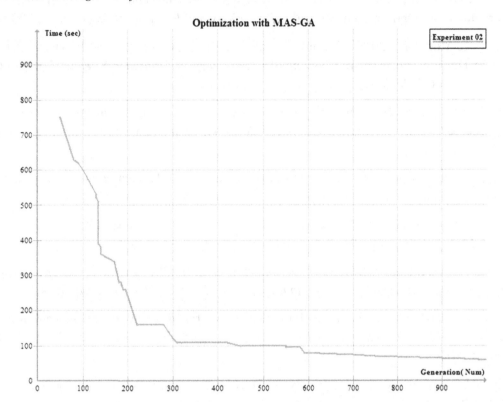

to regulate the maximum energy consumption of the HVAC, depending on the energy demand of the driver and passengers. Also, we should find the available and adaptable charging station according to the distance, the energy amount in the battery and charging time in charging station. The proposed approach can also save the battery of electric vehicles.

REFERENCES

Baouche, F., Billota, R. E. L., Faouzi, N. E., & Trigui, R. (2014). Electric vehicle charging stations allocation models. Transport Research Arena, Paris, France.

DeJong, K., & Sarma, J. (1993). *Generation Gaps Revisited, Foundations of Genetic Algorithms 2.* Morgan-Kaufmann Publishers.

Dong, J., Liu, C., & Lin, Z. (2014). Charging infrastructure planning for promoting battery electric vehicles: An activity-based approach using multiday travel data. *Transportation Research, 38*(Part C), 44–55.

Dong, Z., Navwant, T., & Jiayu, C. (2020). Optimal Design of Energy Storage System to Buffer Charging Infrastructure in Smart Cities. *Journal of Management Engineering, 36*(2).

Ferber, J. (1995). *Les systèmes multi-agents, vers une intelligence collective.* InterEditions.

Holland, J. (1975). *Adaptation in Natural and Artificial Systems.* University of Michigan Press.

Kachroudi, S., Grossard, M., & Abroug, N. (2012). Predictive Driving Guidance of Full Electric Vehicles Using Particle Swarm Optimization. Vehicular Technology. *IEEE Transactions on*, *61*(9), 3909–3919.

Kameda, H., & Mukai, N. (2011). Optimization of Charging Station Placement by Using Taxi Probe Data for On-Demand Electrical Bus System. *Lecture Notes in Computer Science*, *6883*, 606–615. doi:10.1007/978-3-642-23854-3_64

Laroui, Dridi, & Afifi. (2019). Energy Management For Electric Vehicles in Smart Cities: A Deep Learning Approach. *IEEE International Wireless Communications & Mobile Computing Conference (IWCMC 2019)*.

Li, Y., Li., L, Yong, J., Yao, Y., & Li, Z. (2011). Layout Planning of Electrical Vehicle Charging Stations Based on Genetic Algorithm. *Lecture Notes in Electrical Engineering, 1*(99), 661- 668.

Masjosthusmann, C., Kohler, U., Decius, N., & Buker, U. (2012). A vehicle energy management system for a Battery Electric Vehicle. *Vehicle Power and Propulsion Conference (VPPC), 2012 IEEE*, 339 – 344.

Paolo, N., Alberto De, M., Anna Giulio, C. M., & Francesco, S. (2014). Current trends in Smart City initiatives: Some stylised facts. *Cities (London, England)*, *38*, 25–36. doi:10.1016/j.cities.2013.12.010

Roscher, M. A., Leidholdt, W., & Trepte, J. (2012). High efficiency energy management in BEV applications. *International Journal of Electrical Power & Energy Systems*, *37*(1), 126–130. doi:10.1016/j.ijepes.2011.10.022

Sweda, T., & Klabjan, D. (2011). An Agent-Based Decision Support System for Electric Vehicle Charging Infrastructure Deployment. *7th IEEE Vehicle Power and Propulsion Conference*.

Wang, H., Huang, Q., Zhang, C., & Xia, A. (2010). A Novel Approach for the Layout of Electric Vehicle Charging Station. *Apperceiving Computing and Intelligence Analysis Conference*.

Wooldridge, M., & Jennings, N.R. (1995). Intelligent agents: Theory and practice. *The Knowledge Engineering Review, 10*(2), 115-152.

Worley, Klabjan, & Sweda. (2012). Simultaneous vehicle routing and charging station siting for commercial electrice vehicles. *IEVC 2012*.

Chapter 10
Future Blockchain Technology for Autonomous Applications/ Autonomous Vehicle

Arnab Kumar Show
Banaras Hindu University, India

Abhishek Kumar
Banaras Hindu University, India

Achintya Singhal
 https://orcid.org/0000-0003-0242-2031
Banaras Hindu University, India

Gayathri N.
Galgotias University, India

K. Vengatesan
Sanjivani College of Engineering, Savitribai Phule University, India

ABSTRACT

The autonomous industry has rapidly grown for self-driving cars. The main purpose of autonomous industry is trying to give all types of security, privacy, secured traffic information to the self-driving cars. Blockchain is another newly established secured technology. The main aim of this technology is to provide more secured, convenient online transactions. By using this new technology, the autonomous industry can easily provide more suitable, safe, efficient transportation to the passengers and secured traffic information to the vehicles. This information can easily gather by the roadside units or by the passing vehicles. Also, the economical transactions can be possible more efficiently since blockchain technology allows peer-to-peer communications between nodes, and it also eliminates the need of the third party. This chapter proposes a concept of how the autonomous industry can provide more adequate, proper, and safe transportation with the help of blockchain. It also examines for the possibility that autonomous vehicles can become the future of transportation.

DOI: 10.4018/978-1-7998-3295-9.ch010

INTRODUCTION

Nowadays technology has grown rapidly from all points of world. And the cost behind that also grown exponentially. Also, for human need, humans have to travel every time from one location to another. But now the travelling cost, environmental damages, affects, road accidents are increasing rapidly. Thus, as a result it creates the future of transportation as Autonomous vehicle. In upcoming few years, it can be very natural that owning autonomous vehicle for all consumers. Autonomous vehicle can give a best solution to the current issues of transportation. Driving safety experts predict that once driverless technology has been fully developed, traffic collisions (and resulting deaths, injuries and costs), and caused by human error, such as delayed reaction time, tailgating, rubbernecking, and other forms of distracted or aggressive driving should be reduced soon ("Wikipedia Self-driving", n.d.).

Figure 1. Autonomous vehicle

Blockchain is a newly established secured technology. It is a novel approach to the distributed database. A blockchain is a data structure that makes it possible to create a digital ledger of data and share it among a network of independent parties (Hori & Sakajiri, n.d.). It is a growing list of records, called blocks which are linked using cryptography. Each block contains a cryptographic hash value of the previous block, a timestamp and transaction information. It allows a peer-to-peer communication without any intermediary. There are three types of blockchain: First: Public blockchain, Second: Private blockchain, Third: Hybrid blockchain. All the three types of blockchain use cryptography to allow each participant on any given network to manage the ledger in a secure way without the need of central authority (Hori & Sakajiri, n.d.). The last few years, the blockchain has gained widespread traction and is constantly attracting new investments. A wide range of industries, including finance, insurance, healthcare, logistics and supply chain management are starting to discuss and test blockchain technology in a number of use cases (Saranti et al., 2019). The main application of blockchain are in financial system, healthcare, smart grid technology, business and industry, smart parking system, cyber security, information security, big data security etc.

So, from this chapter we want to explore how the combination of blockchain and autonomous industry became the future of transportation. And how by using blockchain autonomous industry can easily provide more security and efficient travel in transportation system.

Fundamentals of Autonomous Vehicle:

The vehicle that can be driven from one location to another location without a human driver within a particular time, for a particular goal is known as autonomous vehicle or autonomous car or self-driving car. The general use of this autonomous vehicle is concluded that the cost of human driven car is reduced for children, elder and for a disabled person (Saranti et al., 2019).

The first experiment on Autonomous Driving System (ADS) was organized in the year 1920 ("Wikipedia Self-driving", n.d.). The first semi-automated car was designed in 1997 by Japan's Tsukuba Mechanical Engineering Laboratory ("Wikipedia Self-driving", n.d.). The first truly autonomous car was developed in the year 1980 when the autonomous highway system was developed (Saranti et al., 2019). According to NHTSA (National Highway Traffic Safety Administration) vehicle automation has been classified into six automation levels ("Vehicles for Safety", n.d.):

Level 0: No Automation
   § Human driver controls all the driving.
Level 1: Driver Assistance
   § An advance driver assistance system (ADAS) technology has been used in this level.
Level 2: Partial Automation
   § An advance driver assistance system (ADAS) technology has been used which controls the steering and accelerating in some condition. Also, the driver pay attention all the time.
Level 3: Conditional Automation
   § An advance driver system (ADS) technology has been used in this level of automation. In this level ADS technology is used while free path of in less congested way. The driver is ready to pay his attention at any time.
Level 4: High Automation
   § In this level of automation, the ADS technology controls all the driving things and monitors all the surroundings in a wider range of environment. The human driver pays his attention in some conditions.
Level 5: Full Automation
   § The human need not be pay his attention at any condition. He feels just like a passenger. The ADS control all the driving at all condition.

It is estimated that the autonomous vehicle's cost per mile will be reduced compared to human driven cars in 2018to 2020 ("Decentralized blockchain", n.d.). In 2018, the cost is 80 cents per mile, but in 2030 the estimated cost will be 50 cents per mile and up to 2040 the cost will be 30 cents per mile ("Decentralized blockchain", n.d.). So, the cost per mile will be cheaper than today compared to normal cars.

Figure 2. Level of Automation

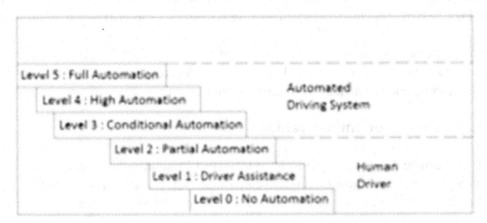

In the autonomous car all the traffic information collected through roadside units, passed vehicles, cameras on the vehicle, sensors like LiDAR (Light Detection and Ranging). Some advance radio sensor technology has been used for more information like RADAR (Radio Detection and Ranging). Multiple sensors and multiple cameras are giving all the traffic information properly. The correctness of this information can be up to 100%. Hence the main purpose of this is to provide more security and safety as much as possible

Advantages of Autonomous Vehicle

The autonomous vehicle has many differences compared to human driven cars. The applications of this vehicle are also advance from normal vehicles (Pete G., 2018). To provide more safety this vehicle never breaks the traffic rules. The main advantages of using autonomous vehicle are as follows:

- Decrease road accidents:

Many people are dead or fallen in injury or paralyzed due to road accidents every day. Generally, human driven cars are driven very roughly, as a result several road accidents are happened, human beings who are not guilty for any reason, are fallen in serious injury or even death.

The autonomous car or self-driving car was projected to reduce these types of traffic accidents. Estimated that, the autonomous vehicles can save 30,000 lives per year or reduce 60% to 80% death per year, which are generally happened by human error or traffic destruction (Fagnant & Kockelman, 2015).

- Reduce Travel Time:

We all know that time is never wait for anyone. So, every human has efficient time to complete their works or jobs. For performing works every man has to change their location with respect to time. All men are trying to complete their task or job within specified time. So human try to done it well and quickly. For this we all are trying to move anywhere as soon as possible, but this small mistake can lead to death or a serious injury. Several road accidents, road congestions and breaking traffic rules are also happening by this problem.

The autonomous vehicle has an advance software technology which follows all the traffic rules carefully. In any condition, the vehicle never breaks the traffic rules, which leads to a safe and smooth transportation system. Also, autonomous vehicle uses a software technology to find the shortest route, less congested path so that the vehicle can take less travel time. So, all the passengers can easily reach to their destination within proper time.

- Reduce road congestion:

The main reason behind the road congestion is several road accidents which are happened due to human error, reckless driving, traffic destruction etc. Sometime road congestion is happened due to breaking traffic rules. Also, several congestions are occurred due to animal interference and road constructions.

Decreasing the number of road accidents should be reducing the road congestions. The autonomous vehicle uses a software technology by which it never breaks the traffic rules. Also, it uses high light and radio detecting sensors which helps it to get correct information about nearby road constructions. Since transportation of autonomous vehicle is safe and smooth, so it reduces so much congestion.

- Reduce fuel and transportation cost:

Generally human driven cars are burning more fuel by driving roughly. Generally, fuel is more burning due to discrete increasing and decreasing of speed. But the autonomous car can easily decrease the economy of fuel by accelerating and decelerating safer and smoothly. As a result, the all over transportation cost was decreased.

- Increase path limit:

Generally, road lanes were blocked due to rough and irregular driving of humans. And these leads to the reduction of path capacity. The State Smart Transportation Initiative (SSTI) says that autonomous vehicles can increase the highway capacity by 100% (Darren C., n.d.). Also platooning of autonomous vehicles can also increase the path capacity up to 50% (Darren C., n.d.).

- Decrease Environmental pollution:

Nowadays human driven cars are a great reason for air pollution. In the smoke of normal vehicles dangerous air polluted gases such as Sulfur dioxide (SO_2), Nitrogen dioxide (NO_2), Carbon monoxide (CO) are released. Also due to road congestions high frequency horns are the reason of noise pollution. These can pollute the entire environment.

But the autonomous car uses modern software technology to drive the car. AVs are highly programmed to reduce fuel economy. And it uses converter that convert the harmful gases into other gases which are not so harmful for environment.

Autonomous Vehicle Requirements

Recent advances in autonomous vehicle guidance have encouraged further investments in industry and academia. Nowadays in common road scenarios the driverless vehicle technology is successful in high percentage. However new research efforts are required to meet the demand for higher performance or for advance technology ("Visual Requirements", 2016). Some requirements for advance features in autonomous vehicles are as follows:

- Advance sensor technology:

Generally, in human driven cars, humans are using their 5 sense to make right decisions at any situation. But the autonomous vehicles are using advance sensor technology such as cameras, LiDAR (Light Detection and Ranging), RADAR (Radio detection and Ranging), ADS (Advance Driving System), HMI (Human Machine Interface), IMU (Inertial Measurement unit) (Pedrosa & Pau, 2018)("CUBE", 2018). By using these sensors, vehicles make decisions based on digital that detects objects such as:

§ Humans walking at surrounding
§ Passing vehicles
§ Road constructions, Road blocks, pot holes, Black cars on dark streets
§ Traffic signals
§ Crossing animals or children

Sometimes in human driven car, humans are not able to recognize pot hole or a large crack on the road. But the autonomous vehicle's side cameras, laser technology and radio technology easily recognize these scenarios.

High resolution cameras are used by this autonomous vehicle, which can take high definition pictures of passing vehicles, directions, surrounding areas, road blocks, traffic signals, high-definition maps for localization.

LiDAR-which stands for Light Detection and Ranging, is a remote sensing method that uses light in the form of a laser o measure ranges to the earth. A LiDAR consists of a Laser technology, a scanner and a specialized GPS technology. In autonomous vehicle, it is used for examine the surface of the earth ("CUBE", 2018).

RADAR-which stands for Radio Detection and Ranging, is an advance sensing technology that uses radio waves to determine the range, the angle, or velocity of another passing vehicle. It is an electromagnetic system that is used to detect the location of another vehicle, distance of another vehicle from the point where the RADAR is placed. It works by radiating energy into space and monitoring the echo or reflected signals from the objects ("CUBE", 2018).

ADS-which is stands for Advance Driving System, is an electronic technology that controls all the driving mechanism in all condition. It is used for increase car safety or more generally for road safety.

HMI-which is stands for Human Machine Interface, is a part of Advance Diver Assistance System (ADAS) that helps automakers ensures a wide range of ADAS related services. In autonomous cars, HMI platforms are used for car-to-car communication (Anderson et al., 2016).

IMU-which is stands for Inertial Measurement unit, is a dynamic sensor to steer the vehicle dynamically. It measures vehicles three linear acceleration component and three rotational rate components

("CUBE", 2018). IMU is said to be unique among all the sensors in autonomous vehicle because it needs no connection or knowledge from the external world.

- Required high speed information:

Driverless cars have advance systems, like multiprocessing high-performance computers, for monitoring surrounding area; high resolution cameras for getting high quality 3D images of roadsides, passing vehicles, road blocks, traffic signals; advance laser technology (LiDAR technology) for examine earth surface; RADAR sensor for calculating speeds, distance, position of other vehicles. From all these sensors a huge amount of information will be collected. Since, the size of information will be vast; all this information can cause congestion in the network system. So, for this reason autonomous vehicle need a high-speed network for getting high speed information. Autonomous vehicle is using electronic support, high speed information links for managing that information.

- Required safe, secured high speed network:

Autonomous vehicles are using multiple sensors to make vehicle faster, smarter and more intelligent. These sensors will produce huge amount of data for the vehicle. Autonomous cars needed the high-speed processors, analyzer for controlling that information. Also, it requires a high-speed network than the existing 4G network system. Autonomous vehicles are requiring the capabilities for processing huge amount of information. According to Dr. Joy Laskar, CTO of Maja systems, future autonomous cars will generate nearly 2 petabits of data, which is equivalent to 2 million gigabits ("Blockchain Cloud", 2019).

The fifth generation (5G) wireless technology will be growing up rapidly. It is expected that almost everything will be connected through this ultra-fast, highly reliable, fully responsive network system. By many researches, it is found that it will offer 100 times faster than 4G network. The autonomous industry is using this technology for vehicle-to-vehicle (V2V), vehicle-to-infrastructure (V2X), vehicle-to-pedestrian (V2P), vehicle-to-network (V2N) connectivity (Leiding B., 2018). This faster network makes this vehicle extraordinarily safe, secure and reliable on the road. High quality infotainment services will be provided by the 5G network in the self-driving cars. More opportunities for 5G innovation to upgrade autonomous car technology. These opportunities are explored by regular examination of the safety performance of the autonomous vehicle (Leiding B., 2018).

- Accuracy of information:

In the autonomous vehicle, all information is gathered through cameras, RADAR, LiDAR, HMI are used to identify traffic signals, road blocks, pot holes, nearby vehicles, objects in the surrounding. New GNSS (Global navigation Satellite System)/INS (Inertial Navigation System) can deliver reliable, cost effective and centimeter level accurate positioning for autonomous cars. It can also provide accurate information for a wide range of autonomous application, including automotive, robotic, construction and agricultural machinery.

In comparison to other sensors in autonomous vehicle, IMU (Inertial Measurement Unit) is unique among them. Because it requires no signals, no information from outside the vehicle. The IMU can measure the forces of acceleration (gravity and motion) and the angular rates of the vehicle, which is required for rotation of the vehicle. The GNSS/INS receiver can provide accurate position with the help of satellites. But when the connections of GNSS/INS are lost with satellites, the IMU completely measures the vehicles speed, direction, rotating speed, estimates its accurate position until the GNSS system can access with the satellites and recalculate the position of the vehicle ("CUBE", 2018).

- Controlled driving system:

The autonomous driving car starts with the perception system, which can estimate the surrounding area, passing vehicles speed, road blocks and traffic signals. The side cameras have taken 3D images from which a map is created, which specifies that where the vehicle is placed. When the location of the vehicle is known, then the system draws a map to reach destination. The ADS system decides through the road map that when rotations are come, where traffic signals are placed.

The ADS control all the driving scenarios at all condition. The IMU system can also percept the path accurately. While driving, the direction of the vehicle is changing through its position. So, while driving the direction of the vehicle is changing dynamically. Dynamic changes of direction require sensors with dynamic response. The IMU system is a fully environment independent technology. It can easily track the dynamically path accurately. It tracks position even in tricky scenarios such as slipping and skidding where tire lose friction.

- Correlativity with environment:

Autonomous cars are promised to modify the transportation system. These autonomous vehicles are saving millions of lives. It will also have an effect on the environment. But the effect of this vehicle on environment is good or bad is depend on technological and policies that have yet to be made. According to research from the Department of Energy (DOE), autonomous vehicle could reduce the energy consumption in transportation by 90% (Anderson et al., 2016). The autonomous vehicle also reduces the fuel economy as well as cost of fuel is also reduced. Ultimately the total transportation cost has been reduced.

Generally human driven cars are polluting the entire environments by disperse harmful gasses in the air which affect entire human beings. The autonomous vehicle is maintaining a relation with environment, so that the environment should not pollute.

Use of Blockchain in Autonomous Industry

Few decades ago, the self-driving cars were so far from reality. But in the upcoming years, the autonomous vehicle can become the future of transportation not only for passengers also for goods. For end user, the Decentralized Autonomous vehicle foundation makes a network which not only connects user to user, or vehicle to vehicle, it can also connect human beings with autonomous vehicle including cars, trucks, rovers and drones. Nowadays blockchain is also a highly growing technology, which is a chain of blocks. Each block contains information. In a blockchain every block is authenticated for a specified person. Each block contains a previous hah value and a current hash value. The current hash value is generated by the information containing that block. And the previous hash value is the current hash value of previous block. By using this advance method, the blockchain technology can provide more security for authenticated person. The blockchain is a peer-to-peer communication between nodes which is spread all over the world. And each node was controlled by specified authenticated person. By using this blockchain technology, the autonomous industry can provide more safe and secured transportation for all end users. It can provide various helps, such as point-to-point network communication, transparency, digital transactions, authentication, smart manufacturing in automotive industry, ride sharing, machine to machine communication, reliable and available network, personalized car insurance, smart contract using blockchain technology.

- P2P network communication:

P2P stands for peer to peer. Peer to peer network communication is also known as node to node network communication. In a peer to peer network system, all the systems that mean computers are connected to each other with a suitable network. In this communication system, there is no need of central server. All devices are connected to each other. If one device fails, no other devices are affected. Blockchain is a distributed ledger that allow to transactions with peers without the help of central authority.

Recently, in August 2019, in an experiment, trucks made machine to machine transactions without any human interaction (Mobility et al., 1997). This is possible in only blockchain platform. This machine to machine transaction is also happened in autonomous vehicle charging station, using blockchain platform this transaction is possible. In the block of both peers, the transaction information was stored. This information can only check by authorized person. In this scenario, blockchain is used for peer to peer network communication. While, a number of major projects can also be done by using peer to peer blockchain technology.

- Transparency:

The main aspect of blockchain technology is how this technology can provide security and privacy. This leads to some confusion about how privacy and transparency are both exist simultaneously. On a blockchain, the block is secured by cryptography. For each block, a hash value was generated by which next block was connected. If anyone try to change any information of any block, the current hash value was changed, and easily that block was detected in that blockchain.

Blockchain is introducing a new technology of a transparent and decentralized ledger. In this transparent ledger information can be verified and stored securely. This technology can be used in autonomous vehicle for verify the accuracy of the information, which are collected by the sensors of the vehicle by the surrounding environment. Thus, blockchain give a secured and transparent storage platform to the customers.

- Ride sharing:

Over the past decade, Lyft and Uber have made waves in auto industry, not only for cars, also provide services to the passengers (Mobility et al., 1997). Now, the multi-billion-dollar industry, ride-sharing offers both blockchain and e-commerce the opportunity to expand. Imagine the possibility to make a payment without a human, or without a central authority, or without a credit card, the passengers can easily pay their amount using blockchain. The most popular ride sharing companies are exploring driverless cars with the help of blockchain. Then after some decades, any type of transactions is happened without human interaction, only through blockchain.

- Reliable and available network:

In autonomous vehicle, a fast and reliable network is required for collecting huge amount of data by the sensors. For this reason, nowadays fast, reliable 5G network is adopted in market. This high-speed network is not available in everywhere. For this somewhere accidents can be taking place. Blockchain can be used as a trusted network. Blockchain follows point to point protocol by which every information can be transmitted to the vehicle at proper time. Furthermore, the autonomous vehicle is travelling many places, the block of the autonomous vehicle stores all the information about climate, weather, road conditions. That information is useful for another vehicle for travelling that place. The autonomous vehicle shares this type of traffic information through the blockchain network. So, the vehicle become faster and more reliable.

- V2X communication:

V2X stands for vehicle to everything. The autonomous vehicle can easily communicate to another vehicle. So, it performs V2V (vehicle to vehicle) communication. Blockchain offers advance technology by which the autonomous vehicle can be communicate with road side units, passing humans, clouds. Since the nature of blockchain is peer to peer, so that the combination of blockchain and the autonomous vehicle communicate at various points like, V2V (vehicle to vehicle), V2I (vehicle to infrastructure), V2P (vehicle to pedestrian), V2C (vehicle to cloud) ("Blockchain Cloud", 2019), that means V2X (vehicle to everything) communication is possible (Leiding B., 2018).

- Smart manufacturing in automotive industry:

The blockchain technology provides security to independent and associate automotive cars. Since, it can make an interface between autonomous industry and environment. It stores information in the block, by which it can ensure transparency, data accuracy, quick detection of problems, instant money transfer, and maintenance with regulations (Park & Tran, 2014). This technology can increase the development of autonomous industry while making it safer, more reliable and less expensive.

- Digital transactions:

Imagine a future transportation system, where everything is delivered to home via driverless car. The question is how the payments of the delivery can happen? Or, is the transaction is secured or not? Or, without a human the transaction is possible or not? Blockchain can give the best answer of all requirements. After delivery or after transportation via driverless car the transaction can be done using blockchain technology. Blockchain can provide safe and secured transactions between nodes. It offers point-to-point network where no third party can be involved. The autonomous vehicle has to passing with a transaction for home delivery for passengers, charging cost, fuel cost, parking charge, toll taxes. All of these payments are done by blockchain.

The autonomous vehicle is using his own blockchain account, that is his own block, where each transactions information is stored at all point. All the passengers contain his own block, from which he or she can make an easy transaction to the autonomous vehicle. In this transaction, no third party will be involved. As a result, using blockchain the transaction at all point is safe and secured.

- Safe and secured transportation:

The autonomous vehicle is launched in market to provide more safety, security to passengers, nearby vehicles. Also launched for reduce congestions, reduce road accidents, maintain all traffic rules, reduce travel time, reduce fuel and transportation cost. For proving more safety, it would require high frequency laser and high frequency radio technology for collecting accurate information. The autonomous vehicle guarantees the passengers for safe and secured transportation (Todd L., 2019).

Blockchain and the autonomous vehicle combine provide more security, since blockchain is a trusted network. Using blockchain technology, all the information is secured, so that the transportation will be safer.

- Authentication:

It is discussed before that the cameras, sensors are gathering a lot of information in the autonomous vehicle from the surrounding environment. This huge amount of data has to be sent to the vehicle securely. That means, a trusted secured policy has been required for secure such type of data. One of the best solutions for such a requirement is blockchain. At first, the blockchain technology has verified all the information, and then it guarantees the vehicle that all the data are collected is accurate and secured ("CUBE", 2018).

In nowadays, it is easy to hack a central server, or bank server, or a railway website. But blockchain is a unique technology which cannot be hackable. Using this advance technology in autonomous vehicle, all the information is collected through road side units, cameras, sensors, multiple sources are safe and secured.

- Smart contract using blockchain technology:

Blockchain can also facilitate safe transactions by allowing users to use smart contract to make payments at all condition. By using this smart contract technology in blockchain, user make payment directly to the charging station, or in toll gates, or in fuel cost. By using this smart contract technology, each block in a blockchain stores information about car records, highest speed, lowest speed, fuel cost, and mileage. This data is cryptographically verified by the blockchain technology. Then this vehicle can easily communicate with another vehicle or with any network. This can also make payments autonomously.

CONCLUSION

This chapter shows small fundamentals of autonomous vehicle, all the advantage, requirements, and solution using blockchain of autonomous vehicle. The blockchain technology is a great innovation in autonomous industry. In future, blockchain can be more effective than now for autonomous cars. Its advancements are exponentially increasing. So, blockchain can become the main part of autonomous vehicle. In future, blockchain is not only the main part of autonomous vehicle; it grows as the future of transportation.

REFERENCES

Anderson, J., Kalra, N., Stanley, K., Sorensen, P., Samaras, C., & Oluwatola, O. (2016). Autonomous Vehicle Technology: A Guide for Policymakers. doi:10.7249/RR443-2

Autonomy International Business Pte Ltd. (2019). *Blockchain Cloud for Autonomous Vehicles Table of Contents*. Author.

Cube Intelligence io. (2018). CUBE-Autonomous Car Network Security Platform based on Blockchain. https://medium.com/@cubeintel/cube-autonomous-car-security-platform-based-on-blockchain-bfc159abce09#:~:text=Blockchain%20Layer&text=CUBE%20uses%20block%2Dchain%20technology,and%20IoT%20or%20traffic%20center

Darren, C. (n.d.) What is vehicle platooning? https://www.drivingtests.co.nz/resources/what-is-vehicle-platooning/

Fagnant, D. J., & Kockelman, K. (2015). Preparing a nation for autonomous vehicles: Opportunities, barriers and policy recommendations. *Transportation Research Part A, Policy and Practice, 77,* 167–181. doi:10.1016/j.tra.2015.04.003

Federal Highway Administration. (2016). *Visual requirements for human drivers and autonomous vehicles*. Author.

Hori, K., & Sakajiri, A. (n.d.). Blockchain For Dummies. Windows, M. *Corporation.*

Leiding, B. (2018). Enabling the V2X Economy Revolution Using a Blockchain-Based Value Transaction Layer for Vehicular Ad-Hoc Networks. *Conference on Information Systems (MCIS),* 1–31.

Mobility, W., Database, D., & Transportation, F. O. R. (1997). *For Transportation.* Academic Press.

National Highway Traffic Safety Administration. (n.d.). Automated Vehicles for Safety. https://www.nhtsa.gov/technology-innovation/automated-vehicles-safety

Park, H.-S., & Tran, N.-H. (2014). Autonomy for Smart Manufacturing. *Journal of the Korean Society for Precision Engineering, 31*(4), 287–295. doi:10.7736/KSPE.2014.31.4.287

Pedrosa, A. R., & Pau, G. (2018). ChargeItUp: On blockchain-based technologies for autonomous vehicles. CRYBLOCK 2018 - Proceedings of the 1st Workshop on Cryptocurrencies and Blockchains for Distributed Systems, Part of MobiSys 2018, (June), 87–92. 10.1145/3211933.3211949

Pete, G. (2018). 10 Advantages of Autonomous Vehicles. https://www.itsdigest.com/10-advantages-autonomous-vehicles

Saranti, P. G., Chondrogianni, D., & Karatzas, S. (2019). Autonomous vehicles and blockchain technology are shaping the future of transportation. Advances in Intelligent Systems and Computing, 879(June), 797–803. doi:10.1007/978-3-030-02305-8_96

Todd Litman. (2019). Autonomous Vehicle Implementation Predictions: Implications for Transport Planning. Transportation Research Board Annual Meeting, 42(January), 36–42. 10.1613/jair.301

United States Department of Transportation. (n.d.). Decentralized blockchain networks that use automated smart contracts can potentially reduce ride-sharing costs by 20 percent. https://www.itsknowledgeresources.its.dot.gov

Wikipedia. (n.d.), Self-driving car. https://en.wikipedia.org/wiki/Self-driving_car

Chapter 11
Blockchain Security Using Secure Multi–Party Computation

Jenila Livingston L. M.
ⓘ https://orcid.org/0000-0002-6333-5751
Vellore Institute of Technology, India

Ashutosh Satapathy
Vellore Institute of Technology, India

Agnel Livingston L. G. X.
St. Xavier's Catholic College of Engineering, India

Merlin Livingston L. M.
Jeppiaar Institute of Technology, India

ABSTRACT

In secure multi-party computation (SMC), multiple distributed parties jointly carry out the computation over their confidential data without compromising data security and privacy. It is a new emerging cryptographic technique used in huge applications such as electronic auction bidding, electronic voting, protecting personal information, secure transaction processing, privacy preserving data mining, and privacy preserving cooperative control of connected autonomous vehicles. This chapter presents two model paradigms of SMC (i.e., ideal model prototype and real model prototype). It also deals with the type and applications of adversaries, properties, and the techniques of SMC. The three prime types of SMC techniques such as randomization, cryptographic techniques using oblivious transfer, and anonymization methods are discussed and illustrated by protective procedures with suitable examples. Finally, autonomous vehicle interaction leveraged with blockchain technology to store and use vehicle data without any human interaction is also discussed.

DOI: 10.4018/978-1-7998-3295-9.ch011

1. INTRODUCTION

Recently, people have started to demand that governments and companies protect their personal information more proactively, especially financial, health, demographic or other sensitive information. Large companies, by being conscientious stewards of their personal data, are now looking to retain the trust of their customers. The combination of encryption, delivery, and distributed computation by SMC in these situations can have a significant effect on data privacy and security. Advancement in cryptography techniques converge to help developers put applications of blockchain closer to the fundamental decentralizing principles on which this technology is based.

In a blockchain model, all parties maintain a global ordered set of records that are referred to as blocks. The blockchain database is not stored in any single location, meaning no centralized version of this information exists for a hacker to corrupt. The records it keeps are truly transparent, public and easily verifiable but the data is cryptographically stored inside. The blockchain is immutable, so no one can tamper with the data, inside the blockchain.

Two or multiple parties wish to conduct a computation based on their private inputs, but neither party is willing to reveal its own personal input to others. Secure Multi-Party Computation creates methods for multiple parties to jointly compute a function on their inputs for keeping their data private. It is a subfield of cryptography also known as Multi Party Computation, secure computation or privacy-preserving computation. This cryptography model protects participants'/ parties' privacy from each other. This chapter provides a framework and serves as a guideline for researchers to define novel SMC related problems for their specific computations.

This chapter is broken into seven sections. First section compacts with the introductory part of Secure Multi-Party Computation; followed by section two which describes different SMC models. Third section deals with type of adversaries and fourth section discusses the properties of SMC. Different SMC techniques are explained elaborately with suitable examples in section five. Section six deliberates SMC in block chain applications and finally this chapter ended with the conclusive part.

2. SMC MODELS

Multiple parties carry out computation over their confidential data without any loss of data security or privacy. Let multiple parties $P_1, P_2.....P_n$ want to perform computation C_i on their private data. $D_1, D_2.....D_n$ be the data corresponding to $P_1, P_2.....P_n$. D_i should not be accessible to any P_j during computation C_i where i^1j and $j = 1,2.....n$. Generally two model paradigms are popular in SMC; Ideal model prototype and Real model prototype (Shukla & Sadashivappa, 2012).

Ideal model prototype of SMC is also called Uncorrupted Trusted Third Party (UTTP). In ideal model, there exists an incorruptible trusted party (UTTP); who can be trusted by all the parties; to whom each protocol participant sends its data/ input to perform computation. This trusted party computes the function on its own and sends back the appropriate output to each party (Figure 1). Thus the privacy of the inputs is preserved. In **real model prototype** of SMC, no external party is used. All the parties agree on a common protocol to exchange data for preserving privacy and maintain correctness result (Figure 2).

Let D_i is private data of P_i, $i = 1,2.....n$. In ideal model, data are send to UTTP directly where as in real model, $f(D_1), f(D_2).....f(D_n)$ exchange between the parties.

In ideal model, the computation result may be wrong, if few parties behave maliciously and supply invalid input to the UTTP. The privacy will be destroyed if an UTTP turns corrupt and it is the major limitation of this model. The implementation process is costly due to the cost of working model of this incorruptible trusted party UTTP.

Figure 1. Ideal model prototype of SMC

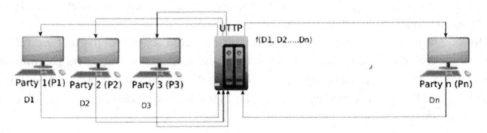

In real model prototype parties do not contribute definite inputs with each other and there will be chance of an adversary (a party) can carry out passive or active attack.

Figure 2. Real model prototype of SMC

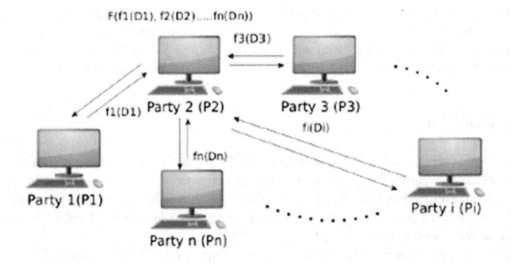

3. ADVERSARIES

Adversaries faced by the different protocols can be categorized according to how willing they are to deviate from the protocol. There are different SMC protocols have been developed to provide security against above adversaries. Some of them are Yao's Garbled Circuit, Ben-Or, Goldwasser and Wigderson (BGW), Goldreich-Micali-Wigderson (GMW), Chaum, Crepeau and Damgard (CCD) etc.

Type of adversaries:

An adversary can be static or adaptive in nature. A **static adversary** is malicious in nature, prior to the execution of protocol. An **adaptive adversary** is malicious during the execution of protocol. There are essentially two types of adversaries, each giving rise to different forms of security.

- A **semi-honest adversary**: It is a passive adversary model that follows a protocol but tries to learn other than the output of the computation without deviate from the protocol, i.e., it gathers information out of the protocol. Protocols in the semi-honest model are quite efficient and starting point for achieving higher levels of security.

- A **corrupt or malicious adversary:** It is an active adversary, does not follows the protocol and tries to learn other than result. The adversary may arbitrarily deviate from the protocol execution in its attempt to cheat.

The applications of adversaries are as follows:

(i) **Private Information Retrieval:** The client requests the server to provide i^{th} bit/word without the server knowing anything about it. The client is also not aware of bit/ word sequence.

(ii) **Privacy-Preserving Data Mining:** One or multiple parties execute data mining operation on the private database of another party without knowing any details.

(iii) **Privacy-Preserving Database Query:** One party has a string S_i and other party has database D to be searched. Such that other party does not know about S_i and first one does not know about D.

(iv) **Privacy-Preserving Intrusion Detection:** Party B enters the hacker's information and searches A's database; B only gets the comparison results.

4. PROPERTIES OF SMC

Let D_i is private data of P_i, i = 1,2.....n. We wish to perform a computation $f(D_1, D_2.....D_n) = (Y_1, Y_2..... Y_n)$ where Y_i is private output value for P_i then the SMC aims to ensure the following basic properties

(a) Correctness: Ensure the parties correctly compute the correct output f or not. This correctness goal comes in two flavors: either the honest parties are guaranteed to compute the correct output, or they abort if they find an error.

(b) Input Privacy: For $P_1, P_2.....P_n$, each party's input remains private. No information about the private data of the parties can be inferred from the messages sent during the execution of the protocol. The only information that can be inferred about the private data is the output of the function.

(c) Output Delivery: The protocol never ends until everyone receives an output.

(d) Fairness: If one party gets the answer, so does everyone else.

The following actions are necessary to be checked for the SMC operations but all these cases need not to be satisfied for all the SMC operations.

- Data stored at remote site must be obscured.
- Data must be obscured during transition.

- Prevent information access patterns of data at remote site from adversaries.
- Perform operations on obscured data at remote site.

5. SMC TECHNIQUES

SMC deals with the problem of jointly computing a function among a set of distrusting parties. Three main techniques used in SMC are:

(i)   Anonymization methods
(ii)   Randomization methods
(iii) Cryptographic techniques

In anonymization methods, the identity of the parties is hidden rather than hiding individual parties' data. It is the ideal model where TTP is used (Shukla & Sadashivappa, 2012). In randomization methods, participants use random numbers for obscuring their input. In cryptographic techniques, secret inputs are encrypted at participant's side and computation is performed on encrypted data. Randomization and cryptographic techniques are elaborately discussed in succeeding session.

5.1 Randomization Technique

In this technique, data distortion methods are used to add noise to the original input. This method uses perturbation methods that produce an appropriate balance between privacy preservation and knowledge discovery. Additive perturbation is based on private summation protocol where randomized noise is added to the data records. In multiplicative perturbation, the random rotation techniques are used to perturb the records. Firstly the participants randomize their data and transmit the randomized data to the other neighboring participants (receiver). Secondly the data receiver estimates the original distribution of the data by employing a distribution reconstruction algorithm. The limitation of randomization technique involves there is no standardize algorithm for a single operation.

5.1.1 Private Summation Protocol

In this protocol the parties use random numbers for obscuring their inputs and perform computation over obscured inputs. Algorithm for private summation protocol is given below.

Algorithm:
Given: Each party P_i with input D_i

Step 1:   Generate random number $r_{i,j}$ to its neighbor Pj.

Step 2:   Wait for $r_{j,i}$ from each neighbor Pj.

Step 3:   Compute $D_i' = D_i + \sum_j r_{j,i} - \sum_j r_{i,j}$

Step 4:   Publish D_i' to each other.

Step 5:   Output $= \sum_i D_i'$

Figure 3. Private summation protocol

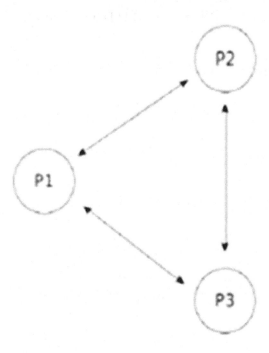

Assume three parties, P_1, P_2 and P_3 with inputs D1,D2 and D3 connected with each other as Figure 3 Each party generates random number $r_{i,j}$ to its neighbor Pj and $D_i^{'}$ is calculated as given below(Kreitz, 2012).

$$D_1^{'} = D_1 + r_{1,2} + r_{1,3} + r_{2,1} + r_{3,1}$$

$$D_2^{'} = D_2 + r_{2,1} + r_{2,3} + r_{1,2} + r_{3,2}$$

$$D_3^{'} = D_3 + r_{3,1} + r_{3,2} + r_{3,1} + r_{2,3}$$

They publish $D_i^{'}$ to each other. Finally output will be calculated by summating the values, $\sum_i D_i^{'} = D_1^{'} + D_2^{'} + D_3^{'}$. The working procedure of three-party protocol algorithm is given below and the five steps process is illustrated with Figure 4.

Three-Party Protocol Algorithm:
Given: Parties P_1, P_2 and P_3 have inputs D_1, D_2, D_3 respectively.
    Step 1: P_1 chooses a random number r_1.
    Step 2:   Computes $r_1 D_1$ and sends it to P_2.
    Step 3: P_2 computes $r_1 D_1 D_2$, sends to P3.

Step 4: P_3 computes $r_1 D_1 D_2 D_3$, sends to P1.

Step 5:   P1 computes $r_1^{-1}(r_1 D_1 D_2 D_3)$; sends $D_1 D_2 D_3$ to P_2 and P_3.

Figure 4. Three party protocol

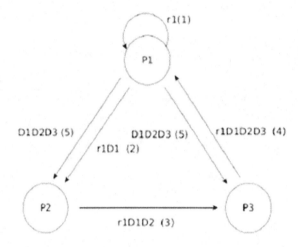

5.2 Cryptographic Techniques

Cryptographic techniques provide well defined model for privacy. There also exists vast toolset of cryptographic algorithms and techniques for privacy preserving in securing multiple party data. The cryptographic techniques solutions for SMC uses basic building blocks for secure computation (Oleshchuk & Zadorozhny, 2007), few of the important building blocks are: Yao's Millionaires Problem, Homomorphic Encryption and Oblivious Transfer.

5.2.1 Oblivious Transfer (OT)

Oblivious Transfer is one of the fundamental building blocks of cryptographic protocols (Chou & Orlandi, 2015). It is a protocol where party P_1 transfer many pieces of information to party P_2 but remain oblivious about which piece of information retrieved by party P_2 as shown in Figure 5.

The working procedure of Oblivious Transfer (Buchanan, 2016) for private information retrieval is shown in Figure 6 and the corresponding algorithm is exemplified below.

Oblivious Transfer Algorithm:

Step 1:   Alice (Party 1) and Bob (Party 2) agree upon shared input 'g' and 'p'.

Step 2:   Party 1 generates a random number 'a' and computes $A = g^a$ mod p. Party 1 sends index number of its messages $m_0 = 0$, $m_1 = 1$ with A to Party 2.

Step 3:   Party 2 generates a random number 'b' and computes $B = g^b$ mod p / $A(g^b$ mod p) based on its choice 0/1 and sends it to Party 1. Party 2 also generate $K_s = A^b$ mod p.

Step 4:   Party 1 generates $K_0 = B^a$ mod p and $K_1 = (B/A)^a$ mod p and Sends $E_{K0}(m_0)$ and $E_{K1}(m_1)$ to Party 2.

Figure 5. Black-box of OT mechanism

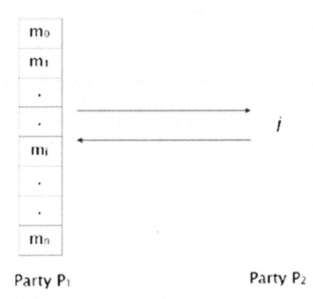

Figure 6. OT for private information retrieval

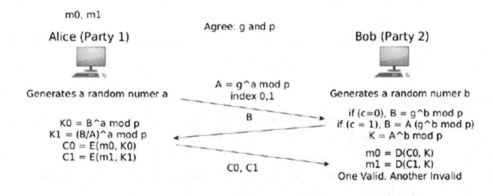

Step 5:   Party 2 decrypts both messages using Ks; but one message only gives valid output.

Example:

Given: Alice's $m_0 = 10$, $m_1 = 12$.

Step 1:   Alice (Party 1) and Bob (Party 2) agree upon shared input $g = 3$ and $p = 77$.

Step 2:   Party 1 generates $a = 5$ and computes $A = 3^5 \bmod 77 = 12$. Party 1 sends index number of its messages $m_0 = 0$, $m_1 = 1$ with A=12 to Party 2.

Step 3:   Party 2 generates $b = 4$ and computes $B = 3^4 \bmod 77/ 12\ (3^4 \bmod 77) = 4 / 48$ based on its choice 0/1 and send it to Party 1. Party 2 also generate $K_s = 12^4 \bmod 77 = 23$

Step 4:   If $c = 0$ at party 2, party 1 generates $K_0 = 23$ and $K_1 = 0.0041$ and sends $E_{K0}(10)$ and $E_{K1}(12)$ to Party 2.

Step 5:   Party 2 decrypts both messages using Ks;
         i.e., $D_K s(E_{K0}(10)) = 10$, $D_K s(E_{K1}(12)) = $ garbage.

5.2.2 Yao's Garbled Circuit (YGC)

YGC is one of the important protocols used for secure m-party computation. It is used to evaluate Boolean function. One of the main issues when working with Yao-based protocol is that the function to be securely evaluated must be represented as a circuit (Yao's Garbled Circuit), usually consisting of XOR and AND gates; as most real-world programs contain loops and complex data structures which is really a high non-trivial task.

Figure 7. Circuit diagram of D1^D2^D3

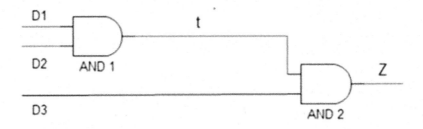

The 2-party computation protocol can be extended to m-party protocol and the algorithm for 2-party protocol is given below.

Algorithm (2-party):
Given a digital circuit where P_1 is a generator and P_2 is an evaluator.
    Step 1: P_1 generates GCT and encrypts each row of GCT.
    Step 2: P_1 sends both GCT and the key associated with its input.
    Step 3: P_1 and P_2 do oblivious transfer. P_2 obtains the key associated with its input.
    Step 4: P_2 computes circuit output and sends to P_1

Figure 8. Circuit diagram of x^y

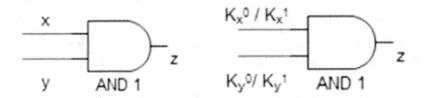

The circuit diagram of $x^\wedge y$ (Figure 8) for 2-party computation protocol and the corresponding GCT truth generation table (Table 1) is given below. Kx^0, Kx^1, Ky^0 and Ky^1 are the random numbers generated by P_1. The steps involved in this processes are

- P_1 shuffles the GCT; send GCT and Kx^a to P_2.
- P_2 does oblivious transfer for Ky^b.
- P_2 decrypts one row successfully and send the output to P_1.

Table 1. AND truth table and its GCT generation

x	y	z
0	0	0
0	1	0
1	0	0
1	1	1

x'	y'	z'	GCT
K_x^0	K_y^0	0	$E_{K_x^0}(E_{K_y^0}(0))$
K_x^0	K_y^1	0	$E_{K_x^0}(E_{K_y^1}(0))$
K_x^1	K_y^0	0	$E_{K_x^1}(E_{K_y^0}(0))$
K_x^1	K_y^1	1	$E_{K_x^1}(E_{K_y^1}(1))$

Assume 3, 5, 7 and 9 are the random numbers generated by P_1. P_1 shuffles the GCT and send GCT and $Kx^a=3$ to P_2. P_2 does the oblivious transfer for Ky^b. If choice = 0 then 7 else 9 will be retrieved. P_2 decrypts one row successfully and send the output to P_1.

Table 2. AND truth table and its GCT generation

x	y	z
0	0	0
0	1	0
1	0	0
1	1	1

x'	y'	z'	GCT
3	7	0	$E_3(E_7(0))$
3	9	0	$E_3(E_9(0))$
5	7	0	$E_5(E_7(0))$
5	9	1	$E_5(E_9(1))$

The 3-party computation protocol can be extended to m-party protocol and the circuit diagram of $D1^\wedge D2^\wedge D3$ (Figure 9) for 3-party computation protocol is given below. For the first circuit, P_1 is a generator and P_2 is an evaluator. For the second circuit, P_2 is a generator and P_3 is an evaluator.

Figure 9. Circuit diagram of D1^D2^D3

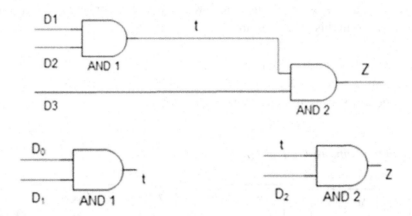

Algorithm (3-party):

Given: For digital Circuit C_1, P_1 is a generator and P_2 is an evaluator. Digital Circuit C_2, P_2 is a generator and P_3 is an evaluator.

    Step 1: P_1 generates GCT_1 and encrypts each row of GCT_1.

    Step 2: P_1 sends GCT_1 and the key associated with its input.

    Step 3: P_1 and P_2 do oblivious transfer. P_2 obtains the key associated with its input.

    Step 4: P_2 computes circuit output and one will be valid.

    Step 5:   Repeat step 1 to step 4 for circuit C_2.

    Step 6: P_3 sends final output to P_1 and P_2.

5.2.3 Improved Yao's Garbled Circuit

Improved Yao's Garbled Circuit is another protocol for secure m-party computation that is used to evaluate both arithmetic and logical functions. Each party creates shares of its secret data based on number of parties' involvement and distributes shares among the parties. After distribution, each party holds shares from different parties' only i.e. one share from each party. Parties perform computation on shares individually. Share their outputs to compute the final output. Yao's backend circuit is a mixture of additive (XOR) and/or multiplicative (AND) gates where intermediate outputs are also secretly shared. The 2-party computation protocol for the Improved Yao's Garbled Circuit is given below.

Algorithm (2-party):

Given: Yao's digital circuit and parties P_1 and P_2 with secret 'u' and 'v'

    Step 1: P_1 creates two shares 'u_1' and 'u_2' for 'u'.

    Step 2:   Similarly P_2 creates 'v_1' and 'v_2' for 'v'.

    Step 3: P_1 and P_2 exchange their shares with each other i.e. 'u_2' to P_2 and 'v_1' to P_1.

    Step 4: P_1 computes $O_1 = f(u_1, v_1)$ on its share (u_1, v_1). Similarly P_2 computes $O_2 = f(u_2, v_2)$ on its share (u_2, v_2).

    Step 5: P_1 and P_2 share their outputs O_1 and O_2.

    Step 6:   At last, P_1 and P_2 compute the final output $f(O_1, O_2)$.

Algorithm explanation with example:

Phase 1: Secret shares generation (2-party)
Given: Parties P_1 and P_2 with secret '7' and '9' respectively.
  Step 1: P_1 selects a random no. '3' and computes $(7 \oplus 3) = 4$.
  Step 2: P_2 selects a random no. '5' and computes $(9 \oplus 5) = 12$.
  Step 3: For P_1, $(u_1, u_2) = (3, 4)$; P_2, $(v_1, v_2) = (5, 12)$.
  Step 4: P_1 sends '$u_2 = 4$' to P_2 and P_2 sends '$v_1 = 5$' to P_1.
  Step 5: After exchange, P_1 holds $(u_1, v_1) = (3, 5)$ and P_2 holds $(u_2, v_2) = (4, 12)$.
Note: Finally, P_1 and P_2 will have $(3, 5)$ and $(4, 12)$ respectively

Phase 2: Addition (2-party)
  After secret shares generation 2-party addition will be done. Here u and v values will be taken from P_1 and P_2.
  Step 6: The final output (w) is computed by using addition gate (XOR), $w = u \oplus v$

The first party (P_1) sets its output to be, $w_1 = u_1 \oplus v_1$
The second party (P_2) sets its output to be $w_2 = u_2 \oplus v_2$
So the final output (Canetti & Rosen, 2009),

$$w_1 \oplus w_2 = u_1 \oplus v_1 \oplus u2 \oplus v2 = u1 \oplus u2 \oplus v1 \oplus v2 = u \oplus v$$

Figure 10 represents the addition gate over secret inputs. The 2-party addition process is illustrated below with the same example.

Figure 10. Addition over secret inputs

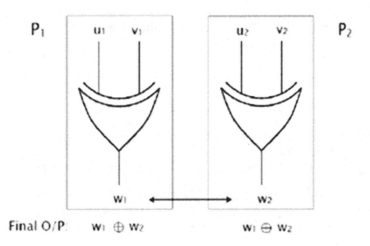

Example (2-party Addition):

Given: Consider the previous example, P_1's secret shares $(u_1, v_1) = (3, 5)$ and P_2's secret shares (u_2, v_2) = (4, 12).

Step 1: P_1 performs $(u_1 \oplus v_1) = (3 \oplus 5) = 6$.

Step 2: P_2 performs $(u_2 \oplus v_2) = (4 \oplus 12) = 8$.

Step 3:   Both P_1 and P_2 share their outputs; i.e., 6 to P_2 and 8 to P_1.

Step 4: P_1 computes $(6 \oplus 8) = 14$. <final output>.

Step 5: P_2 computes $(6 \oplus 8) = 14$. <final output>.

Note: Final output 14, same as XOR of P_1's input and P_2's input $(7 \oplus 9) = 14$.

Multiplication Gate (AND)

Let $w = u \times v$

$$= (u_1 \oplus u_2) \times (v_1 \oplus v_2)$$

$$= (x_n...x_2x_1 \oplus y_n...y_2y_1) \times (t_n...t_2t_1 \oplus z_n...z_2z_1)$$

where u, v are the inputs from P_1, P_2; $u_1 = x_n...x_2x_1$ (Binary Representation).
    Similarly

$$v_2 = y_n...y_2y_1, t_n...t_2t_1, z_n...z_2z_1]$$

Here one party generates all possible output which is called generator. The other party is an evaluator which retrieves correct output based on its secret shares (y_i, z_i) using oblivious transfer.
    Assume P1 is a generator and it generates $(w_{00}, w_{01}, w_{11}, w_{10})$ then

$$w_{ab} = w_i \oplus (x_i \oplus y_i) \times (t_i \oplus z_i) [w_i = x_i \oplus t_i]$$

The below table 3 describes the GCT generation for the known (x_i, t_i)

Table 3. GCT generation

index	(y_i, z_i)	w_{ab}
1	(0, 0)	$w_{00} = (x_i \oplus t_i) \oplus (x_i \oplus 0).(t_i \oplus 0)$
2	(0, 1)	$w_{01} = (x_i \oplus t_i) \oplus (x_i \oplus 0).(t_i \oplus 1)$
3	(1, 1)	$w_{11} = (x_i \oplus t_i) \oplus (x_i \oplus 1).(t_i \oplus 1)$
4	(1, 0)	$w_{10} = (x_i \oplus t_i) \oplus (x_i \oplus 1).(t_i \oplus 0)$

P_1 Transfers index numbers 1, 2, 3, 4 with w_i to the evaluator P_2. The evaluator (P_2) retrieves correct output based on its secret shares A.

At Evaluator (P_2):
If choice = 1 then w_{00}, output $w_i \oplus w_{00} = w$.
If choice = 2 then w_{01}, output $w_i \oplus w_{01} = w$.
If choice = 3 then w_{11}, output wi $\oplus w_{11} = w$.
If choice = 4 then w_{10}, output wi $\oplus w_{10} = w$.

Based on the choice, corresponding output will be correctly retrieved and others will be left in garbage. This procedure is illustrated with the below example

Example (2-party Multiplication):
Known: P_1's $(u_1, v_1) = (3, 5)$

The binary representation of $(u_1, v_1) = (0011, 0101)$

Step 1: Start from LSB of u_1 and v_1. $(x_1, t_1) = (1, 1)$
Step 2: P_1 generates w_{ab} . $(w_{00}, w_{01}, w_{11}, w_{10}) = (1, 0, 0, 0)$.
Step 3: P_1 and P_2 use oblivious transfer; here P_1 has $(w_{00}, w_{01}, w_{11}, w_{10})$
Step 4: P_1 transfers index numbers 1, 2, 3, 4 with $w_1 = 0$ to P_2.
Step 5: At P_2, $(u_2, v_2) = (4, 12) = (0100, 1100)$. As, $(y_1, z_1) = (0, 0)$ so, choice = 1.
Step 6: P_2 successfully retrieves $w_{00} = 1$. Final O/P bit = $0 \oplus 1 = 1$.
Step 7: Repeat the above steps until $(x_i, t_i) = (x_4, t_4)$.

5.2.4 Digital Circuit Representation: Improved Yao's Garbled Circuit

The digital circuit of full adder for two parties (P1 + P2) is shown in Figure 11.

Figure 11. Digital circuit of full adder (P1 + P2)

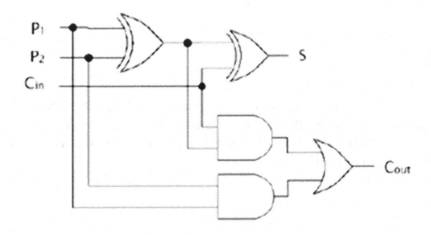

In Yao's circuit, OR gate will be replaced by AND and XOR gates as in Figure 12.

Figure 12. Yao's circuit representation of full adder (P1 + P2)

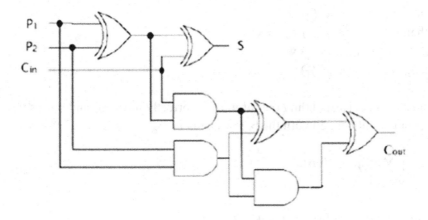

The digital circuit of full adder for three parties (P1 + P2 + P3) is shown in Figure 13.

Figure 13. Digital circuit of full adder (P1 + P2 + P3)

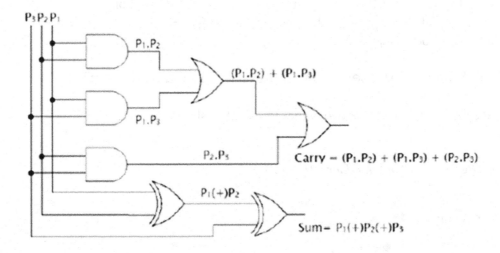

In Yao's circuit (Gkikas, 2014), OR gates will be replaced by AND and XOR gates. Thus the digital circuit of full adder for three parties (P1 + P2 + P3) after replacement is shown in Figure 14.

For each XOR and AND gate, result is computed as discussed earlier. The parties' inputs and intermediate outputs are secretly shared between parties.

Figure 14. Yao's circuit representation of full adder (P1 + P2 + P3)

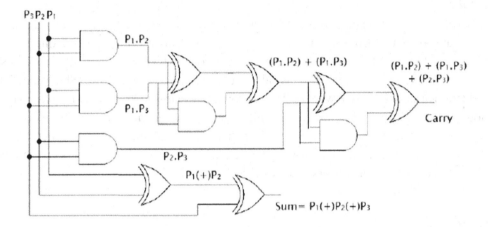

6. SMC IN BLOCKCHAIN APPLICATIONS

SMC can be used to solve dining cryptographer and Yao's millionaire problems. In dining cryptographer problem, there are 'n' cryptographers who respect each other want to make an anonymous payment, i.e., they do not want to reveal who has done the actual payment, but they will get to know only the paid status. In Yao's millionaire problem, 'm' millionaires wish to find who is wealthier without revealing their data. These problems can be solved using SMC.

Bitcoin application allows the users to transfer bitcoins or currency, securely over a blockchain. In fair MPC protocol all parties receive the output or no party does. This is extremely important for applications like contract signing, bidding and auctions. The computing parties register on the blockchain and connect to other registered parties to form the distributed network. The blockchain is entrusted with doing the entire book keeping, as well as identifying cheaters and handling disputes (Zyskind, 2016).

6.1 SMC: Blockchain Technology in Autonomous Vehicles

Autonomous driving or transport technologies have drawn considerable interest from both academia and industry. Blockchain technology has become a tool that is quickly being integrated into the world of finance, governance, logistics as well as the motor industry. Researches carried out a test run in which autonomous vehicles made machine-to-machine payments to facilitate financial settlement using a blockchain platform without any human interaction. The vehicle can communicate with various networks and pay for parking or tolls autonomously. The data of the vehicle can only be accessed by permissible parties. This would then allow service providers or government entities to verify credentials and track certain data in real time.

The range of data shared using this advanced technology would be anything from navigation, charging and refueling services, validity of licenses as well as paying and recording balances for payable services like tolls and parking. By storing data on a blockchain, digital certificates for information including vehicle identity, ownership, warranties and current mileage can be securely stored in an electronic wallet. This data will be cryptographically verified and immutably stored on the blockchain. This platform could also be used for ride sharing and secure exchange of traffic information to alleviate congestion (Jenkinson, 2019).

Connected vehicle technologies, on the other hand, are also being used to enhance the safety and mobility of our transport network by the situational awareness and traffic state estimation through vehicle-to-vehicle (V2V) and vehicle-to-infrastructure communications, which can allow applications such as cooperative collision alert, providing traffic signal status information in real time (Shladover, 2018).

The introduction of autonomous powered vehicles provides possibilities for cleaner, faster, and smarter transportation. Broadcasting information to the vehicles and infrastructures around, however, threatens protection and privacy. Command decisions based on this knowledge are therefore vulnerable to malicious attacks. Cooperative management strategy integrating effective multi-stakeholder computation improves resistance to latency and adverse attacks (Li et al., 2019).

7. CONCLUSION

In this chapter, the secure Multi-Party computation, SMC models and its applications, type of adversaries such as static, adaptive, semi-honest and malicious adversaries, goals and actions required to achieve SMC are concisely discussed. Different types of SMC techniques, primarily randomization; cryptographic techniques using oblivious transfer and Yao's garbled circuit protocol are exemplified with suitable examples. This blockchain technology used in vehicles allows for digital currency transactions and other confidentiality services to happen autonomously in a cryptographically secure network.

REFERENCES

BuchananB. (2016). *Oblivious Transfer.* https://asecuritysite.com/encryption/ot

Canetti, R., & Rosen, A. (2009). General secure two party and multi party computation. *Cryptography & Game Theory.* https://www.cs.tau.ac.il/~canetti/f09-materials/f09-scribe4.pdf

Chou, T., & Orlandi, C. (2015). The Simplest Protocol for Oblivious Transfer, *Technische Universieit Eindhoven and Aarhus University.* https://eprint.iacr.org/2015/267.pdf

Gkikas, K. (2014). *Yao's Garbled Circuit.* https://homepages.cwi.nl/~schaffne/courses/crypto/2014/presentations/Kostis_Yao.pdf

Jenkinson, G. (2019). *Can Blockchain Become an Integral Part of Autonomous Vehicles?* https://cointelegraph.com/news/can-blockchain-become-an-integral-part-of-autonomous-vehicles

Kreitz, G. (2012). Secure Multi-Party Computation. *KTH - Royal Institute of Technology.* http://www.csc.kth.se/~buc/PPC/Slides/kreitz-pet-course-mpc.pdf

Li, T., Lin, L., & Gong, S. (2019). *AutoMPC: Efficient Multi-Party Computation for Secure and Privacy-Preserving Cooperative Control of Connected Autonomous Vehicles.* http://ceur-ws.org/Vol-2301/paper_13.pdf

Oleshchuk, V. & Zadorozhny, V. (2007). Secure Multi-Party Computations and Privacy Preservation: Results and Open Problems. *Telektronikk: Telenor's Journal of Technology*, *103*(2).

Shladover, S. E. (2018). Connected and automated vehicle systems: Introduction and overview. *Journal of Intelligent Transport Systems*, *22*(3), 190–200. doi:10.1080/15472450.2017.1336053

Shukla, S., & Sadashivappa, G. (2012). Secure Multi-Party Computation (SMC): A Review. *International Conference on Communication, Computing and Information Technology (ICCCMIT)*.

Zyskind, G. (2016). *Efficient Secure Computation Enabled by Blockchain Technology*. Massachusetts Institute of Technology. https://dspace.mit.edu/ bitstream/handle/1721.1/ 105933/964695278-MIT. pdf?sequence=1&isAllowed=y

ADDITIONAL READING

Cramer, R. (2003). *Efficient Multi-party Computation over Rings*, from https://homepages.cwi.nl/~fehr/mypapers/CFIK03.pdf

Dhooghe, S. (2018). *Applying Multiparty Computation to Car Access Provision*, from https://www.esat.kuleuven.be/cosic/publications/thesis-296.pdf

Evans, D., Kolesnikov, V., & Rosulek, M. (2018). *A Pragmatic Introduction to Secure Multi-Party Computation*. NOW Publishers, from https://www.cs.virginia.edu/~evans/pragmaticmpc/pragmaticmpc.pdf

Fattaneh Bayatbabolghani & Marina Blanton. (2018). *Secure Multi-Party Computation Tutorial*, from http://people.ischool.berkeley.edu/~fbayatba/Publications/CCS_Presentation.pdf

Hirt, M. (2001). Multi-Party Computation: Efficient Protocols, General Adversaries, and Voting. Dissertation submitted to Eth Zurich, from https://www.it.iitb.ac.in/~madhumita/research_topics/Multi-Party%20Computation.pdf

Nikolaj Volgushev et al. (2019). *Conclave: secure multi-party computation on big data*, from https://people.csail.mit.edu/malte/pub/papers/2019-eurosys-conclave.pdf

Zhao, C., Zhao, S., Zhao, M., Chen, Z., Gao, C.-Z., Li, H., & Tan, Y. (2019). Secure Multi-Party Computation: Theory, practice and applications. *Information Sciences*, *476*, 357–372. doi:10.1016/j.ins.2018.10.024

Chapter 12
Issues and Challenges (Privacy, Security, and Trust) in Blockchain-Based Applications

Siddharth M. Nair
Vellore Institute of Technology, Chennai, India

Varsha Ramesh
Vellore Institute of Technology, Chennai, India

Amit Kumar Tyagi
iD https://orcid.org/0000-0003-2657-8700
Vellore Institute of Technology, Chennai, India

ABSTRACT

The major issues and challenges in blockchain over internet of things are security, privacy, and usability. Confidentiality, authentication, and control are the challenges faced in security issue. Hence, this chapter will discuss the challenges and opportunities from the prospective of security and privacy of data in blockchain (with respect to security and privacy community point of view). Furthermore, the authors will provide some future trends that blockchain technology may adapt in the near future (in brief).

1. INTRODUCTION

Blockchain introduced the world's most famous cryptocurrency concept, bitcoin (Tomov, 2019). It is an improvement on the ideals of a peer to peer network and creates a universal data set which can be trusted by all users despite the fact that they do not trust each other. It creates a database or a record of transactions that are shared, trusted and protected, where stable and encrypted copies of data are saved on every node in the system. Financial incentives like native network tokens are applied onto the system to make it more immune to faults and collision.

DOI: 10.4018/978-1-7998-3295-9.ch012

Blockchain has been useful in other sectors of technology. For example, it has been implemented in IoT to improve security and efficiency of IoT based devices. For example, in the agriculture industry, research shows that Blockchain allows food to be tracked from farms to supermarkets in a few seconds. So, it helps in reducing illegal harvesting and shipping scams (Hackernoon, n.d.a). It is also used to keep tabs on overflowing commodities. This works on the principle that data tampering cannot take place using Blockchain, thereby making hacking difficult. Using Blockchain in IoT has its own issue. Data mining in Blockchain needs a large amount of computation and processing power. Most IoT devices do not have the required power to do so.

Blockchain is also hinted to be able to improve security and efficiency in cyber physical systems. For example, studies show that Blockchain can be used in autonomous automobile industry. A Blockchain based database can be used to store the identity information of newly created vehicles (Dorri, Steger, Kanhere et al, 2017). Thus, the information of newly created vehicles can be stored securely in an E-wallet. The data stored cannot be tampered with and will be cryptographically verified. This will enable the vehicle to communicate with a number of networks and thus pay bills, tolls, fines autonomously.

Blockchain technology has been used in social media and networks, to fix many issues. On social media, fake news spreads as quickly as good content. Blockchain helps in fighting fake news using its ledger system. Content and identification can be verified at any time. This also makes collection of data a lot simpler. Blockchain also makes it possible to track data and monitor user interaction with the content. This helps social media channels estimate the likes, shares and views more accurately.

In recent times, the popularity of crowdsourcing systems has increased massively despite the certain privacy issues and challenges faced by it. Blockchain based crowdsourcing systems were employed to solve the problem of small value transactions in crowdsourcing (Li et al., 2019). Similarly, the acquisition and computation of data using some sensing devices to share the gathered data, also known as crowdsensing has been growing in popularity in recent times. Blockchain, being a distributed database in which data cannot be tampered, has the right characteristics to improve the security of crowdsensing applications.Another important where Blockchain is used is the cloudlet (Xu et al., n.d.). Cloudlet is a group of computer systems designed to swiftly render cloud computing resources to the users to enhance the performance of multimedia applications. The security and integrity of the offloaded data that are processed by cloudlets have to be preserved especially with the increasing user requirements of migrating tasks. The characteristics of Blockchain prove to be favorable in these circumstances.

Blockchain is also used to improve security and trust in fog, edge and cloud computing. Fog computing is a decentralized computing foundation in which data, computation, storage and applications are placed some place between the cloud and the source of data. Fog computing has a distributed architecture and requires a technique to protect network resources and transactions. Similarly, edge is a distributed structure in which data is computed at the edge of the network where generation of data takes place instead of computing it in a centralized data processing repository.Cloud computing, is a technology that makes computing services like database, storage, software and analytics available on the internet. For these purposes, an equally distributed security structure is required. Blockchain is a distributed ledger in which data cannot be tampered. So, it creates distributed trust and security.

Note that many useful/ possibleapplications of blockchain have been discussed in (**Sawal et al., 2019**). Hence, now the remaining part of this chapter is organized as:

- Section 2 discusses related work Blockchain technology and Blockchain enabled applications

- Section 3 discusses motivation behind this work, interested/ useful facts/ points behind writing this chapter.
- Section 4 discusses importance and benefits of Blockchaintechnology in current era, i.e., useful to society or citizens/ business (i.e., in present and future).
- Section 5 discusses many critical issues towards existing Blockchain based applications.
- Section 5 discusses several tools, methods,existing algorithms, available for Blockchain based applications.
- Further, section 7 discusses/ provides several opportunities for future researchers (with identifying several research gaps towards Blockchain based applications).
- Section 8 provides an open discussion with discussing that "Is really Blockchain technology is the necessity of future technology, or just a trend"?
- In last in section 9, this chapter will be concluded in brief.

2. RELATED WORK

In this chapter, we use block chain technology to analyze some of the different applications. We also address the problems of security and privacy, as well as the approaches suggested.

Blockchain in finance: Initially Blockchain was established as a framework for the common decentralized digital currency Bitcoin. In many digital currencies like Altercoin, Peercoin, Ethereum (Wood, 2014), Karma (Vishumurthy et al., 2003), Hashcash(Back, n.d.) and BinaryCoin, Blockchain off late is used. Although they use different consensus algorithms to verify and validate blocks, the majority of digital currencies are based on a blockchain structure. (Tschorsch & Scheuermann, 2016) examines in detail the bitcoin currency and the financial blockchain and points out that the biggest import of the blockchain in the financial sector, which is the use of smart contracts. In any organization security related issues are more concentrated. Organization that uses Block chain is the one which ensures authorization among parties to access accurate data. The main goal of blockchain is to give warranty for data secure and data access. Blockchain guarantees data integrity based on its basic immutability and traceability characteristics. The merging of sequential hashing and encryption makes it extremely difficult to manipulate blockchain data for any user or nodes in the network. The right to be forgotten guarantees the user's privacy in any network, which is particularly important in terms of data immutability. The main challenge is to ensure that the right is applied in a technology based on no content loss. Also, blockchain provides many solutions.

Blockchain in healthcare: In the healthcare sector, Blockchain should be transparent and scalable, protected and data protection should be preserved. The health care blocks primarily contain medical records, reports and images. (Linn & Koo, 2016) Discusses the healthcare blockchain in context and has demonstrated that the data have storage impacts and performance limitations. Each user would have a copy of every individual's health record in the network while data is stored in Bitcoin-patterned blockchains. This is not an acceptable method of storing and bandwidth-intensive system for processing. It generates a waste of network resources and data transmission issues. We have to implement a system that Access Control Manager for data management and processing to incorporate the use of blockchains in the healthcare sector. Only an index or list of all the authorized user information are in the actual blockchain. It operates like a metadata catalog about patients and locations and stores the data for an authorized user to access. The data is encrypted, time-stamped, and retrieved by a unique identifier to increase data access efficiency. In blockchain data repositories called data lakes all health-related data is stored. Data in data lakes is encrypted and digitally signed for privacy purposes, and only authenticated users are allowed to access them.

Blockchain in Defense: The defense has to dependent on cyber-physical systems and their data stored in it, to overcome highly congested environments in the future. The current cyber defense appears to be turbulent and progressive improvements fall short of the growing cyber threat. Blockchain technology overturns the cyber security paradigm, which reduces the probability of data compromise by its untrustworthy, transparent and fault-tolerant. (Barnas, n.d.) discusses the need of blockchain technology in global defense in detail. The core elements in blockchain functioning such as secure hashing, backlinked data structure and consent mechanism play a major role in attributing the blockchain security factor. Since any authorized Network user can access the network data, the confidentiality of data is a major problem with blockchain security. This can be overcome through data encryption and access control maintenance by stored in blockchains. Blockchain may be used by acting as operational or support roles in the defense application.

Cyber defense: It's a low-cost, high-paid blockchain technology. First, blockchain ensures the widespread perception of all digital events by transmitting them to all network nodes and then employs various consensus algorithms to validate and verify. Once the data is stored it cannot be manipulated. If the information is altered or modified, it will be time-marked again and a record will be maintained. One can image, hash and secure modern weapons and component information in the database and continuously track them with blockchain devices. The specifics are mentioned in (Tirenin & Faatz, 1999).

3. MOTIVATION

For building a secure cyber infrastructure in above discussed (mentioned) applications like cloudlet, cyber physical systems, internet of things, we need to provide some innovation, reliable mechanism to protect our/ device communication (data). Blockchain is the best ever solution for achieving a certain level of security and building trust among users in this current (smart) era. It is because, till no attack has been faced on a Blockchain network, on Bitcoin (a popular cryptocurrency).There are few chances (possibility)that Blockchain will be fail for (in) providing a secure communication (to industries). There are many uses of blockchain are introducing now days in manysectors like agriculture, transportation, manufacturing, smart grids, etc., but every application cannot use (digest) Blockchain technology easily. There are various issues like time required for authentication, lesser privacy preservation, etc., raised in Blockchain technology. Also, there is a possibility of 51 percent attack on a Blockchain network or blockchain based applications.

Hence, this section discusses reason/ our motivation behind writing this chapter. Now, next section will discuss scope and importance of this work or Blockchain concept in many applications/ technology components in near future.

4. SCOPE OF THE WORK/ BLOCKCHAIN BASED APPLICATIONS IN PRESENT AND FUTURE

We are at the culmination of a historical change in technology that is making a massive impact in the technology. In this chapter, we will discuss how Blockchain has made an impact, making an impact and will make an impact in the future.

The emergence of Blockchain: Twenty years ago, a company called Netscape released the whole software of the navigator of internet, this movement kickstarted the concept of open source and hence coined the same as 'open source'. Without the concept of open source, Blockchain would have nerve started.

A computationally practical solution for time stamping digital documents such that it could not be backdated or tampered with was the need of the hour. This issue is being resolved by the system which uses a cryptographically secured chain of blocks to store the time stamped documents. In 1992, Merkle trees were incorporated into the design to make it more efficient by allowing several documents to be collected into one block.This technology was not made use of for a brief period of time and the had been taken down in 2004, four years before the inception of bitcoin.In 2004, cryptographic activist Hal Finney introduced a system called RPoW,Reusable Proof ofWork (Changelly, n.d.), the system worked by receiving a non-exchangeable hash cash-based proof of work token and in return created an RSA-signed token that could then be transferred from client to client. RPow solved the double spending problem by keeping the ownership of tokens registered on a trusted server that was designed to allow users throughout the world to verify its correctness and integrity in real time.RPoW can be considered as an early prototype and a significant early step in the history of cryptocurrencies.In late 2008 a white paper introducing a decentralized peer to peer electronic cash system called bitcoin-was posted to a cryptography mailing list by a person or group using the pseudonym. Based on the hashcash proof of work algorithm, but rather than using a hardware trusted computing function like the RPoW, the double spending protection in bitcoin was provided by a decentralized peer to peer protocol for tracking and verifying the transactions.In short,Bitcoins are 'mined' for a reward using the proof work mechanism by individual miners and then verified by the decentralized nodes in the network. However, it was not very well appreciated. Hence, a scripting functionality called smart contracts came up. Note that Smart contracts are decentralized Turing machine, they can be also known as complete virtual machine.

Moving Beyond the Hype

Blockchain 1.0 is the present reality of Blockchain while Blockchain 2.0 is a new paradigm of collectivity and Blockchain 3.0 are the self-organizing networks (decentralized governance). Also, now a days Blochain 4.0 is in ternds for distributed and decentralized applications**(Sawal et al., 2019)**. In Blockchain 1.0, the entire network agreed with consensus about the records, in Blockchain 2.0, the entire network consents to the records, the agreements over the records and the execution of those agreements. In terms of analogy, Blockchain 1.0 **OS** some sort of public ledger, then Blockchain 2.0 is a public computer, a decentralized computer. United nations are actually contemplating about adding the right to internet access to the Human Rights. In the future, a completely transparent entry of data will be available which will be audited by everyone. For example, Estonia (Rivera et al., 2017) is known for being innovative in their governance, they already implemented a digital ID and online voting for the citizens and they are now moving forward as one of the first countries in the world to issue their own cryptocurrency, it is coined as East corn. One important key point of Blockchain is digital assets which is nothing but decentralized tokens which has given rise to 'icos', i.e. initial coin offerings and this technology is used for centrally crowd funding money for Blockchain products but Blockchain is more similar to a digital IPO. There is an already a movement towards the decentralization of opinion and the decentralization of coordination. In Blockchain 3.0, shares of the network will be distributed to the participants, according to their contribution; the value of their contribution as perceived by other peers in that network, in last Blockchain 4.0 belongs to Dapps (Decentralized Applications).

Hence, this section discusses scope of the blockchain technology or block based applications to people/ society. Further, section will discuss several open issues in existing Blockchain based applications (in detail).

5. OPEN ISSUES IN BLOCKCHAIN BASED APPLICATIONS

Analogically quoting, like 'Every coin has two sides', similarly, 'the power to authenticate digital information and its transparent nature' has its downfalls. Often the power is misused and fake news spreads which leads to cyber-attacks. The key concern to Blockchain is how to design a system which is resistant to fraudulent behavior. How to incentivize people to participate in their best professional way? And how to maximally align everyone's interests (Hackernoon, n.d.b)?

a) The First and foremost concern is the mounting attention and engagement into renowned social networking sites. Platforms like Facebook and twitter use marketing strategies to increase their growth, however certain consumers prefer to underplay their identity.

b) The second issue is sending wrong information. This becomes a major issue when the information sent is confidential and to an unknown server who can use it to his advantage.

c) The third issue is crypto jacking, it is the type of malware, although they don't directly steal money from the members, they decrease the efficiency rate of the system which opens the door for criminals to access hostile codes which causes unwanted problems for the users.

d) The fourth issue is selfish miners, who increase their productivity or rewards by keeping their blocks private and not revealing their true identity making the whole process incomplete.

e) The fifth issue is the fact that the block data is searched using the index method, the block does not contain the hash value of the next block; it should be looked into as it resembles a linked list.

f) The sixth issue is only according to a study, an attacker can realize illegal gain with only 25% operating capability through a malicious mining process instead of 51%.

g) The seventh issue is the bitcoin wallet, it has become the attackers main subject to seek.It leads to hacking attacks and thefts, weak spots are being exploited

h) The eighth issue is double spending, this issue has been pertaining for a while now and irreversibility of data makes the transaction invalid

i) The ninth issue is the software used and how secure it is. As efficient as it is, it is not free from small bugs which makes huge transaction errors.

j) The tenth issue is they have proposed to protect the personal key by using a hardware token, which again might be misused or mishandled

k) The eleventh issue is by creating unwanted collisions which are timestamp attacks and also by cannibalizing the data.

l)   The next issue is falsifying the ledger, this is a very critical issue as it changes the whole blueprint of the information sent.

m)   The thirteenth issue is that the base foundation of the Blockchain, that is, the technology which is being made use of must be verified and cross checked.

Note that some useful issues and challenges towards blockchain based applications have been discussed in **(Hassan et al., 2019)** and in table 1 (refer appendix A). Hence, this section discusses or list about existing all open issues available in blockchain based applications. Now, next section will provide a summary on existing tools, method and algorithms for available Blockchain based applications.

6. TOOLS, METHODS AND ALGORITHMS FOR BLOCKCHAIN BASED APPLICATIONS

Blockchain is renowned for its application in cryptocurrencies like Bitcoin and Ethereum but it has the ability and potential to evolve many industries such as agriculture, finance, healthcare, defense etc. Blockchain is one of the fastest growing technologies on the planet. Thus, with its scaling importance and usage, the need for simple tools to develop Blockchain applications has risen. There are many Blockchain development tools available at the moment. A few of the most widely used tools are (Hackernoon, n.d.c),

a. Remix IDE

This is an uncomplicated tool which is based on the browser and is used to produce and deploy smart contracts. Smart contracts are an integral part of cyber physical systems and cryptocurrencies like Ethereum use Remix IDE tool to create and deploy smart contracts into the Blockchain. This tool is used with the help of the programming language 'Solidity', where it can write, debug, test and deploy smart contracts

b. Solc

Solidity is a programming language used to create smart contracts. The syntax of this programming language has a certain similarity to JavaScript. The generated script has to be converted into a format which can be read by Ethereum. This is where the Solc tool comes into play

c. Solium

Security is of utmost importance when it comes to developing Blockchain applications. The generated Solidity code must be free from all sorts of security loopholes. A tool has been developed to format the generated Solidity code and resolve all the security issues in them. This tool is called Solium. It checks if the code is formatted and also checks the vulnerability of the code.

d. Blockchain as a Service

This is a tool created to offer solutions based on the cloud to construct, host and utilize Blockchainapplications on the Blockchain, wherein the service provider from the cloud controls operations to develop a flexible and operational foundation. This benefits the companies and the individuals who want to utilize the Blockchain technology but have had trouble in implementing it because of technical difficulties or operational expenses.

e. Metamask

This is a tool that acts as a link or a connection between EthereumBlockchain and web browsers like Firefox and Chrome. It works as an extension to the browser. It is extensively used for storing keys for Ether and ERC20. This tool is also used for selling tokens. It links with various Ethereum testing networks to make it an exemplary tool for developers.

As discussed above and in (Sawal et al., 2019), Blockchain is a decentralized, distributed, and open digital ledger in which transactions are registered by users across many computers such that a record cannot be tampered with, without the modification of all the blocks on the Blockchain along with the consensus of the network. The mechanism by which nodes are added to the end of the Blockchain, along with checking the validity of records, is called the Blockchain algorithm. The algorithm in Blockchain is used to validate signatures, approve balances, check is a created block is valid or not, establish how miners are allowed to validate a block, authorize the method to report a block to move, define the consensus of the network. The different Blockchain algorithms are,

i. Consensus Algorithm (Bach et al., 2018)

These algorithms are complicated but very useful when it comes to running a node or to purchase coins. They deliver reliability on those particular networks in which many nodes are present such that they adhere to the said protocols. Consensus in a Blockchain is defined by the nodes, not the miners. The chain with most work defines the consensus. If the Blockchain forks and the Proof of Work changes, there will not be any mining power left to secure it. Nodes accept, verify and replicate the transactions. The also verify and replicate the blocks along with serving and storing in the Blockchain. The proof of work algorithm is defined by the nodes and not the miners.

- Proof of Work: This is the first consensus algorithm established for a Blockchain. This algorithm is used to authenticate transactions and create new blocks onto the Blockchain. Proof of work is based on the competition of miners against each other to authenticate transactions and get remunerated. Digital tokens are sent to each user in a network. In a decentralized ledger, all transactions are aggregated into blocks. During this process, the validation of transactions should be done carefully.
- Proof of Stake: This algorithm was designed to solve some issues in the Proof of Work algorithm. It states that a user can verify or mine block transactions based on the number of coins they hold. Thus, the more coins a user has, the more mining power he/she will possess.
- Delegated Proof of Stake: This is a consensus algorithm that preserves conclusive agreements on the facts across the network, verifies transactions and acts like a digital republic.This algorithm uses voting which takes place in real time, along with reputation consideration to attain consensus. Among all the consensus protocols, this is the least centralized, thus making it the most inclusive
- Practical Byzantine Fault tolerance: This is a system for a dispersed network to attain consensus in the Blockchain, even if some nodes are fake or malicious. According to this, for a transaction to be

confirmed, an agreement on the subject must be made by most nodes. Basically, it is the hallmark of the Blockchain to confirm a particular transaction even if some nodes do not approve it.

- Raft Consensus: This algorithm works on two basic principles which are as follows. In a term, one leader only can be chosen. Also, a leader cannot append or erase entries in the log, only the new entries can be appended by it. This algorithm is used when the number of servers is relatively less. The servers are assigned as leader, follower and candidates. The followers acknowledge the requests sent by the leaders. During the start of each term, all the candidates contest for the position of the leader.

ii. Mining Algorithms

Mining of data has three major segments namely, Clustering, Sequence Analysis and Association Rules. The analysis of a collection of data to create a collection of grouping laws by which future data is classified is called Clustering or Classification. The examination of patterns that transpire in a particular sequence is called Sequence Analysis. An association rule is a law which dictates particular association rules and relationships between a collection of objects in a database.

iii. Traceability Chain Algorithm (Chen, 2018)

Traceability confirms the start and working following a transaction when in the background, additional data is also being accumulated to enhance the performance of internal processes and to plan the ventures of every node in the chain. The purpose of this algorithm is to obtain traceability decisions swiftly. Due to the presence of an inference mechanism, this algorithm operates quicker than a consensus algorithm. Traceability in Blockchain is responsible for supporting and enhancing the coordination that is possessed by the chain so that more data can be collected about the location and status of the transactions taking place and this information can be used by the nodes to plan the rest of its ventures. Using this algorithm, every single digital asset used in the Blockchain can be traced. This algorithm involves marking of nodes so that they can be identified easily. With the flow of information electronically, many scans are run so that data retrieval can be done efficiently. Links are established so that sharing of data between different chains can be made efficient.

Hence, this section discusses many existing tools, methods and algorithms for blockchain based applications in detail. Now, next section will provide some useful and future reserch directions for future reserchers (towards possible blockhain based applications).

7. FUTURE RESEARCH DIRECTIONS USING BLOCKCHAIN APPLICATIONS

Blockchain is a technology that has taken the world by storm. It has shown its prospects in various industries. This section discusses a few possible future directions of this technology.

a) Big Data (Karafiloski & Mishev, 2017): The combination of big data and Blockchain has shown an immense amount potential. The couple can be used for the management of data as well as the analysis of data. For the management of data, Blockchain can be used to save valuable data as it is a distributed, decentralized and a secure ledger for records. It can also verify the authenticity of the data as the information stored in the Blockchain cannot be tampered with. For analysis of data, the different transactions taking place on the Blockchain could be analysed to detect patterns of trade. Using this, an algorithmic assumption of the trading patterns of the users of the Blockchain would be available.

b) Artificial Intelligence (Marwala & Xing, n.d.): Blockchain technology has had many developments in recent times and research suggests that the technology has a massive scope in the field of artificial intelligence. Artificial intelligence could resolve many hurdles present in Blockchain technology. For instance, a trusted third party is required in Blockchain to check if a particular condition is fulfilled for a contract. Artificial intelligence could help remove the need for a trusted third party. A virtual third party could be created which would learn from the background and educate itself. This way, all conflicts would be resolved. Blockchain can also be used to make sure that Artificial intelligence devices do not misfire. As the information in Blockchain cannot be tampered with there can be no changes made to the protocols which the devices will have to adhere to.

c) Testing of Blockchains: In recent times, new kinds of Blockchains have been created and several hundred different cryptocurrencies have been recorded. But some Blockchain developers may fake the execution of their Blockchain to draw investors and gain huge amounts of money. Also, when a person wants to incorporate Blockchain into their business, they need to know which type of Blockchain to use so that it is suitable for their needs. This is where Blockchain testing comes in handy. For example, the need for different characteristics of a Blockchain like throughput, scalability, verification speed or crash fault tolerance has to be judged and administered into the application accordingly. Thus, Blockchains can be used for testing as well.

Hence, this section provides a several future research directions with blockchain technology with many new emerging areas/sectors. Now, next section will provide an open discussion, which will tell that blockchain is really necessary for future or not with providing some useful facts.

8. AN OPEN DISCUSSION: BLOCKCHAIN BASED APPLICATIONS IS A NECESSITY OR JUST A TREND

According to what we have seen in the paper so far, it will be right to say that Blockchain based applications was a trend when the concept of Blockchain kicked in but now it's become a necessity. Blockchains revolution was a beginning, which means to continue it, change is the only guarantee to revolutionize it. The applications become internally self-organizing which reduces the number of faults, since the information is stored in a database, we can use logistics to update ourselves with the best routes, traffic analysis and the best schedule which can be efficiently produced. In this way, the transportation can be greatly improvised. The most advanced form of Blockchain which is used in Blockchain application is steemBlockchain (Davidson et al., 2018), steem can be compared to a real estate system, it is basically *open-source immutable database which distributes resources in a decentralized way*. With resources like steem, you can post content which can never be deleted, in Facebook, they own our data and can remove the same, usingsteemBlockchain no one can remove our account without our consent. Thus, Blockchain will impact every facet of our life in the near future.

Hence, this section discusses about an open discussion, i.e., provide an opinion with some basic facts which prove that Blockchain is necessity of future technology. It will be used in many sectors and businesses for improving profit and building trust in (of) the same. Now next section will conclude this work in brief with some future remarks.

9. SUMMARY

Now a days, Blockchain network is growing and using by many industries/ organizations. In near future, blockchain technology will change every possible business in next few years (10 or 20) due to having its unique features of decentralization, distributed (or using no intermediary). Blockchain is an open, decentralized ledger, can transform business and society. Blockchain based transformation can be made with (in) short-term reality. Some popular advantages of using blockchain (using proof of work) in manipulations (like cloudlet, internet of things, cloud computing, edge computing, etc.) are great transparency, enhanced security, improved traceability, increased efficiency, and speed (with reduced cost). For future, work, we need to improve blockchain technology or removing several implications of blockchain transformation. A technology should be adopted by many and affordable (accessible) and should not harm environment (basic fundamentals of human being)/ nature. With blockchain technology, we can create a disruptive/ sustainable life (reduce negative impact of blockchain to our life/ business).

REFERENCES

Azaria, A., Ekblaw, A., Vieira, T., & Lippman, A. (2016). MedRec: Using Blockchain for Medical Data Access and Permission Management. *2016 2nd International Conference on Open and Big Data (OBD)*, 25-30. 10.1109/OBD.2016.11

Bach, L. M., Mihaljevic, B., & Zagar, M. (2018). Comparative analysis of blockchain consensus algorithms. *2018 41st International Convention on Information and Communication Technology, Electronics and Microelectronics (MIPRO)*, 1545-1550. 10.23919/MIPRO.2018.8400278

Back. (n.d.). *Hashcash-a denial of service counter-measure*. Academic Press.

Barnas. (n.d.). *Blockchains in national defense: Trustworthy systems in a trustless world*. Blue Horizons Fellowship, Air University, Maxwell Air Force Base.

Changelly. (n.d.). https://changelly.com/blog/what-is-blockchain

Chen. (2018). A traceability chain algorithm for artificial neural networks using T–S fuzzy cognitive maps in blockchain. *Future Generation Computer Systems*, *80*(March), 198–210.

Davidson, De Filippi, & Potts. (2018). Blockchains and the economic institutions of capitalism. *Journal of Institutional Economics*, *14*(4), 639–658.

Dorri, A., Kanhere, S. S., Jurdak, R., & Gauravaram, P. (2017). Blockchain for IoT security and privacy: The case study of a smart home. *2017 IEEE International Conference on Pervasive Computing and Communications Workshops (PerCom Workshops)*, 618-623. 10.1109/PERCOMW.2017.7917634

Dorri, A., Steger, M., Kanhere, S., & Jurdak, R. (2017). Blockchain: A Distributed Solution to Automotive Security and Privacy. *IEEE Communications Magazine*, *55*(12), 119–125. Advance online publication. doi:10.1109/MCOM.2017.1700879

Hackernoon. (n.d.a). https://hackernoon.com/how-will-blockchain-agriculture-revolutionize-the-food-supply-from-farm-to-plate-f8fe488d9bae

Hackernoon. (n.d.b). https://hackernoon.com/how-blockchain-is-solving-the-biggest-problems-in-social-networking-87e4e0753e39

Hackernoon. (n.d.c). https://hackernoon.com/top-12-blockchain-development-tools-to-build-blockchain-ecosystem-371a1b587248

Hassan, M. U., Rehmani, M. H., & Chen, J. (2019). Privacy preservation in blockchain based IoT systems: Integration issues, prospects, challenges, and future research directions. *Future Generation Computer Systems*, *97*, 512-529.

Investopedia. (n.d.). https://www.investopedia.com/terms/1/51-attack.asp

Karafiloski, E., & Mishev, A. (2017). Blockchain solutions for big data challenges: A literature review. *IEEE EUROCON 2017 -17th International Conference on Smart Technologies*, 763-768. 10.1109/EUROCON.2017.8011213

Kogias. (2019). Toward a Blockchain-Enabled Crowdsourcing Platform. *IT Professional, 21*(5), 18-25.

Li, M., Weng, J., Yang, A., Lu, W., Zhang, Y., Hou, L., Liu, J.-N., Xiang, Y., & Deng, R. H. (2019, June 1). CrowdBC: A Blockchain-Based Decentralized Framework for Crowdsourcing. *IEEE Transactions on Parallel and Distributed Systems*, *30*(6), 1251–1266. doi:10.1109/TPDS.2018.2881735

Linn, L. A., & Koo, M. B. (2016). Blockchain for health data and its potential use in health it and health care related research. In *ONC/NIST Use of Blockchain for Healthcare and Research Workshop*. ONC/NIST.

Lu, Wang, Qu, Zhang, & Liu. (n.d.). A Blockchain-Based Privacy-Preserving Authentication Scheme for VANETs. *IEEE Transactions on Very Large-Scale Integration (VLSI) Systems*.

Marwala & Xing. (n.d.). *Blockchain and Artificial Intelligence*. https://arxiv.org/ftp/arxiv/papers/1802/1802.04451.pdf

Mohanta, B. K., Panda, S. S., & Jena, D. (2018). An Overview of Smart Contract and Use Cases in Blockchain Technology. *2018 9th International Conference on Computing, Communication and Networking Technologies (ICCCNT)*, 1-4. 10.1109/ICCCNT.2018.8494045

Rivera, R., Robledo, J. G., Larios, V. M., & Avalos, J. M. (2017). How digital identity on blockchain can contribute in a smart city environment. *2017 International Smart Cities Conference (ISC2)*, 1-4. 10.1109/ISC2.2017.8090839

Sanghi, N., Bhatnagar, R., Kaur, G., & Jain, V. (2018). BlockCloud: Blockchain with Cloud Computing. *2018 International Conference on Advances in Computing, Communication Control and Networking (ICACCCN)*, 430-434. 10.1109/ICACCCN.2018.8748467

Sawal, N., Yadav, A., & Tyagi, D. (2019). *Necessity of Blockchain for Building Trust in Today's Applications: An Useful Explanation from User's Perspective.* Available at SSRN: https://ssrn.com/abstract=3388558

Taylor, Dargahi, Dehghantanha, Parizi, & Choo. (2019). A systematic literature review of blockchain cyber security. *Digital Communications and Networks.*

Tirenin, W., & Faatz, D. (1999). A concept for strategic cyber defense. *Military Communications Conference Proceedings*, 458–463. doi: 10.1109/MILCOM.1999.822725

Tomov, Y. K. (2019). Bitcoin: Evolution of Blockchain Technology. *2019 IEEE XXVIII International Scientific Conference Electronics (ET)*, 1-4.

Tschorsch & Scheuermann. (2016). Bitcoin and beyond: A technical survey on decentralized digital currencies. *IEEE Communications Surveys & Tutorials, 18*, 2084-2123. doi: .2535718 doi:10.1109/COMST.2016

Vishumurthy, V., Chandrakumar, S., & Sirer, E. G. (2003). Karma: A secure economic framework for peer-to-peer resource sharing. *Proceedings of the 2003 Workshop on Economics of Peer-to-Peer Systems.*

Wood, G. (2014). Ethereum: A secure decentralizedgeneralised transaction ledger. *Ethereum Project Yellow Paper, 151*, 1–32.

Xu, X. (2018). An Energy-Aware Virtual Machine Scheduling Method for Cloudlets in Wireless Metropolitan Area Networks. *2018 IEEE International Conference on Internet of Things (iThings) and IEEE Green Computing and Communications (GreenCom) and IEEE Cyber, Physical and Social Computing (CPSCom) and IEEE Smart Data (SmartData)*, 517-523. 10.1109/Cybermatics_2018.2018.00110

Xu, X., Chen, Y., Yuan, Y., Huang, T., & Zhang, X. (n.d.). Blockchain-based cloudlet management for multimedia workflow in mobile cloud computing. *Multimedia Tools and Applications.* Advance online publication. doi:10.100711042-019-07900-x,2019

KEY TERMS AND DEFINITIONS

Bitcoin: Bitcoin is a digital or virtual currency developed in 2009 that allows instant transactions easier by using peer-to-peer technology.

Blockchain: A process in which records are maintained on several computers connected in a pair-to-pairs network of transactions in Bitcoin or other cryptocurrency.

Cloud Computing: On-demand computer system resources available without direct active user management, especially data storage and computing power.

Cryptocurrency: Digital currency used to control authentication techniques for the generation of currency units and the confirmation of transactions, working without a central banking authority.

Ethereum: It is the smart contract (scripting) operating system and open source, public, distributed computing platform based on blockchain.

Internet of Things: Interconnect computer devices embedded in everyday objects via the Internet to enable data to be transmitted and received.

APPENDIX

Table 1. A Taxonomy of Blockchain Based Applications

APPLICATION	CHARACTERISTICS	ADVANTAGES	DISADVANTAGES	RESEARCH CHALLENGES	OPEN ISSUES	SOLUTIONS TO THE CHALLENGES
CYBER PHYSICAL SYSTEMS (Taylor et al., 2019)	Aims to synchronise the realistic world with computational space of the internet	It helps in identifying the potential aspects of Blockchain to include and boom technologies of Blockchain 4.0	The components which fail exhibit this unusual behaviour which arises when you send conflicting information to different parts of the system	The need to include an explicit focus on the cybersecurity	Security and availability is still an ongoing issue	Increasing resilience, robustness and reliability to save against cyberattacks
IOT (Dorri, Kanhere, Jurdak et al, 2017)	Blockchain prevents duplication and personal thefts	The information is sent to trusted resources and the ledger grants information after a lot of analyzation by different groups of resourceful parties	Often false alerts are sent and the sensors are not that powerful to adapt information	There is less transparency and the end to end visibility has to be taken into account	The risk of losing data and gaining other unimportant data makes it an unambiguous situation	
Vehicular Ad Hoc Network(VANET) (Lu et al., n.d.)	Effectively gives a solution to maintain the trust between the VANET entities.	Blockchain is used to quantify the available of the anonymous entities, this helps in valuation of VANET	The processing time is more than the actual time required	The identity of the owner should not be disclosed	The privacy of the location has to be taken into account	VANET time, Effective distance between the systems, Connectivity rate and privacy should be maintained
COMPUTING (Sanghi et al., 2018)	Helps in transporting data, processing and protecting and storing data is done by Blockchain.	The traceability of the entitiescloud is improved using Blockchain.	There are a lot of unauthorised service providers who have vendors which send false information and there is no one cross checking	The time taken to take massive amounts of data is impossible to handle	Monitoring the data keeping the time in check becomes very difficult and the cost of transferring the complex data requires a lot of money	A data portability is necessary where they cannot switch and send data without restraints, they should be no lock in period for switching data
SMART PROPERTY (Mohanta et al., 2018)	A non-physical property which cannot be accessed all the time is solved by authentication using an ownership key, the device used a trustable sourceof time	It decreases the risk of running into fraud, reduces taxes and fees and disables the possibility of duplicates.	The key is in a physical form, for example, a car key and a sim card which makes it very difficult to transfer information or copy information.	In a smart property it will function only if you enter the right pin code, so if the phone has no battery or the phone is disabled, accessing the device. becomes difficult	The dividends are not divided equally and the cost is not equally distributed.	The Blockchain solves this issue by a 'replace and replicate a lost protocol'.
MEDICAL FIELDS (Azaria et al., 2016)	Used in transparently tracking prescription medicines	It is very useful in identifying the right medicine using serial or batch numbers to ensure that the consumers get the right medicine	There may be cases when the expiry data might be reached while the medicine is till being delivered	A large amount of time is taken to deliver the medicines and the effective cost increases	Due to high security and technological advances, the service technician won't be able to access the medicines or won't be sure of which medicine to send	Maintaining regular compliance and a ledge for transport and access of medicines and feasibility is required
CROWDSOURCING (Kogias, 2019)	Uses the idea of a third party to fulfil the exchange between the shared data and in return the rewards are gained as information exchange	Its legal and has structural restrictions	It is vulnerable to manipulate huge amount of data	Leveraging the Blockchain to infuse incentives but can't reveal the confidential inputs of incentive mechani	They have the access to generate their own ids which gives malicious workers to create fake ids and hence forge ideas and signatures	Data confidentiality and transparency and identification if users is a necessity.
CLOUDLET [32]	Cloudlet acts as a high end platform that can run the virtual machines	It support low-latency secure, anonymous, and always-within an on-demand data-sharing scenario	The necessity to be online and offline simultaneously is a necessity	It is still ambiguous about whether to choose the blocks according to proof of work or delegated proof of work	The transaction is fee based and it is based on the stipulated time duration Thus,time is directly proportional to fees	A bridge is required to connect the different types of models to maintain and support the chains

Chapter 13
Blockchain, Cybersecurity, and Industry 4.0

Abhishek Bhattacharya
https://orcid.org/0000-0001-8441-7871
Independent Researcher, India

ABSTRACT

The world is going digital, and the wave of automation is sweeping across all facets of our corporate and personal lives. Industry 4.0 is all about leveraging IoT (internet of things) devices to facilitate further the process of automation that helps all organisations to rapidly scale by leveraging technology. The amount of data and information generated by the connected things is being harnessed with the help of advanced algorithm empowered analytics to induce intelligence into all the actions undertaken for the functioning of these connected devices. This chapter is geared towards giving a representative outlook on the concepts of blockchain that see a base in the concepts of cybersecurity. Further to that, this chapter explores the very imminent use cases of what we call the Industry 4.0. This includes use cases from remmitance, insurance, governance, internet of things (IoT), and supply chain, including the kinds of challenges we currently face.

CYBERSECURITY

In the early years of cyberattacks, organizations would wait to be attacked before they developed a comprehensive plan and response to the attacker. The attack would render the organizations' network presence useless and down for days. Several reasons cyberattacks could severely cripple a network in the early days of this malicious behavior are not enough concentrated research on defending and preventing and the lack of a coordinated effort between private industry and the government.

Since the first well known and wide spread cyberattack in the mid-1990's, many professionals in public and private organizations have diligently been studying and working on the problem of cyberattacks. Initially security companies like Norton, McAfee, Trend Micro, etc. approached the problem from a reactive posture. They knew hackers/malicious attackers were going to strike. The goal of what is now called Intrusion Detection Systems (IDS) was to detect a malicious attacker before an anti-virus, Trojan

DOI: 10.4018/978-1-7998-3295-9.ch013

horse, or worm was used to strike. If the attacker was able to strike the network, security professionals would dissect the code. Once the code was dissected, a response or "fix" was applied to the infected machine(s). The "fix" is now called a signature and they are consistently downloaded over the network as weekly updates to defend against known attacks. Although IDS is a wait and see posture, security professionals have gotten much more sophisticated in their approach and it continues to evolve as part of the arsenal.

Security professionals began looking at the problem from a preventive angle. This moved the cybersecurity industry from defensive to offensive mode. They were now troubleshooting how to prevent an attack on a system or network. Based on this line of thinking, an Intrusion Prevention Systems (IPS) called Snort was soon introduced. Snort is a combination IDS and IPS open source software available for FREE download. Using IDS/IPS software like Snort allows security professionals to be proactive in the cybersecurity arena. Though IPS allows security professionals to play offense as well as defense, they do not rest on their laurels nor do they stop monitoring the work of malicious attackers which fuels creativity, imagination, and innovation. It also allows security professionals that defend the cyberworld to stay equal or one step ahead of attackers.

Cybersecurity also plays an offensive and defensive role in the economy. In its cybersecurity commercial, The University of Maryland University College (2012) states there will be "fifty-thousand jobs available in cybersecurity over the next ten years." The school has been running this commercial for more than two years. When the commercial first began running they quoted thirty-thousand jobs. They have obviously adjusted the forecast higher based upon studies as well as the government and private industry identifying cybersecurity as a critical need to defend critical infrastructure.

Cybersecurity can play economic defense by protecting these jobs which deal with national security concerns and must remain the in the United States. The cybersecurity industry is driven by national security in the government realm and intellectual property (IP) in the private industry space. Many U.S. companies complain to the government about foreign countries hi-jacking their software ideas and inventions through state sponsored and organized crime hackers. Given that foreign countries condone state sponsored national security and intellectual property attacks, it would be to the benefit of companies to find human capital within the shores of the United States to perform the duties and tasks needed.

On the offensive side, Cybersecurity can spur development and increase the skill sets of residents in counties like Prince George's County, Maryland which sits in the epicenter of Cybersecurity for the state of Maryland and the nation. Prince George's Community College is the home of Cyberwatch and the central hub for cybersecurity training and best practices that gets pushed out to other community colleges that are part of the consortium. The goal of these community colleges is to align the education offered to students with skills that companies say are needed to be "workforce ready." It is also a rich recruiting ground for tech companies across the country to identify and hire human capital to put on the front lines of the U.S. fight in cybersecurity.

In conclusion, cybersecurity has come a long way since the publicized hacking cases of the 1990's. These cases brought awareness to the need for the best and brightest to enter the field of computer and network security with the purpose of devising strategies and techniques to defend against "bad actors" that would use technology to commit malicious acts. Because computer and network security require STEM (Science, Technology, Engineering, Math) skills, the pool of U.S. born applicants is presently small. This presents an economic development opportunity for locales that use their community colleges as technology training grounds that are closely aligned with technology companies who need the human capital. The overarching goal of the stakeholders is to produce "workforce ready" students.

WHAT IS SYMMETRIC KEY CRYPTOGRAPHY?

How Does Symmetric Encryption Work?

Symmetric encryption schemes rely on a single key that is shared between two or more users. The same key is used to encrypt and decrypt the so-called plaintext (which represents the message or piece of data that is being encoded). The process of encryption consists of running a plaintext (input) through an encryption algorithm called a cipher, which in turn generates a ciphertext (output) (Brilliant.org, 2020).

If the encryption scheme is strong enough, the only way for a person to read or access the information contained in the ciphertext is by using the corresponding key to decrypt it. The process of decryption is basically converting the ciphertext back to plaintext.

The security of symmetric encryption systems is based on how difficult it randomly guess the corresponding key to brute force them. A 128-bit key, for example, would take billions of years to guess using common computer hardware. The longer the encryption key is, the harder it becomes to crack it. Keys that are 256-bits length are generally regarded as highly secure and theoretically resistant to quantum computer brute force attacks.

Two of the most common symmetric encryption schemes used today are based on block and stream ciphers. Block ciphers group data into blocks of predetermined size and each block is encrypted using the corresponding key and encryption algorithm (e.g., 128-bit plaintext is encrypted into 128-bit ciphertext). On the other hand, stream ciphers do not encrypt plaintext data by blocks, but rather by 1-bit increments (1-bit plaintext is encrypted into 1-bit ciphertext at a time).

Symmetric vs. Asymmetric Encryption

Symmetric encryption is one of the two major methods of encrypting data in modern computer systems. The other is asymmetric encryption, which is the major application of public key cryptography. The main difference between these methods is the fact that asymmetric systems use two keys rather than the one employed by the symmetric schemes. One of the keys can be publicly shared (public key), while the other must be kept in private (private key).

The use of two keys instead of one also produces a variety of functional differences between symmetric and asymmetric encryption(Ahmad et al., 2015). Asymmetric algorithms are more complex and slower than the symmetric ones. Because the public and private keys employed in asymmetric encryption are to some degree mathematically related, the keys themselves must also be considerably longer to provide a similar level of security offered by shorter symmetric keys.

Uses in Modern Computer Systems

Symmetric encryption algorithms are employed in many modern computer systems to enhance data security and user privacy. The Advanced Encryption Standard (AES) that is widely used in both secure messaging applications and cloud storage is one prominent example of a symmetric cipher.

In addition to software implementations, AES can also be implemented directly in computer hardware. Hardware-based symmetric encryption schemes usually leverage the AES 256, which is a specific variant of the Advanced Encryption Standard that has a key size of 256 bits.

It is worth noting that Bitcoin's blockchain does not make use of encryption like many tend to believe. Instead, it uses a specific kind of digital signatures algorithm (DSA) known as Elliptic Curve Digital Signature Algorithm (ECDSA) that generates digital signatures without using encryption.

A common point of confusion is that the ECDSA is based on elliptic-curve cryptography (ECC), which in turn may be applied for multiple tasks, including encryption, digital signatures, and pseudo-random generators (Jeremy Wohlwend, n.d). However, the ECDSA itself cannot be used for encryption at all.

Advantages and Disadvantages

Symmetric algorithms provide a fairly high level of security while at the same time allowing for messages to be encrypted and decrypted quickly. The relative simplicity of symmetric systems is also a logistical advantage, as they require less computing power than the asymmetric ones. In addition, the security provided by symmetric encryption can be scaled up simply by increasing key lengths. For every single bit added to the length of a symmetric key, the difficulty of cracking the encryption through a brute force attack increases exponentially.

While symmetric encryption offers a wide range of benefits, there is one major disadvantage associated with it: the inherent problem of transmitting the keys used to encrypt and decrypt data. When these keys are shared over an unsecured connection, they are vulnerable to being intercepted by malicious third parties. If an unauthorized user gains access to a particular symmetric key, the security of any data encrypted using that key is compromised. To solve this problem, many web protocols use a combination of symmetric and asymmetric encryption to establish secure connections. Among the most prominent examples of such a hybrid system is the Transport Layer Security (TLS) cryptographic protocol used to secure large portions of the modern internet().

It should also be noted that all types of computer encryption are subject to vulnerabilities due to improper implementation. While a sufficiently long key can make a brute force attack mathematically impossible, errors in implementation made by programmers often create weaknesses that open up the way for cyber attacks.

ASYMMETRIC CRYPTOGRAPHY (PUBLIC KEY CRYPTOGRAPHY)

Asymmetric cryptography, also known as public key cryptography, uses public and private keys to encrypt and decrypt data. The keys are simply large numbers that have been paired together but are not identical (asymmetric). One key in the pair can be shared with everyone; it is called the public key. The other key in the pair is kept secret; it is called the private key. Either of the keys can be used to encrypt a message; the opposite key from the one used to encrypt the message is used for decryption.

Many protocols like SSH, OpenPGP, S/MIME, and SSL/TLS rely on asymmetric cryptography for encryption and digital signature functions. It is also used in software programs, such as browsers, which need to establish a secure connection over an insecure network like the Internet or need to validate a digital signature. Encryption strength is directly tied to key size and doubling the key length delivers an exponential increase in strength, although it does impair performance. As computing power increases and more efficient factoring algorithms are discovered, the ability to factor larger and larger numbers also increases.

For asymmetric encryption to deliver confidentiality, integrity, authenticity and non-repudiability, users and systems need to be certain that a public key is authentic, that it belongs to the person or entity claimed and that it has not been tampered with nor replaced by a malicious third party. There is no perfect solution to this public key authentication problem. As mentioned by JR Vacca (2004), a public key infrastructure (PKI) where trusted certificate authorities certify ownership of key pairs and certificates is the most common approach, but encryption products based on the Pretty Good Privacy (PGP) model including OpenPGP -- rely on a decentralized authentication model called a web of trust, which relies on individual endorsements of the link between user and public key.

How Asymmetric Encryption Works

Asymmetric encryption algorithms use a mathematically-related key pair for encryption and decryption; one is the public key and the other is the private key. If the public key is used for encryption, the related private key is used for decryption and if the private key is used for encryption, the related public key is used for decryption.

Only the user or computer that generates the key pair has the private key. The public key can be distributed to anyone who wants to send encrypted data to the holder of the private key. It's impossible to determine the private key with the public one.

The two participants in the asymmetric encryption workflow are the sender and the receiver. First, the sender obtains the receiver's public key. Then the plaintext is encrypted with the asymmetric encryption algorithm using the recipient's public key, creating the ciphertext. The ciphertext is then sent to the receiver, who decrypts the ciphertext with his private key so he can access the sender's plaintext.

Because of the one-way nature of the encryption function, one sender is unable to read the messages of another sender, even though each has the public key of the receiver.

Examples of Asymmetric Cryptography

Ø   RSA (Rivest-Shamir-Adleman) -- the most widely used asymmetric algorithm -- is embedded in the SSL/TSL protocols which is used to provide communications security over a computer network. RSA derives its security from the computational difficulty of factoring large integers that are the product of two large prime numbers (Ninghui Li, n.d.).

Ø   Multiplying two large primes is easy, but the difficulty of determining the original numbers from the product -- factoring -- forms the basis of public key cryptography security. The time it takes to factor the product of two sufficiently large primes is considered to be beyond the capabilities of most attackers, excluding nation-state actors who may have access to sufficient computing power. RSA keys are typically 1024- or 2048-bits long, but experts believe that 1024-bit keys could be broken in the near future, which is why government and industry are moving to a minimum key length of 2048-bits.

Ø   Elliptic Curve Cryptography (ECC) is gaining favor with many security experts as an alternative to RSA for implementing public key cryptography. ECC is a public key encryption technique based on elliptic curve theory that can create faster, smaller, and more efficient cryptographic keys (Hankerson et al., n.d.; Lauter, 2004). ECC generates keys through the properties of the elliptic curve equation.

To break ECC, one must compute an elliptic curve discrete logarithm, and it turns out that this is a significantly more difficult problem than factoring. As a result, ECC key sizes can be significantly smaller than those required by RSA yet deliver equivalent security with lower computing power and battery resource usage making it more suitable for mobile applications than RSA.

Uses of Asymmetric Cryptography

The typical application for asymmetric cryptography is authenticating data through the use of digital signatures. Based on asymmetric cryptography, digital signatures can provide assurances of evidence to the origin, identity and status of an electronic document, transaction or message, as well as acknowledging informed consent by the signer.

To create a digital signature, signing software such as an email program creates a one-way hash of the electronic data to be signed. The user's private key is then used to encrypt the hash, returning a value that is unique to the hashed data. The encrypted hash, along with other information such as the hashing algorithm, forms the digital signature. Any change in the data, even to a single bit, results in a different hash value.

This attribute enables others to validate the integrity of the data by using the signer's public key to decrypt the hash. If the decrypted hash matches a second computed hash of the same data, it proves that the data hasn't changed since it was signed. If the two hashes don't match, the data has either been tampered with in some way -- indicating a failure of integrity or the signature was created with a private key that doesn't correspond to the public key presented by the signer indicating a failure of authentication.

A digital signature also makes it difficult for the signing party to deny having signed something the property of non-repudiation. If a signing party denies a valid digital signature, their private key has either been compromised or they are being untruthful. In many countries, including the United States, digital signatures have the same legal weight as more traditional forms of signatures.

Asymmetric cryptography can be applied to systems in which many users may need to encrypt and decrypt messages, such as encrypted email, in which a public key can be used to encrypt a message, and a private key can be used to decrypt it.

The SSL/TSL cryptographic protocols for establishing encrypted links between websites and browsers also make use of asymmetric encryption.

Additionally, Bitcoin and other cryptocurrencies rely on asymmetric cryptography as users have public keys that everyone can see and private keys that are kept secret. Bitcoin uses a cryptographic algorithm to ensure that only the legitimate owners can spend the funds.

In the case of the Bitcoin ledger, each unspent transaction output (UTXO) is typically associated with a public key (Neha Narula, n.d). So if user X, who has an UTXO associated with his public key, wants to send the money to user Y, user X uses his private key to sign a transaction that spends the UTXO and creates a new UTXO that's associated with user Y's public key.

Asymmetric vs. Symmetric Cryptography

The main difference between these two methods of encryption is that asymmetric encryption algorithms makes use of two different but related keys -- one key to encrypt the data and another key to decrypt it -- while symmetric encryption uses the same key to perform both the encryption and decryption functions.

Another difference between asymmetric and symmetric encryption is the length of the keys. In symmetric cryptography, the length of the keys -- which is randomly selected -- are typically set at 128-bits or 256-bits, depending on the level of security that's needed.

However, in asymmetric encryption, there has to be a mathematical relationship between the public and private keys. Because hackers can potentially exploit this pattern to crack the encryption, asymmetric keys need to be much longer to offer the same level of security. The difference in the length of the keys is so pronounced that a 2048-bit asymmetric key and a 128-bit symmetric key provide just about an equivalent level of security.

Additionally, asymmetric encryption is slower than symmetric encryption, which has a faster execution speed.

Benefits and Disadvantages of Asymmetric Cryptography

The benefits of asymmetric cryptography include:

Ø   the key distribution problem is eliminated because there's no need for exchanging keys.
Ø   security is increased as the private keys don't ever have to be transmitted or revealed to anyone.
Ø   the use of digital signatures is enabled so that a recipient can verify that a message comes from a particular sender.
Ø   it allows for non-repudiation so the sender can't deny sending a message.

Disadvantages include:

Ø   it's a slow process compared to symmetric crytography, so it's not appropriate for decrypting bulk messages.
Ø   if an individual loses his private key, he can't decrypt the messages he receives.
Ø   since the public keys aren't authenticated, no one really knows if a public key belongs to the person specified. Consequently, users have to verify that their public keys belong to them.
Ø   if a hacker identifies a person's private key, the attacker can read all of that individual's messages.

THE 51% ATTACK

Before diving into the 51% attack, it is crucial to have a good understanding of mining and blockchain-based systems.

One of the key strengths of the Bitcoin and its underlying blockchain technology is the distributed nature of building and verifying data. The decentralized work of the nodes ensures that the protocol rules are being followed and that all network participants agree on the current state of the blockchain. This means that the majority of nodes need to regularly reach consensus in regards to the process of mining, to the version of the software being used, to the validity of transactions, and so forth.

The Bitcoin consensus algorithm (Proof of Work) is what assures that miners are only able to validate a new block of transactions if the network nodes collectively agree that the block hash provided by the miner is accurate (i.e. the block hash proves that the miner did enough work and found a valid solution for that block's problem) (M Conti et. al., 2017) (Conti et al., 2017).

The blockchain infrastructure - as a decentralized ledger and distributed system - prevents any centralized entity from making use of the network for its own purposes, which is the reason why there is no single authority on the Bitcoin network.

Since the process of mining (in PoW-based systems) involves the investment of huge amounts of electricity and computational resources, a miner's performance is based on the amount of computational power he has, and this is usually referred to as hash power or hash rate. There are many mining nodes in various locations and they compete to be the next to find a valid block hash and be rewarded with newly generated Bitcoins.

In such a context, the mining power is distributed over different nodes across the world, which means the hash rate is not in the hands of a single entity. At least it is not supposed to be.

But what happens when the hash rate is no longer distributed well enough? What happens if, for example, one single entity or organization is able to obtain more than 50% of the hashing power? One possible consequence of that is what we call a 51% attack, also known as majority attack.

What is a 51% Attack?

A 51% attack is a potential attack on a blockchain network, where a single entity or organization is able to control the majority of the hash rate, potentially causing a network disruption. In such a scenario, the attacker would have enough mining power to intentionally exclude or modify the ordering of transactions. They could also reverse transactions they made while being in control - leading to a double-spending problem.

A successful majority attack would also allow the attacker to prevent some or all transactions from being confirmed (transaction denial of service) or to prevent some or all other miners from mining, resulting in what is known as mining monopoly.

On the other hand, a majority attack would not allow the attacker to reverse transactions from other users nor to prevent transactions from being created and broadcasted to the network. Changing the block's reward, creating coins out of thin air or stealing coins that never belonged to the attacker are also deemed as impossible events.

How Likely is a 51% Attack?

Since a blockchain is maintained by a distributed network of nodes, all participants cooperate in the process of reaching consensus. This is one of the reasons they tend to be highly secure. The bigger the network, the stronger the protection against attacks and data corruption.

When it comes to Proof of Work blockchains, the more hash rate a miner has, the higher the chances of finding a valid solution for the next block. This is true because mining involves a myriad of hashing attempts and more computational power means more trials per second. Several early miners joined the Bitcoin network to contribute to its growth and security. With the rising price of Bitcoin as a currency, numerous new miners entered the system aiming to compete for the block rewards (currently set as 6.25 BTC per block since May 11 (Chavez-Dreyfuss, 2020)). Such a competitive scenario is one of the reasons why Bitcoin is secure. Miners have no incentive to invest large amounts of resources if it is not for acting honestly and striving to receive the block reward.

Therefore, a 51% attack on Bitcoin is rather unlikely due to the magnitude of the network. Once a blockchain grows large enough, the likelihood of a single person or group obtaining enough computing power to overwhelm all the other participants rapidly drops to very low levels.

Moreover, changing the previously confirmed blocks gets more and more difficult as the chain grows, because the blocks are all linked through cryptographic proofs. For the same reason, the more confirmations a block have, the higher the costs for altering or reverting transactions therein. Hence, a successful attack would probably only be able to modify the transactions of a few recent blocks, for a short period of time.

Going further, let's imagine a scenario where a malicious entity is not motivated by profit and decides to attack the Bitcoin network only to destroy it, no matter the costs. Even if the attacker manages to disrupt the network, the Bitcoin software and protocol would be quickly modified and adapted as a response to that attack. This would require the other network nodes to reach consensus and agree on these changes, but that would probably happen very quickly during an emergency situation. Bitcoin is very resilient to attacks and is considered the most secure and reliable cryptocurrency in existence.

Although it is quite difficult for an attacker to obtain more computational power than the rest of the Bitcoin network, that is not so challenging to achieve on smaller cryptocurrencies. When compared to Bitcoin, altcoins have a relatively low amount of hashing power securing their blockchain. Low enough to make it possible for 51% attacks to actually happen. A few notable examples of cryptocurrencies that were victims of majority attacks include Monacoin, Bitcoin Gold and ZenCash.

GENERATIONS OF BLOCKCHAIN

In the development of the internet, one can point to landmark events that can be used to divide the process into stages. Among these important landmarks are the creation of the first wide-area computer networks in the 1960s, the development of an electronic mail system in the 1970s, the creation of ethernet later in that decade, the launching of the world wide web in the 1990s and the creation of the first browsers and search engines later in that decade, among others. Following each of these hallmark developments, the internet changed in a dramatic way. Each step was pivotal in creating the internet that we know and rely on today.

In a similar way, it's possible to look back on the development of blockchain and also divide it into stages, which are marked off by important developments and inventions. Blockchain technology has only been in existence for a fraction of the time that the internet has, so it's likely that there are still important developments to come. Even now, though, experts have begun to divide the history of blockchain into at least three important stages.

Stage 1: Bitcoin and Digital Currencies

While the ideas that would go into the blockchain were swirling around in computer science communities, it was the pseudonymous developer of bitcoin, Satoshi Nakamoto, who outlined the blockchain as we know it in the white paper for BTC. In this way, blockchain technology began with bitcoin. According to Coin Insider, "many ardent developers around the world still consider that blockchain technology might be perfectly suited" for this digital currency and for advancing the goals of digital currencies more broadly.

In the earliest stages, blockchain set up the basic premise of a shared public ledger that supports a cryptocurrency network. Satoshi's idea of blockchain makes use of 1 megabyte (MB) blocks of information on bitcoin transactions (Satoshi Nakamoto, 2008)(Nakamoto, 2008). Blocks are linked together through a complex cryptographic verification process forming an immutable chain. Even in its earliest guises, blockchain technology set up many of the central features of these systems, which remain today. Indeed, bitcoin's blockchain remains largely unchanged from these earliest efforts.

Stage 2: Smart Contracts

As time went on, developers began to believe that a blockchain could do more than simply document transactions. Founders of ethereum, for instance, had the idea that assets and trust agreements could also benefit from blockchain management. In this way, ethereum represents the second-generation of the blockchain technology.

The major innovation brought about by ethereum was the advent of smart contracts. Typically, contracts in the mainstream business world are managed between two separate entities, sometimes with other entities assisting in the oversight process. Smart contracts are those that are self-managing on a blockchain. They are triggered by an event like the passing of an expiration date or the achievement of a particular price goal; in response, the smart contract manages itself, making adjustments as needed and without the input of outside entities.

At this point, many analysts believe that we are still in the process of harnessing the untapped potential of smart contracts. Thus, whether we have truly moved on to the subsequent stage of the development of blockchain is debatable.

Stage 3: The Future

One of the major issues facing blockchain is scaling. Bitcoin remains troubled by transaction processing times and bottlenecking. Many new digital currencies have attempted to revise their blockchains in order to accommodate these issues, but with varying degrees of success. In the future, one of the most important developments paving the way for blockchain technology going forward will likely have to do with scalability.

Beyond this, new applications of blockchain technology are being discovered and implemented all the time. It's difficult to say exactly where these developments will lead the technology and the cryptocurrency industry as a whole. Supporters of blockchain are likely to find this incredibly exciting; from their perspective, we are living in a moment with an epochal technology that is continuing to grow and unfold.

DECENTRALIZED CONSENSUS

There's no argument that cryptocurrencies have an exciting air of disruption about them, with the potential to change core aspects of everyday life, like creating programmable economies. It's difficult to measure the degree of disruption objectively but it is possible to examine the indicators that historically coincide with profound technological innovation.

One of the largest disruptions of modern time was without a doubt the birth of the Internet, which created the ability to interconnect the world digitally in a matter of milliseconds. An indicator coinciding with this event was the dot-com bubble of 1997–2001, a period of excessive market speculation and wild growth.

There are similarities between this period to today's crypto bubble and evidence that the crypto bubble is even greater in magnitude. While we should approach bubbles cautiously, they are a requirement for extreme growth over a short period of time.

Many companies did not survive the collapse of the dot-com bubble, but the giants of today's digital world, companies like Amazon and Google, emerged from the wreckage. We believe that the key for doing the same is planting firm roots in substantiated value and ignoring hype in general. These are guiding principles for Orbs and will be covered in greater depth throughout this paper.

If the Internet was the technological breakthrough driving the dot-com era, what is the underlying technology driving today's crypto era? Cryptocurrencies are not a technology unto themselves but applications of a technology. This technology is decentralized consensus.

Decentralized systems are distributed systems where a group of independent but equally privileged nodes operate on local information to accomplish global goals. These systems lack a central controller that exercises governance, supervision and control over the system, thus allowing power to be distributed over the network in a more uniform and fair manner. Distributed systems are not new, with applications such as Napster driving the peer-to-peer boom of the early 2000s.

Consensus is a shared view of reality that is agreed upon between different parts of a system. Consider the most trivial example of a consumer application — an instant messenger where users can chat amongst themselves. This system requires consensus to operate, allowing every user to authenticate and speak only on their own behalf. All members must reach a shared view of reality regarding which user is which, who owns every username and so forth. The consensus property is very easy to achieve in centralized systems, where a single governing body is trusted by all members to define this shared reality.

Whereas decentralized systems are easy to build without consensus and consensus is easy to achieve in centralized systems, maintaining both properties in the same system proves difficult. This is the underlying innovation in the field of decentralized consensus. The ability to build decentralized systems where a group of independent but equally privileged nodes are able to reach a shared view of reality. Cryptocurrencies are an excellent example of an application that requires such a system, where agreement upon the ledger of transactions and balances can be reached without a governing body.

Is There Really one Blockchain to Rule Them all?

The term blockchain originates from a core implementation construct of cryptocurrencies such as Bitcoin and refers to a continuously growing list of records, called blocks, which are linked and secured using cryptography. This chain of blocks holds the journal of all transactions in the network and forms the distributed ledger. The term blockchain has become synonymous with the core technology providing the infrastructure for such applications.

Building the next generation of blockchain infrastructure has become a fertile ground for innovation and dozens of teams are currently racing to deliver the "best" one. Many of these projects position themselves, sometimes even explicitly, as candidates for the blockchain to rule all blockchains. We believe that this mentality is flawed.

History shows that silver bullets are rare: complex problems are not solved by a single, simple solution. We believe that there will be no blockchain to rule all blockchains. A general-purpose blockchain can only optimize for the lowest common denominator. Therefore, the first step towards building a practical blockchain is articulating a clear use case — defining a real world need that this blockchain infrastructure is attempting to resolve and determining whether or not a market for this need actually exists.

DIGITAL SIGNATURES

Understanding the Technology Behind 'Digital Signatures'

There are reliable software applications and products available that generate digital signatures merging both digital technologies with electronic graphical signatures of their handwritten signatures. This is both secure and is easily deployed. The process is based on the 'Public Key Infrastructure' industry standard - or putting it technically asymmetric cryptography. In a PKI system, user is assigned a key pair that includes a private and a public key (R Perlman, 1999)(Perlman, 1999). These keys are used for encrypting/decrypting document information primarily for digitally signing an electronic document and for verification of the owner's signature. This private key is kept exclusively with the document owner and stored in complete confidentially, hence sustaining security of the data.

This digital technology uses a cryptographic function, "hashing" which is used for generating and authenticating the signature. The 'hash' function uses an algorithm to produce a digital 'fingerprint', or encoded message. This encrypted message is technically unique to the signing parties as well as the document. This gives the guarantee that the person signing it is indeed the originator of the document. This way, the document cannot be reused, re-printed or assigned to someone else, once signed by the originator. It's similar to 'locking' the document with a protective seal. Any changes, if made to the document after signing it using this digital process, are considered illegal or 'forged', hence invalidating the signatures hereafter.

How Does it Work?

When the owner (who has the private key) wants to send a document to someone, he signs it using that private key. The process is initiated with a mathematical function that occurs to generate a document hash or message digest. This document hash is signed digitally using the owner's private key and then is added into the message. The owner can then send the original document with the digital signature on it with his public key. The receiver validates that the document if it actually belongs to the owner by using that public key which further initiates a signature verification process for authentication. This hash value from the received message is calculated and compared to the values of the original document and if it matches, it validates the owner's signature.

What are the Benefits that Digital Signatures can Bring?

To describe them concisely:

- A digital signature validates the signatures and protects the document from non-repudiation.

- The process is easier, seamless and saves time by allowing you to digitally signing documents in a click, even if you are living far away from the document owner.
- It saves organizations or corporate sectors thousands of dollars spent annually on printing, purchasing paper and ink, and posting important documents locally or internationally.
- It encourages a 'green' environment practice by going paperless.
- It protects the documents' data integrity and ensures greater legal compliance.

Pros and Cons of Digital Signatures

Before we begin let's discuss the difference between an electronic signature and a digital signature. There are distinctive differences which are important to understand.

Electronic Signatures

This is a signature that you add to a document located on the Internet. It could be an email, or a PDF file. In each case there are different ways to create and add them to the document.

Another electronic signature you may be becoming more familiar with is the one used when getting a package delivered to your home which you need to sign for. Or, even in retail outlets where you use your credit cards. It seems that electronic signature devices are being used more frequently.

It might look like an electronic pad or gadget and will have a field that looks like this x_____. This is where you sign your name. This is as good as if you were signing a piece of paper. It indicates that a transaction has taken place and you have agreed to it by signing your name.

Pro: No cumbersome papers to sign, convenient and secure for the merchant. It serves as proof of agreement for any charge back issues.

Con: Cost of Equipment.

Digital Signatures

Digital signatures are different and more complicated. Digital signatures are obtained from services like Verisign.

Digital signatures are used to authenticate the author of documents that are sent electronically. You get them from a 'certificate authority' site. There are quite a few identity checks required before you can receive your digital signature (R Rivest et. al., 1978)(Rivest et al., 1978).

A digital signature comes with a public key authority or PKI. When you apply and receive a digital signature, you get two keys. One signature is a public key and the other is a private key.

Pro: Very secure, involves encryption between sending and receiving the document.

When you digitally sign a document you use your private key signature. Then, the document is 'hashed', encrypted and sent to the receiver. They use your public key, which you previously provided them. If no changes have been made to the document as confirmed by the private key, the item is then decrypted and appears in normal reading format.

If for any reason the public key doesn't work, then it means that the item has been tampered with.

Con: Some certificates are easier to obtain than others.

Digital signatures are more for technology based protection and the laws regarding them will depend on state law. Certificates expire so it is the responsibility of the receiver to confirm the pubic key is valid. If you own the key, you need to take responsibility for keeping it safe. Common sense should prevail. If you've gone to all the trouble to obtain one, don't give it to others to use.

What are zk-SNARKs?

Zcash is the first widespread application of zk-SNARKs, a novel form of zero-knowledge cryptography. The strong privacy guarantee of Zcash is derived from the fact that shielded transactions in Zcash can be fully encrypted on the blockchain, yet still be verified as valid under the network's consensus rules by using zk-SNARK proofs.

The acronym zk-SNARK stands for "Zero-Knowledge Succinct Non-Interactive Argument of Knowledge," and refers to a proof construction where one can prove possession of certain information, e.g. a secret key, without revealing that information, and without any interaction between the prover and verifier.

"Zero-knowledge" proofs allow one party (the prover) to prove to another (the verifier) that a statement is true, without revealing any information beyond the validity of the statement itself (Capkun, n.d.). For example, given the hash of a random number, the prover could convince the verifier that there indeed exists a number with this hash value, without revealing what it is.

In a zero-knowledge "Proof of Knowledge" the prover can convince the verifier not only that the number exists, but that they in fact know such a number – again, without revealing any information about the number. The difference between "Proof" and "Argument" is quite technical and we don't get into it here.

"Succinct" zero-knowledge proofs can be verified within a few milliseconds, with a proof length of only a few hundred bytes even for statements about programs that are very large. In the first zero-knowledge protocols, the prover and verifier had to communicate back and forth for multiple rounds, but in "non-interactive" constructions, the proof consists of a single message sent from prover to verifier. Currently, the most efficient known way to produce zero-knowledge proofs that are non-interactive and short enough to publish to a block chain is to have an initial setup phase that generates a common reference string shared between prover and verifier. We refer to this common reference string as the public parameters of the system.

If someone had access to the secret randomness used to generate these parameters, they would be able to create false proofs that would look valid to the verifier. For Zcash, this would mean the malicious party could create counterfeit coins. To prevent this from ever happening, Zcash generated the public parameters through an elaborate, multi-party ceremony. To learn more about our parameter generation ceremony and see the precautions we've taken to prevent the secret randomness essential to Zcash from being exposed (e.g. computers being blowtorched)

How zk-SNARKs are Constructed in Zcash

In order to have zero-knowledge privacy in Zcash, the function determining the validity of a transaction according to the network's consensus rules must return the answer of whether the transaction is valid or not, without revealing any of the information it performed the calculations on. This is done by encoding some of the network's consensus rules in zk-SNARKs. At a high level, zk-SNARKs work by first turning what you want to prove into an equivalent form about knowing a solution to some algebraic equations. In the following section, we give a brief overview of how the rules for determining a valid transaction get transformed into equations that can then be evaluated on a candidate solution without revealing any sensitive information to the parties verifying the equations.

Computation → Arithmetic Circuit → R1CS → QAP → zk-SNARK

The first step in turning our transaction validity function into a mathematical representation is to break down the logical steps into the smallest possible operations, creating an "arithmetic circuit". Similar to a boolean circuit where a program is compiled down to discrete, single steps like AND, OR, NOT, when a program is converted to an arithmetic circuit, it's broken down into single steps consisting of the basic arithmetic operations of addition, subtraction, multiplication, and division (although in our particular case, we will avoid using division).

How zk-SNARKs are Applied to Create a Shielded Transaction

In Bitcoin, transactions are validated by linking the sender address, receiver address, and input and output values on the public blockchain. Zcash uses zk-SNARKs to prove that the conditions for a valid transaction have been satisfied without revealing any crucial information about the addresses or values involved (Bowe et al., 2016). The sender of a shielded transaction constructs a proof to show that, with high probability:

Ø   the input values sum to the output values for each shielded transfer.
Ø   the sender proves that they have the private spending keys of the input notes, giving them the authority to spend.

The private spending keys of the input notes are cryptographically linked to a signature over the whole transaction, in such a way that the transaction cannot be modified by a party who did not know these private keys.

In addition, shielded transactions must satisfy some other conditions that are described below.

Bitcoin tracks unspent transaction outputs (UTXOs) to determine what transactions are spendable. In Zcash, the shielded equivalent of a UTXO is called a "commitment", and spending a commitment involves revealing a "nullifier". Zcash nodes keep lists of all the commitments that have been created, and all the nullifiers that have been revealed. Commitments and nullifiers are stored as hashes, to avoid disclosing any information about the commitments, or which nullifiers relate to which commitments (Bowe et al., 2016).

For each new note created by a shielded payment, a commitment is published which consists of a hash of: the address to which the note was sent, the amount being sent, a number "rho" which is unique to this note (later used to derive the nullifier), and a random nonce.

Commitment = HASH(recipient address, amount, rho, r)

When a shielded transaction is spent, the sender uses their spending key to publish a nullifier which is the hash of the secret unique number ("rho") from an existing commitment that has not been spent, and provides a zero-knowledge proof demonstrating that they are authorized to spend it. This hash must not already be in the set of nullifiers tracking spent transactions kept by every node in the blockchain.

Nullifier = HASH(spending key, rho)

The zero-knowledge proof for a shielded transaction verifies that, in addition to the conditions listed above, the following assertions are also true:

Ø For each input note, a revealed commitment exists.
Ø The nullifiers and note commitments are computed correctly.
Ø It is infeasible for the nullifier of an output note to collide with the nullifier of any other note.

In addition to the spending keys used to control addresses, Zcash uses a set of proving and verifying keys to create and check proofs. These keys are generated in the public parameter ceremony discussed above, and shared among all participants in the Zcash network. For each shielded transaction, the sender uses their proving key to generate a proof that their inputs are valid. Miners check that the shielded transaction follows consensus rules by checking the prover's computation with the verifying key. The way that Zcash's proof generation is designed requires the prover to do more work up-front, but it simplifies verifying, so that the major computational work is offloaded to the creator of the transaction (this is why creating a shielded Zcash transaction can take several seconds, while verifying that a transaction is valid only takes milliseconds).

The privacy of Zcash's shielded transactions relies upon standard, tried-and-tested cryptography (hash functions and stream ciphers), but it's the addition of zk-SNARKs, applied with the system of commitments and nullifiers, that allows senders and receivers of shielded transactions to prove that encrypted transactions are valid. Other methods of providing privacy for cryptocurrencies rely upon obscuring the linkage between transactions, but the fact that Zcash transactions can be stored on the blockchain fully encrypted opens up new possibilities for cryptocurrency applications. Encrypted transactions allow parties to enjoy the benefits of public blockchains, while still protecting their privacy. Planned future upgrades will allow users to selectively disclose information about shielded transactions at their discretion.

Future Applications of zk-SNARKs

Creating shielded transactions in Zcash is only one example out of many possible applications of zk-SNARKs. Theoretically, you can use a zk-SNARK to verify any relation without disclosing inputs or leaking information. Generating proofs for complex functions is still too computationally intensive to be practical for many applications, but the Zcash team is pushing the boundaries for optimizing zk-SNARKs, and is already breaking new ground with more efficient implementations.

zk-STARKs

zk-STARKs were created by Eli-Ben Sasson, a professor at the Technion-Israel Institute of Technology. As an alternative version of zk-SNARK proofs, zk-STARKs are, generally, considered a more efficient variant of the technology - potentially faster and cheaper depending on the implementation. But more importantly, zk-STARKs do not require an initial trusted setup (hence, the "T" for transparent) (Xie T et. al., 2019)(Boldyreva et al., 2019).

Technically speaking, zk-STARKs do no require an initial trusted setup because they rely on leaner cryptography through collision-resistant hash functions. This approach also eliminates the number-theoretic assumptions of zk-SNARKs that are computationally expensive and theoretically prone to attack by quantum computers.

In other terms, zk-STARK proofs present a simpler structure in terms of cryptographic assumptions. However, this novel technology comes with at least one major disadvantage: the size of the proofs is bigger when compared to zk-SNARKs. Such a difference in data size may present limitations depending on the context of use, but it is probably something that can be figured out as the technology is further tested and investigated.

Scaling Benefits of Using STARKs

STARKs improve two of the problems of permissionless blockchains: scalability and privacy. The pioneer in STARK technology StarkWare Industries' current ZK-STARK research is focusing on scalability first and then privacy later on.

STARKs improve scalability by allowing developers to move computations and storage off-chain. Off-chain services will be able to generate STARK proofs that attest the integrity of off-chain computations. These proofs are then placed back on chain for any interested party to validate the computation. Moving the bulk of computational work off-chain using STARKs allows existing blockchain infrastructure to scale exponentially while trustlessly maintaining computational integrity.

Differences Between ZK-SNARKs and ZK-STARKs

Ø   ZK-SNARKs require a trusted setup phase whereas ZK-STARKs use publicly verifiable randomness to create trustlessly verifiable computation systems.
Ø   ZK-STARKs are more scalable in terms of computational speed and size when compared to ZK-SNARKs.
Ø   ZK-SNARKs are vulnerable to attacks from quantum computers due to the cryptography they use. ZK-STARKs are currently quantum-resistant.

INDUSTRY 4.0 USE CASES

Blockchain Use Case in Remittance

In short, remittance can be defined as the transfer of money to a distant location, usually between individuals that live in different countries. In most cases, it consists of an immigrant worker sending money to their home country.

Today, remittances represent the largest flow of funds into the developing world, surpassing foreign direct investments and official development assistance. According to the World Bank Group, the remittance industry experienced significant growth in the past years, up 8.8% in 2017, and 9.6% in 2018.

Some developing economies are heavily dependent on cash that comes from abroad, making remittances a substantial component of their economy. As such, migrant workers' transfers are now one of the main sources of income for many countries. For example, Haiti received international remittances that accounted for roughly 29% of its GDP in 2017. The percentage raised to 30.7% in 2018.

The Problem

The World Bank estimates that the current cost for sending a $200 remittance is around 7% (global average)(Ratha, 2019). Considering that worldwide remittances made up to $689 billion in 2018, 7% would count for roughly $48 billion paid in operational costs.

In addition to the high fees, most remittance solutions rely on third-party services and financial institutions. The need for multiple intermediaries makes the current system highly inefficient. Not only because the services are expensive but also because transfers may take days or even weeks.

In this context, blockchain technology may provide viable and more efficient alternatives to the remittance industry. This article introduces some of the possibilities and existing solutions, along with a few examples of companies working on the space.

Is Blockchain the Solution?

The main goal of blockchain remittance companies is to simplify the entire process, removing unnecessary intermediaries. The idea is to provide frictionless and nearly instant payment solutions. Unlike traditional services, a blockchain network doesn't rely on a slow process of approving transactions, which usually goes through several mediators and requires a lot of manual work.

Instead, a blockchain system can perform worldwide financial transactions based on a distributed network of computers. This means that several computers participate in the process of verifying and validating transactions - and this can be done in a decentralized and secure way. When compared to the traditional banking system, blockchain technology can provide faster and more reliable payment solutions at a much lower cost.

In other words, blockchain technology may solve some of the major problems faced by the remittance industry, such as high fees and long transaction time. The operational costs can drop substantially simply by reducing the numbers of intermediaries.

USE CASES

Mobile Application

Many companies are now experimenting with blockchain technology to deliver new payment solutions. Some mobile crypto wallets allow users to send and receive digital assets worldwide, and to quick exchange between crypto and fiat currencies.

Coins.ph is one example of a mobile wallet app that provides multiple features. Users are able to do international remittances, pay bills, buy game credits, or simply trade Bitcoin and other cryptocurrencies. Also, some financial services don't require a bank account.

Digital Platforms

Some companies are operating an infrastructure that interacts directly with the traditional financial system. For instance, BitPesa is an online platform that deploys blockchain technology in Africa. Founded in 2013, they are providing payment solutions and currency exchange at lower rates and increased speed.

The Stellar protocol is another example of a blockchain platform serving the remittance industry. Stellar was founded in 2014 with the alleged goal of promoting financial access, connecting people and financial institutions worldwide.

The Stellar network counts with a distributed ledger that has its own currency, named Stellar lumens (XLM). Their native token can be used as a bridge currency, facilitating global trades between fiat and cryptocurrency assets. Similar to BitPesa, users and financial institutions can use the Stellar platform to send and receive money with reduced transaction costs.

ATMs

Along with mobile applications and online platforms, the use of ATMs may provide an interesting solution for sending and receiving money worldwide. Such an approach may be especially useful in underdeveloped areas that still lack a good Internet connection or banking system.

Companies like Bit2Me and MoneyFi are developing new remittance systems that combine blockchain technology with ATMs. Their goal is to issue prepaid cards that support multiple functionalities.

The combined use of blockchain ledgers with ATMs has the potential to greatly reduce the need for intermediaries. Users won't need a bank account, and the ATM companies will likely charge a small fee in the process.

Current Challenges and Limitations

While it's clear that blockchain technology can bring many advantages to the remittance industry, there is still a long way to go. Following are some of the potential barriers and major limitations, along with possible solutions.

Ø   Crypto-fiat conversion. The worldwide economy is still based on fiat currencies, and converting between crypto and fiat is not always an easy task. In many cases, a bank account is required. Peer to peer (P2P) transactions can remove the need for a bank, but users will likely need to convert from fiat to crypto in order to use the money.

Ø   Mobile and Internet dependence. Millions of people living in underdeveloped countries still lack access to the Internet, and many don't have a smartphone. As mentioned, blockchain-compatible ATMs may be part of the solution.

Ø   Regulation. Cryptocurrency regulation is still in very early stages. It is either unclear or inexistent in several countries, especially the ones that rely on foreign cash inflow. But further adoption of blockchain technology will certainly push regulation forward.

Ø   Complexity. Using cryptocurrencies and blockchain technology require certain technical knowledge. Most users still rely on third-party service providers because running and using blockchain autonomously is not an easy task. Also, many crypto wallets and exchanges still lack educational guides and intuitive interfaces.

Ø   Volatility. Cryptocurrency markets are still immature and subject to high volatility. As such, they are not always suitable for everyday use, as their market value may change very quickly. Other than that, highly-volatile currencies are not ideal for people that just want to transfer money from one place to another. This problem is less concerning, though, and stablecoins may offer a viable solution.

BLOCKCHAIN USE CASE IN INSURANCE

The most significant, essential types of insurance are key cogs in the American economic sector and are critical to the well-being of countless individuals and families. The life/health insurance sector was responsible for $638 billion in new premiums written in 2015, and the property/casualty sector grew three percent to a record high of $520 billion. But it's not all roses and lilacs when it comes to the insurance industry. Tellingly, 35% of insurer directors at a PwC forum said that they believe the industry landscape will remain the same, but the players will change substantially in a matter of 5–10 years. 44% said that "most insurers will not survive, at least in their existing form."

This indicates that, among other factors, innovation and embracing technological differentiators will be key in determining which players have staying power and which will slide into irrelevance. The blockchain possesses the potential to be one of the most impactful developments for insurers and their customers, encompassing use cases that include fraud prevention, reducing administrative costs, asset tracking and assessment, and even new forms of insurance, such as microinsurance.

Fraud Prevention: Detecting Fraudulent Claims

It's not as if insurers aren't dedicating ample time and resources to fighting fraud. Insurance companies lose over USD 6.25 billion to frauds which results in higher premiums for genuine consumers(Insurance Fact Book, 2019). As much as 95% of insurers employ anti-fraud technology, and 71% of those respondents said that detecting claims fraud is the primary aim of such technology. Legislators have done their part, too. 48 states plus Washington, D.C. categorize insurance fraud as a specific crime. 41 states plus the District have a fraud bureau that deals exclusively with insurance-specific fraud cases.

Yet insurers continue to be burned by fraudsters. One conservative estimate pegs the losses in the industry from fraud at $80 billion per year. It's not just the insurance companies whose pockets are robbed by insurance fraudsters, either. Insurance fraud costs the average family between $400 and $700 per year in the form of higher premiums. Auto insurance represents the most prevalent, costly form of insurance fraud, and studies claim that 25% of bodily injury claims resulting from car crashes are exaggerated or outright fraudulent. This can mean an extra $200–$300 per year on your car insurance premium alone.

Many forms of insurance fraud are made possible by the lack of shared information across the insurance industry. Limited observation space allows fraudulent claims to slip through the cracks, and whether it is due to competitive instincts, legal concerns, technological shortcomings, or other reasons, insurance companies are often not equipped to sniff out bad claims. If the blockchain can be used as the basis for an industry-wide store of information into which algorithms could be fashioned to detect repeat claims, chronic offenders, and other signs of fraud, it would be a major win for the industry and non-fraudsters who continue to pay out the nose for the cost of false claims.

Expediting Policy Creation and Claims Processing

The healthcare industry serves as a prime example of how errors and inefficiencies in the claims review process can cause exorbitant costs that are ultimately reflected in higher premiums. A 2017 report found that nine percent of medical insurance claims, or roughly $262 billion, were initially denied. Those denials led to $8.6 billion in appeals-related administrative costs, and approximately 63% of those appeals proved successful. Those initial denials not only necessitated additional billions in costs, they put at risk approximately $4.9 million per hospital in net patient revenue.

Like any industry, the trend toward convenience, including 24-hour shopping, one-click purchasing, and digitization, is coming in the insurance industry. From policy creation to claims monitoring, it's only a matter of time until excess human intermediaries must adapt or be forced out, and there's reason to think that automation will streamline policy creation and claims processing as much, if not more so, than any other facet of the insurance sector.

In discussions about how the industry can better detect fraud, an industry-wide information database is often mentioned, and this store of shared information could serve several purposes for the sake of insurance. Aside from fraud detection, it could serve as a resource by which claims could be processed, paid out, or denied with greater rapidity. The price one pays for insurance is based upon several factors that can be ever-changing. When it comes to policy creation and claims processing, a catch-all database that contains information including but not limited to accident history, medical procedures, and filing records could create much-needed efficiency.

Streamlining Routine Interactions

Fraud accounts for approximately 10% of the property-casualty insurance sector's annual losses, constituting $34 billion in losses over a four-year stretch between 2011 and 2015[1]. While this fraud takes many forms, the exchange of false information is a major pain point that leads to costs falling disproportionately on one party and their insurer, ultimately raising premiums across the entire industry. Providing false information on insurance-related documents carries weighty consequences.

If caught maliciously providing false information on a health insurance application, the civil penalty can cost as much as $250,000. When exchanging information post-crash, the penalties for dishonesty are not quite as steep. If law enforcement gets involved and false information is given — which is often the case in an accident — the penalty is up to 1 year in jail, 12 months probation, and a $1,000 fine. For a second offense, the offender risks 5 years in prison, 5 years probation, and/or a $5,000 fine. However, these cases can be difficult to prove and prosecute, and better systems of catching false insurance claims and securitizing routine insurance-related interactions is needed.

Envision a world where the details of one's insurer were stored on a database, tied directly to one's verified identity. No longer would one have to jot down information, hoping that the person who rear-ended them did not give them bogus information. Quicker, more reliable systems for making the routine insurance-related interaction more trustless and pain-free would lessen not only countless instances of fraud, but headaches.

Risk Prevention

The insurance industry is massive, consisting of over 7,000 companies collecting over $1 trillion in premiums annually. That makes the industry ripe for rip-off, and fraudsters are estimated to incur a cost of over $40 billion each year on insurers. These immense costs eventually end up costing purchasers of insurance policies, though many don't realize how much fraudulent claims impact their policy's price tag.

Insurance companies have the duty of employing the most stringent risk prevention and fraud detection apparatuses, and the blockchain is at the frontier of cutting-edge fraud prevention tools. The technology can be utilized as a method to seamlessly and securely share fraud intelligence among decentralized institutions, and may also minimize counterfeiting, double booking, and document or contract alterations by establishing clear, timeless records of asset ownership.

On-Demand Insurance

Insurers of all kinds face inefficiencies that ultimately manifest as increased costs to the policy buyer. With $1.1 trillion in net premiums written in 2016, and a form of insurance for virtually any aspect of life available for purchase, the need for greater efficiency in the industry is ever-present. As it stands, the industry requires humans to pass a policy from quote to underwriting to eventually issuance, costing time, money, and exposing the policy buyer to risk in the interim. Those who seek to employ smart contracts in insurance see the opportunity for built-in "triggers" to activate and terminate policies based on predetermined criteria. This would mean quicker establishment of policies based on a database of required information for on-demand policy creation, as well as quicker claims processing and payouts.

Property and Casualty Insurance

Property and casualty insurance covers risk related to lost or damaged property, and it accounted for 47% of all premiums written in 2016. The collective P/C insurance umbrella of home, auto, and commercial constituted by far the largest number of insurers in the nation that year, with 2,538 P/C insurance businesses. The sheer size of these insurers' responsibilities — $533.7 billion in premiums were written in 2016 — is illustrative of the difficulties inherent to assessing claims. Gathering data on assets such as a home or vehicle is notoriously costly and time-consuming, and accounts for many of the inefficiencies in property and casualty insurance.

With the blockchain, a completely new system of tracking the lifetime of an asset could be established, eschewing a fragmented network that varies by insurer for a unified record database built on the blockchain. Smart contracts could digitize paper contracts and process claims based on coded criteria, calculating liabilities for all parties based on universal criteria and standards. Better yet, this record could be updated in real time by insurers and policyholders when the status of an asset or policy changes.

Reinsurance

Reinsurance allows insurers to mitigate their risk by offloading policies on other insurers. However, the offloading process often ends up with tangled wires and inefficiencies. Altogether, reinsurance expense ratios typically account for 5–10% of premiums, an indication that leaps can be made in the efficiency of reinsurance processes. PricewaterhouseCoopers estimates that the introduction of blockchain technology in reinsurance could remove 15–25% of expenses, delivering an industry-wide savings of $5 billion–$10 billion. The primary way to achieve these savings is through the adoption of a blockchain ledger by which insurers could communicate intel pertaining to reinsured policies. Considering that aspects of a single policy are routinely divvied up between numerous insurers, the need for unification of recordkeeping in reinsurance is particularly great.

Microinsurance

Microinsurance is a lifeline covering specific insurance needs, typically for low-income families and individuals, and strong demand for microinsurance has been met with increasing adoption. In 2009, microinsurance covered approximately 135 million risks worldwide. Today, that number stands at 500 million. In Africa, microinsurance coverage — primarily funeral insurance — grew 200% between 2008 and 2012, and the 172 million lives covered in some way by microinsurance in Asia and Oceania represents a 40% annual increase between 2010 and 2012.

The potential market for microinsurance is estimated to be a whopping 4 billion people, and the blockchain can help the industry accommodate those in need of specified, affordable insurance. By facilitating transparent, peer-to-peer contracts and transactions, as well as bypassing often corrupt bureaucracy, the nations that need it most will be granted access to simple, understandable, and effective means of coverage.

Peer-to-Peer Insurance

Peer-to-peer insurance is a relatively new term, but the roots of the industry — lending with as few intermediaries as possible to reduce waste and eschew profits — goes back to old-school mutual insurance. With a $64 billion valuation in 2015 and an anticipated value of $1 trillion by 2025, P2P insurance is on an undeniable upswing. It's clear to see why the market is expected to grow: members pool their resources, and unpaid premiums are returned to the members instead of being kept by an investor or insurer as revenue.

This general vision of insuring only what you need if you need it is being fitted to blockchain technology, with members placing their funds in digital wallets and those funds representing the amount of exposure from which they are protected. If a claim is made, their investment is used, and if not, the funds are returned to them. These sort of blockchain-based P2P insurance models are being used for unemployment insurance and a select few other forms of coverage, and more iterations are sure to emerge.

PARAMETRIC INSURANCE

Parametric insurance, aka index insurance, refers to a policy — typically related to weather events — that pays out a predetermined amount only when a specific parameter is triggered. This makes it fairly simple to install the parameters of a policy — if X amount of rain falls, the homeowner is paid X — into a self-executing smart contract, and this formula can be followed across the many forms of parametric policies. These parametric insurance policies are uniquely suited to smart contracts built on the blockchain, and adopting the technology could save insurers and policyholders a boatload in administrative costs. Because parametric insurance policies are defined by specific parameters, the subjectivity that is required to determine damages in traditional insurance is not in play, rendering the human element of claims processing virtually moot.

Blockchain Use Case in Governance

Blockchain Technology (also called Distributed Ledger Technology (DLT)) is a potential vehicle to improve government services and foster more transparent government-citizen relations. The distributed tech can work to dramatically optimize business processes through more efficient and secure data sharing.

Blockchain has numerous possible applications for the public sector. Through blockchain technology, governments can improve the way they deliver services, prevent tax fraud, eliminate bureaucracy, and reduce waste. Digital cash transactions can help reshape financial transactions between the government and its citizens.

The existing inefficient pen-and-paper way of doing things plagues the public sector and has made the hallmark of government offices: bureaucracy and corruption. Mistrust in government services to effectively problem solve and provide services to the population is a baseline for public perceptions. Blockchain creates a trustless environment for regulatory activity and works to combat slow, expensive multi-step processes that require several intermediaries. Sounds like government and blockchain are a match made in heaven.

Blockchain interventions in government practices have strong use cases for various departments from healthcare benefits to social security benefit distribution to improved document management and storage. Decentralized tech offers hope that governments can achieve more streamlined operations and pare down back-office operations. Blockchain could potentially alleviate populations worldwide from high taxation and smooth ruffled relationships, instilling trust through a new kind of technological infrastructure that is decentralized and autonomous. Unbiased technology is the next frontier of public sector management with blockchain as the vehicle for trustless web 3.0 solutions.

Centralized Government & Public Sector Operations

Centralized government functions have earned public services a bad name over the years. People often dread having to do anything involving government offices from the long lines and excruciating wait times at the DMV to the arduous process of filing taxes; citizens feel government offices are inefficient. The simplest tasks become elongated when bureaucracy is the only thing protecting us from fraud and security breaches.

Here are the main pain-points for government departments that contribute to the low public opinion:

Opaque Operations

Everything the government does seems to be shrouded in mystery, and perceptions of low accessibility to information and direct representation are only mounting. Citizens even have trouble accessing their personal information at times. People are forced to wait for annual reports to find out where their tax dollars have already been spent. There are no real-time updates to follow transactions or cash flow. The money seems to disappear into thin air. With a lack of transparency, there is a lack of accountability that follows. Federal bodies meet behind closed doors, and subjective news reports then trickle down to the public. Additionally, it is those in power who seems to dictate the flow of information.

Slow and Inefficient

Filing for benefits is a perfect example of a slow and inefficient process that damages government-citizen relations. Receiving benefits is a multi-step process that requires potential recipients to file at least three to four months in advance in the U.S. All government programs require people to collect personal documentation and mail in or submit it through online portals. Then the documents must pass human several verification processes and audits. Fund distribution also relies on snail mail and other ineffective forms of dispensation. Checks don't always come on time and fraud is rampant.

Privacy issues

"Big brother is watching." While we might not know exactly where our money goes after we pay our taxes or what the government is doing, the government collects and stores our private information. Defense departments worldwide use existing technology to invade privacy in the name of security. Our cell phones are used as government surveillance tools. If the government had alternative means to collect the information they needed to provide adequate national security they would not need to infringe on citizens' privacy.

Widespread Corruption

There is tax fraud, identity theft, falsified data and more within the government and its population. Corruption in developing countries is nearly guaranteed when it comes to local elections. Dishonesty is commonplace in political landscapes. Citizens have their own mixed bag of scams like tax evasion and in some more extreme cases staged death to collect social security. Corruption exists from the smallest local government offices up through federal presidential elections.

Expensive and Wasteful

With all the need for document verification, multi-step registrations, and the human hands needed to perform these duties, public sector service delivery is expensive and generally wasteful. If specific processes were abridged and simplified, billions could be saved annually. As the government becomes bigger and bigger and involves more and more actors, it becomes more difficult to track spending, and more waste is added as citizens reluctantly foot the bill.

How Blockchain Works

The blockchain is a digital ledger where digital asset transactions are recorded chronologically and publicly. It can also function to store and exchange information between parties via distributed peer-to-peer networks. Transaction verification is executed autonomously through cryptography and requires no third-party. Smart contracts can be written and live atop the blockchain. Smart contracts are event-based and can release funds or verify processes automatically upon being triggered by a pre-determined event. Some of the famed benefits of the technology are its chronological public ledger, trustless transactions, data storage potential, real-time results/analytics, and smart contract automation.

How Blockchain Can Improve Government & Public Sector Operations

Blockchain technology, in its most basic form, is designed to function as an asset management platform. Almost all government departments and services require transactions and basic asset management. As detailed above, the way the government currently handles asset management is outdated and ineffective. As we move away from paper-based practices blockchain can serve as the perfect platform to accommodate modern operational needs. The web 3.0 technology has the potential to revolutionize management ushering in new voting systems, new record storage, new tax portals, new healthcare delivery and more (R Potluri et. al., 2018)(Potluri & Vajjhala, 2018). It will also improve governments abilities to collaborate with other countries' governments worldwide. As the private sector rises to the occasion to meet citizens' expectations for speed, transparency, and trustless transactions governments are starting to discuss the possibilities and solutions blockchain could bring to their operations and governed populations.

Here are some of the main benefits of blockchain applications in government:

Ø   Trustless Transactions & Interactions

An important feature of blockchain is its ability to facilitate transactions that aren't predicated on trust and the need for paper-trails of verification. Blockchain-based citizen registration could create a blockchain I.D. that could then be used (even separate of personal identity) for fraud-free, real-time monetary transactions between governments and citizens via distributed ledger technology. When citizens share access to documents, and they will be stored securely on the blockchain and bolster personal privacy, interactions become trustless and require less bureaucratic paper-based verification making them additionally more affordable.

Security

Governments are now a target for web hackers, and these hacks cost citizens' their privacy and the government large sums of money. These security breaches are easily preventable thanks to improved blockchain data storage with ledger separation on a distributed network. This makes hacking worlds more difficult. Traditionally a hacker would only have to break into just one single server or cloud-based storage solution. Blockchain eliminates a single point of failure to enhance security.

Ø   Immutable Record Storage

The government uses our data to make projections and predictions, plan budgets, and perform demographic analysis. The more secure and accurate a government's data stores are the better the government can make decisions about the future. Immutability ensures that data is not being tampered with and therefore immutability also contributes to transparency and trust. We can trust that statistics are real because they are permanent and immutable. This improves identity and residency management, which is a huge global issue.

Ø   Lower cost and improved efficiency

If we can verify and authenticate without third-parties on the blockchain and make updates in real-time, we can eliminate time and cost from government supply chains. With instant transactions and verifications, there is less need for personnel and the associated resources previously needed to perform tasks that could now be automated via smart contract.

Ø   Transparency and corruption reduction

With immutability and publicly stored records, citizens could view the cash flow and transactions verified via blockchain. Public records would be more accurate and trustworthy. This kind of unfettered access to tamper-proof public ledgers and data would work to repair broken government-citizen trust. People would need to rely less on biased and unreliable news sources. Voting could also happen on-chain for improved transparency and corruption reduction.

POTENTIAL VERTICALS FOR GOVERNMENT APPLICATIONS IN BLOCKCHAIN

Blockchain could be applied to nearly any public sector supply chain vertical. The benefits of decentralization in government aren't just limited to administrative tasks it can help to make all of the following departments more efficient and affordable.

Ø   Defense and Military
Ø   Public Health
Ø   Sanitation
Ø   Agriculture
Ø   Energy
Ø   Housing
Ø   Social welfare
Ø   Justice
Ø   Transportation
Ø   Treasury
Ø   Veteran Affairs
Ø   Land Management

USE CASES FOR BLOCKCHAIN APPLICATIONS IN GOVERNMENT

Improved Taxation Processes

Blockchain has several use cases that could help streamline complex taxation protocols. It could potentially allow citizens to allocate their tax dollars themselves towards the programs they support, increasing and overall sense of democracy. Taxes could be held in smart contracts, and tax returns could be released automatically triggered by filing.

Reconciling Intragovernmental Transfers

When large sums of money are considered unreconciled funds in the federal budget the process of reconciling is unnecessarily lengthy and costly. It also prevents accurate future budget projects and makes things difficult to account for. These sometimes trillions of dollars could benefit from blockchain accounting systems that would offer immutable transaction ledgers that could allow for even automated reconciliation with a pre-programmed smart contract designed to reconcile transfers based on specific events.

E-residency Programs

Government IDs verified on the blockchain could help residents vote, file taxes, and perform other related citizenship processes in a more secure and streamlined fashion. Virtual residency authentication could help to immutable provide citizenship. All government transactions could be moved onto the blockchain using virtual e-residency identities to streamline all interactions between the government and citizens. For countries with universal healthcare, patient portals could be integrated, and everything from banking to medical prescriptions could be performed in one e-resident portal. Nearly one-sixth of the world's population does not have documented proof of their existence. Blockchain could help establish identity for this one-sixth giving them access to education, banking, mobile communication, and more.

Reduce Voter Fraud

Blockchain could be the perfect solution (especially in developing nations with openly corrupt voting processes) to eliminate voter fraud. Votes made via blockchain could be stored on the public ledger anonymously with verifiable audit trails thanks to its innate immutable nature. Blockchain-based voting systems could help to repair trust between government and citizen.

Blockchain Identity

Blockchain-based identity management can help governments give citizens control of their information and allow them to decide who can access their data. This will make it easier to authenticate individuals and save the government effort in verifying identity. Thanks to the blockchain ledger's immutable ledger, once the blockchain I.D. is created it will become a permanent and accurate record.

Courtroom Evidence Authentication

Blockchain can be used to authenticate evidence admissible in a courtroom. Through recognizing digital data and timestamps stored on the blockchain courtrooms can use hash value verification as proof in court. This can help improve the justice system and create trustless evidence sources to validate rulings without third-party bias.

Improved Healthcare Coverage Platforms

Blockchain-based healthcare platforms can improve coverage and health service delivery for low-income and the elderly while reducing overall costs. In countries with national public healthcare services, medical records can be integrated with all other blockchain identity records to create accurate, consolidated, and tamper-proof data stores. Updated healthcare records on the blockchain can help contribute to improved medical interventions thanks to real-time data analysis across hospital locations.

Shared Energy Sources

Public energy management via blockchain could help to reduce expenses while saving the environment. The blockchain is an ideal platform for energy sharing and automated distribution. Citizens can buy and sell their solar power on the blockchain to others in their neighborhood.

Government Record Storage

The blockchain offers more secure and tamper-proof storage for marriage certificates, divorce records, death documentation, passports, visa records, property titles, vehicle titles, and corporate registrations. The government performs an enormous amount of record management that could be made easier and more affordable if it was brought on-chain.

The Future of Blockchain Applications in Government

While governments and political structures might remain centralized in nature, there is room for decentralization through technology to bring more transparency to the public sector. Distributed Ledger Technology offers these improvements in government-citizen relations. Global economic competition is already forcing countries to start at least consider researching the potential for blockchain, while others nations have already launched national cryptocurrencies.

We will continue to see varying degrees of adoption globally on a government level. Whether it will stop political corruption or redistribute political power to the people, it will at the very least optimize notoriously bureaucratic and inefficient services saving everyone time and money. Preventing corruption and fraud without the need for third-party watchdog groups minimizes feelings of surveillance, that "big brother is watching," and allows the automated verification technology to create trustless interactions instead.

The old way of doing things creates a maze of red tape around government departments that foster mistrust and dissatisfaction. If governments want to be able to deliver services on par with the private sector and early blockchain adopting nations, they will need to begin integration sooner rather than later.

Blockchain can help bring transparency, speed, security, privacy, immutability, and more to government practices in hundreds of use cases across departments. Those with national healthcare programs can work to integrate identity management with health record management to limit personal information sprawl that currently plagues citizens who are forced to reveal their private details in multiple locations on paper and online.

Blockchain could potentially bring tax relief and help to make governing and being governed a trustless dynamic. Building trust through decentralized technology is applicable across verticals and industries. Blockchain technology even in its infancy has so much to offer governments as a tool for improved operations full stop.

Blockchain IoT Use Cases

Blockchain empowers the IoT devices to enhance security and bring transparency in IoT ecosystems. According to IDC, 20% of all IoT deployments will enable blockchain based solutions by 2019.

Blockchain offers a scalable and decentralized environment to IoT devices, platforms, and applications.

Banks and Financial institutes like ING, Deutsche Bank, and HSBC are doing PoC to validate the blockchain technology. Apart from financial institutes, a wide range of companies have planned to experience the potential of the blockchain.

On the other hand, the Internet of Things (IoT) opens up countless opportunities for businesses to run smart operations. Every device around us is now equipped with sensors, sending data to the cloud. Therefore, combining these two technologies can make the systems efficient.

Here are a few Blockchain Enterprise use cases on how combining IoT with Blockchain can have a significant impact across multiple industries:

- Supply Chain and Logistics
- Automotive Industry
- Smart Homes
- Sharing Economy
- Pharmacy Industry
- Agriculture

SUPPLY CHAIN AND LOGISTICS

A global supply chain network involves many stakeholders such as brokers, raw material providers, and so on, complicating the end-to-end visibility.

Also, the supply chain can extend over months of time and consist of a multitude of payments and invoices.

Due to the involvement of multiple stakeholders, delivery delays become the biggest challenge.

Therefore, companies are working on making the vehicles IoT-enabled to track the movement throughout the shipment process.

Due to the lack of transparency and complications in the current supply chain and logistics, Blockchain and IoT combined can help enhance the reliability and traceability of the network.

IoT sensors like motion sensors, GPS, temperature sensors, vehicle information or connected devices provide crisp details about the status of shipments. Sensor information is then stored in the blockchain.

Once the data is saved on the Blockchain, stakeholders listed in the Smart Contracts get access to the information in real-time. Supply chain participants can accordingly prepare for transshipment and run cross-border transactions.

AUTOMOTIVE INDUSTRY

Digitization is experienced nowadays as a competitive demand. Automotive industries are using IoT-enabled sensors to develop fully automated vehicles.

Connecting IoT enabled vehicles with the decentralized network enables multiple users to exchange crucial information easily and quickly.

The automotive industry is one of the interesting blockchain IoT use cases where the combined technology can disrupt automated fuel payment, autonomous cars, smart parking and automated traffic control.

SMART HOMES

Smart iot-enabled devices play a crucial role in our day-to-day lives. Iot blockchain enables the home security system to be managed remotely from the smartphone.

But the traditional centralized approach to exchange information generated by IoT devices lacks the security standards and ownership of information.

Blockchain could elevate the smart home to the next level by solving security issues and removing centralized infrastructure.

SHARING ECONOMY

Sharing economy has become a widely adopted concept around the world. Blockchain could help create decentralized, shared economy applications to earn considerable revenue by sharing the goods seamlessly.

Can you imagine an Airbnb apartment which leases itself? Slock.it is doing it precisely by using Blockchain IoT.

How is Slock.it transforming the Sharing Economy business? Slock.it is using blockchain technology for sharing of IoT-enabled objects or devices.

They have planned to develop a Universal Sharing Network (USN) to create a secure online market of connected things. With USN, any object can be rented, sold or shared securely without requiring intermediaries.

It could be possible for third-parties like manufacturers to onboard any object to the USN without seeking permission. Smart contracts ensure data privacy and transparency by controlling access to information.

PHARMACY INDUSTRY

The issue of the counterfeit medicines in the pharmaceutical sector is increasing with every passing day. The pharmacy industry is responsible for developing, manufacturing and distributing drugs; therefore tracking the complete journey of drugs is difficult.

The transparent and traceable nature of the blockchain technology can help to monitor the shipment of drugs from its origin to the destination of the supply chain.

AGRICULTURE

Growing more food for the increased population while minimizing environmental footprints and ensuring transparency across the supply chain is essential for maximum customer satisfaction.

Blockchain coupled with IoT has the potential to reshape the food production industry- from farm to grocery to home. By installing IoT sensors in the farms and sending its data directly to the blockchain can help enhance the food supply chain to a greater extent.

Summary

Several industries have begun to explore the potential applications of IoT and Blockchain to improve efficiency and bring automation. In this article, we discussed some real-world products, employing this technology to build robust business solutions.

Blockchain Use Cases in Supply Chain

A supply chain is a network of people and businesses involved in creating and distributing a particular product or service - all the way from the initial suppliers to the end users and customers. A basic supply chain system often involves the suppliers of food or raw materials, the manufacturers (processing stage), the logistics companies, and the final retailers.

Currently, the supply chain management system is plagued by a lack of efficiency and transparency and most networks face difficulties when trying to integrate all parties involved. Ideally, the products and materials, as well as money and data need to move seamlessly throughout the various stages of the chain.

However, the current model makes it difficult to maintain a consistent and efficient supply chain system - which impacts negatively not only the profitability of the companies but also the final retail price.

Some of the supply chain's most pressing issues can be addressed through the use of blockchain technology as it provides novel ways to record, transmit, and share data.

THE BENEFITS OF USING BLOCKCHAIN FOR THE SUPPLY CHAIN

Since blockchains are designed as distributed systems, they are highly resistant to modification and can suit very well on supply chain networks. A blockchain consists of a chain of data blocks, which are linked through cryptographic techniques that ensure the stored data cannot be altered or tampered with - unless the whole network agrees.

Therefore, blockchain systems provide a secure and reliable architecture for conveying information. Although often used for recording cryptocurrency transactions, blockchain technology can be extremely useful for securing all kinds of digital data, and applying it to the supply chain network can bring many benefits.

Transparent and Immutable Records

Imagine that we have several companies and institutions working together. They may use a blockchain system to record data about the location and ownership of their materials and products. Any member of the supply chain can see what is going on as resources move from company to company. Since data records cannot be altered, there would be no question as to who the responsible party was if something goes wrong.

Cutting Costs

A lot of waste occurs through the inefficiencies within the supply chain network. This problem is especially prevalent in industries that have perishable goods. The improved tracking and data transparency help companies identify these wasteful areas so they can put cost-saving measures in place.

The blockchain can also eliminate fees associated with funds passing into and out of various bank accounts and payment processors. These fees cut into profit margins, so being able to take them out of the equation is significant.

Creating Interoperable data

One of the most significant problems with the current supply chain is not being able to integrate data across every partner in the process. Blockchains are built as distributed systems that maintain a unique and transparent data repository. Each node of the network (each party) contributes to adding new data and verifying their integrity. This means that all information stored on a blockchain is accessible to all parties involved, so one company can easily verify what information is being broadcasted by the other.

Replacing EDI

Many companies rely on Electronic Data Interchange (EDI) systems to send business information to each other. However, this data frequently go out in batches, rather than in real-time. If a shipment goes missing or pricing changes rapidly, other participants in the supply chain would only get this information after the next EDI batch goes out. With blockchain, the information is updated regularly and can be quickly distributed to all entities involved.

Digital Agreements and Document Sharing

A single version of the truth is important for any type of supply chain document sharing. The necessary documentation and contracts can be associated with blockchain transactions and digital signatures, so all participants have access to the original version of the agreements and documents.

The blockchain ensures document immutability, and the agreements can only be changed if all involved parties reach consensus. This way, organizations can spend less time with their lawyers going over the paperwork or at the negotiating table, and more time developing new products or promoting business growth.

The challenges of blockchain adoption in supply chain management

Although the blockchain technology has a huge potential for the supply chain industry, there are some challenges and limitations worth considering.

Deploying new Systems

Systems that are purpose-built for the organization's supply chain may not be capable of adapting to a blockchain-based environment. Overhauling the company's infrastructure and business processes is a significant undertaking that can disrupt operations and take away resources from other projects. Thus, upper management may be hesitant to sign off on this type of investment before seeing widespread adoption by other major players in their industry.

Getting Partners On-board

The partners involved in the supply chain also need to be willing to get on-board with blockchain technology. While organizations still get benefits from having only part of the process covered by the blockchain, they can't take full advantage of it when there are holdouts. Moreover, transparency is not something that all companies desire.

Change Management

Once the blockchain-based system is in place, businesses have to promote the adoption of it to their employees. A change management plan should address what the blockchain is, the ways that it improves their job duties, and how to work with the new systems that include it. An ongoing training program can address new features or innovations in blockchain technology, but that certainly requires time and resources.

Looking Into the Future

Several large players of the supply chain industry are already embracing blockchain-based distributed systems and setting up resources to encourage its use. We are likely to see global supply chain platforms leveraging blockchain technology to streamline the way companies share information as products and materials move around.

Blockchain technology can transform organizations in many different ways, from production and processing to logistics and accountability. Every event can be registered and verified to create transparent and immutable records. Therefore, the use of blockchain in supply chain networks certainly has the potential to eliminate areas of inefficiency that are so common in the traditional management models.

REFERENCES

Ahmad, S., Alam, K. M. R., Rahman, H., & Tamura, S. (2015). A comparison between symmetric and asymmetric key encryption algorithm based decryption mixnets. *2015 International Conference on Networking Systems and Security (NSysS)*, 1-5. 10.1109/NSysS.2015.7043532

Bowe, Hopwood, Hornby, & Wilcox. (2016). *Zcash Protocol Specification, Semantic Scholar*. Academic Press.

Butterworth, P. (2019). *Intertrust.* https://www.intertrust.com/blog/what-is-tls-and-how-to-ensure-a-secure-implementation/

Capkun, S. (n.d.). *Practical zkSNARKS for ZCash in ethz.ch.* https://ethz.ch/content/dam/ethz/special-interest/infk/inst-infsec/system-security-group-dam/education/available_projects/zksnarks.pdf

Chavez-Dreyfuss. (2020). https://www.reuters.com/article/us-crypto-currencies-bitcoin-halving/bitcoin-undergoes-third-halving-falls-vs-u-s-dollar-idUSKBN22N2X8

Conti, M., Kumar, S., Lal, C., & Ruj, S. (2017). *A Survey on Security and Privacy Issues of Bitcoin.* arXiv:1706.00916v3

Hankerson, Menezes, & Vanstone. (n.d.). *Guide to Elliptic Curve Cryptography.* Springer.

Insurance Fact Book. (2019). https://www.iii.org/sites/default/files/docs/pdf/insurance_factbook_2019.pdf

Internet Society. (n.d.). https://www.internetsociety.org/deploy360/tls/basics/

Lauter, K. (2004, February). The advantages of elliptic curve cryptography for wireless security. *IEEE Wireless Communications, 11*(1), 62–67. doi:10.1109/MWC.2004.1269719

Nakamoto. (2008). *Bitcoin: A Peer-to-Peer Electronic Cash System.* Bitcoin.org

Perlman, R. (1999, November-December). An overview of PKI trust models. *IEEE Network, 13*(6), 38–43. doi:10.1109/65.806987

Potluri, R., & Vajjhala, N. (2018). A Study on Application of Web 3.0 Technologies in Small and Medium Enterprises of India, The Journal of Asian Finance. *Economics and Business, 5*(2), 73–79.

Ratha, D. (2019). *Remittances on track to become the largest source of external financing in developing countries in World Bank Blogs.* https://blogs.worldbank.org/peoplemove/remittances-track-become-largest-source-external-financing-developing-countries

Rivest, R. L., Shamir, A., & Adleman, L. (1978, February). A method for obtaining digital signatures and public-key cryptosystems. *Communications of the ACM, 21*(2), 120–126. doi:10.1145/359340.359342

Wohlwend, J. (2016). *Elliptic Curve Cryptography - Pre and Post Quantum - MIT Math.* http://www-math.mit.edu/~apost/courses/18.204-2016/18.204_Jeremy_Wohlwend_final_paper.pdf

Xie, T., Zhang, J., Zhang, Y., Papamanthou, C., & Song, D. (2019). Libra: Succinct Zero-Knowledge Proofs with Optimal Prover Computation. In A. Boldyreva & D. Micciancio (Eds.), Lecture Notes in Computer Science: Vol. 11694. *Advances in Cryptology – CRYPTO 2019. CRYPTO 2019.* Springer. doi:10.1007/978-3-030-26954-8_24

ENDNOTE

[1] "2019 Insurance Fact Book - Insurance Information Institute." 16 Apr. 2019, https://www.iii.org/sites/default/files/docs/pdf/insurance_factbook_2019.pdf. Accessed 5 Jul. 2020.

Chapter 14
Use of Smart Contracts and Distributed Ledger for Automation

Abhishek Kumar Gautam
https://orcid.org/0000-0001-7345-380X
Indian Institute of Management, Shillong, India

Nitin Nitin
https://orcid.org/0000-0001-5686-1131
Indian Institute of Management, Shillong, India

ABSTRACT

Blockchain as a service has evolved significantly from where it started as an underlying technology for Bitcoin cryptocurrency when introduced in 2008. Realization of the immense opportunities this technology possesses encouraged the development of several other Blockchain solutions such as Ethereum, which focused more on the unique competencies much beyond just the digital currency. In this chapter, the authors provided insights into the unmatchable capabilities of Blockchain to evade cyber-attacks that can facilitate a much-needed push for the scalable operation of autonomous vehicles by providing a safer and trustable ecosystem through smart contracts. The chapter also discusses the integration of Ethereum Blockchain with Confidential Consortium Framework (CFF) to overcome the shortcomings of Blockchain in terms of speed and volume. Towards the end, they talked about some of the modern technologies such as IoT and AI that can be benefitted by Blockchain.

INTRODUCTION

Purpose/Motivation: Many organizations have already invested huge amounts in research and development of Autonomous Vehicles in efforts to commercialize them with a transformational amalgamation of technologies, Blockchain being one of them. The purpose of the chapter is to find the opportunities and challenges of using Blockchain-based smart contracts deployed on distributed ledger technology for AVs.

DOI: 10.4018/978-1-7998-3295-9.ch014

Objective: To find the appropriate Blockchain solution for Autonomous Vehicles that can act as a platform-based ecosystem where AVs can interact with other vehicles, carry out transactions, avail various services, share valuable data and resources, etc. Moreover, to suggest a viable solution with a supporting architecture model that can assist in the development and implementation of the solution.

Methodology/Approach: Our approach for research and literature review comprises of identification of the goal of the study, followed by the screening of high-quality research papers from several sources such as IEEE, HBR, Springer, Emerald Insights and white papers from various websites to understand the latest developments. A systematic mapping study is conducted to bring together facts and analyses that form the foundation for developing new ideas to device frameworks and architecture that can provide safe, scalable, and efficient Blockchain solutions for Autonomous Vehicles.

Scope of Work and Limitations: With so many Blockchain solutions emerging every day that hold the potential to make the previous technologies obsolete, a thorough comparison of all the technologies that can highlight their pros and cons, can be studied thoroughly. Also, new ways of making the technology more standardized and economically viable can be analyzed with a special focus on building expertise in exception handling.

Findings: After extensive research and literature review, the researchers believe that an integration of the Consortium Ethereum Blockchain with Microsoft Confidential Consortium Framework (CFF) would be the most effective solution to build an ecosystem of connected Autonomous Vehicles.

Managerial Implication: Major inferences from the study include designing ground-breaking solutions that would bring Autonomous Vehicles, even more, closer to its prospective customers and promote the adoption of the technology on a large scale to make it more sustainable for day to day transit purposes. It is a technology that will impact our way of doing business, managing travel, handling logistics, and even our daily routine; hence it is imperative to build solutions that are safe and reliable.

Background: Blockchain Networks are not centralized, unlike traditional networks, and consist of nodes that are interconnected to each other, as shown in Figure 1. The two most popular Blockchains are Bitcoin and Ethereum, Bitcoin being the largest usually used for cryptocurrencies. Ethereum Blockchain has built-in functionality for smart contracts to deploy Decentralized Applications (DApps). Smart Contracts are computer codes that enforce agreements between parties based on the simple logic of IFTTT (If This Then That). Smart Contracts in a Blockchain works in a way similar to legal contracts in the real world. Through smart contracts, Blockchain can automate business by facilitating automatic real-

Figure 1. Traditional Network vs Blockchain Network

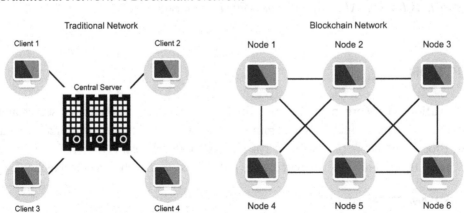

time record management, invoice and receipt verification, payments, inventory management, logistics management, internal auditing & quality check, information sharing, etc. while keeping high-quality data secure and immutable. It can be used to automate the supply chain of various industries, including Manufacturing, Banking & Insurance, Legal, Health-Care, etc.

Table 1. Comparison between Public, Consortium and Private Blockchain

Property	Public Blockchain	Consortium Blockchain	Private Blockchain
Consensus Determination	All miners	Selected set of nodes	One organization
Read Permission	Public	Could be public or restricted	Could be public or restricted
Immutability	Nearly Impossible to tamper	Could be tampered	Could be tampered
Efficiency	Low	High	High
Centralized	No	Partial	Yes
Consensus Process	Permissionless	Partially/ Fully Permissioned	Partially/ Fully Permissioned

Source: Wang, H., Zheng, Z., Xie, S., Dai, H. N., & Chen, X. (2018). Blockchain challenges and opportunities: a survey. International Journal of Web and Grid Services, 14(4), 352. doi:10.1504/ijwgs.2018.10016848

It is crucial to identify the business needs and requirements to decide upon the best Blockchain platform. It is a vital business decision to choose the right Blockchain platform else it can turn out to be a costly affair that might not even serve the purpose and will be utterly unviable for the business. Some Blockchain platforms don't allow high transaction rates, and adding each block is very expensive, e.g., each bitcoin transaction uses enough energy to run one US household for one entire week making high rate large scale global solutions unsustainable. Based on the features as listed in Table 1, researchers can start with deciding between Public or Private Blockchain, or do we need a hybrid one? What technologies can be integrated for better control of functionality? What kind of permissions do we need to assign to participants for accessing the Blockchain database? Answers to these questions depend on the Business needs of various industries. The Table 2 depicts the Segment Forecast for Blockchain Market in various sectors.

Table 2. Segment Forecast for Blockchain Market

	2020	2021	2022	2023	2024
Banking, Finance, Insurance	60.7%	63.2%	63.8%	64.4%	65.1%
Healthcare	3.8%	4.7%	4.9%	5.0%	5.1%
Cybercurrency	22.0%	18.6%	17.7%	16.9%	16.0%
Supplychain	5.5%	5.1%	4.7%	4.4%	4.1%
Internet of Things (IoT)	8.0%	8.4%	8.8%	9.3%	9.7%
Total	100.0%	100.0%	100.0%	100.0%	100.0%
Growth	186.4%	83.9%	45.0%	25.0%	20.0%
Total (MM $)	**15108.6**	**27779.6**	**40280.4**	**50350.5**	**60420.5**

Source: WinterGreen Research, Inc. via https://www.ibm.com/downloads/cas/PPRR983X

Here, our objective is to find possible Blockchain-based solutions for automation of vehicles, which might interact with several stakeholders, including suppliers, owners, vendors, transportation, and logistics service provider, banks, advertising agency, buyers, etc. (Yuan & Wang, 2016). The organization will not need a Public Blockchain for their business as an organization would not like to make their confidential internal data public and would like to control the access to the participants of the Blockchain. Figure 2 depicts the access mechanism in a Blockchain, controlled through asymmetric cryptography.

Figure 2. Asymmetric Cryptography

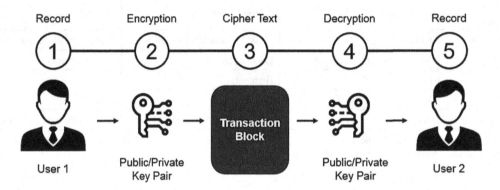

The researchers propose to find opportunities of using Hybrid or Private Ethereum Blockchain integrated with either Microsoft Confidential Consortium Framework (CCF) or Hyperledger Fabric or VeChain Thor for enhanced transaction rate of 1600 transactions/sec, 15000 transactions/sec and 10000 transactions/sec respectively. IoT concepts could be used to track supply chain objects using Barcodes, QR Codes, RFIDs, Arduino, and Sensors throughout the product journey (Samaniego & Deters, 2017). Ethereum uses ERC20 tokens to represent real-world physical objects as digital tokens through smart contracts using entities called "oracles." Ethereum uses high-level language Solidity (influenced by JavaScript and C++) (Lee, 2019a) for developing smart contracts in Development Frameworks such as Truffle and testing in Testnet such as TestRPC, Rinkeby or Ganache before deploying and finally running using GGC Compiler or Ethereum Virtual Machine(EVM) (Lee, 2019b). Ethereum platform provides integrated APIs such as JSON RPC and Web3JS for user interaction with the Blockchain. The Blockchain solutions are intended to benefit businesses in terms of Reduction in Operational Costs, Stabilizing Financial Position, Enhanced Customer Satisfaction by automating operational processes. The basic framework of a Blockchain is shown in Figure 3 (Rathee & Iqbal, 2019).

The chapter presents a step by step approach of identifying the best solution that could fulfill defined requirements. The initial part of the chapter is dedicated to a literature review of some fundamental topics that provide background knowledge on Ethereum Blockchain, Smart Contracts, Consensus Algorithm, The Decentralized Autonomous Organization, and Ethereum Virtual Machine. The review is followed by a discussion on some of the common smart contract vulnerabilities and their mechanism presented in a tabular format for better understanding.

The researchers further discussed the Confidential Consortium Framework (CCF), highlighting some of its most important features and how it can help make the traditional Blockchain more efficient, fast, and scalable. The researchers then talked about Autonomous Vehicles and provided basic literature

Figure 3. Blockchain Framework

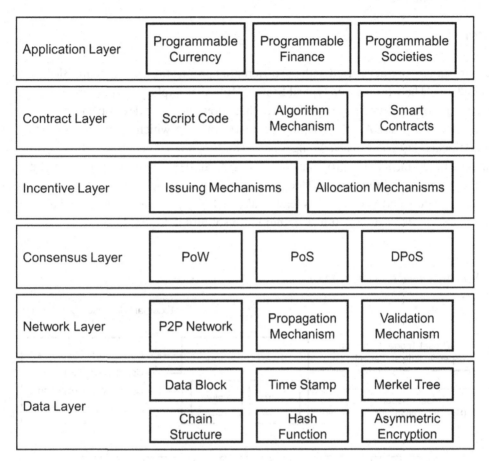

regarding the same. The five levels of automation in vehicles are described, followed by twelve critical challenges; the industry is currently facing. With a central focus on autonomous vehicles in the chapter, researchers identified Hybrid Ethereum Blockchain integrated with Microsoft Confidential Consortium Framework to be the best approach for solving issues in the Automobile Industry working on AVs. The researchers delved deep into the mechanism of Ethereum as a platform and how solutions can be derived from it using Smart Contracts and Decentralized Applications. With a brief analysis of Autonomous Vehicles, researchers listed some of the key solutions that Blockchain can provide to solve stated challenges explained with the help of a detailed Architectural Model of the Ecosystem. The researchers also identified some of the organizations or groups currently working in the field of Automation and discussed their progress journey. The researchers finally concluded the chapter with some of the future trends and research opportunities in the field of Blockchain and Smart Contracts.

LITERATURE REVIEW

Ethereum

The concept of smart contract started with the differential proposition of Ethereum Blockchain (Alharby & Moorsel, 2017). The working of a typical Smart Contract is explained in Figure 4. Ethereum is a development centric open-source software platform that allows nodes to develop and deploy decentralized applications, also known as DApps, for deploying smart contracts, which are generally monitored by peers on the same Blockchain (Wang, Yuan, Wang et al, 2018). Ethereum is generally called a Complete Turing, which fundamentally means that programs or contracts can be written to solve computation problems with the ability to perform branching and looping statements with local state storage using programming languages like Solidity and Serpent. This feature allows EVM to write sophisticated algorithmic codes in other compatible languages and translate them into solidity if required.

Figure 4. Smart Contract Mechanism

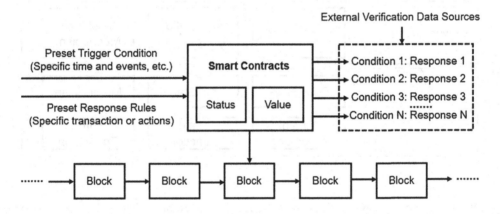

Ethereum fundamentally works on the following principles: -

1. *Simplicity*: Ethereum protocols are designed to keep the simplicity alive at all costs and any complexity to be added only if it brings immense benefits to the system. The reason why Ethereum gained so much popularity is mostly because of its simplicity. While it allows sophisticated operations and functionalities for developers and architects, it can still be used by many users who are not very tech-savvy.
2. *Universality*: Ability to implement smart contracts with algorithms based on any mathematical model where Ethereum acts as a platform to add customized features to the solution. It is compatible with numerous frameworks, and various technologies such as cloud computing and machine learning can be integrated into it to fulfill the business requirement of the user.
3. *Modularity*: Ethereum protocols are modular and separable to accommodate any quick changes without interrupting the complete environment. It allows deriving new functionalities using a soft fork to create applications that might not be very suitable with the original version of the Ethereum.

4. *Agility*: Protocols are flexible to the modifications at any given stage that can improve scalability and security. New Blockchain solutions have already been derived by many organizations augmenting a particular aspect or feature, which may also include adding features that were mostly considered as the drawbacks of the Blockchain. Agility is one of the primary reasons why the Blockchain solutions are being adapted for the changing business needs every day and used in newer applications.
5. *Non-Censorship*: The protocol will not make any attempt to restrict any specific category of usage. In fact, as the technology matures, it has allowed more and more use cases. Blockchain is considered unsuitable for numerous applications, and their probable use case is discarded quite quickly. However, few changes to the existing Blockchain can sometimes do wonders, and that has been proved time and again.

Smart Contracts

So, how Ethereum has been able to implement its values into the functionalities of smart contracts? A smart contract architecture is depicted in Figure 5 (Wang et al., 2019). When anyone initiates a transaction, the underlying smart contract is triggered, and subsequent processes occur based on the algorithm coding. Solidity compiler compiles codes in EVM byte code, which is uploaded into the Blockchain in the form of a transaction. Ether(ETH) is used as the crypto-fuel of the Ethereum Blockchain, which can be traded on any centralized and decentralized currency exchange. These Ethers can be used to pay transaction fees as a GAS on Ethereum Network (Lauslahti et al., 2017). The smallest unit of Ether is Wei, and one ether is equal to 10^{18} Wei. GAS is a fee required to carry out the transaction, which will be transferred to the miner. As complexity increases, the transaction will require more GAS. Since the sender needs to pay the certain GAS amounts to execute the transaction, it prevents the abuse of the facility to carry out any malicious activity such as Denial of Service as it requires an infinite loop of transactions, which is not possible with limited GAS. The latest GAS prices can be easily determined online through EthGasStation or Etherscan. Ethereum has an unlimited supply, while the supply of Bitcoin is limited to only 21 million. State in an Ethereum network is made up of objects known as Accounts. An Ethereum account that has a 20-byte address is an object in the state. An account in Ethereum typically consists of four fields:

1. *Nonce*: A counter that makes sure that each transaction can be processed only once
2. *Balance*: The current ether balance of the account that can be used to pay the transaction fees
3. *Contract Code*: Code that implements the smart contract into the system
4. *Storage*: Account storage of the Ethereum which remains empty in a default state

A transaction in Ethereum refers to a signed data package to be sent from an externally owned account that stores a specific message. Any transaction in Ethereum consists of a receiver of the message, a signature that identifies the sender, the amount of ether being sent to the receiver, and the data field. STARTGAS value that represents the maximum number of steps allowed for a transaction to complete can never be zero. GASPRICE value that represents the fees paid by the sender for each computational step is provided by the sender. A transaction fee is calculated as STARTGAS * GASPRICE, where STARTGAS has a value that prevents the code from going into a hostile infinite loop. Usually, a computation step costs one gas but not limited to this amount and increases as the transaction becomes computationally expensive.

Figure 5. Smart Contract Architecture

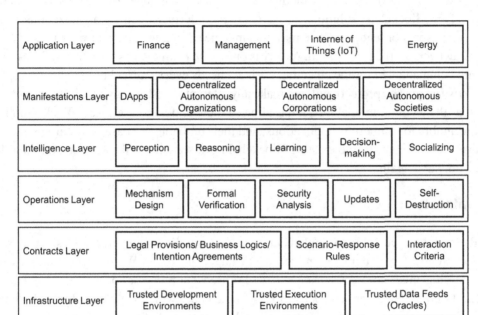

Consensus Algorithm

Currently, Ethereum is working on Proof of Work but is planning to shift to Proof of Stake(POS) algorithm in future calling it Casper. In the current protocol of Proof of Work(POW), the miner gets the reward for mining a block by guessing the nonce. However, In the POS system, there will be no reward; however, the transaction fee is given to the miner. Miner is determined by the wealth of the node, or we could say the stake on the Blockchain. In fact, In POS, a miner is called Forger (Saleh, 2018). Some of the key differences in various consensus algorithms are outlined in Table 3 (Wang, Zheng, Xie et al, 2018). Users join a validator pool to be selected as Forger, which put their bet on the block and get rewarded accordingly. Proof of Work creates a race situation, and every miner works on the same block at a time, causing duplicity and waste of computational energy. It is called mining in the context of the gold analogy, i.e., mining of precious metals. Similarly, Blockchain tokens are also precious and require effort to be earned.

Table 3. Comparison of Consensus Algorithms

Property	PoW	PoS	PBFT	DPOS
Node Identity	Open	Open	Permissioned	Open
Energy Saving	No	Partial	Yes	Partial
Tolerance	< 25%	< 51%	< 33.3%	< 51%
Power of Adversary	Computing Power	Stake	Faulty Replicas	Validators
Example	Bitcoin	Peercoin	Hyperledger Fabric	Bitshares

Source: Wang, H., Zheng, Z., Xie, S., Dai, H. N., & Chen, X. (2018). Blockchain challenges and opportunities: a survey. International Journal of Web and Grid Services, 14(4), 352. doi:10.1504/ijwgs.2018.10016848

There are generally two strategies that are used by the miners, i.e., Solo Mining and Pool Mining. Solo Mining is the one in which a single miner adds the block in which both cost and reward are high for the miner. Cost is high since all the computational power required to add the block is used by one miner alone; though, the miner alone takes all the reward without any need to share it with anyone. Conversely, Pool Mining is a strategy in which miners form a group and mine together to increase chances of acceptance of block, and proportionally, the reward is shared. Miners usually require computational expertise to remain competitive to earn profits. They can either do CPU mining or GPU mining, whichever servers the purpose. Central Processing Unit (CPU) Mining is used on a Private Blockchain using virtual ether for testing while the Graphics Processing Unit (GPU) Mining use Real Ether through Hardware.

Ether can be sold or bought through exchanges, and some famous exchanges are- Bitfinex, Bittrex, Kraken, Coinbase, Poloneix, etc. Participants of a Blockchain generally use one of the two strategies for trading, namely, Buy and Hold Strategy and Active Trading. As the name suggests, Buy and Hold strategy is used to keep currency safe in cold storages like paper wallets and hardware wallets. On the other hand, Active Trading is all about buying the currency and selling as the prices go high. Users usually hold access to a wallet to store their currency. Paper Wallet and Hardware are the two types of wallets that users may use for storing Ethers. My Ether Wallet is the most popular paper wallet and is generally a paper with a code on it which people use for storing Ethers for a long term purpose. The best thing about paper wallets is; that it isn't connected to the internet in any way, which makes it hack-proof, but that is also the worst part about it because there is no way to retrieve your currency back if you lose the paper or if it gets spoiled. Most active users use Hardware Wallet rather than Paper Wallet so that they perform transactions quickly and more frequently while keeping their currency safe. Trezor is the most popular Hardware Wallet, which is a USB based Wallet along with a recovery card. Hardware is not connected to the internet to remove any possibility of hacking, but if anyone has access to PIN and the recovery card, one can find ways to steal the Ethers from your wallet. Either it is a Paper Wallet or a Hardware Wallet, it is imperative to keep it safe from the external environment and robbers. Provided that you have safe physical storage for your wallet, it is safe from any vulnerabilities. Now that we have a safe way to store our Ether, how to convert them into dollars for everyday use? Converting Ether into Fiat currency and transferring to the bank account can take up to 1 week while Tether solves this problem and can be transferred between bank and cryptocurrency exchanges instantaneously (Pedrosa & Pau, 2018). The price of Tether never changes and is always equal to 1 USD. A detailed comparison of some of the most popular cryptocurrencies is outlined in Table 4.

Decentralized Autonomous Organization

Decentralized Autonomous Organization(DAO) or Decentralized Autonomous Corporation(DAC) is a decentralized system with no governing body that runs on smart contracts removing the need of any third party for governance. The system works with developers writing the code that will run the organization. Initial Funding Process lets people invest in the DAO system to earn stakes. The process is called Initial Coin Offering(ICO), similar to IPO, which provides necessary resources to the DAO application. After the funding process is over, the DAO starts to operate on top of Ethereum. In the past, there had been an attack on the 'The DAO,' which caused it to split into two parts. This DAO was launched in 2016 when more than 11000 participants raised USD 150m in just 28 days.

Now that all the participants have a particular stake in the DAO, they all follow a specific protocol to reach a consensus. Many of the participants may not agree with all the consensus and may wish to leave

Table 4. Comparison of Popular Cryptocurrencies

	Bitcoin (BTC)	Ethereum (ETC)	Bitcoin Cash (BCH)	Litecoin (LTC)
Price($)	6400	225	510	55
Market Capitalization ($B)	111.5	22.9	8.8	3.3
Number of Transactions (24h)	264000	592000	20000	29000
Avg. Transaction Value ($'000)	30.9	1.1	5.9	7.7
Avg. Block Time	9m 21s	14s	12m 19s	2m 29s
Circulating Supply (M tokens)	17.3	101.8	17.3	58.2
Blocks Last 24 Hours	155	5980	100	562
Avg. Blocks per Hour	6	249	4	23
Current Reward Per Block (# tokens)	12.50 BTC	3 ETH	12.5 BCH	25 LTC
Current Reward Per Block ($)	81800	790	6400	1400
First Block	39822	42215	39822	40824

Source: What is Blockchain Technology? (2018, September 11). Retrieved from https://www.cbinsights.com/research/what-is-blockchain-technology/

the system. If a participant doesn't want to be part of the DAO, a Split Function acts as an Exit Door to get back the Ethers the person has invested, but can only use those Ethers after 28 days. However, this feature also gave rise to a system vulnerability known as "Recursive Call Bug" that can allow the attacker to take more Ethers than what was invested. The Exit function is concluded using a 2 step process, i.e., Returning the Ether in exchange of DAO tokens and registering the transaction to update the ledger with last internal token balance. But, using a recursive function attacker was able to repeat the first step of transferring Ethers before the transaction could be updated on the network. Just a few months after the creation of the DAO, an attacker indeed was able to exploit the loophole to carry out the biggest attack in the history of Blockchain by drawing 1/3rd of the DAO's funds, i.e., approximately USD 50m (O'Hara, 2017). It is also vital to understand that the loophole was present in the DAO application, which was built on the Ethereum platform and not the Ethereum itself. The attacker, though, couldn't access those Ethers for 28 days, which allowed The DAO to take corrective action on the attack.

The DAO had three options, which include taking No Action, performing a Soft Fork, and the last extreme option of performing a Hard Fork. Some participants were in favor of "No Actions," reasoning the underlying nature of the Blockchain that the rules never change and keeping this idea alive. Since it was a massive loss of assets, most people voted in favor of "Soft Fork." A Soft Fork, as shown in Figure 6, allows the introduction of new rules while the old rules are still valid and followed by users. The method is backward compatible, and it is the choice of the participants to follow the new rules or not. The idea behind implementing a soft fork is to lock down the stolen ether and ignoring any transaction with those ethers. But, this idea can give rise to another issue, i.e., "Denial of Service(DoS)" attack in which the attacker may send infinite transaction requests using stolen ethers. Hence finally, a Hard Fork was used to deal with the attack. Unlike Soft Fork, in a Hard Fork, all the participants need to upgrade and follow new protocols making it backward-incompatible (Kim & Zetlin-Jones, 2019). This forceful method is usually used to recover any damage from the attack. As per the Hard Fork, as shown in Figure 7, the previously mined blocks were declared invalid and deriving a new branch from

Figure 6. Soft Fork

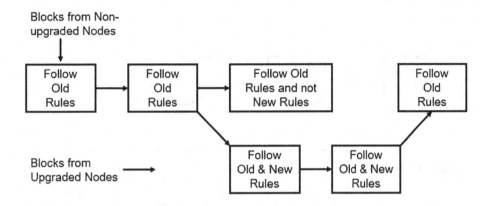

the point just before the attack happened. This was a plastic damage attack in private Blockchain. The new branch was called Ethereum(ETH), which was a result of a hard fork to refund the money lost using a "Withdraw" function, and 1 ETH will be given for every 100 DAO from DAO token holders. Those who were against the Hard Fork remained in the old chain, which was called "Ethereum Classic(ETC)." Ethereum Classic opposes Hard Fork and stays true with philosophy- "Blockchain is immutable." Today, it is the 12th largest cryptocurrency in the world, with a market cap of over USD 1bn. ETH, however, has now grown to a whopping USD 28bn holding the 2nd largest position right after Bitcoin Blockchain. ETH was formed for the sole purpose of refunding the stolen tokens from "The DAO Attack." Although many criticized the Hard Fork executed on Ethereum, it is successful since the decision is backed by its stakeholders and made a positive impact on people about how the technology deals with such a crisis.

Ethereum Virtual Machine

Ethereum Virtual Machine(EVM), as depicted in Figure 8, is one of the main components of the Ethereum Blockchain, which allows DApps on the platform to implement smart contracts. It enables the development of hundreds of potential applications on a single platform. It is usually implemented using programming languages such as JavaScript, Python, C++, etc. The use of smart contracts is not at all limited to the cryptocurrency and, used mostly for implementing other Business applications, Automation being one of them. Each node of the network runs the same smart contract. The downside of this philosophy is that it is more computational and expensive, but it is much more fault-tolerant, forever permanent, and ensures zero downtime. Hence, the decision of selection of Blockchain to solve a business challenge is of utmost importance. EVM executes smart contracts written in a solidity programming language, which is converted in byte code for compilation (Mohanta et al., 2018). It is very much similar to JavaScript & C and supports inheritance and libraries. Some of the most popular apps on Ethereum are Provenance, Weifund, Uport, BlockApps, Augur, etc.

Figure 7. Hard Fork

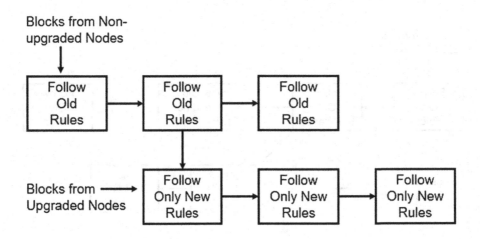

The user can connect to the Ethereum network through an Ethereum Client on the system consisting of an EVM on which the DApps can be developed and tested. Some of the most popular Ethereum Clients are Go-Ethereum, EthereumH, Parity, etc. Ethereum Foundation is a leader in developing Clients for connecting to the network. While a Client is used to connect to the network for developing smart contracts or applications, a Wallet is used to connect to the Ethereum network to make Ether transactions. The light wallet is used by many users as it doesn't download the complete Blockchain on the device. A full node wallet is used when the user wishes to keep the complete Blockchain on the device. Some of the most popular wallets are Mist Wallet, Jaxx, Myetherwallet, Trezor, etc.

Figure 8. Ethereum Distributed Network

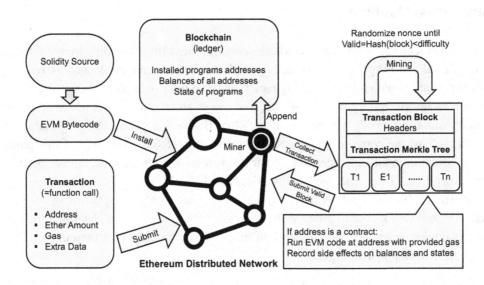

Ethereum Explorer is a graphical user interface for the users to manage their Blockchain account. It has various features such as a catalogue of all the transactions, the current and historical price of Ether, recently mined blocks, etc. Ethereum Token standards, i.e., ERC20 Tokens, are the set of protocols that will be used while developing your cryptocurrency and how they will function. Mostly used ERC20 functions are totalSupply(), transfer(A,x) etc. Ethereum supports the idea of Smart Contracts to a great extent as compared to the rival Bitcoin, which mostly talks about the payment methods on the platform. Smart Contracts remove any possible bottlenecks that might occur during the flow of the process, creating a truly autonomous environment ensuring fast and smooth decision making. The well-implemented smart contract would be a blessing to the organization, but a bad code written for the implementation of contracts can cause havoc for the participants of equally high magnitude, which can be in terms of financial loss as well as the loss of trusted and respectful partnerships among organizations. Whenever anything unfortunate happens with the smart contract, a hard fork can be used to make the correction. This action splits the chain into two, and the longer chain now grows with the new contracts. However, a bigger problem is the loopholes and bugs in the code, which can make the smart contract vulnerable to attacks putting all that we have on the Blockchain at stake. While bugs in the code can be corrected through thorough testing before implementation, loopholes, which are majorly due to the flaw in the algorithm, are hard to detect and correct, creating a major problem for the Blockchain architects.

Smart contracts allow users to carry out operations like exchanging money, shares, content, or anything of value in a transparent manner. Smart contracts are triggered as soon as the conditions are met, and the operation is carried out as designed. It establishes a high level of trust among the parties since contracts are supervised by the computers that run the Blockchain. Although Smart contracts can be used on any Blockchain, Ethereum provides better processing capabilities. Other than Ethereum, RootStock(RSK) platform can be used for implementing smart contacts through Sidechain Technology on Bitcoin Blockchain. Although, RSK is compatible with smart contracts developed for Ethereum, but is not as powerful as Ethereum. NXT is another public Blockchain platform for implementing smart contracts that are available in the form of the template as you cannot create a smart code of your own. Smart contracts are made up of two components, namely, Smart Contract Code and Smart Legal Contract. These are the codes that are stored, verified, and executed on the Network. In Automation, a smart contract can detect who was at fault, the sensor, or the driver. Understanding the environment from the data and communicating with other machines. It is evident that Ethereum is the best platform to implement smart contracts.

SMART CONTRACT VULNERABILITIES

There are various challenges associated with the deployment of smart contracts and thus require testing through security analysis tools to perform formal verification methods for the identification of any vulnerabilities. The limited knowledge of the developers and users is one major reason why all smart contracts aren't absolutely bug-free. Moreover, the technology is still in its early stage and lacks standard practices for developing and testing of smart contracts (Bhargavan et al., 2016). Smart Contracts deployed with bugs cannot be updated in traditional ways like the software but has to be terminated before deploying the corrected one.

As shown in Table 5 (Praitheeshan et al., 2019), the researchers have summarized vulnerabilities that can affect the smart contract code and its execution. A common attack vector can be a transaction ordering problem as smart contracts execute asynchronously. The issue can be solved through a locking mechanism for the transaction to keep the counter in the FIFO order. A timestamp dependence issue is the one that has a constant variable assigned to the block, and thus, it is suggested to avoid assigning a timestamp to the variable in contract code. Exception handling issues can be a critical issue in solidity programming. Such issues can be handled by some of the best practices of the try-catch exception mechanism (Swan, 2016). Moreover, newer solidity compiler versions through an error or warning when the code is being compiled without the appropriate implementation of exception handling. The DAO attack, discussed in the chapter, was caused by the Reentrancy issue occurred due to the call method that

Table 5. Ethereum Smart Contract Vulnerabilities and Security Issues

Smart Contract Vulnerabilities	Mechanism	Attacks	Security Issue
Re-entrancy problem	Calling a function recursively from FALLBACK function	The DAO Attack	Failing to protect or store data
Transaction Ordering	Inconsistent time of invocation for transaction orders	-	Race condition
Block timestamp dependency	Assignment of constant variables to block timestamp	-	Not using cryptographically random numbers
Exception handling	Discrepancy in return values of the called function	Ether Throne Attack	Unable to handle errors
Call stack depth limitation	Exceeding number of calls beyond limit	-	Buffer overflows
Integer overflow/underflow	Big value after subtracting positive integer from zero	Integer Over	Error in Integer range
Unchecked and failed SEND	Sending Ethers without checking conditions	The DAO Attack	Failing to protect or store data
Destroyable/suicidal contract	Due to unauthorized user	Parity Multisig Wallet	File Access issues
Unsecured balance	Exposed Ether balance due to modifier public	Parity Multisig Wallet	Failing to protect or store data
Misuse of ORIGIN	Using return value of ORIGIN instead of CALLER for contract authentication	-	Failing to protect or store data
No restricted write	Restriction on storage variable by modifier private	Parity Multisig Wallet	Failing to protect or store data
No restricted transfer	Unable to transfer Ether by an independent user to the sender	The DAO Attack	Failing to protect or store data
Non-validated arguments	Contract function arguments not validated before use	Under Flow Attack	Unable to handle errors
Greedy contract	Indefinitely locking the Ether balance	Parity Multisig Wallet	Failing to protect or store data
Prodigal contract	Arbitrarily leaking Ether balance to users	The DAO Attack	Leakage of Information
Gas overspent	Consumption of unnecessary amount of Gas by contract	-	Poor usability

Source: Praitheeshan, P., Pan, L., Yu, J., Liu, J., & Doss, R. (2019, August 22). Security Analysis Methods on Ethereum Smart Contract Vulnerabilities: A Survey. Retrieved from https://ui.adsabs.harvard.edu/abs/2019arXiv190808605P/abstract

can be executed without any GAS limit if not assigned any value manually. This vulnerability triggers the usage of the GAS until exhausted. ReGuard is a dynamic analyzing tool that can be used to detect Reentrancy issues (Westerkamp, 2019).

While smart contracts can be an excellent way to automate several processes for autonomous vehicles, timestamp dependence issues, transaction ordering issues, and other vulnerabilities can cause discrepancies in the data and payment methods. This may even lead to the autonomous vehicle getting stuck on tolls or parking spots if smart contracts fail to execute or throw exceptions (Wohrer & Zdun, 2018). Moreover, since all vehicles are also communicating with other vehicles in the vicinity, the inability to execute the desired procedure can impact the smooth flow of traffic. In some cases, the impact can be hazardous, and therefore the mechanism to detect and correct the loopholes of smart contracts for such a use case becomes even more critical.

CONFIDENTIAL CONSORTIUM FRAMEWORK (CCF)

Quite frequently, it happens that a Blockchain seems like the best option to solve a business problem or to create a new offering for the customers, but few issues with the typical Blockchain make the organizations to dump the idea of implementing Blockchain-based solution. The most prominent of such problems is its incapability to hold data at a large scale, and it executes the transactions at a much slower rate than many other technologies. However, Ethereum Blockchain has some of the unique features that force the enterprise to look for opportunities to overcome these issues and build an application to support business needs. Luckily, the Ethereum Blockchain is very flexible and agile to accommodate these changes and develop solutions relevant to the business. One such approach has been used by CFF, formerly known

Figure 9. Confidential Consortium Framework

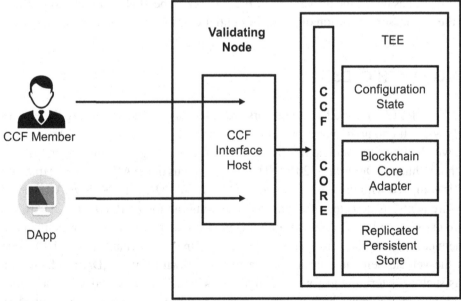

as CoCo Framework, developed by Microsoft under the umbrella Microsoft Azure (Microsoft Research & Microsoft Azure, 2019). It simplifies the consensus in a way that node identities are known and controlled in the network. It is typically a framework compatible not only with Ethereum Blockchain but with many other derived Blockchain such as Corda, Hyperledger, and Quorum.

The significant benefits that are being offered by the CCF are:

1. Better throughput of databases increasing the transmission speed
2. Flexible and richer confidentiality features in the model
3. Management of network policy through distributed governance
4. Increased assistance in non-deterministic transaction
5. Reduction in the consumption of computational energy

Confidential Consortium Framework, as shown in Figure 9, use Trusted Execution Environments (TEEs) through Intel's SGX and Windows VSM to achieve these benefits that are creating immense value for the users. The framework validates the participants on the network to create a network of trusted nodes and simultaneously verify the code at runtime using TEE. CCF interface act as a gateway for the end-user to interact with the Validating Nodes (VNs). It consists of a persistent store that holds the ledger state. A CCF configuration is used to create the network constitution. TEE consists of Blockchain core and adapter, which is used to execute all the smart contracts in the DApps of the Ethereum Blockchain. Typically, a CC Framework consists of two types of users, and both use a private/public key pair along with an X.509 certificate required for identification within the network. Members of the consortium are the governing bodies who run the VNs and define the rules of the ecosystem. Decisions within the ecosystem regarding any changes are taken by the members through a system of casting votes. On the other hand, participants don't have any operational control and are added by the members of the consortium through the voting process. A CCF network consists of a complete list of members, a list of validating nodes, and a code manifest that defines which code will run on the network. A Blockchain-based application on CCF can perform transactions approximately 100 times faster as compared to the one without the CCF. Microsoft has tested the throughput of the network to be 1600 transactions per second, which has become the strongest proposition of the Confidential Consortium Framework.

AUTONOMOUS VEHICLES

Autonomous Vehicles (AV) or Self Driving Cars are vehicles capable of sensing the environment and moving safely with little to no human input. It is made possible by making use of Artificial Intelligence Technology, which allows the vehicle to understand its surrounding environment and take appropriate actions (Muthukrishnan & Duraisamy, 2019). The primary focus of the AVs is to make transit smooth and safe. An AV is equipped with various IoT devices such as RADAR, LIDAR, SONAR, GPS, Odometry, Inertial Measurements, as depicted in Figure 10. The combination of RADAR, LIDAR, and SONAR help an AV in drawing a picture of the surrounding environment by sending waves in all direction and collecting them back to calculate the distance and shape of the object (Pahl et al., 2018). Video cameras mounted on the vehicle helps in coloring in the picture drawn by the LIDAR, which could identify colored signs such as determining if a traffic light is switched green or red. Similarly, most AVs are also equipped with microphones both inside the vehicle and outside vehicle. One outside the vehicle

Figure 10. Autonomous Driving Platform Environment

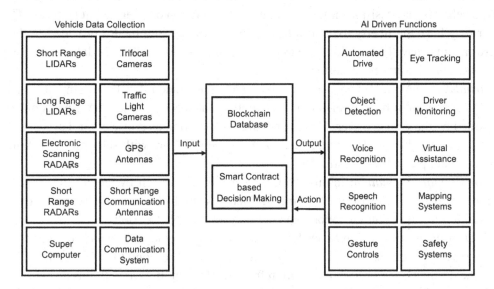

assists in identifying horn sounds or sirens from any emergency vehicle, while the one inside the cabin is much more sophisticated to take commands from humans and identifying meaning through Natural Language Processing (NLP). These devices can generate approximately 300TB of data in just one year from a single autonomous car (Polyzos & Fotiou, 2017). Detailed information on how much data each sensor can generate individually is shown in Table 6.

Table 6. Data Generated by Sensors

Sensor	Quantity	Data generated/sec
RADAR	4 to 6	0.1-15 Mbit/s
LIDAR	1 to 5	20-100 Mbit/s
Camera	6 to 12	500-3500 Mbit/s
Ultrasonic	8 to 16	<0.01 Mbit/s
Vehicle Motion, GNSS, IMU	-	<0.1 Mbit/s

Source: Autonomous cars will generate more than 300 TB of data per year. (2019, August 19). Retrieved from https://www.tuxera.com/blog/autonomous-cars-300-tb-of-data-per-year/

As per SAE (Society of Automotive Engineers), there are five levels of automation defined on the extent of automation:

Level 0- No Automation: This level typically means the absence of any automation and require complete performance of human driver to use all the functionalities of the vehicle to drive it. These are the vehicles that we have been driving for years now, which might have some new technologies such as proximity warning systems.

Level 1- Driver Assistance: Introductory level of automation in which the human driver drivers the car, but the vehicles may assist in either acceleration/deceleration or steering but not both. The human driver may have the liberty to choose from some of the driving modes provided in the vehicle. These cars may have features like lane assist in steering the car back in the lane or automatic braking system on identifying an obstacle.

Level 2- Partial Automation: Moving one step further from the previous level, the computer in the vehicle could take control of both acceleration/deceleration and steering. All other aspects of driving are controlled by the human driver. These cars have an autonomous cruise control system to not only move left and right but also control the speed of the car. Cars with self-parking features are an excellent example of such automation.

Level 3- Conditional Automation: In this level, the car will drive itself by understanding the environment by analyzing the real-time data from the sensors and IoT. The computer will request human intervention in case of an exception, which it may not be able to resolve on its own.

Level 4- High Automation: A significant leap in autonomous vehicles in which the car may still be able to perform necessary action even if the human doesn't respond to the exception. The car can reach the destination with zero intervention from any human. If a car with this level of automation encounters a situation outside its scope, it should be able to abort the drive and park the car in a safe zone to wait for human action. In fact, the car can drive around without any human inside in a geo-fenced area.

Level 5- Full Automation: This level talks about a futuristic approach of automating vehicles where a vehicle may just act as a cabin for the passengers. The vehicle probably may not have the typical tools such as steering wheel or pedals for acceleration and brakes, etc.

Figure 11. Autonomous Vehicle Market

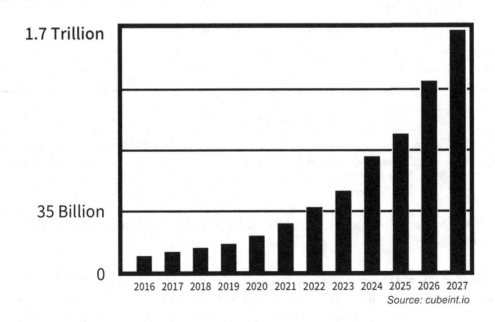

As shown in Figure 11, the Autonomous Vehicle market size is rising rapidly, with nearly an exponential growth rate. Currently, companies such as Tesla, BMW, Nvidia, Google, Volkswagen, and many others are currently working on concept cars but may not be commercialized for a few more years (Ayvaz & Cetin, 2019). Reportable miles per disengagement for the Number of test miles in California in the year 2018, for some of the leading companies are shown in Table 7.

Table 7. Reportable miles per disengagement for the Number of test miles

Companies	Miles	Miles per Disengagement
Waymo	1271587	11154.3
GM Cruise	447621	5204.9
Zoox	30764	1922.8
Nuro	24680	1028.3
Pony.AI	16356	1022.3
Nissan	5473	210.5
Baidu	18093	205.6
Aurora	32858	99.9
Drive.ai	4617	83.9
Nvidia	4142	20.1
Mercedes-Benz	1749	1.5
Apple	79745	1.1
Uber	26899	0.4

Source: DMV via thelastdriverlicenseholder.com

CHALLENGES WITH AUTONOMOUS VEHICLES

1.   Losing control of the vehicle due to possible cyber-attacks on the technology

As technology progress, new methods to disrupt those technologies have also been devised by unethical hackers from time to time across the globe. Using technologies that continuously work with IoT devices and interact using the internet can all come to an abrupt stop if a hacker could hack into the Wi-Fi. Moreover, all devices play an important role in understanding the environment, and failure of even one equipment due to external hacks can put the complete system in danger. Also, an elevated level could be possible where a hacker may be able to tweak how the device work or to send fudged information contaminating the complete data set to trick the vehicle into making wrong decisions (Barabás et al., 2017).

2.   Need for real-time data that can be shared with other vehicles in proximity

Driving at higher speeds, especially on the road with many other vehicles moving at similar or different speeds would require making decisions based on the real-time data collected from the devices mounted on the car. However, these decisions will not be limited to the data from own vehicle but also from other vehicles such as a change in speed or lane of another vehicle will have an impact on the way the vehicle is moving. Sharing data among vehicles as quickly as possible with mainstream wireless technologies is a big challenge.

3. Need for standard and trusted source of data for all vehicles

Just like the speed at which the data is transferred had been a challenge, the quality of the data is also vital. A stream of data that is not standard across the network would be hard to use, especially during the drive. A study suggests that most of the data collected during the transit is not used at all, but is generally used for learning patterns through AI when the vehicle is idle.

4. Decision-making speed and consensus between multiple vehicles

A combination of the two issues, i.e., speed of data transfer and standardization of data, gives rise to the challenge of incompetence to arrive at a quick consensus among vehicles. It is quite possible that more than one autonomous vehicle would like to use a lane or a parking spot or even the more complex decision of crossing an approaching intersection. The speed, distance, and various other factors can contribute to such decisions with a pre-requisite that both the parties reach a consensus quickly.

5. Instant Payments for various services such as parking and toll payments

The need for a widely accepted solution for an automatic payment system is the need of the hour to smoothen the driving experience to a large extent. Human involvement in making payments will make this process more time consuming and will interfere with the natural movement of an autonomous vehicle. While we make a shift to automating the cars to the extent that require zero-intervention of human, instant payments to make vehicles truly autonomous is extremely important.

6. The huge cost of storing real-time data

As discussed earlier, autonomous cars set to produce approximately 300TB of data in a single year; this number would increase exponentially with more and more AVs and further advancement of the technologies. Most car manufacturers would thrive to add more advanced technologies for better features creating a greater need to expand data storage facilities. Finding a solution that provides the best proposition while minimizing the tradeoff between storage capacity and transfer speed is a big task.

7. Building complex yet efficient AI algorithms that understand patterns

An Autonomous Vehicle typically consists of 100 Million Lines of Code. Writing programs that possess the ability to learn and evolve with increased testing and experience should remain efficient, avoiding any overload that can prove fatal while an AV is on the road. Various technology companies are competing to write the finest codes and algorithms to understand the patterns in the best way possible and retaining the memory for future use.

8.   The ambiguity of handling multiple exceptions during transit

Vehicles being tested and built today possess different levels of automation with diverse mechanisms to deal with exceptions. With an increasing level of automation, the ability to handle exception increases, but the computer still needs appropriate geo-fencing, proper roads, correct signboards to identify exceptional situations to take action. An autonomous system needs to go through intensive trials, which improve the ability of the system to deal with even the most unlikely situation. Most companies have already invested much for testing of their concept vehicles, but how much is enough, being still contentious.

9.   Lack of proper supportive Infrastructure especially in remote locations

The infrastructure required for autonomous vehicles to be a success is no more limited to better roads, adequate signage, marking for lanes, etc. but extended to the advanced technological ecosystem that consists of strong internet connectivity throughout for communication, charging stations, standardized payment methods at parking lots and tolls, etc.

10.   Possibility of failure of technologies in bad weather

Most devices work best only in a certain range of favorable conditions and tend to fail in hostile weather conditions. Moreover, capturing data from surrounding by the devices mounted on the vehicle becomes difficult in extreme cold, rain, fog, and heat/sunlight.

11.   Legal regulations of government to deal with liabilities

Autonomous Vehicles will bring a huge shift in the liabilities related to any minor or major accidents that are caused due to AVs. It is still questionable that who will be held liable, owner, or the manufacturer for any unfortunate incident. Given the uncertainty, most locations aren't suitable and hence not approved for any trails or use of autonomous vehicles, and only a few technologically advanced locations have been granted permits to conduct trails.

12.   Effect on the environment with the increased use of devices on the vehicle

With increased consumption of energy due to more devices used in cars, which will rise as autonomous vehicles become more common will have a negative impact on the environment. Although eco-driving, along with better fuel options, would try to balance the effects of increased energy consumption and decreased fuel economy, the overall impact can still have an adverse effect on the environment. More-over, people staying closer to roads or are frequent travelers will be exposed to a higher level of radio waves for a prolonged period.

BLOCKCHAIN SOLUTION FOR DECENTRALIZED AUTONOMOUS VEHICLES(DAV)

Designing a Blockchain-based solution for any real-world problem should go through a step by step approach of asking fundamental questions. We need to identify the use cases of the Blockchain in the industry followed by identifying the platform, the type of data that the Blockchain will work with, and lastly, the kind of consensus algorithm that should be used within the Blockchain. As a result of thorough research and analysis of the pros and cons of various Blockchain technologies available, the researchers believe that using Ethereum Blockchain integrated with CC Framework (Confidential Consortium Framework) by Microsoft Azure would be the best choice for Decentralized Autonomous Vehicles as shown in Figure 12. Ethereum Blockchain is selected because of its several features that are not completely offered by other Blockchain, such as Simplicity, Universality, Modularity, Agility, etc. It is quite easy to develop Decentralized Applications on Ethereum Network and implementing various Smart Contracts to build consensus and trust among peers. Moreover, the implementation of smart contracts will automate several operations in a speedy way without the need for human intervention. The researchers are integrating the Confidential Consortium Framework to extend the ability of Ethereum Blockchain to perform transactions as fast as 1600 transactions per second and better handling of data. The researchers have opted for a Consortium or Hybrid Ethereum Blockchain where a part of record management will rely highly on permissions on Private Network for handling sensitive data while some part would be recorded on a Public Network such that the data can be used by stakeholders, vehicle manufacturers, developers for developing Artificial Intelligence models, etc. (Xing & Marwala, 2018). Distributed Ledger will be used to store real-time data or to perform transactions for payment of services. Also, organizations into Research and Development can trade their data to other organizations decreasing the testing and development time of Autonomous Vehicles.

Figure 12. Ethereum and CCF Architecture for Autonomous Vehicles

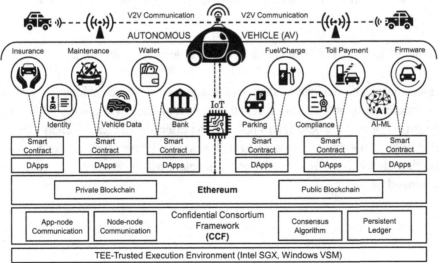

Ethereum currently uses Proof of Work-based consensus algorithm but is set to make a shift to Proof of Stake very soon. The computer of the vehicle will act as a Blockchain node, and APIs like JSON RPC or Web3JS can be used for interacting with the DApps (Norta, 2017). While implementing the solution, some necessary configurations are required regarding the permission to nodes on the Blockchain. For Autonomous Vehicles, access to data should be restricted in a way that a particular vehicle is able to access only data relevant for its operation and don't have access to data that is personal and specific to another vehicle. Some parts of the data can be put on the network through the on-chain transactions by mirroring the transaction, and the data can be used by other peers. Conversely, private data can be put on to the ledger through off-chain transactions so that it remains confidential to the particular user. Sending real-time data on the network should require a single signature while sensitive operations, such as access to the Control Unit of the car to update the firmware, should require multiple signatures to avoid any malicious attack. To avoid any monetary loss, a higher degree of security would be required while performing transactions. In order to pay for services, Vehicle Owners can use Tether, which always remains equal to one USD and can be used to pay for services such as toll payments, fuel payments, etc. Asset re-issuance should be done gradually on a half-yearly or annual basis to increase the total tokens in circulation for better usage and stability of token prices in the market, as the requirement may increase as more users join the network. A robust Blockchain should be able to handle data in an efficient way. With each record that is added in the Blockchain, a unique signature is published that identifies the record. All the records are stored in a logical sequence, which can be verified later to identify any tampering in case of an attack on the system. There will be no need for any authorization since all the records that are stored will be generated directly from the IoT devices. A permission-based Blockchain application, also known as DApps (Kapitonov et al., 2017), will be used to make sure that only authorized users can add or read the data once the permission is granted. It is necessary to ensure that the data is not misused and also can be traded with other users if the data is related to research and testing. Moreover, all the invoices and receipts that are paid by the users for various purposes can be stored in the Blockchain that can be verified by the user if required. However, any fraud is very unlikely since the vendor will not risk charging the user inappropriately, given the fact that all the data will be stored on the network permanently. Similarly, an insurance-related smart contract will be initiated in case of any damage to the vehicle, and the introduction of the smart contracts will only speed up the process of amount disbursals (Lamberti et al., 2018).

A large chunk of data transmitted by an Autonomous Vehicle is generated by the IoT devices, which work in 4 layers, namely; Create, Aggregate, Integration, and Analyze (Atlam & Wills, 2019). Firstly, Data is created from various sensors embedded in the vehicle, such as a camera, LIDAR, microphone, etc. This data will be aggregated that includes combining the data from multiple devices into one place followed by Integration, i.e., the transmission of data for storage and analysis on Blockchain networks. Finally, the data will be analyzed by using artificial intelligence to build a model that can help in making real-time decisions (Bahga & Madisetti, 2016). The suggested Blockchain will be able to hold a variety of data, which include vehicle registration number, data generated by the vehicle while driving, real-time updates on the state of the vehicle, etc. AI would learn from the data on Blockchain and transmitting back useful models that can be used by other vehicles in the ecosystem, as shown in Figure 13. Moreover, Silo Machine Learning (ML) can also be deployed on a particular part of the chain on which the analysis can be conducted (Shreyas Ramachandran et al., 2019). Based on the information, Vehicles would avail services such as predictive maintenance, insurance payments, etc. The insurance companies can easily conduct audits through Blockchain to verify any damage since the data will be readily available if a user requests for any claim. Likewise, due to the availability of permanent data on the ledger, information about Original Equipment Manufacturer (OEM) of any vehicle can be traced back to its manufacturer, including detailed statistics such as which supplier delivered parts to the OEM. All the data will become very much transparent to any of the auditor if the need arises.

Figure 13. Autonomous Vehicle Data Transmission and Storage Ecosystem

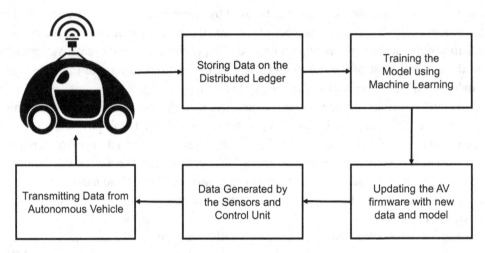

IMPACT OF BLOCKCHAIN

The biggest reason why a tamper-proof Blockchain distributed ledger is the most suitable technology for Autonomous Vehicles is due to the fact that a cyber-attack on the Self-Driving Vehicle can cause damage which is beyond monetary loss. A car without control can put the safety of humans, both inside and outside the vehicle, in danger. Many new technologies may provide immense benefits in terms of efficiency, scalability, and cost-effectiveness, but the security in AVs cannot be compromised. Blockchain is extremely good at being tamper-proof and much more advanced in avoiding cyber-attacks than any known technology today. While databases can fail due to downtimes bringing the whole idea of AVs to an abrupt stop, Blockchain, with so many nodes working all the time, will barely run out of service. As the network increases, the probability of downtime decreases even further.

Using a Blockchain solution, as discussed in this chapter or the one similar to this will have the following impacts on the Autonomous Vehicles:

1. Real-time data from IoT devices in the Autonomous Cars can be stored on the network in a tamper-proof way, which can later be used for verification or analysis purposes.
2. Organizations can trade their research data with other players and build a partnership to create synergies, which otherwise wouldn't be possible. Also, as more organizations join the consortium, the Blockchain ecosystem will grow and become very powerful.
3. Identity management such as vehicle or registration numbers of all the cars can be stored on the network identifying each one of them as a node that interacts with other nodes in a peer-to-peer network.

4. Car performance data of the vehicles can be recorded to build models that can be used for making the experience of the rider better.

5. Insurance firms will be able to cover the vehicles financially by charging customers a price deduced in a transparent manner from the vehicle details such as past performance, depreciation, and the life of the vehicle.

6. Predictive Maintenance can be used as a tool to extract the best from an AV by performing repairs and maintenance of the vehicle on the right parts at the right time, leaving behind the concept of preventive maintenance.

7. Car owners can earn and store digital currency or token in a cryptocurrency wallet to facilitate smooth transactions on the network as and when required based on the execution of smart contracts to disburse payments.

8. Wallet users can convert their digital currency into fiat currency to receive money directly into the bank accounts and vice versa. Currency, such as Tether, is quite stable and always remains equal to one dollar and can be converted into other forms of currency very quickly through exchanges.

9. Blockchain can facilitate automatic payment for services such as parking based on the smart contracts, which might calculate charges for a certain type of vehicle that used a parking space for a specific duration.

10. Similarly, Vehicles can automatically disburse payments to vendors for regular and necessary services like refueling/recharging, tolls, challans, without any human intervention from either side (Pustisek et al., 2016).

11. Manufacturers of the vehicle can send firmware updates through the Blockchain network that can be executed automatically when the vehicle is not in use or as per the schedule suggested by the owner.

12. Several vehicles can share real-time data among themselves to facilitate the uninterrupted movement of the vehicle, based on the short-range and long-range data from another vehicle. Moreover, predictive modeling can be done through technologies such as Artificial Intelligence for making the journey safer.

Now that we will have almost every possible data from the vehicle, many more operations can also be automated by using Blockchain once the adoption of the technology starts to increase rapidly as the understanding of this technology among people improves.

CASE STUDIES

IOTA and Volkswagen

IOTA is an emerging Machine to Machine economy based network of Internet of Things (IoT) that ensures data integrity for micropayments and other applications in a decentralized system. The strongest proposition of IOTA is a Directed Acyclic Graph(DAG) named Tangle for primarily storing the transactions. Transactions represented on the tangle graph are known as sites that are validated by the nodes on the network. The key idea behind the technology is to get the users to work to validate the transactions of the other users so that their own transaction can be issued on the network. A transaction is approved if it doesn't conflict with other transactions in history in a direct or indirect manner. More the number of approvers of a transaction, the higher will be the confidence to accept the transaction.

IOTA has partnered with one of the largest auto manufacturers in the world, Volkswagen. The two entities are set to release Digital CarPass, with a focus on the reliable and secure collection of vehicle data as announced by the Blockchain Head at VW, Benjamin Sinram. Digital CarPass is based on the Proof of Concept consensus algorithm via Tangle Network to improve the efficiency of the vehicle through trusted vehicle software. The technology delivered by IOTA will be used for delivering new services to customers with an ability to pay for those services instantaneously. VW is also working on a Blockchain-based identity management solution that allows multiple individuals to use the vehicle. Moreover, VW is integrating manufacturing supply chain with Blockchain for better tracking of parts on an open ledger as well as charging protocol using Ethereum Blockchain-based solution developed by Energy Web Foundation. In its futuristic missions, Volkswagen has focused largely on e-mobility solutions and Autonomous Driving. Likewise, VW has invested in Artificial Intelligence in its major projects of Industry 4.0 and AVs. The foremost reason for VW's collaboration with IOTA is to build a relationship with other organizations, which can create a synergy to benefit all. The restriction in using the capabilities of each other in the Auto Industry is inhibiting the overall growth of an ecosystem where vehicles can exchange their data, and use resources of other brands to create more value and better driving experience. Volkswagen is using Blockchain to create a secure network that can deploy the application to keep track of various parameters in various verticals of the business, which include Operation, Maintenance, and Logistics.

MOBI- Mobility Open Blockchain Initiative

MOBI is a consortium for smart mobility, working with leaders in the auto and technology industry, governments, and NGOs with a pursuit to create efficient, safer, greener, less congested, and affordable mobility services through adoption and standardization of distributed ledger technology. Blockchain holds the quality to reduce the cost of mobility and related activities by establishing coordination among partner organizations. Some of the founding members of the consortium include Ford, BMW, GM, Renault, and others, which represent 80% of the overall manufacturing across the globe. Moreover, Technology giants such as Accenture and IBM are actively contributing in helping auto manufacturers implement Blockchain technologies in their solutions for automotive vehicles. The consortium is also supported by coveted institutions such as the World Economic Forum.

MOBI projects include developing possible use cases and standards of technology usage in various applications. For instance, the ability to track the odometer of the vehicle and storing the data on the distributed ledger where it can be used as the data stream for Artificial Intelligence. Moreover, Compliance and Trust are built among the partner members, which will enhance the collaboration between them. As more & more members contribute to the development of a global database, the worldwide adoption of the Blockchain as a service will become even more promising. MOBI is set to apply standards such as Proof of Concept Protocol at the industrial scale. The objective is to share R&D standards to leverage the potential of the industry and the way we transit from one location to another. This will not only save the development time of the technology but also allow a safer implementation of the technology. Gone are the days when an organization used to work and develop technologies inside the closed walls without sharing knowledge. Each company use to exhaust its resource into exorbitant R&D and would take years to release any new and innovative feature for its customers. Vehicles are now shifting from being an industrial product to a technology-based product leveraging high impact technologies such as IoT, AI all along with Blockchain.

Cube

CUBE is a Blockchain-based security system for autonomous cars, which also includes data sharing between the producers of the data and their customers. It is an organization making an effort to solve the possible issue of cyber-attacks on autonomous cars and various malicious attacks using Blockchain technology while making use of AI tools like deep learning and quantum hash cryptography. The project under Cube is to be implemented using Decentralized Autonomous Organization, as discussed in a previous section. Big Data generated by an automobile consists of data related to patterns of driving, fuel utilization, vehicle condition, which can be sold to consumers of this data, that include automobile manufacturers, insurance companies, etc. in exchange for CUBE Tokens. CUBE Token owners can be those who produce the information, i.e., the car owners. These owners can use these tokens to avail CUBE affiliated services such as maintenance, fuel refilling, insurance payments, etc.

The primary reason to collect the data from the user is to better analyze the probability of an attack on the vulnerable system of the autonomous vehicle. The possibility of attack is quite high when the data is being transmitted from one device to another. An autonomous vehicle communicates with the surrounding vehicle through V2V Communication for sharing two types of data, namely Short Range Data and Long-Range Data. Short Range Data gathers information regarding the relative location and the behavior while the Long Range Data has information about road conditions, traffic congestion, accident information, etc. An autonomous car consistently sends the data to the nearest Base Station and continuously switch the Base Station as it moves through a process of a handshake.

CUBE aspires to implement Blockchain to store data on the network, which has shown remarkable ability to avert the risk of cyber-attacks since the hacker needs to hack multiple nodes at a time, which is quite difficult. CUBE has identified the basic issues of scalability and speed of current Blockchain solutions. CUBE consists of a private Blockchain for autonomous cars to solve the mentioned issues of transaction speed and constitutes an overall architecture of Hybrid Blockchain. CUBE's Over-the-Air(OTA) technology will automatically update the car's firmware to patch any vulnerability in the system. In order to enhance the security, CUBE is using Artificial Intelligence-Deep Learning that will predict the malicious attack and the strategy to defend the system through passive methods. Although in the past, AI has not been as effective in dealing with such attacks. CUBE has deployed TensorFlow, a library of Google that is open-source and uses dataflow graphs that can be developed with Python to improve its ability to deal with any attack. Largely, CUBE is one of the most promising developers of Blockchain-based solution for Autonomous Vehicles and have immense growth opportunities.

BiTA- Blockchain in Transport Alliance

It is an alliance of approximately 500 members in 25 countries founded in 2017, primarily consisting of members from industries related to Transportation, Freight, Logistics, etc. BiTA is headquartered in Chattanooga, TN, USA. The common goal of the member organization is to automate and standardize the unstructured business practices through technology. The alliance is not only progressing towards finding new Blockchain-based solutions but also educating other organizations about distributed ledger technologies. BiTA uses Blockchain technology to track events such as payment, supply chain, sensor data, mobile app data, and telematics. BiTA is actively researching and finding everyday solutions for companies to increase efficiency. The network of the alliance has increased quite exponentially, with many leading companies joining the group. As the network grows bigger, the applications to use Blockchain will become even more profitable.

FUTURE TRENDS AND RELATED WORK

Smart Contracts have proved out to be very helpful in extending the capabilities of Blockchain, but that gave rise to some severe vulnerabilities, as discussed in the chapter. Significant research is being put into making smart contracts more secure and bug-free. Various tools and techniques have been developed in recent times. Examples of such tools include Mainan, ZEUS, SmartCheck, ContactFuzzer, Oyente, Vandal, teEther, Sereum, MadMax, etc. These tools have been quite helpful in identifying issues with smart contracts and possible loopholes, but the lack of a standardized approach to deal with vulnerabilities needs immense improvement. Also, it is quite tricky to find and correct the buggy part of codes in a smart contract already deployed on the Blockchain. Research in the field of detection and an easy way to update smart contracts can be extended to make smart contracts efficient. A robust system that can verify and provide proof that the smart contract is working as per the designed specifications could help to gain the confidence of stakeholders to invest in the technology. Future research has been initiated in this field and called Formal Verification. Another solution named Layer 2 is under development that overcomes the current inefficiencies of smart contracts in terms of performance quality, total throughput, and capacity of handling complex algorithms. Currently, Blockchain and smart contracts are cyber-physical systems of management, while recent trends depict that this may shift to cyber-physical-social systems abbreviated as CPSSs, which takes into account the social and individual factors that may help in solving the principal-agent dilemma. In future developments, we can also expect the active integration of Blockchain with Big Data for better data management and enriched data analytics.

CONCLUSION

Blockchain-based solutions are growing rapidly and have become a hot topic among technology enthusiasts and innovators. Many Blockchain Platforms have emerged along with several cryptocurrencies in a very short span of time, which can sometimes be overwhelming, impacting the decisions of individuals, firms, and governments as they try to figure out the best fitting Blockchain that can serve their needs. Several players in the automobile industry are making significant efforts to not only build autonomous cars but also to build an environment that is appropriate and necessary for their effective operation. AVs are highly technology-driven machines and use some of the most sophisticated devices. To support such a modern vehicle, technologies that will help in transmission and storage of data need to be quite advanced with a high level of security features. Because of its unmatched capability to avoid cyber-attacks, the researchers concluded that Blockchain is the best-known solution to handle data securely. A tamper-proof trail of data from AVs on a decentralized network provides a clean source of information for analyses and model building tools. Smart contracts that can be deployed on these distributed ledgers to carry out processes like payments or predictive maintenance are extremely essential to form a truly autonomous ecosystem that will enable organizations to achieve the highest level of automation.

However, Blockchain being an evolving technology, require more research and standardization in terms of the development of smart contracts, which are quite vulnerable to loopholes and its integration with other technologies such as Microsoft Azure, AI, and IoT, as discussed in the chapter. The researchers have made an attempt to provide possible integration of various technologies that can create a synergy to solve real-world problems of gaps in the performance of existing tools and techniques. Since the smart contract is one of the unique proposition of the Ethereum Blockchain, other Blockchain technologies are mostly underestimated in various studies. The possibility of better solutions on other Blockchain can be studied as future work by the researchers.

REFERENCES

Alharby, M., & Moorsel, A. V. (2017). *Blockchain Based Smart Contracts: A Systematic Mapping Study. Computer Science & Information Technology*. CS & IT. doi:10.5121/csit.2017.71011

Atlam, H. F., & Wills, G. B. (2019). Technical aspects of blockchain and IoT. *Advances in Computers*, 1–39. doi:10.1016/bs.adcom.2018.10.006

Ayvaz, S., & Cetin, S. C. (2019). Witness of Things. *International Journal of Intelligent Unmanned Systems*, 7(2), 72–87. doi:10.1108/IJIUS-05-2018-0011

Bahga, A., & Madisetti, V. K. (2016). Blockchain Platform for Industrial Internet of Things. *Journal of Software Engineering and Applications*, 09(10), 533–546. doi:10.4236/jsea.2016.910036

Barabás, I., Todoruţ, A., Cordoş, N., & Molea, A. (2017). Current challenges in autonomous driving. *IOP Conference Series. Materials Science and Engineering*, 252, 012096. doi:10.1088/1757-899X/252/1/012096

Bhargavan, K., Swamy, N., Zanella-Béguelin, S., Delignat-Lavaud, A., Fournet, C., Gollamudi, A., … Sibut-Pinote, T. (2016). Formal Verification of Smart Contracts. *Proceedings of the 2016 ACM Workshop on Programming Languages and Analysis for Security - PLAS'16*. doi:10.1145/2993600.2993611

Kapitonov, A., Lonshakov, S., Krupenkin, A., & Berman, I. (2017). Blockchain-based protocol of autonomous business activity for multi-agent systems consisting of UAVs. *2017 Workshop on Research, Education and Development of Unmanned Aerial Systems (RED-UAS)*. 10.1109/RED-UAS.2017.8101648

Kim, T. W., & Zetlin-Jones, A. (2019). The Ethics of Contentious Hard Forks in Blockchain Networks With Fixed Features. *Frontiers in Blockchain*, 2, 9. Advance online publication. doi:10.3389/fbloc.2019.00009

Lamberti, F., Gatteschi, V., Demartini, C., Pelissier, M., Gomez, A., & Santamaria, V. (2018). Blockchains Can Work for Car Insurance: Using Smart Contracts and Sensors to Provide On-Demand Coverage. *IEEE Consumer Electronics Magazine*, 7(4), 72–81. doi:10.1109/MCE.2018.2816247

Lauslahti, K., Mattila, J., & Seppala, T. (2017). *Smart Contracts How Will Blockchain Technology Affect Contractual Practices?* SSRN Electronic Journal. doi:10.2139srn.3154043

Lee, W. (2019a). Getting Started with Smart Contract. *Beginning Ethereum Smart Contracts Programming*, 127-146. doi:10.1007/978-1-4842-5086-0_6

Lee, W. (2019b). Connecting to the Ethereum Blockchain. *Beginning Ethereum Smart Contracts Programming*, 61-69. doi:10.1007/978-1-4842-5086-0_3

Microsoft Research & Microsoft Azure. (2019, April 10). *CCF: A Framework for Building Confidential Verifiable Replicated Services*. Retrieved from https://github.com/microsoft/CCF/blob/master/CCF-TECHNICAL-REPORT.pdf

Mohanta, B. K., Panda, S. S., & Jena, D. (2018). An Overview of Smart Contract and Use Cases in Blockchain Technology. *2018 9th International Conference on Computing, Communication and Networking Technologies (ICCCNT)*. doi:10.1109/icccnt.2018.8494045

Muthukrishnan, S., & Duraisamy, B. (2019). Blockchain Technologies and Artificial Intelligence. *Studies in Big Data*, 243-268. doi:10.1007/978-981-13-8775-3_12

Norta, A. (2017). Designing a Smart-Contract Application Layer for Transacting Decentralized Autonomous Organizations. *Communications in Computer and Information Science, 721*, 595–604. doi:10.1007/978-981-10-5427-3_61

O'Hara, K. (2017). Smart Contracts - Dumb Idea. *IEEE Internet Computing, 21*(2), 97–101. doi:10.1109/MIC.2017.48

Pahl, C. E. L., Ioini, N., & Helmer, S. (2018). A Decision Framework for Blockchain Platforms for IoT and Edge Computing. *Proceedings of the 3rd International Conference on Internet of Things, Big Data and Security*. 10.5220/0006688601050113

Pedrosa, A. R., & Pau, G. (2018). ChargeItUp. *Proceedings of the 1st Workshop on Cryptocurrencies and Blockchains for Distributed Systems - CryBlock'18*. doi:10.1145/3211933.3211949

Polyzos, G. C., & Fotiou, N. (2017). Blockchain-Assisted Information Distribution for the Internet of Things. *2017 IEEE International Conference on Information Reuse and Integration (IRI)*. 10.1109/IRI.2017.83

Praitheeshan, P., Pan, L., Yu, J., Liu, J., & Doss, R. (2019, August 22). *Security Analysis Methods on Ethereum Smart Contract Vulnerabilities: A Survey*. Retrieved from https://ui.adsabs.harvard.edu/abs/2019arXiv190808605P/abstract

Pustisek, M., Kos, A., & Sedlar, U. (2016). Blockchain Based Autonomous Selection of Electric Vehicle Charging Station. *2016 International Conference on Identification, Information and Knowledge in the Internet of Things (IIKI)*. 10.1109/IIKI.2016.60

Rathee, S., & Iqbal, A. (2019). A Blockchain Framework for Securing Connected and Autonomous Vehicles. *Sensors (Basel), 19*(14), 3165. doi:10.339019143165 PMID:31323870

Saleh, F. (2018). *Blockchain Without Waste: Proof-of-Stake*. SSRN Electronic Journal. doi:10.2139srn.3183935

Samaniego, M., & Deters, R. (2017). Internet of Smart Things - IoST: Using Blockchain and CLIPS to Make Things Autonomous. *2017 IEEE International Conference on Cognitive Computing (ICCC)*. 10.1109/IEEE.ICCC.2017.9

Shreyas Ramachandran, S., Veeraraghavan, A. K., Karni, U., & Sivaraman, K. (2019). Development of Flexible Autonomous Car System Using Machine Learning and Blockchain. *Lecture Notes in Electrical Engineering*, 63-72. doi:10.1007/978-3-030-20717-5_8

Swan, M. (2016). Blockchain Temporality: Smart Contract Time Specifiability with Blocktime. Rule Technologies. *Research, Tools, and Applications*, 184-196. doi:10.1007/978-3-319-42019-6_12

Wang, H., Zheng, Z., Xie, S., Dai, H. N., & Chen, X. (2018). Blockchain challenges and opportunities: A survey. *International Journal of Web and Grid Services*, *14*(4), 352. doi:10.1504/IJWGS.2018.10016848

Wang, S., Ouyang, L., Yuan, Y., Ni, X., Han, X., & Wang, F. (2019). Blockchain-Enabled Smart Contracts: Architecture, Applications, and Future Trends. *IEEE Transactions on Systems, Man, and Cybernetics. Systems*, *49*(11), 1–12. doi:10.1109/TSMC.2019.2895123

Wang, S., Yuan, Y., Wang, X., Li, J., Qin, R., & Wang, F. (2018). An Overview of Smart Contract: Architecture, Applications, and Future Trends. *2018 IEEE Intelligent Vehicles Symposium (IV)*. 10.1109/IVS.2018.8500488

Westerkamp, M. (2019). Verifiable Smart Contract Portability. *2019 IEEE International Conference on Blockchain and Cryptocurrency (ICBC)*. 10.1109/BLOC.2019.8751335

Wohrer, M., & Zdun, U. (2018). Smart contracts: security patterns in the ethereum ecosystem and solidity. *2018 International Workshop on Blockchain Oriented Software Engineering (IWBOSE)*. 10.1109/IWBOSE.2018.8327565

Xing, B., & Marwala, T. (2018). *The Synergy of Blockchain and Artificial Intelligence*. SSRN Electronic Journal. doi:10.2139srn.3225357

Yuan, Y., & Wang, F. (2016). Towards blockchain-based intelligent transportation systems. *2016 IEEE 19th International Conference on Intelligent Transportation Systems (ITSC)*. doi:10.1109/itsc.2016.7795984

ADDITIONAL READING

Academic Papers. (n.d.). Retrieved from https://www.iota.org/research/academic-papers

Artificial Intelligence Based Autonomous Car. (2018, January 1). Retrieved from https://www.researchgate.net/publication/325183067_Artificial_Intelligence_Based_Autonomous_Car

Ashish. (2018, June 22). Coco Framework a game changer in Blockchain technology. Retrieved from https://medium.com/coinmonks/coco-framework-a-game-changer-in-blockchain-technology-throughput-of-around-1600-transactions-per-fb1ffd79822d

Automotive Vehicle Cyber Security - Blockchain Technology Platform - CUBE. (2019, March 4). Retrieved from https://cubeint.io/

Autonomous cars will generate more than 300 TB of data per year. (2019, August 19). Retrieved from https://www.tuxera.com/blog/autonomous-cars-300-tb-of-data-per-year/

Contracts, S. The Blockchain Technology That Will Replace Lawyers. (n.d.). Retrieved from https://blockgeeks.com/guides/smart-contracts/

ethereum/wiki. (n.d.). Retrieved October 10, 2019, from https://github.com/ethereum/wiki/wiki/White-Paper

Gadam, S. (2019, January 12). Artificial Intelligence and Autonomous Vehicles. Retrieved from https://medium.com/ datadriveninvestor/artificial-intelligence- and-autonomous-vehicles-ae877feb6cd2

Gadam, S. (2019, January 12). Artificial Intelligence and Autonomous Vehicles. Retrieved from https://medium.com/ datadriveninvestor/artificial-intelligence -and-autonomous-vehicles-ae877feb6cd2

Hollander, L. (2019, February 2). The Ethereum Virtual Machine? How does it work? Retrieved from https://medium.com/ mycrypto/the-ethereum-virtual- machine-how-does-it-work-9abac2b7c9e

MOBI – mobility open blockchain initiative. (n.d.). Retrieved from https://dlt.mobi/

Standard for Self-Driving Vehicles. (n.d.). Retrieved from https://www.sae.org/ news/press-room/2018/12/ sae-international-releases-updated- visual-chart-for-its-%E2%80%9 Clevels-of-driving-automation%E2%80%9 D-standard-for-self-driving-vehicles

The key technology toward the self-driving car. (2018, January 2). Retrieved from https://www.emerald.com/insight/content/doi/10.1108/IJIUS-08-2017-0008/full/html

What is Blockchain Technology? (2018, September 11). Retrieved from https://www.cbinsights.com/research/what-is-blockchain-technology/

KEY TERMS AND DEFINITIONS

Artificial Intelligence: Artificial intelligence refers to human-like intelligence that can be adopted by machines, especially computers. Intelligence may include learning, reasoning, and self-correction.

Autonomous Vehicles: Also known as a Self-Driving Vehicle or Driverless Vehicle that can guide itself without any human intervention by sensing the environment with the help of multiple sensors and IoT devices.

Blockchain: Blockchain is a decentralized database that controls records of digital data or actions of each participant who has a copy of the ledger and may access, inspect, or add to the data, but can't change or delete it making it tamper-proof since each new block of transactions links back to previous blocks providing enhanced immutability to the complete system. It is based on Distributed Ledger Technology(DLT), which works on the principle of game theory, cryptography, and P2P technology.

Confidential Consortium Framework: CFF is a framework developed by Microsoft which is compatible with various Blockchain Solutions and can be used to increase the throughput of the system up to 1600 transactions per sec along with low energy consumption.

Decentralized Applications: Decentralized applications or DApps is a system application that runs on a distributed network which acts as an interface amongst the user and the provider which are basically of three types, i.e., the one that can be used to manage money, the one used for smart contracts and the last one for the voting & governance system.

Ether: Crypto token used in Ethereum is known as Ether, which can be used to pay transaction fees or a computational service in the form of GAS. Wei is the smallest unit of Ether.

Ethereum: Ethereum is an open-source Blockchain-based computing platform that works as a distributed network featuring smart contracts and decentralized applications. It provides a virtual machine to execute scripts using a network of nodes and currently has two basic versions, i.e., Ethereum (ETH) and Ethereum Classic.

Ethereum Virtual Machine: Ethereum virtual machine (EVM) allows the development of various decentralized applications like Smart Contracts that can be used on Ethereum Blockchain and can be implemented using common programming languages like Python, C++, etc.

Hard Fork: Hard fork is an upgrade in the protocol, functionalities, and rules that aren't backward compatible, which means that a node cannot continue to follow the old protocols and necessarily follows the new protocol.

Internet of Things: IoT is an integrated system of connected devices that are assigned a unique identifier and could transfer data over a network.

Mining: Mining is the process of validating the transaction or records and adding them to the chain in the form of Blocks. Miners usually solve a computational problem to guess the nonce of the block to add it to the chain for which they are rewarded as per the consensus algorithm.

Proof of Stake: In Proof of stake, the creator or the miner of the block is chosen from a pool of miners that hold a particular stake in the network. There is no reward for adding a block in the Blockchain. However, the miner gets the transaction fees.

Proof of Work: Proof of work is an algorithm in which a difficult mathematical puzzle is solved by the miner to prove that the miner worked to solve the block so that it can be added to the chain. Multiple miners compete to solve the block as quickly as possible to get the reward making the process competitive and full of work.

Smart Contracts: Computer codes that are capable of executing a term of negotiation, partnership rules, or an agreement between parties on the Blockchain network are known as Smart Contracts

Soft Fork: Soft fork is an upgrade in the protocol, functionalities, and rules that are backward compatible, which means that a node can continue to follow the old protocols without necessarily accepting the new changes.

Solidity: Solidity is a programming language specially used for writing codes for Smart Contracts. It was proposed in 2014 and is very similar to other programming languages such as JavaScript & C making it quite easy to learn.

Chapter 15
Blockchain in Clinical Trials

Shaveta Malik
Terna Engineering College, India

Archana Mire
Terna Engineering College, India

Amit Kumar Tyagi
iD https://orcid.org/0000-0003-2657-8700
Vellore Institute of Technology, Chennai, India

Arathi Boyanapalli
SRM University, Chennai, India

ABSTRACT

Clinical research comprises participation from patients. Often there are concerns of enrolment from patients. Hence, it has to face various challenges related to personal data, such as data sharing, privacy and reproducibility, etc. Patients and researchers need to track a set plan called study protocol. This protocol spans through various stages such as registration, collection and analysis of data, report generation, and finally, results in publication of findings. The Blockchain technology has emerged as one of the possible solutions to these challenges. It has a potential to address all the problem associated with clinical research. It provides the comfort for building transparent, secure services relying on trusted third party. This technology enables one to share the control of the data, security, and the parameters with a single patient or a group of patients or any other stakeholders of clinical trial. This chapter addresses the use of blockchain in execution of secure and trusted clinical trials.

1) INTRODUCTION

In biomedical research prodigious challenge is the background fixing methodology issues from the background .Certainly related to wide range of scientific misconduct facets, lock of responsibility, from errors to fraud, concessions the outcome of a clinical study and the quality of undermines research. Clinical trials may also compare a new treatment to a treatment that is already available. Every clinical trial has a

DOI: 10.4018/978-1-7998-3295-9.ch015

protocol, or action plan, for conducting the trial. The plan describes what will be done in the study, how it will be conducted, and why each part of the study is necessary. Each study has its own rules about who can participate. Some studies need volunteers with a certain disease. Some need healthy people. Others want just men or just women. In the United States, an independent committee of physicians, statisticians and members of the community must approve and monitor the protocol. They make sure that that the risks are small and are worth the potential benefits. Blockchain (Zheng et al., 2017) can have a wide impact on clinical research because it allows sharing, caring and tracking for data, it also encoded with the tracking system which is secure and decentralized for any interaction of data and that could occur in the clinical trial context. This lead to more belief in clinical research .A steps towards better transparency on the basis to improved clinical research methodology and develop trust within communities of research and between research and communities of patients. Previously, blockchain known to be for bitcoin (Bonneau et al., 2015) as it is distributed public ledger that record all the transaction of a bitcoin in a conformable and secure way without the involvement of the third party to process payment. It is a decentralized storage of data or ordered records, events which is called blocks. In which every block having the timestamp and linked with previous block. The architecture of blockchain agree for storing the existence of proof of data. As the only of data is the proof of data and believe that this is the exapler shift for the medical methodology of research. Indeed to prevent the posteriori reconstruction analysis blockchain ensures that the events that pursued in chronological order. Blockchain technology is just like a new operating system for belief Indeed in health care (Mettler, 2016)has made substantial treads in the last few years. For example IBM entered into research projects (Brodl, 2019)with the U.S food and drug administration and center for disease control and more recently announced and multi-company health utility network being designed to create an complete blockchain network that can value multiple members of the healthcare ecosystem in a protected, joint environment. The great challenges in clinical trials are sharing of data, personal data privacy concerns and enrolment of patient and Boehringer Ingelheim's commitment to healthcare innovation and marks the first time that blockchain technology will be explored in a clinical trial setting in Canada.

Blockchain technology as a new operating system for trust (Sawal et al., 2016). This collaboration is another great example of the ways stakeholders are coming together

However, blockchain remains a vague concept with unclear benefits for many in the clinical research and brader healthcare industries.

Tools used for Securing the Data

Authentication:-The common form of authentication is user id and password and other form is biometric and eye scanner or fingerprint that is the form to identify someone through physical appreance and the other is RSA secure id is token that is a device which generate secure id code by every sixty seconds to log in by using RSA device use the four digit pin with the code which will be generated by the device.

Access Control:- It decide or determine which users have access to read, modify, add or delete the data or information .The administrator can work to add or delete but it is difficult to maintain by ACL (Access Control List) and the improved method is RBAC (Role Based Access Control).In which right will assign according to the roll. It help in to increase the security.

Encryption:-It is a method to encode the data so that any authorized person /user can access the information .It has public or private key .In public key encryption has two keys used one is public and other is private for sending the message .For sending the message public key used and for receiving or decrypt the message private key used for security.

Firewalls: - To increase the security in network is a firewall. It can be as a hardware or software .It restrict the flow of packets or data leaving from the organization's network.

Virtual Private Network (VPN):-Firewall will work in organization but in outside the corporate network or VPN will work through this organization allow limited access to its network and also the same time ensure the security also.

Indulgent Blockchain in Clinical Trials

To make a shared and continually reconciled database on a distributed network is to store digital information that is the central purpose of blockchain .To keep the track of data, whether that data is related to financial transactions, product inventory, healthcare data, or anything else that is in the essence of blockchain that is distributed electronic ledger .The validity of a transaction by recording every change across the entire distributed network is one of the most valuable features.

To locate and share large quantities of data with specific individuals, often across long distances is depends upon having a fast, easy and transparent way. Through audit trails blockchain is conceivably most immediately applicable to clinical trials. As much transparency as possible regarding where and when data was entered, and by whom—as well as other information such as who has permission to access what data good clinical practice requires. By improving privacy, security, and transparency audit trails provide this insight, and blockchain can take it to the next level.

To make operations at sites, CROs, and sponsor organizations much more efficient that is the benefits of being able to control access to data via a decentralized ledger like blockchain are many, not least of which is that it would .Several blockchain hacks in thecryptocurrency (Koblitz & Menezes, 2016) world—organizations can protect against risk by keeping their blockchain technology private rather than publicly distributable as industries are still coming to terms with the security implications of the technology.

What About the Monitoring Side?

Slow adoption of technology in healthcare is often the result of the regulatory scrutiny the industry works under. This scrutiny is no surprise: the work of researchers and developers of medical products, after all, has a tremendous impact on public health. As a result, any time a technology from outside the traditional eClinical space enters a clinical research setting, compliance becomes a major question. Will the use of blockchain—or other innovations such as mHealth (Ichikawa et al., 2017), wearables, AI, and bring-your-own-device, for that matter—meet the regulatory guidelines that were developed around the use of EDC, eSource, and other traditional eClinical platforms?

The first regulatory question raised around a publicly-accessible data storage network like blockchain is likely to center around data security. Clinical trials contain a wealth of sensitive data (Shamila et al., 2019), whether it's proprietary information on a medical product's safety and efficacy or personally-identifiable information belonging to clinical trial patients. Implementing new ways of storing and accessing that data raises important questions and concerns about security and accessibility. But one of the things that makes blockchain so groundbreaking is its ability to make data completely visible, completely password protected, or somewhere in the middle. Users can allow access to certain pieces of information while blocking others.

The implications for clinical trials, in which there has long been a tug-of-war between those advocating for increased data transparency and those fighting to keep sensitive data private, are significant. This can go a long way toward, for example, enabling researchers to meet regulatory requirements around reporting clinical trial results without putting personally-identifiable information at risk.

Clinical trial regulators have already started work to pave the way for blockchain. The FDA, for example, spearheaded an initiative last year to define the best way of using blockchain to exchange health data. With these efforts underway, and with the potential of blockchain becoming increasingly clearer, we could be on the cusp of a new era of data storage in healthcare and clinical research

Blockchain Practice in Research

An Encrypted way (Zhang & Liu 2010) of distributing, sharing, and storing information—seem appealing for health data is the core views of blockchain technology –decentralized. In health care the excitement around using blockchain technology is also growing. Proponents point to blockchain's potential to liberate data from entrenched silos, empowering patients to securely "own" their data. This is a shared source of truth and has the capability to transform the clinical research industry. And what drives this technology is the drive to revolutionize patient care.

Today's researchers face the challenges of precisely reproducing data, efficiently sharing data, privacy concerns, and patient conscription strategies in addition to increased costs. To drives this technology forward where this level of "unsettling innovation" steps in too. Data stored in a blockchain is essentially impossible to menial, overstep, or steal, because the record is not kept on a single repository this is the superlative part about blockchain but the record is feast throughout several databases in duplicate copies. The dawn of companies connecting their devices to mobile apps and the cloud will rightly necessitate The greater consideration of the companies to connecting their devices to mobile apps and the cloud will rightly necessitate and discussion of cyber security risks. To overcome big data hurdles (Prosperi et al., 2018) there is a pressure from commercial and regulatory agencies because every day large amount of clinical trials data is generated, it's becoming obvious that bequest data management systems are not influential adequate to procedure and hold the data mined from all the recent research studies, artifice problems for patient secrecy, as well as data veracity.

The biopharma industry can be seen in how patient data is collected, stored and its accessibility it is the major win for using a blockchain.With current technologies the ability to locate individuals for studies is imperative for investigators, Though, data is scattered across multiple exclusive systems that are often autonomous and discordant with each other, making it extremely difficult to novice personages for trials.

A blockchain could also modernize while communication among the patient and doctors during the trail. To provide smart contracts that endorse transparency and traceability over clinical trial sequences the AI has these kind of tool and can afford financial motivations for a patient's involvement and allotment of their data. To empower patients and doctors and expand the delivery of care this kind of organizational limpidity and inclusivity.

Moreover the benefit of utilizing the innovation level is the capability for patients to well join with persons who have similar conditions (e.g., in rare disease populations), that can enhance trial transfer potential. It is necessity it is a key driver for any research to remember that patient engagement and necessity to ensure that patients can find information that is available and has factual value.

According to writers at Beyond Standards, some of these concern include:-In today's clinical trials that concern is some discouraging facts relating to patient engagement:

- Cancer patients participate in oncology trials is Less than 5% of adult
- From where to find relevant information on trials Fewer than 1 in 20 people know
- To meet Enrolment timeline 80% of clinical trials fail

2) CHALLENGES IN CLINICAL TRIALS

There are number of challenges while directing clinical trials, It is a time consuming, affluent affair which encompasses close association between multiple stakeholders, often geographically distributed, and in the process high level of monitoring, regulation and precision require.

Challenges are describe below:-

- DATA MANAGEMENT
  - Dynamic access management of data - As determined by blinding/unblinding of data, database lock access rights are time based.
  - From variety of sources multiple version of data created – external labs, CROs, other vendors. By increasing globalization of clinical trials the issue gets compounded. Difficulties in accessing the required data as data is kept in a extensive variability of siloed system and its lead to duplication also.
  - Non-aggregation of Clinical Data –The simplest research question is a big challenge as data is not easy to access .Its very time consuming to pull the data from the multiplicity of sources and mending composed reports.
  - Data Entry –Investigator does not have tools to analyze the data in real time and wastage of time to integrate data with a centralized repository,
  - Involvement of several vendors in the studies and manage strategic partnerships and sites of study.
- DATA SHARING AND SECURITY
  - Precluding leak, fraud, abuse of private information.
  - Verification of data through multi party channels.
  - Sharing of data in a measured manner: It must be ensured that the data sharing is consistent with federal and local regulations.
- SUBJECT ENROLLMENT
  - Capability to recruit, enroll, and hold appropriate volunteers.
  - In the form of personal benefits for subjects absence of suitable return of investment, and it leads to increase the burden for subjects in study participation.
  - Guaranteeing Subject Safety – Development of safety oversight that include Serious adverse event (SAE) and adverse event (AE) reporting, compliance with GCP, local regulations, and trial protocol, remote or onsite monitoring and setup of a safety review committee and an independent data safety monitoring board (DSMB).
  - Inefficient Study Recruitment - effort in finding the right subjects.
- SPIRALING COSTS

    ○   The cost of conducting clinical trials is very high all time. On the already stretched out resources the increasing complexity of clinical trials and tight delivery timelines is tapping more pressure indeed new discoveries are getting overdue and chances to participate in new forms of treatment get abridged and patient suffers.

3) ISSUES IN BLOCKCHAIN TECHNOLOGY WHILE IMPLEMENTING IN HEALTHCARE SECTOR

Figure 1. Issues in Healthcare

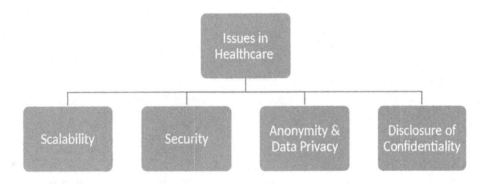

1) **Scalability**:-In healthcare system users comes with sensors device then limitations of storage will come .In blockchain network the processing or execution of transaction takes more time. So, the throughput will be slow .Moreover speed issue will come and may limit the scalability .In distributed system of blockchain all the blocks and stored on every node it also conquer the issue of speed and scalability.(Sobia Yaqoob et al, 2019)

2) **Security**:- Since the blockchain works on the consent of the information providers. In case over 50% people providing information are fake then they might reject the honest miners' information and hence the confidential information may get seized, but being such a large number of network that block chain is this would be rare scenario.

3) **Disclosure of confidentiality**: - Due to the nature of blockchain another issue comes that is transparency discloses confidentiality, it is a more serious issue because records related to patient are highly sensitive because of the transparency nature of blockchain, healthcare and patient records shown to everyone.

4) **Anonymity and Data Privacy**: - The uncertainty and fraud hype in the blockchain is another challenge .Criminals are taking advantage by using cryptocurrencies with the blockchain network. Using 'Ransomware' to seize computer network by hackers with blockchain network .In public blockchain network data privacy is compromised. Moreover in regards of privacy of healthcare patient is more concerned.

4) BLOCKCHAIN-BASED HEALTHCARE APPLICATIONS

In many healthcare applications blockchain technology is redefining data modelling and governance deployed and in many current development it is at the centre This is mainly due to its flexibility and capabilities to fragment, safe and share medical data and services in an unprecedented way. Evolving blockchain-based technology of healthcare are theoretically ordered into two layers, with blockchain technology, data sources.s

Figure 2. Workflow for healthcare applications Blockchain Based (Khezr et al., 2019)

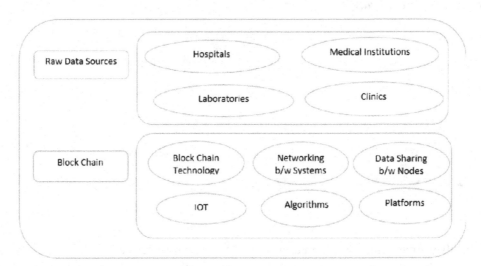

Figure 2. It is a workflow of healthcare application that is based on the blockchain.It consists of two layer that includes raw data sources and blockchain as it is a decentralized technology which permits manifold stakeholders to profit from healthcare claims.

Initially, Raw data subsequently created from medical devices, labs, social media and many other sources that grew in scale to big data and for the whole blockchain based health care this data is the essential ingredient .It is creates the first layer of the stack and it is the principle component .It create a secure healthcare architecture and divided into four component .It sits on the top of the raw data layer(Khezr et al., 2019) To create and manage their transactions, blockchain provides platforms for the ease to users as this platform has diverse features such as protocol and consensus algorithm .There are several platforms were created and are presently in use such as Hyperledger Fabric(Choudhary et al., 2019) , Ripple, Ethereum (Bogner et al., 2016).

The main components of the blockchain are smart contracts, membership, digital assets, signatures, wallet and events. An inclusive range of protocols could be used for collaborating with other programs and frameworks, or uniform through different networks.

It may contain for occurrence, P2P, centralized, decentralized, and distributed. Policymakers could mark a special either public, private or even unify based on the range of requirements they need to fulfill. The applications are integrated with the whole system once the platform is created by implementing blockchain technology, the next phase is to confirm Blockchain-based healthcare applications can be classified into three broad classes.

Firstly, the managing of the data that include global scientific sharing of data for the research & development (R&D) and for the storage that is based on the cloud based application and EHRs. The next class represents SCM applications that includes the pharmaceuticals and clinical trials .Finally, the third class shields the IoMT, including a convergence of healthcare IoT and medical devices, healthcare IoT infrastructure, data security and AI.

Use of IOT in Healthcare with Blockchain:-Healthcare in terms IOT (IoHT) Internet of Healthcare Things, Many health organization using IoHT to monitor the newborn baby and tracking the inventory also.

IoHT in Healthcare divided into two categories one for the clinical service and other for support operations.

In clinical service we can monitor the patient and also tracking the sign and indication of the patient those are communicate for the study such as blood sugar level.

For the support operations. It is equipment centric sensors and also reduce the cost with good utilization of the resources of the medical.

Through sensors we can track the record and location of medical equipment e.g digital X ray equipment, ventilators. So that it can easily located when need.

5) APPLICATION OF BLOCKCHAIN IN HEALTHCARE:-

1) **Supply Chain Management**:-At manufacture center drugs are manufacture through blockchain, we can track the ingredients of the drug and track the counterfeit drug through blockchain and it also help in to find the source of counterfiling.

2) **Integrity of Medical Records**:-Track all the records of medical through blockchain whenever you want to produced medical records then through block chain we can track all the records from starting or can store all the records.

3) **Single Patient Identification**:- In healthcare duplicate and mismatch of patient's record is not rare but through blockchain whole data can be store and track and no one can modify the data in between or without any concern. E.g while looking for the address of patient you can search with different keys but you will find out the single patient identification.

4) **Change in Business model**:- In healthcare profession, a doctor or nurse can easily access the record of the patient and also update the status of the current stage of the patient .

6) HOW CLINICAL TRIALS WORK

Clinical Trial (Kuehn, 2012) is research to study a test or treatment that's given to people and it also study how benign those tests are because new tests or treatment directly aren't offered to the public. Once the experiments have done or when it found to be safe and helpful they may become tomorrow's standard of care.

There are following things that clinical trials can study:

- Clinical trials can be study a lot of many things, namely:

- U.S. agency of Food and Drug Administration (FDA) have not yet approved any new drug.
- Approved new drugs usage.
- Some more methods to help patients inhale/take drugs, i.e. can be pill form.
- Usage of herbs and vitamins as substitute for medicines.
- To find and track disease by new tests and
- Drugs or procedures that release symptoms.

Clinical Trials Process

There is principle investigator (PI) who take the charge of the trials, it's his or her responsibility to take care designed, revised and concluded. The PI takes prime in designing the clinical trials and he or she is a subject matter expert in the clinical trials and along with the research team and carries out the study.

Clinical trials needs to be approved and also needs some sponsors to get the financial aid required to do the trials. Usually government agencies, non-profit organizations, pharmaceutical (drug) companies are the major sponsors for the clinical trials. Getting or finding a sponsors of the clinical trial research plan that is also called protocol. After the research plan is approved the sponsor gives the financial support.

First IBR review the clinical trials and it includes of five members .These members must be scientist ("someone not a scientist and someone not from health care center").After the review through IBR, DSMB ("**D**ata and **S**afety **M**onitoring **B**oards") review the progress but not all clinical trials are reviewed by DSMBs if IRB needs more review than IRB does.DSMB are the experts and they take care of the working of test or treatment.

Nevertheless there are four general benefits:-

1) Most current cancer care you will have access.
2) Experts involve in the process
3) Tracked Results of the treatment (good & bad both)
4) Help other patients with cancer

But there may be side effects like any other test or treatment and risk too .As good as or improved than the one now in use new tests or treatments may not work

Phases of Clinical Trials

There are number of phases of clinical trials in which with the health intercession scientists do experiments to find the proof for a process that can be useful as a medical treatment

In the pharmaceutical, drug design and drug discovery are the starting phases then lead to animal testing. If this is efficacious, they begin the clinical phase of improvement by testing for wellbeing in a few human subjects and inflate to test in many study participants to regulate if the treatment is operative.

The reason behind the clinical trial is to believe that new test or treatment may improve the care of patients. Before clinical trials, tests and treatments are assessed in preclinical research. Preclinical research assesses the feature of test or treatment and it is not done with people. For example if a device is harmful to living tissue, the research may aim to learn. Tests and treatments go through a series of clinical trials after preclinical research, Clinical trials assess if tests or treatments are safe for and work in people.

Figure 3. Process of Clinical trials

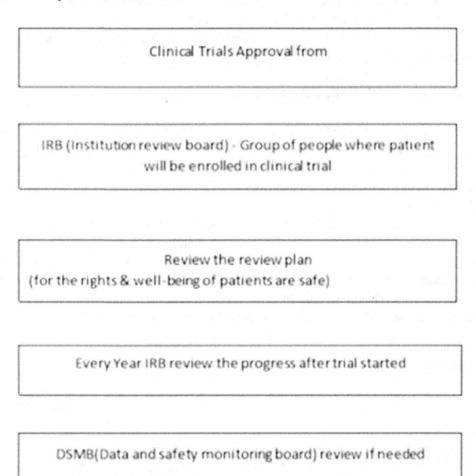

Clinical Trials Approval from

IRB (Institution review board) - Group of people where patient will be enrolled in clinical trial

Review the review plan
(for the rights & well-being of patients are safe)

Every Year IRB review the progress after trial started

DSMB(Data and safety monitoring board) review if needed

There are number of phases of clinical trials, the phases are described next using the example of a new drug treatment. If the clinical trials will take new treatment it is divided into different stages that is called phases.

The phases are divided into two part. The earliest phase trials tell the drug is safe or side effects it causes and later phases trials are to test the new treatment and find whether the new treatment or test is better than the previous test.

The following phases are given below:-

Phase 0:- In which small group of people will work e.g 10 .The first clinical trials done among people is phase 0. In which used to see how the drug is responding in the body and how it effect in the body. In this stage or phase 0. If cancer disease is taking for the test then in phase 0 lots of different types can take. It is not a randomized.

Phase 1:-It is also for the small group of people e.g 20 to 50 .In which also works on the types of cancer but in phase 1 focuses on the side effect and what happens to the treatment in the body.

Phase 2:-In phase 2 medium group of people work e.g 100 people. In which one or more cancer type can take for test and sometimes can take more than two.

Phase 3:- In phase 3 lots of people work e.g hundreds or thousands of people .In which focuses on the new treatment and comparison with the previous standard treatment.

How Block Chain Work With Clinical Trials

Data generated by clinical trials can be used as datasets by regulatory bodies for approval of newer treatments. The trustworthiness of the data plays a major role as million dollars are invested by stakeholder in research findings and the data can be used by researchers, stakeholders for further investigations on the diseases and finding new pharmaceutical drugs based on the study made on the datasets which is generated by clinical trials.

Clinical trials may undermine several threats. Data can be altered or lost accidentally or by contemptible as data is generated in various sites. Commercial and regulatory agencies are under pressure to overcome big data hurdles, legacy data management systems are not powerful enough to process and retain the data extracted from all of the current research studies, posing problems for patient privacy, as well as data integrity. This may result in zero percent results. The unpredictable nature of clinical trials results in high costs for pharmaceutical drugs and for everyone from the researcher to consumer.

Figure 4. Traditional method for clinical trials (Choudhary et al., 2019)

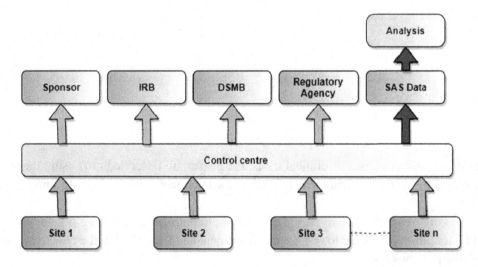

The above discussed drawbacks in clinical trials can be prevailed over by using blockchain technology. Blockchain technology uses transparent distributed ledger (Kuo et al., 2017) and distributed network that enable every stakeholder to store time-stamped transactions. Each and every transaction is verified and can be tracked by all the stakeholders. The data cannot be altered as it is stored in a distributed database and encrypted by keeping a track of previous transactions, so one change in one part of data creates a chain of changes which is not possible due to permissions required to validate. Blockchain is a platform that stores and processes information securely and can be useful for clinical trial analysis, patient's medical data.

Blockchain technology benefits applications other than finance such as healthcare, supply-chain management, smart city, smart agriculture and many more. Blockchain technology can be used for supporting or for superseding the old-style infrastructure for data used in clinical trials Blockchain can establish a permanent record agreed up on by all related parties, hence it has can mitigate quite a few threats to data validity. Biomedical research can see an upsurge in the public trust, safer medicine, better life and an increase in the confidence in its veracity etc. when using the data recorded for the clinical trials using block chain. Clinical Trials can be managed by Hyper Ledger Fabric platform.

HyperLedger Fabric

Hyperledger Fabric (Choudhary et al., 2019) is a private blockchain framework developed by The Linux Foundation. It offers a modular architecture supporting pluggable components, such as consensus protocol, encryption, identity management, and membership services. The private network comprises multiple nodes, a smart contract or chain code, and a ledger containing a state database and a log of transactions. A node can be maintained by an individual or multiple user. Based on their functionalities, the nodes can be categorized into client (invokes transactions), peer (maintains and updates ledger), and ordered (supports communication and maintains order of transactions).

- Client node: It submits transaction-invocation to the endorsers and transaction-proposals to the orderer. It is connected to both peer and orderer nodes.
- **Peer node**: It commits transactions and maintains the world state of the ledger. It updates the ledger after receiving ordered states from the orderer. A peer node can act as an endorser to sign a proposed transaction before it is sent to the orderer.
- **Orderer node**: It runs a broadcast communication service to guarantee delivery. It delivers transactions to the peer nodes after verifying the endorsement message.

A smart contract, also known as chaincode in Hyperledger Fabric, is a self-executing logic that represents agreements or a set of rules which govern transactions in a blockchain network. The rules are implemented as functions in chaincode. All data transactions that require accessing the ledger invoke corresponding chaincode functions. Hyperledger Fabric implements endorsement policies or conditions to validate proposed transactions. Once a transaction is proposed by a client, it must be endorsed by the pre-defined endorsing nodes. The endorsement signatures are collected and sent to the orderer. The orderer verifies the endorsement message, such as valid number of endorser signatures and simulated transaction results, from all endorsers. The collected transactions are then sent as a new block to all peers. A trusted Membership Service Provider (MSP) enrolls the participants in the network. MSP provides a verifiable digital identity to all entities in the blockchain network, such as peers, orderers, and clients. It serves as a trusted authority which abstracts the process of issuing cryptographic certificates and user authentication.

Some of the other notable features of Hyperledger Fabric include:

- **Confidentiality**: In addition to a private network, it allows creation of private channels comprising a sub-group of network participants. All information related to a channel are accessible only to the members of that channel, thereby elevating the level of confidentiality.
- **Cryptographic identity management**: A membership identity service manages user IDs and authenticates all participants on the network. Additional access control can be implemented for specific network operations.
- **Modular design**: It supports a modular architecture that allows different components, such as membership function and consensus, to be plug-and-play.

Formation of Blockchain

Figure 5. Clinical Trials using Blockchain Technology (Choudhary et al., 2019)

1) **Principal Investigator (PI)** — Principal Investigator —The responsibilities of the PI is to defend the safety, rights and welfare of subject that joined in the trial and the prime responsibility for leading and concocting the study at each site of the multi-site clinical trial.
2) **Coordinating Center (CC)** — In which report can generate, edit and schedule the activities and the center is also responsible coordinating a multi-site clinical trial. They also help in to connect with suitable stakeholders.
3) **Data Safety and Monitoring Board (DSMB)** —In which h they are accountable for study improvement evaluate and review the accrued study data for study progress and participant safety. They also concern about alteration or finish of the trial.
4) **Institutional Review Board (IRB)** — The board review the study material and all facets of trial and also careful to protect the rights and safety.

5) **Regulatory agencies** — Medical treatments are safe and operative for subjects to use as regulatory agencies, such as The Food and Drug Administration (FDA) ensured. They verified the veracity of data and the quality .They examine the study sites with respect to shield the rights of subjects.

6) **Sponsors** —An individual, institution, or organization that recruit, achieve, and fund a clinical trial, but does not essentially bearing it.

7) **Analysts** — Researchers or statisticians who fold, review, and establish trial results, including de-identified data collected from subjects.

Summary:- Clinical trials is an important area to get the best of medicines out in the market for the various sorts of diseases that is happening to human beings now a days due to the changes in the various elements of his living. Block chain is the technology that helps in carving a niche in the data security and safety related to quite a few study areas and clinical trials is one such area. Block chain helps in maintaining the privacy of the data related to the patients and various treatments they are undergoing and also maintains the privacy of the data.

REFERENCES

Bogner, A., & Chanson, M. (2016). A Decentralised Sharing App running a Smart Contract on the Ethereum Blockchain. *Proceedings of the 6th International Conference on the Internet of Things - IoT'16.* 10.1145/2991561.2998465

Bonneau, J., Miller, A., Clark, J., Narayanan, A., Kroll, J. A., & Felten, E. W. (2015). SoK: Research Perspectives and Challenges for Bitcoin and Cryptocurrencies. *2015 IEEE Symposium on Security and Privacy* 10.1109/SP.2015.14

Brodl, U. (2019). *Testing blockchain technology for clinical trials in Canada. IBM blog.* Watson Health Perspectives.

Choudhary, O., Fairoza, N., Sylla, I., & Das, A. (2019). A Blockchain Framework for Managing and Monitoring Data in Multi-Site Clinical Trials. *Journal of Biomedical Informatics.*

Ichikawa, D., Kashiyama, M., & Ueno, T. (2017). Tamper-Resistant Mobile Health Using Blockchain Technology. *JMIR mHealth and uHealth, 5*(7), e111. doi:10.2196/mhealth.7938 PMID:28747296

Khezr, S., Moniruzzaman, M., Yassine, A., & Benlamri, R. (2019). Blockchain Technology in Healthcare: A Comprehensive Review and Directions for Future Research. *Applied Sciences (Basel, Switzerland), 9*(9), 1736. doi:10.3390/app9091736

Koblitz, N., & Menezes, J. (2016). *Cryptocash, cryptocurrencies, and cryptocontracts.* Springer. doi:10.100710623-015-0148-5

Kuehn, B. M. (2012). Few Studies Reporting Results at US Government Clinical Trials Site. *Journal of the American Medical Association, 307*(7), 651–653. doi:10.1001/jama.2012.127 PMID:22337663

Kuo T, Kim H, & Ohno-Machado L. (2017). Blockchain distributed ledger technologies for biomedical and health care applications. *J Am Med Inform Assoc., 24*(6), 1211–1220.

Mettler, M. (2016). Blockchain technology in healthcare: The revolution starts her*e. 2016 IEEE 18th International Conference on e-Health Networking, Applications and Services (Healthcom).*

Prosperi, M., Min, J. S., Bian, J., & Modave, F. (2018). Big data hurdles in precision medicine and precision public health. *BMC Medical Informatics and Decision Making, 18*(1), 139. doi:10.118612911-018-0719-2 PMID:30594159

Sawal, N., Anjali, T., Amit, T., Sreenath, N., & Rekha, G. (2016). *Necessity of Blockchain for Building Trust in Today's Applications: An Useful Explanation from User's Perspective.* Academic Press.

Shamila, M., & Vinuthna, K. (2019). A Review on Several Critical Issues and Challenges in IoT based e-Healthcare System. IEEE.

Yaqoob, Khan, Talib, Butt, & Saleem, Arif, & Nadeem. (2019). Use of Blockchain in Healthcare: A Systematic Literature Review. *International Journal of Advanced Computer Science and Applications, 10*(5).

Zhang, R., & Liu, L. (2010). Security Models and Requirements for Healthcare Application Clouds. *2010 IEEE 3rd International Conference on Cloud Computing.*

Zheng, Z., Xie, S., Dai, H., Chen, X., & Wang, H. (2017). An Overview of Blockchain Technology: Architecture, Consensus, and Future Trends. *2017 IEEE International Congress on Big Data.*

Compilation of References

2014. Revision of World Urbanization Prospects. (n.d.). Available: https://esa.un.org/unpd/wup/

AbouZahr, C., Jha, P., Macfarlane, S. B., Mikkelsen, L., Setel, P. W., Szreter, S., & Stout, S. (2007). A scandal of invisibility: Making everyone count by counting everyone. *Lancet*, *370*(9598), 1569–1577. doi:10.1016/S0140-6736(07)61307-5 PubMed

Abuelela, M., & Olariu, S. (2010). *Taking VANET to the Clouds*. Academic Press.

Ahishakiye, E., Wario, R., & Niyonzima, I. (2018). Developing Countries and Blockchain Technology : Uganda ' s Perspective. *International Journal of Latest Research in Engineering and Technology*, *4*(August), 94–99.

Ahmad, F., Kazim, M., & Adnane, A. (2015). Vehicular Cloud Networks : Architecture, Applications and Security Issues. *2015 IEEE/ACM 8th International Conference on Utility and Cloud Computing (UCC)*, 571–576. 10.1109/UCC.2015.101

Ahmad, S., Alam, K. M. R., Rahman, H., & Tamura, S. (2015). A comparison between symmetric and asymmetric key encryption algorithm based decryption mixnets. *2015 International Conference on Networking Systems and Security (NSysS)*, 1-5. 10.1109/NSysS.2015.7043532

Ahmed, S., Soaibuzzaman, Rahman, S. M., & Rahaman, S. M. (2019). A Blockchain-Based Architecture for Integrated Smart Parking Systems. *2019 IEEE International Conference On Pervasive Computing and Communications Workshops (PerCom Workshops)*. 10.1109/PERCOMW.2019.8730772

Alharby, M., & Moorsel, A. V. (2017). *Blockchain Based Smart Contracts: A Systematic Mapping Study. Computer Science & Information Technology*. CS & IT. doi:10.5121/csit.2017.71011

Ali, M. S., Vecchio, M., Pincheira, M., Dolui, K., Antonelli, F., & Rehmani, M. H. (2019). Applications of Blockchains in the Internet of Things: A Comprehensive Survey. *IEEE Communications Surveys and Tutorials*, *21*(2), 1676–1717. doi:10.1109/COMST.2018.2886932

Alonso-Ayuso, A., Escudero, L. F., & Martín-Campo, F. J. (2011, March). Collision avoidance in air traffic management: A mixed-integer linear optimization approach. *IEEE Transactions on Intelligent Transportation Systems*, *12*(1), 47–57. doi:10.1109/TITS.2010.2061971

Amiri, A. I. W., Baza, M., Banawan, K., Mahmoud, M., Alasmary, W., & Akkaya, K. (2019). *Privacy-Preserving Smart Parking System Using Blockchain and Private Information Retrieval*. https://arxiv.org/abs/1904.09703

Anderson, J., Kalra, N., Stanley, K., Sorensen, P., Samaras, C., & Oluwatola, O. (2016). Autonomous Vehicle Technology: A Guide for Policymakers. doi:10.7249/RR443-2

Andreas, M. (2014). *Mastering Bitcoin: Programming the Open Blockchain*. Academic Press.

Andrew, M., Malte, M., Kevin, L., & Arvind, N. (2017). *An Empirical Analysis of Linkability in the Monero Blockchain.* arXiv:1704.04299

Arif, M., Wang, G., Bhuiyan, A. Z., Wang, M., Chen, T., & Jianer. (2019). A survey on security attacks in VANETs: Communication, applications and challenges. *Vehicular Communications, 19*, 100-179. www.elsevier.com/locate/vehcom

Arushi, A., & Sumit, Y. (2018). *Block chain Based Security Mechanism for Internet of Vehicles (IoV). In 3rd International Conference on Internet of Things and Connected Technologies, (ICIoTCT).* Elsevier. https://www.ssrn.com/link/3rd-iciotct-2018

Atlam, Alenezi, Alassafi, & Wills. (2018). Blockchain with Internet of Things: Benefits, Challenges, and Future Directions. *International Journal of Intelligent Systems and Applications.*

Atlam, H. F., & Wills, G. B. (2019). Technical aspects of blockchain and IoT. *Advances in Computers*, 1–39. doi:10.1016/bs.adcom.2018.10.006

Autonomy International Business Pte Ltd. (2019). *Blockchain Cloud for Autonomous Vehicles Table of Contents.* Author.

Ayvaz, S., & Cetin, S. C. (2019). Witness of Things. *International Journal of Intelligent Unmanned Systems, 7*(2), 72–87. doi:10.1108/IJIUS-05-2018-0011

Azaria, A., Ekblaw, A., Vieira, T., & Lippman, A. (2016). MedRec: Using Blockchain for Medical Data Access and Permission Management. *2016 2nd International Conference on Open and Big Data (OBD)*, 25-30. 10.1109/OBD.2016.11

Bach, L. M., Mihaljevic, B., & Zagar, M. (2018). Comparative analysis of blockchain consensus algorithms. *2018 41st International Convention on Information and Communication Technology, Electronics and Microelectronics (MIPRO)*, 1545-1550. 10.23919/MIPRO.2018.8400278

Back. (n.d.). *Hashcash-a denial of service counter-measure.* Academic Press.

Bahga, A., & Madisetti, V. K. (2016). Blockchain Platform for Industrial Internet of Things. *Journal of Software Engineering and Applications, 09*(10), 533–546. doi:10.4236/jsea.2016.910036

Baldini, G. (2019). Zone Keys Trust Management in Vehicular Networks based on Blockchain. 2019 Global IoT Summit (GIoTS), 1–6.

Baliga. (2017). *Understanding blockchain consensus models.* Persistent Systems Ltd, Tech. Rep.

Baouche, F., Billota, R. E. L., Faouzi, N. E., & Trigui, R. (2014). Electric vehicle charging stations allocation models. Transport Research Arena, Paris, France.

Barabás, I., Todoruţ, A., Cordoş, N., & Molea, A. (2017). Current challenges in autonomous driving. *IOP Conference Series. Materials Science and Engineering, 252*, 012096. doi:10.1088/1757-899X/252/1/012096

Barnas. (n.d.). *Blockchains in national defense: Trustworthy systems in a trustless world.* Blue Horizons Fellowship, Air University, Maxwell Air Force Base.

Basharuddin, N., Yusnita, R., & Norbaya, F. (2012). Intelligent Parking space detection system based on image Processing. *International Journal of Innovation, Management and Technology, 3*(3), 232–253.

Benet, J. (n.d.). IPFS - Content self-addressed, Versioned, P2P File System (DRAFT 3).

Benson, J. P., O'Donovan, T., O'sullivan, P., Roedig, U., & Sreenan, C. (2006). Car-Park management using wireless sensor networs. Proceedings of 31 IEEE coif. Local Computer Networks, 588-595.

Bentov & Gabizon. (2016). Cryptocurrencies without proof of work. In *International Conference on Financial Cryptography and Data Security* (pp. 142-157). Springer. 10.1007/978-3-662-53357-4_10

Bhargavan, K., Swamy, N., Zanella-Béguelin, S., Delignat-Lavaud, A., Fournet, C., Gollamudi, A., … Sibut-Pinote, T. (2016). Formal Verification of Smart Contracts. *Proceedings of the 2016 ACM Workshop on Programming Languages and Analysis for Security - PLAS'16.* doi:10.1145/2993600.2993611

BioThink Futuristic Vehicle for Mega-Cities. (2015) Available online: www.mohammadghezel.com

Biswas, S., Sharif, K., Li, F., Nour, B., & Wang, Y. (2019). A Scalable Blockchain Framework for Secure Transactions in IoT. IEEE Internet of Things Journal, 6(3).

Blockchain-Base Structures for a Secure and Operate Network of Semi-Autonomous Unmanned Aerial Vehicles. (2018). IEEE.

Bocek, T., Rodrigues, B. B., Strasser, T., & Stiller, B. (2017). Blockchains everywhere—A use-case of blockchains within the pharmaceutical company supply-chain. *Proc. IFIP/IEEE Symp. Integr. Netw. Service Manage.*, 772–777.

Boda, V. K., Nasipuri, A., & Howitt, I. (2007). Design Considerations for a Wireless Sensor Network for Locating Parking Spaces. *Proceedings of IEEE Southeastcon*, 698–703. doi:10.1109/SECON.2007.342990

Bogner, A., & Chanson, M. (2016). A Decentralised Sharing App running a Smart Contract on the Ethereum Blockchain. *Proceedings of the 6th International Conference on the Internet of Things - IoT'16.* 10.1145/2991561.2998465

Bonde, D. J., Rohit, S. S., Akshay, S. K., Suresh, K., & Uday, B. (2014). Automated car parking system commanded by mobile application. *International Conference on Computer Communication and Informatics (ICCCI -2014).* 10.1109/ICCCI.2014.6921729

Bonneau, J., Miller, A., Clark, J., Narayanan, A., Kroll, J. A., & Felten, E. W. (2015). SoK: Research Perspectives and Challenges for Bitcoin and Cryptocurrencies. *2015 IEEE Symposium on Security and Privacy* 10.1109/SP.2015.14

Bowe, Hopwood, Hornby, & Wilcox. (2016). *Zcash Protocol Specification, Semantic Scholar.* Academic Press.

Brodl, U. (2019). *Testing blockchain technology for clinical trials in Canada. IBM blog.* Watson Health Perspectives.

BuchananB. (2016). *Oblivious Transfer.* https://asecuritysite.com/encryption/ot

Butterworth, P. (2019). *Intertrust.* https://www.intertrust.com/blog/what-is-tls-and-how-to-ensure-a-secure-implementation/

Cai, W., Wang, Z., Jason B. E., Hong, Z., Feng, C., & Leung, C. M. V. (2018). Decentralized Applications: The Blockchain-Empowered Software System. *IEEE Access*, 6, 53019-53033. doi: . doi:10.1109/ACCESS.2018.2870644

Caliskan, C., Graupner, D., & Mauve, M. (2006). Decentralized discovery of free parking places. *Proceedings of the 3rd international workshop on Vehicular ad hoc networks.*

Canetti, R., & Rosen, A. (2009). General secure two party and multi party computation. *Cryptography & Game Theory.* https://www.cs.tau.ac.il/~canetti/f09-materials/f09-scribe4.pdf

Capkun, S. (n.d.). *Practical zkSNARKS for ZCash in ethz.ch.* https://ethz.ch/content/dam/ethz/special-interest/infk/inst-infsec/system-security-group-dam/education/available_projects/zksnarks.pdf

Catalani & Gans. (2019). *Some Simple Economics of the Blockchain.* Academic Press.

Chang, Y. (2019). Blockchain Technology for e-Marketplace. 2019 IEEE International Conference on Pervasive Computing and Communications Workshops (PerCom Workshops), 429–430. doi:10.1109/PERCOMW.2019.8730733

Changelly. (n.d.). https://changelly.com/blog/what-is-blockchain

Chavez-Dreyfuss. (2020). https://www.reuters.com/article/us-crypto-currencies-bitcoin-halving/bitcoin-undergoes-third-halving-falls-vs-u-s-dollar-idUSKBN22N2X8

Chen. (2018). A traceability chain algorithm for artificial neural networks using T–S fuzzy cognitive maps in blockchain. *Future Generation Computer Systems, 80*(March), 198–210.

Chou, T., & Orlandi, C. (2015). The Simplest Protocol for Oblivious Transfer, *Technische Universieit Eindhoven and Aarhus University.* https://eprint.iacr.org/2015/267.pdf

Choudhary, O., Fairoza, N., Sylla, I., & Das, A. (2019). A Blockchain Framework for Managing and Monitoring Data in Multi-Site Clinical Trials. *Journal of Biomedical Informatics.*

Conoscenti, M., Vetro, A., & De Martin, J. C. (2016). Blockchain for the internet of things: A systematic literature review. *3th International Conference of Computer Systems and Applications*, 1–6. 10.1109/AICCSA.2016.7945805

Conti, M., Kumar, S., Lal, C., & Ruj, S. (2017). *A Survey on Security and Privacy Issues of Bitcoin.* arXiv:1706.00916v3

Croman, Decker, Eyal, Gencer, Juels, Kosba, Miller, Saxena, Shi, GunSirer, Song, & Wattenhofe. (n.d.). *On Scaling Decentralized Blockchains.* Academic Press.

Crosby, Nachiappan, Pattanayak, Verma, & Vignesh. (2016). Blockchain Technology: Beyond Bitcoin. *Applied Innovation Review.*

Crosby, M., Pattanayak, P., Verma, S., & Kalyanaraman, V. (2016). Blockchain technology: Beyond bitcoin. *Appl. Innov., 2*, 6–10.

Cube Intelligence io. (2018). CUBE-Autonomous Car Network Security Platform based on Blockchain. https://medium.com/@cubeintel/cube-autonomous-car-security-platform-based-on-blockchain-bfc159abce09#:~:text=Blockchain%20Layer&text=CUBE%20uses%20block%2Dchain%20technology,and%20IoT%20or%20traffic%20center

Dai, H. N., Zheng, Z., & Zhang, Y. (2019). Blockchain for Internet of Things: A Survey. IEEE Internet of Things Journal, 6(5).

Dai, H.-N., Zheng, Z., & Zhang, Y. (2019). *Blockchain for Internet of Things: A Survey. IEEE Internet of Things Journal.*

Darren, C. (n.d.) What is vehicle platooning? https://www.drivingtests.co.nz/resources/what-is-vehicle-platooning/

Davidson, De Filippi, & Potts. (2018). Blockchains and the economic institutions of capitalism. *Journal of Institutional Economics, 14*(4), 639–658.

DeJong, K., & Sarma, J. (1993). *Generation Gaps Revisited, Foundations of Genetic Algorithms 2.* Morgan-Kaufmann Publishers.

Dong, J., Liu, C., & Lin, Z. (2014). Charging infrastructure planning for promoting battery electric vehicles: An activity-based approach using multiday travel data. *Transportation Research, 38*(Part C), 44–55.

Dong, Z., Navwant, T., & Jiayu, C. (2020). Optimal Design of Energy Storage System to Buffer Charging Infrastructure in Smart Cities. *Journal of Management Engineering, 36*(2).

Dorri, A., Kanhere, S. S., Jurdak, R., & Gauravaram, P. (2017). Blockchain for IoT security and privacy: The case study of a smart home. *2017 IEEE International Conference on Pervasive Computing and Communications Workshops (PerCom Workshops)*, 618-623. 10.1109/PERCOMW.2017.7917634

Dorri, A., Steger, M., Kanhere, S. S., & Jurdak, R. (2017). BlockChain : A Distributed Solution to Automotive Security and Privacy. *IEEE Communications Magazine*, *55*(December), 119–125. doi:10.1109/MCOM.2017.1700879

Dorri, A., Steger, M., Kanhere, S., & Jurdak, R. (2017). Blockchain: A Distributed Solution to Automotive Security and Privacy. *IEEE Communications Magazine*, *55*(12), 119–125. Advance online publication. doi:10.1109/MCOM.2017.1700879

ElMahdy. (2015). Available online: ww.behance.net/

Energypedia. (n.d.). https://energypedia.info/ wiki/Blockchain_Opportunities _for_Social_Impact_in_Developing _Countries#Possible_Advantages _of_Blockchain_Technology_for_Developing_Countries

Event data recorder. (2017). Available: https://en.wikipedia. org/wiki/Eventdatarecorder

Fagnant, D. J., & Kockelman, K. (2015). Preparing a nation for autonomous vehicles: Opportunities, barriers and policy recommendations. *Transportation Research Part A, Policy and Practice*, *77*, 167–181. doi:10.1016/j.tra.2015.04.003

Federal Highway Administration. (2016). *Visual requirements for human drivers and autonomous vehicles*. Author.

Ferber, J. (1995). *Les systèmes multi-agents, vers une intelligence collective*. InterEditions.

Fernandez-Caramals & Fraga-Lamas. (2018). A review on the use of blockchain for the internet of things. *IEEE Access, 6*.

Finney. (2004). *RPOW - Reusable Proofs of Work*. Academic Press.

Gervais, A., Wüst, K., & Ritzdorf, H. (n.d.). On the Security and Performance of Proof of Work Blockchains. Academic Press.

Gkikas, K. (2014). *Yao's Garbled Circuit*. https://homepages.cwi.nl/~schaffne/courses/crypto/2014/presentations/Kostis_Yao.pdf

Guo, S., Hu, X., Zhou, Z., Wang, X., Qi, F., & Gao, L. (2019). Trust Access Authentication in Vehicular Network Based on Blockchain. *China Communications*, *16*(June), 18–30. doi:10.23919/j.cc.2019.06.002

Guy, Z., Oz, N., & Alex, P. (2015). Decentralized Privacy: Using Blockchain to Protect Personal Data. *IEEE Security and Privacy Workshops (SPW)*. Doi:10.1109/SPW.2015.27

Hackernoon. (n.d.a). https://hackernoon.com/how-will-blockchain-agriculture-revolutionize-the-food-supply-from-farm-to-plate-f8fe488d9bae

Hackernoon. (n.d.b). https://hackernoon.com/how-blockchain-is-solving-the-biggest-problems-in-social-networking-87e4e0753e39

Hackernoon. (n.d.c). https://hackernoon.com/top-12-blockchain-development-tools-to-build-blockchain-ecosystem-371a1b587248

Hankerson, Menezes, & Vanstone. (n.d.). *Guide to Elliptic Curve Cryptography*. Springer.

Harris, C. G. (2018). The risks and dangers of relying on blockchain technology in underdeveloped countries. IEEE/IFIP Network Operations and Management Symposium: Cognitive Management in a Cyber World, NOMS 2018, 1–4. doi:10.1109/NOMS.2018.8406330

Hasib Anwar. (2018). *What is ZKP? A Complete Guide to Zero Knowledge Proof*. https://101blockchains.com/zero-knowledge-proof/

Hassan, M. U., Rehmani, M. H., & Chen, J. (2019). Privacy preservation in blockchain based IoT systems: Integration issues, prospects, challenges, and future research directions. *Future Generation Computer Systems*, *97*, 512-529.

Holland, J. (1975). *Adaptation in Natural and Artificial Systems*. University of Michigan Press.

Hori, K., & Sakajiri, A. (n.d.). Blockchain For Dummies. Windows, M. *Corporation.*

Huang, J., Kong, L., Kong, L., Liu, Z., Liu, Z., & Chen, G. (2019). Blockchain-based Crowd-sensing System. *Proceedings of 2018 1st IEEE International Conference on Hot Information-Centric Networking, HotICN 2018*, 234–235. 10.1109/HOTICN.2018.8605960

Ichikawa, D., Kashiyama, M., & Ueno, T. (2017). Tamper-Resistant Mobile Health Using Blockchain Technology. *JMIR mHealth and uHealth*, *5*(7), e111. doi:10.2196/mhealth.7938 PMID:28747296

INC42. (n.d.). https://inc42.com/resources/how-will-blockchain-technology-help-developing-countries/

Insurance Fact Book. (2019). https://www.iii.org/sites/default/files/docs/pdf/insurance_factbook_2019.pdf

IntelliPaat Blogs. (n.d.). *What is Blockchain Technology?* https://intellipaat.com/blog/tutorial/blockchain-tutorial/what-is-blockchain/

Internet Society. (n.d.). https://www.internetsociety.org/deploy360/tls/basics/

Investopedia. (n.d.). https://www.investopedia.com/terms/1/51-attack.asp

Jaoude, J. O. E. A., & Saade, R. G. (2019). Blockchain Applications – Usage in Different Domains. *IEEE Access : Practical Innovations, Open Solutions*, *7*, 45360–45381. doi:10.1109/ACCESS.2019.2902501

Jenkinson, G. (2019). *Can Blockchain Become an Integral Part of Autonomous Vehicles?* https://cointelegraph.com/news/can-blockchain-become-an-integral-part-of-autonomous-vehicles

Jiang, T., Fang, H., & Wang, H. (2019). Blockchain-Based Internet of Vehicles : Distributed Network Architecture and Performance Analysis. IEEE Internet of Things Journal, 6(3), 4640–4649. doi:10.1109/JIOT.2018.2874398

Kachroudi, S., Grossard, M., & Abroug, N. (2012). Predictive Driving Guidance of Full Electric Vehicles Using Particle Swarm Optimization. Vehicular Technology. *IEEE Transactions on*, *61*(9), 3909–3919.

Kamau, G., Boore, C., Maina, E., & Njenga, S. (2018). Blockchain technology: Is this the solution to EMR interoperability and security issues in developing countries? 2018 IST-Africa Week Conference, IST-Africa 2018.

Kameda, H., & Mukai, N. (2011). Optimization of Charging Station Placement by Using Taxi Probe Data for On-Demand Electrical Bus System. *Lecture Notes in Computer Science*, *6883*, 606–615. doi:10.1007/978-3-642-23854-3_64

Kanimozhi & Jacob. (2019). *Artificial Intelligence primarily based Network Intrusion Detection with Hyper-Parameter improvement standardisation on the Realistic Cyber Dataset CSE-CICIDS2018 mistreatment Cloud Computing*. IEEE.

Kapitonov, A., Lonshakov, S., Krupenkin, A., & Berman, I. (2017). Blockchain-based protocol of autonomous business activity for multi-agent systems consisting of UAVs. *2017 Workshop on Research, Education and Development of Unmanned Aerial Systems (RED-UAS)*. 10.1109/RED-UAS.2017.8101648

Karafiloski, E., & Mishev, A. (2017). Blockchain solutions for big data challenges: A literature review. *IEEE EUROCON 2017 -17th International Conference on Smart Technologies*, 763-768. 10.1109/EUROCON.2017.8011213

Khelifi, H., Luo, S., Nour, B., Moungla, H., & Ahmed, S. H. (2018). Reputation-based Blockchain for Secure NDN Caching in Vehicular Networks. 2018 IEEE Conference on Standards for Communications and Networking (CSCN), 1–6. doi:10.1109/CSCN.2018.8581849

Khezr, S., Moniruzzaman, M., Yassine, A., & Benlamri, R. (2019). Blockchain Technology in Healthcare: A Comprehensive Review and Directions for Future Research. *Applied Sciences (Basel, Switzerland)*, *9*(9), 1736. doi:10.3390/app9091736

Kim, S. (2019). Impacts of Mobility on Performance of Blockchain in VANET. *IEEE Access : Practical Innovations, Open Solutions, 7*, 68646–68655. doi:10.1109/ACCESS.2019.2918411

Kim, T. W., & Zetlin-Jones, A. (2019). The Ethics of Contentious Hard Forks in Blockchain Networks With Fixed Features. *Frontiers in Blockchain, 2*, 9. Advance online publication. doi:10.3389/fbloc.2019.00009

Koblitz, N., & Menezes, J. (2016). *Cryptocash, cryptocurrencies, and cryptocontracts.* Springer. doi:10.100710623-015-0148-5

Kogias. (2019). Toward a Blockchain-Enabled Crowdsourcing Platform. *IT Professional, 21*(5), 18-25.

Kreitz, G. (2012). Secure Multi-Party Computation. *KTH - Royal Institute of Technology.* http://www.csc.kth.se/~buc/PPC/Slides/kreitz-pet-course-mpc.pdf

Kshetri, N., & Voas, J. (2018). Blockchain in Developing Countries. *IT Professional, 20*(2), 11–14. doi:10.1109/MITP.2018.021921645

Kuehn, B. M. (2012). Few Studies Reporting Results at US Government Clinical Trials Site. *Journal of the American Medical Association, 307*(7), 651–653. doi:10.1001/jama.2012.127 PMID:22337663

Kuo T, Kim H, & Ohno-Machado L. (2017). Blockchain distributed ledger technologies for biomedical and health care applications. *J Am Med Inform Assoc., 24*(6), 1211–1220.

Lamberti, F., Gatteschi, V., Demartini, C., Pelissier, M., Gomez, A., & Santamaria, V. (2018). Blockchains Can Work for Car Insurance: Using Smart Contracts and Sensors to Provide On-Demand Coverage. *IEEE Consumer Electronics Magazine, 7*(4), 72–81. doi:10.1109/MCE.2018.2816247

Larimer, D. (2018). DPOS Consensus Algorithm – The Missing Whitepaper. *Steemit.* Available: https://steemit. com/dpos/dantheman/dpos-consensus-algorithm-this-missingwhite-paper

Larimer. (2018). *Delegated proof-of-stake consensus.* Academic Press.

Laroui, Dridi, & Afifi. (2019). Energy Management For Electric Vehicles in Smart Cities: A Deep Learning Approach. *IEEE International Wireless Communications & Mobile Computing Conference (IWCMC 2019).*

Lauslahti, K., Mattila, J., & Seppala, T. (2017). *Smart Contracts How Will Blockchain Technology Affect Contractual Practices?* SSRN Electronic Journal. doi:10.2139srn.3154043

Lauter, K. (2004, February). The advantages of elliptic curve cryptography for wireless security. *IEEE Wireless Communications, 11*(1), 62–67. doi:10.1109/MWC.2004.1269719

Lee, W. (2019a). Getting Started with Smart Contract. *Beginning Ethereum Smart Contracts Programming, 127-146.* doi:10.1007/978-1-4842-5086-0_6

Lee, W. (2019b). Connecting to the Ethereum Blockchain. *Beginning Ethereum Smart Contracts Programming,* 61-69. doi:10.1007/978-1-4842-5086-0_3

Leiding, B. (2018). Enabling the V2X Economy Revolution Using a Blockchain-Based Value Transaction Layer for Vehicular Ad-Hoc Networks. *Conference on Information Systems (MCIS),* 1–31.

Leiding, B., & Vorobev, W. V. (2018). *Enabling the Vehicle Economy Using a Blockchain-Based Value Transaction Layer Protocol for Vehicular Ad-Hoc Networks.* Academic Press.

Li, T., Lin, L., & Gong, S. (2019). *AutoMPC: Efficient Multi-Party Computation for Secure and Privacy-Preserving Cooperative Control of Connected Autonomous Vehicles.* http://ceur-ws.org/Vol-2301/paper_13.pdf

Li, X., Jiang, P., Chen, T., Luo, X., & Wen, Q. (n.d.). A Survey on the Security of Blockchain Systems. Academic Press.

Li, Y., Li., L, Yong, J., Yao, Y., & Li, Z. (2011). Layout Planning of Electrical Vehicle Charging Stations Based on Genetic Algorithm. *Lecture Notes in Electrical Engineering, 1*(99), 661- 668.

Liang, X., Zhao, J., Shetty, S., & Li, D. (2017). Towards data assurance and resilience in IoT using blockchain. *IEEE Military Communications Conference (MILCOM)*. 10.1109/MILCOM.2017.8170858

Li, M., Weng, J., Yang, A., Lu, W., Zhang, Y., Hou, L., Liu, J.-N., Xiang, Y., & Deng, R. H. (2019, June 1). CrowdBC: A Blockchain-Based Decentralized Framework for Crowdsourcing. *IEEE Transactions on Parallel and Distributed Systems, 30*(6), 1251–1266. doi:10.1109/TPDS.2018.2881735

Lin, J., Yu, W., Zhang, N., Yang, X., Zhang, H., & Zhao, W. (2017). A survey on internet of things: Architecture, enabling technologies, security and privacy, and applications. *IEEE Internet of Things Journal, 4*(5), 1125–1142. doi:10.1109/JIOT.2017.2683200

Linn, L. A., & Koo, M. B. (2016). Blockchain for health data and its potential use in health it and health care related research. In *ONC/NIST Use of Blockchain for Healthcare and Research Workshop*. ONC/NIST.

Lin, W.-H., & Liu, H. (2010, December). Enhancing realism in modeling merge junctions in analytical models for system-optimal dynamic traffic assignment. *IEEE Transactions on Intelligent Transportation Systems, 11*(4), 838–845. doi:10.1109/TITS.2010.2050880

Liu, B., Yu, X. L., Chen, S., Xu, X., & Zhu, L. (2017). Blockchain based data integrity service framework for IoT data. In *IEEE International Conference on Web Services (ICWS)*. IEEE. 10.1109/ICWS.2017.54

Loi, L., Duc-Hiep, C., & Hrishi, O. (2016). Making Smart Contracts Smarter. *Proceedings of the 2016 ACM SIGSAC Conference on Computer and Communications Security*, 254-269. DOI: 10.1145/2976749.2978309

Lu, R., Lin, X., Zhu, H., & Shen, X. (2009). SPARK: A New VANET-based Smart Parking Scheme for Large Parking Lots. *IEEE Communications Society subject matter experts for publication in the IEEE INFOCOM 2009 Proceedings*, 1413-1421. doi:. doi:10.1109/ ACCESS.2018.2864189

Lu, Wang, Qu, Zhang, & Liu. (n.d.). A Blockchain-Based Privacy-Preserving Authentication Scheme for VANETs. *IEEE Transactions on Very Large-Scale Integration (VLSI) Systems*.

Lu, Z., Wang, Q., Qu, G., & Liu, Z. (2018). Article. 2018 17th IEEE International Conference On Trust, Security And Privacy In Computing And Communications/ 12th IEEE International Conference On Big Data Science And Engineering (TrustCom/BigDataSE), 98–103. 10.1109/TrustCom/BigDataSE.2018.00025

Luoto, J., McIntosh, C., & Wydick, B. (2007). *Credit Information Systems in Less Developed Countries: A Test with Microfinance in Guatemala*. University of San Francisco.

Lu, Z., Wang, Q., Qu, G., Member, S., Zhang, H., & Liu, Z. (2019). *A Blockchain-Based Privacy-Preserving Authentication Scheme for VANETs*. Academic Press.

Mark Gates. (2017). *Blockchain: Ultimate Guide to Understanding Blockchain*. Bitcoin, Cryptocurrencies, Smart Contracts and the Future of Money.

Marwala & Xing. (n.d.). *Blockchain and Artificial Intelligence*. https://arxiv.org/ftp/arxiv/papers/1802/1802.04451.pdf

Masjosthusmann, C., Kohler, U., Decius, N., & Buker, U. (2012). A vehicle energy management system for a Battery Electric Vehicle. *Vehicle Power and Propulsion Conference (VPPC), 2012 IEEE*, 339 – 344.

Medium. (n.d.). https://medium.com/swlh/what-blockchain-means-for-developing-countries1ec25a416a4b

Mengelkamp, E., Notheisen, B., Beer, C., Dauer, D., & Weinhardt, C. (2018). A blockchain-based smart grid : Towards sustainable local energy markets. Computer Science -. *Research for Development*, *33*(1), 207–214. doi:10.100700450-017-0360-9

Mettler, M. (2016). Blockchain technology in healthcare: The revolution starts her*e. 2016 IEEE 18th International Conference on e-Health Networking, Applications and Services (Healthcom).*

Microsoft Research & Microsoft Azure. (2019, April 10). *CCF: A Framework for Building Confidential Verifiable Replicated Services.* Retrieved from https://github.com/microsoft/CCF/blob/master/CCF-TECHNICAL-REPORT.pdf

Mike, A. H. (1995). *Crossbow Technologies.* http://www.xbow.com

Miller, D. (2018). Blockchain and the internet of things in the industrial sector. *IT Professional*, *20*(3), 15–18. doi:10.1109/MITP.2018.032501742

Min, X., Li, Q., Liu, L., & Cui, L. (2016). A Permissioned Blockchain Framework for Supporting Instant Transaction and Dynamic Block Size. 2016 IEEE Trustcom/BigDataSE/ISPA, 90–96. doi:10.1109/TrustCom.2016.0050

Mobility, W., Database, D., & Transportation, F. O. R. (1997). *For Transportation.* Academic Press.

Mohanta, B. K., Panda, S. S., & Jena, D. (2018). An Overview of Smart Contract and Use Cases in Blockchain Technology. *2018 9th International Conference on Computing, Communication and Networking Technologies (ICCCNT),* 1-4. 10.1109/ICCCNT.2018.8494045

Mohanta, B. K., Panda, S. S., & Jena, D. (2018). An Overview of Smart Contract and Use Cases in Blockchain Technology. *2018 9th International Conference on Computing, Communication and Networking Technologies (ICCCNT).* doi:10.1109/icccnt.2018.8494045

Mousannif, H., Khalil, I., & Al Moatassime, H. (2011). (20110 "Cooperation as a service in VANETs,". *Journal of Universal Computer Science*, *17*(8), 1202–1218.

Muftah, F., & Mikael, F. (2016). Investigation of Smart Parking Systems and their technologies Completed Research Paper. *Thirty Seventh International Conference on Information Systems*, 1-14.

Mulder, M., Abbink, D. A., van Paassen, M. M., & Mulder, M. (2011, March). Design of a haptic gas pedal for active car-following support. *IEEE Transactions on Intelligent Transportation Systems*, *12*(1), 268–279. doi:10.1109/TITS.2010.2091407

Muralidharan, S., Roy, A., & Saxena, N. (2016). An Exhaustive Review on Internet of Things from Korea's Perspective. *Wireless Personal Communications*, *90*(3), 1463–1486. doi:10.100711277-016-3404-8

Muthukrishnan, S., & Duraisamy, B. (2019). Blockchain Technologies and Artificial Intelligence. *Studies in Big Data*, 243-268. doi:10.1007/978-981-13-8775-3_12

Nakamoto, S. (2008). Bitcoin: A Peer-to-Peer Electronic Cash System. www.bitcoin.org

Nakamoto, S. (2008). *Bitcoin: A peer-to-peer electronic money system.* Tech. Rep. Available: https://archive.is/rMBtV

Nakamoto. (2008). *Bitcoin: A Peer-to-Peer Electronic Cash System.* Academic Press.

Nakamoto. (2008). *Bitcoin: A Peer-to-Peer Electronic Cash System.* Bitcoin.org

Nakomoto. (2009). *Bitcoin: A Peer-to-Peer Electronic Cash System.* bitcoin.org.

National Highway Traffic Safety Administration. (n.d.). Automated Vehicles for Safety. https://www.nhtsa.gov/technology-innovation/automated-vehicles-safety

Nebula Ai (NBAI). (2018). *Decentralized ai Blockchain white paper*. Nebula AI Team.

Norta, A. (2017). Designing a Smart-Contract Application Layer for Transacting Decentralized Autonomous Organizations. *Communications in Computer and Information Science, 721*, 595–604. doi:10.1007/978-981-10-5427-3_61

O'Hara, K. (2017). Smart Contracts - Dumb Idea. *IEEE Internet Computing, 21*(2), 97–101. doi:10.1109/MIC.2017.48

Olariu, S., Eltoweissy, M., & Younis, M. (2011, July–September). Toward autonomous vehicular clouds. *ICST Trans. Mobile Commun. Comput., 11*(7–9), 1–11.

Oleshchuk, V. & Zadorozhny, V. (2007). Secure Multi-Party Computations and Privacy Preservation: Results and Open Problems. *Telektronikk: Telenor's Journal of Technology, 103*(2).

Ostermaier, B., Florian, D., & Strassberger, M. (2007). *Enhancing the Security of Local Danger Warnings in VANETs - A Simulative Analysis of Voting Schemes*. Academic Press.

Pahl, C. E. L., Ioini, N., & Helmer, S. (2018). A Decision Framework for Blockchain Platforms for IoT and Edge Computing. *Proceedings of the 3rd International Conference on Internet of Things, Big Data and Security*. 10.5220/0006688601050113

Panarello, A., Tapas, N., Merlino, G., Longo, F., & Puliafito, A. (2018). Blockchain and IoT integration: A systematic survey. *Sensors (Basel), 18*(8), 2575. doi:10.339018082575 PMID:30082633

Paolo, N., Alberto De, M., Anna Giulio, C. M., & Francesco, S. (2014). Current trends in Smart City initiatives: Some stylised facts. *Cities (London, England), 38*, 25–36. doi:10.1016/j.cities.2013.12.010

Park, H.-S., & Tran, N.-H. (2014). Autonomy for Smart Manufacturing. *Journal of the Korean Society for Precision Engineering, 31*(4), 287–295. doi:10.7736/KSPE.2014.31.4.287

Parkres. (2018). https://www.parkres.org

Pathak, N., & Bhandari, A. (2018). *IoT, AI, and Blockchain for. NET : Building a next-generation application from the ground up*. doi:10.1007/978-1-4842-3709-0

Pedrosa, A. R., & Pau, G. (2018). ChargeItUp: On blockchain-based technologies for autonomous vehicles. CRYBLOCK 2018 - Proceedings of the 1st Workshop on Cryptocurrencies and Blockchains for Distributed Systems, Part of MobiSys 2018, (June), 87–92. 10.1145/3211933.3211949

Performance Analysis and Optimization of the Blockchain Technology. (n.d.). https://assignmenthelp4me.com/article-performance-analysis-and-optimization-of-the-blockchain-technology-869.html

Perlman, R. (1999, November-December). An overview of PKI trust models. *IEEE Network, 13*(6), 38–43. doi:10.1109/65.806987

Pete, G. (2018). 10 Advantages of Autonomous Vehicles. https://www.itsdigest.com/10-advantages-autonomous-vehicles

Pew Research Center. (n.d.). http://www.pewinternet.org/2017/10/04/americansattitudes- toward-driverless-vehicles/

Pham, N. T., Ming-Fong, T., Nguyen, B., Chyi-Ren, D., & Der-Jiunn, D. (2015). *A Cloud-Based Smart-Parking System Based on Internet-of-Things Technologies. Emerging Cloud-Based Wireless Communications and Networks, 3, 1581-1591*.

Polyzos, G. C., & Fotiou, N. (2017). Blockchain-Assisted Information Distribution for the Internet of Things. *2017 IEEE International Conference on Information Reuse and Integration (IRI)*. 10.1109/IRI.2017.83

Potluri, R., & Vajjhala, N. (2018). A Study on Application of Web 3.0 Technologies in Small and Medium Enterprises of India, The Journal of Asian Finance. *Economics and Business, 5*(2), 73–79.

Praitheeshan, P., Pan, L., Yu, J., Liu, J., & Doss, R. (2019, August 22). *Security Analysis Methods on Ethereum Smart Contract Vulnerabilities: A Survey.* Retrieved from https://ui.adsabs.harvard.edu/abs/2019arXiv190808605P/abstract

Prashanth Joshi, A., Han, M., & Wang, Y. (2018). *A survey on security and privacy issues of blockchain technology.* Mathematical Foundations of Computing., doi:10.3934/mfc.2018007

Prosperi, M., Min, J. S., Bian, J., & Modave, F. (2018). Big data hurdles in precision medicine and precision public health. *BMC Medical Informatics and Decision Making*, *18*(1), 139. doi:10.118612911-018-0719-2 PMID:30594159

Pustisek, M., Kos, A., & Sedlar, U. (2016). Blockchain Based Autonomous Selection of Electric Vehicle Charging Station. *2016 International Conference on Identification, Information and Knowledge in the Internet of Things (IIKI)*. 10.1109/IIKI.2016.60

Qin, Y., & Huang, D. (2012). VehiCloud : Cloud Computing Facilitating Routing In Vehicular Networks. 2012 IEEE 11th International Conference on Trust, Security and Privacy in Computing and Communications, 1438–1445. 10.1109/TrustCom.2012.16

Quora. (2017). *What makes blockchain trusted?* https://www.quora.com/What-makes-blockchain-trusted

Rad, F., Pazhokhzadeh, H., & Parvin, H. (2017). A Smart Hybrid System for Parking Space Reservation in VANET. *Journal of Advances in Computer Engineering and Technology*, *3*(1).

Ratha, D. (2019). *Remittances on track to become the largest source of external financing in developing countries in World Bank Blogs.* https://blogs.worldbank.org/peoplemove/remittances-track-become-largest-source-external-financing-developing-countries

Rathee, S., & Iqbal, A. (2019). A Blockchain Framework for Securing Connected and Autonomous Vehicles. *Sensors (Basel)*, *19*(14), 3165. doi:10.339019143165 PMID:31323870

Ravallion, M., & Chen, S. (2005). Hidden impact? Household saving in response to a poor-area development project. *Journal of Public Economics*, *89*(11-12), 2183–2204. doi:10.1016/j.jpubeco.2004.12.003

Reyna, A., Martín, C., Chen, J., Soler, E., & Díaz, M. (2018). On blockchain and its integration with IoT Challenges and opportunities. *Future Generation Computer Systems*, *88*, 173–190. doi:10.1016/j.future.2018.05.046

Rivera, R., Robledo, J. G., Larios, V. M., & Avalos, J. M. (2017). How digital identity on blockchain can contribute in a smart city environment. *2017 International Smart Cities Conference (ISC2)*, 1-4. 10.1109/ISC2.2017.8090839

Rivest, R. L., Shamir, A., & Adleman, L. (1978, February). A method for obtaining digital signatures and public-key cryptosystems. *Communications of the ACM*, *21*(2), 120–126. doi:10.1145/359340.359342

Roscher, M. A., Leidholdt, W., & Trepte, J. (2012). High efficiency energy management in BEV applications. *International Journal of Electrical Power & Energy Systems*, *37*(1), 126–130. doi:10.1016/j.ijepes.2011.10.022

Runyon, J. (2017, May 15). How Smart Contracts [Could] Simplify Clean Energy Distribution. Retrieved 10 July 2017, from https://www.renewableenergyworld.com/articles/2017/05/how-smart-contracts-could-simplify-clean-energy-distribution.html

Rutkin, A. (2016, March 2). Blockchain-based microgrid gives power to consumers in New York. Retrieved 10 July 2017, from https://www.newscientist.com/article/2079334-blockchain-based-microgrid-gives-power-to-consumers-in-new-york/

Safi, Q., Luo, S., Limin, P., Liu, W., Hussain, R., &Bouk, H. S. (2018). SVPS: Cloud-Based Smart Vehicle Parking System Over Ubiquitous VANETs. *Computer Networks*. doi: .2018.03.034 doi:10.1016/j.comnet

Salahuddin, M. A., Al-fuqaha, A., Guizani, M., & Cherkaoui, S. (2014). RSU Cloud and its Resource Management in support of Enhanced Vehicular Applications. 2014 IEEE Globecom Workshops (GC Wkshps), 127–132. doi:10.1109/GLOCOMW.2014.7063418

Salan, Rehman, Nizamuddin, & Al-Fuqaha. (n.d.). Blockchain for AI: Review and Open analysis Challenges. *IEEE Access: Practical Innovations, Open Solutions*. Advance online publication. doi:10.1109/ACCESS.2018.2890507

Saleh, F. (2018). *Blockchain Without Waste: Proof-of-Stake*. SSRN Electronic Journal. doi:10.2139srn.3183935

Samaniego, M., & Deters, R. (2016). Blockchain as a service for IoT. *IEEE International Conference on Internet of Things (iThings) and IEEE Green Computing and Communications (GreenCom) and IEEE Cyber, Physical and Social Computing (CPSCom) and IEEE Smart Data (SmartData)*, 433–436. 10.1109/iThings-GreenCom-CPSCom-SmartData.2016.102

Samaniego, M., & Deters, R. (2017). Internet of Smart Things - IoST: Using Blockchain and CLIPS to Make Things Autonomous. *2017 IEEE International Conference on Cognitive Computing (ICCC)*. 10.1109/IEEE.ICCC.2017.9

Sanghi, N., Bhatnagar, R., Kaur, G., & Jain, V. (2018). BlockCloud: Blockchain with Cloud Computing. *2018 International Conference on Advances in Computing, Communication Control and Networking (ICACCCN)*, 430-434. 10.1109/ICACCCN.2018.8748467

Saranti, P. G., Chondrogianni, D., & Karatzas, S. (2019). Autonomous vehicles and blockchain technology are shaping the future of transportation. Advances in Intelligent Systems and Computing, 879(June), 797–803. doi:10.1007/978-3-030-02305-8_96

Sarkar, M. A. R., Rokoni, A. A., Reza, M. O., & Ismail, M. F. (2012). Smart Parking system with image processing facility. *Intelligent Systems and Applications, 3*, 41–47.

Sawal, N., Anjali, T., Amit, T., Sreenath, N., & Rekha, G. (2016). *Necessity of Blockchain for Building Trust in Today's Applications: An Useful Explanation from User's Perspective*. Academic Press.

Sawal, N., Yadav, A., & Tyagi, D. (2019). *Necessity of Blockchain for Building Trust in Today's Applications: An Useful Explanation from User's Perspective*. Available at SSRN: https://ssrn.com/abstract=3388558

Sebastian, P., & Hamada, R. H. (2010). Vision based automated parking System. *10th International conference on Information Science, Signal Processing and their Applications (ISSPA 2010), 1*, 757-760.

Security, D., Security, D., & Security, D. (n.d.). Toward a Distributed Trust Management scheme for VANET. Academic Press.

Shamila, M., & Vinuthna, K. (2019). A Review on Several Critical Issues and Challenges in IoT based e-Healthcare System. IEEE.

Shieh, W.-Y., Hsu, C.-C., Tung, S.-L., Lu, P.-W., Wang, T.-H., & Chang, S.-L. (2011, March). (20110 "Design of infrared electronic-toll-collection systems with extended communication areas and performance of data transmission,". *IEEE Transactions on Intelligent Transportation Systems, 12*(1), 25–35. doi:10.1109/TITS.2010.2057508

Shladover, S. E. (2018). Connected and automated vehicle systems: Introduction and overview. *Journal of Intelligent Transport Systems, 22*(3), 190–200. doi:10.1080/15472450.2017.1336053

Shrestha, R. (2018). *Challenges of Future VANET and Cloud-Based Approaches*. Academic Press.

Shrestha, R., & Nam, S. Y. (2017). *Trustworthy Event-Information Dissemination in Vehicular Ad Hoc Networks*. Academic Press.

Shreyas Ramachandran, S., Veeraraghavan, A. K., Karni, U., & Sivaraman, K. (2019). Development of Flexible Autonomous Car System Using Machine Learning and Blockchain. *Lecture Notes in Electrical Engineering*, 63-72. doi:10.1007/978-3-030-20717-5_8

Shukla, S., & Sadashivappa, G. (2012). Secure Multi-Party Computation (SMC): A Review. *International Conference on Communication, Computing and Information Technology (ICCCMIT)*.

Siemens, A. G. (2012). *Intelligent Traffic Systems*. https://www.siemens.com/traffic

Singh, D., Singh, M., Singh, I., & Lee, H. J. (2015). Secure and reliable cloud networks for smart transportation services. *2015 17th International Conference on Advanced Communication Technology (ICACT)*, 358-362. 10.1109/ICACT.2015.7224819

Sompolinsky & Zohar. (2016). *Bitcoin's Security Model Revisited*. Academic Press.

Song, J. C., Demir, M. A., Prevost, J. J., & Rad, P. (2018). Blockchain design for trusted decentralized iot networks. In *13th Annual Conference on System of Systems Engineering (SoSE)*. IEEE. 10.1109/SYSOSE.2018.8428720

Stephen, R., & Alex, A. (2018). A Review on BlockChain Security. *IOP Conference Series. Materials Science and Engineering*, *396*(1). Advance online publication. doi:10.1088/1757-899X/396/1/012030

Stuart, H., & Stornetta, W. S. (1991). Bellcore, How to stamp a digital document. *Journal of Cryptology*, *3*.

Sung, Y., Sharma, P. K., Lopez, E. M., & Park, J. H. (2016). FS-OpenSecurity: A taxonomic modeling of security threats in SDN for future sustainable computing. *Sustainability*, *8*(9), 919–944. doi:10.3390u8090919

Sussman, J. M. (2005). *Perspectives on Intelligent Transportation Systems (ITS)*. Springer-Verlag.

Swan, M. (2016). Blockchain Temporality: Smart Contract Time Specifiability with Blocktime. Rule Technologies. *Research, Tools, and Applications*, 184-196. doi:10.1007/978-3-319-42019-6_12

Sweda, T., & Klabjan, D. (2011). An Agent-Based Decision Support System for Electric Vehicle Charging Infrastructure Deployment. *7th IEEE Vehicle Power and Propulsion Conference*.

Tang, Y. W. S., Zheng, Y., & Cao, J. (2006). An Intelligent Car Park Management System based on Wireless Sensor Networks. *Proceedings of the 1st international Symposium on Pervasive Computing and Applications*, 65 - 70. 10.1109/SPCA.2006.297498'

Taylor, Dargahi, Dehghantanha, Parizi, & Choo. (2019). A systematic literature review of blockchain cyber security. *Digital Communications and Networks*.

Technologies, I. (2010). *VANET : Vehicular Applications and Inter-Networking*. Academic Press.

Tirenin, W., & Faatz, D. (1999). A concept for strategic cyber defense. *Military Communications Conference Proceedings*, 458–463. doi: 10.1109/MILCOM.1999.822725

Todd Litman. (2019). Autonomous Vehicle Implementation Predictions: Implications for Transport Planning. Transportation Research Board Annual Meeting, 42(January), 36–42. 10.1613/jair.301

Tomov, Y. K. (2019). Bitcoin: Evolution of Blockchain Technology. *2019 IEEE XXVIII International Scientific Conference Electronics (ET)*, 1-4.

Tschorsch & Scheuermann. (2016). Bitcoin and beyond: A technical survey on decentralized digital currencies. *IEEE Communications Surveys & Tutorials, 18*, 2084-2123. doi: .2535718 doi:10.1109/COMST.2016

Understanding Blockchain Technology and the way to urge involved. (2018). In *The ordinal International Scientific Conference eLearning and software system for Education Bucuresti.*. doi:10.12753/2066-026X-18-000

United Nations. (2007). *Urbanization: A Majority in Cities*. United Nations Population Fund. Available online: https://www.unfpa.org/pds/urbanization.htm

United Nations. (2012). *Current status of the social situation, well-being, participation in development and rights of older persons worldwide*. United Nations Department of Economic and Social Affairs 2012. Available online: https://www.un.org/esa/socdev/ageing/whatsnew%20PDF/Ageing% 20Comprehensive%20report%202010%202%20September.pdf

United States Department of Transportation. (n.d.). Decentralized blockchain networks that use automated smart contracts can potentially reduce ride-sharing costs by 20 percent. https://www.itsknowledgeresources.its.dot.gov

Uslaner, E. M. (2002). *The Moral Foundations of Trust*. Cambridge University Press.

Viriyasitavat, W., & Li Da Xu. (2019). Blockchain Technology for Applications in Internet of Things—Mapping from System Design Perspective. IEEE Internet of Things Journal, 6(5).

Vishumurthy, V., Chandrakumar, S., & Sirer, E. G. (2003). Karma: A secure economic framework for peer-to-peer resource sharing. *Proceedings of the 2003 Workshop on Economics of Peer-to-Peer Systems*.

Walport, M. (2016). *Distributed ledger technology: beyond block chain*. Available: https://www.gov.uk/ government/ publications/distributed-ledger-technology-blackett-review

Walport, M. (2106). *Distributed ledger technology: beyond block chain*. Available: https://www.gov.uk/government/publications/distributed-ledger-technology-blackett-review

Wang, Dong, & Wang. (2019). Securing knowledge with Blockchain and AI. *IEEE Access*.

Wang, H., & He, W. (2011). A Reservation-based Smart Parking System. *The First International Workshop on Cyber-Physical Networking Systems*, 701-706.

Wang, C., Wang, Q., Ren, K., & Lou, W. (2010). Privacy-preserving public auditing for data storage security in cloud computing. *Proc. IEEE INFOCOM*, 1–9. 10.1109/INFCOM.2010.5462173

Wang, H., Huang, Q., Zhang, C., & Xia, A. (2010). A Novel Approach for the Layout of Electric Vehicle Charging Station. *Apperceiving Computing and Intelligence Analysis Conference*.

Wang, S., Ouyang, L., Yuan, Y., Ni, X., Han, X., & Wang, F. (2019). Blockchain-Enabled Smart Contracts: Architecture, Applications, and Future Trends. *IEEE Transactions on Systems, Man, and Cybernetics. Systems*, 49(11), 1–12. doi:10.1109/TSMC.2019.2895123

Wang, S., Yuan, Y., Wang, X., Li, J., Qin, R., & Wang, F. (2018). An Overview of Smart Contract: Architecture, Applications, and Future Trends. *2018 IEEE Intelligent Vehicles Symposium (IV)*. 10.1109/IVS.2018.8500488

Wang, W., Hoang, D. T., Hu, P., Xiong, Z., Niyato, D., Wang, P., Wen, Y., & Kim, D. I. (2019). A Survey on Consensus Mechanisms and Mining Strategy Management in Blockchain Networks. *IEEE Access : Practical Innovations, Open Solutions*, 7, 22328–22370. doi:10.1109/ACCESS.2019.2896108

Wang, X., Zeng, P., Patterson, N., Jiang, F., Doss, R., & Member, S. (2019). An Improved Authentication Scheme for Internet of Vehicles Based on Blockchain Technology. *IEEE Access : Practical Innovations, Open Solutions*, 7, 45061–45072. doi:10.1109/ACCESS.2019.2909004

Wang, Y., Su, Z., Zhang, N., & Member, S. (2019). BSIS : Blockchain-Based Secure Incentive Scheme for Energy Delivery in Vehicular Energy Network. *IEEE Transactions on Industrial Informatics*, *15*(6), 3620–3631. doi:10.1109/TII.2019.2908497

Westerkamp, M. (2019). Verifiable Smart Contract Portability. *2019 IEEE International Conference on Blockchain and Cryptocurrency (ICBC)*. 10.1109/BLOC.2019.8751335

Wikipedia. (n.d.), Self-driving car. https://en.wikipedia.org/wiki/Self-driving_car

Wikipedia. (n.d.). *Privacy and blockchain.* https://en.wikipedia.org/wiki/Privacy_and_blockchain

Wohlwend, J. (2016). *Elliptic Curve Cryptography - Pre and Post Quantum - MIT Math.* http://www-math.mit.edu/~apost/courses/18.204-2016/18.204_Jeremy_Wohlwend_final_paper.pdf

Wohrer, M., & Zdun, U. (2018). Smart contracts: security patterns in the ethereum ecosystem and solidity. *2018 International Workshop on Blockchain Oriented Software Engineering (IWBOSE)*. 10.1109/IWBOSE.2018.8327565

Wood, W., & Carter, B. Dodd, & Bradley. (2016). How Blockchain technology Can Enhance HER operability. Academic Press.

Wood, G. (2014). Ethereum: A secure decentralizedgeneralised transaction ledger. *Ethereum Project Yellow Paper*, *151*, 1–32.

Wood, G. (2014, April). Ethereum: A secure decentralized generalized group action ledger. *Ethereum Project Yellow Paper*, *151*, 1–32.

Wooldridge, M., & Jennings, N.R. (1995). Intelligent agents: Theory and practice. *The Knowledge Engineering Review*, *10*(2), 115-152.

Worley, Klabjan, & Sweda. (2012). Simultaneous vehicle routing and charging station siting for commercial electrice vehicles. *IEVC 2012*.

Wu, D., Rosen, D. W., Wang, L., & Schaefer, D. (2015). Cloud-based design and manufacturing: A new paradigm in digital manufacturing and design innovation. *Computer Aided Design*, *59*, 1–14. doi:10.1016/j.cad.2014.07.006

Xie, T., Zhang, J., Zhang, Y., Papamanthou, C., & Song, D. (2019). Libra: Succinct Zero-Knowledge Proofs with Optimal Prover Computation. In A. Boldyreva & D. Micciancio (Eds.), Lecture Notes in Computer Science: Vol. 11694. *Advances in Cryptology – CRYPTO 2019. CRYPTO 2019*. Springer. doi:10.1007/978-3-030-26954-8_24

Xing, B., & Marwala, T. (2018). *The Synergy of Blockchain and Artificial Intelligence*. SSRN Electronic Journal. doi:10.2139srn.3225357

Xu, Song, Goh, & Li. (n.d.). *Building AN Ethereum and IPFS-based decentralized Social Network System*. Academic Press.

Xu, X. (2018). An Energy-Aware Virtual Machine Scheduling Method for Cloudlets in Wireless Metropolitan Area Networks. *2018 IEEE International Conference on Internet of Things (iThings) and IEEE Green Computing and Communications (GreenCom) and IEEE Cyber, Physical and Social Computing (CPSCom) and IEEE Smart Data (SmartData)*, 517-523. 10.1109/Cybermatics_2018.2018.00110

Xu, X., Chen, Y., Yuan, Y., Huang, T., & Zhang, X. (n.d.). Blockchain-based cloudlet management for multimedia workflow in mobile cloud computing. *Multimedia Tools and Applications*. Advance online publication. doi:10.100711042-019-07900-x,2019

Yahiatene, Y. (2018). Towards a Blockchain and Software-Defined Vehicular Networks approaches to secure Vehicular Social Network. 2018 IEEE Conference on Standards for Communications and Networking (CSCN), 1–7. doi:10.1109/CSCN.2018.8581756

Yan, G., Yang, W., Rawat, D. B., &Olariu, S. (2011). SmartParking: A Secure and Intelligent Parking System. *IEEE Intelligent Transportation Systems Magazine, 3*(1), 18-30.

Yang, J., Portilla, J., & Riesgo, T. (2012). Smart parking service based on Wireless Sensor Networks. *IECON Proceedings (Industrial Electronics Conference),* 6029-6034. 10.1109/IECON.2012.6389096

Yang, Z., Yang, K., Lei, L., Member, S., Zheng, K., Member, S., & Leung, V. C. M. (2019). Blockchain-Based Decentralized Trust Management in Vehicular Networks. IEEE Internet of Things Journal, 6(2), 1495–1505. doi:10.1109/JIOT.2018.2836144

Yan, G., & Olariu, S. (2011, December). A probabilistic analysis of link duration in vehicular ad hoc networks. *IEEE Transactions on Intelligent Transportation Systems, 12*(4), 1227–1236. doi:10.1109/TITS.2011.2156406

Yaqoob, Khan, Talib, Butt, & Saleem, Arif, & Nadeem. (2019). Use of Blockchain in Healthcare: A Systematic Literature Review. *International Journal of Advanced Computer Science and Applications, 10*(5).

Yuan, Y., & Wang, F. (2016). Towards blockchain-based intelligent transportation systems. *2016 IEEE 19th International Conference on Intelligent Transportation Systems (ITSC).* doi:10.1109/itsc.2016.7795984

Yuan, Y., & Wang, F.-Y. (2016). Towards blockchain-based intelligent transportation systems. *Intelligent Transportation Systems (ITSC), 2016 IEEE 19th International Conference on,* 2663–2668.

Zero Knowledge Proof. (2018). *An Introduction to Zero Knowledge Proof.* https://101blockchains.com/wp-content/uploads/2018/11/Zero_knowledge_Proof_ZKP.png

Zhai, Y. (2017). 4 Ways Blockchain Will Disrupt the Energy Sector. https://blogs.adb.org/blog/4-ways-blockchain-will-disrupt-energy-sector.fckLR

Zhang, R., & Liu, L. (2010). Security Models and Requirements for Healthcare Application Clouds. *2010 IEEE 3rd International Conference on Cloud Computing.*

Zhang, X., Li, R., & Cui, B. (2018, August). A Security architecture of VANET based on blockchain and mobile edge computing. In 2018 1st IEEE International Conference on Hot Information-Centric Networking (HotICN) (pp. 258-259). IEEE. doi:10.1109/HOTICN.2018.8605952

Zhang, R., & Xue, R. (2019). Security and Privacy on Blockchain. *ACM Computing Surveys, 1*(1).

Zhang, X., & Chen, X. (2019). Data Security Sharing and Storage Based on a Consortium Blockchain in a Vehicular Ad-hoc Network. *IEEE Access : Practical Innovations, Open Solutions, 7,* 58241–58254. doi:10.1109/ACCESS.2018.2890736

Zhao, L., Peng, X., Li, L., & Li, Z. (2011, March). A fast signal timing algorithm for individual oversaturated intersections. *IEEE Transactions on Intelligent Transportation Systems, 12*(1), 280–283. doi:10.1109/TITS.2010.2076808

Zheng, Z., Xie, S., Dai, H. N., Chen, X., & Wang, H. (2018). Blockchain challenges and opportunities: A survey. *International Journal of Web and Grid Services, 14*(4), 352. doi:10.1504/IJWGS.2018.095647

Zheng, Z., Xie, S., Dai, H., Chen, X., & Wang, H. (2017). An Overview of Blockchain Technology: Architecture, Consensus, and Future Trends. *2017 IEEE International Congress on Big Data.*

Zinon, Z., Christodoulou, P., Andreou, A., & Chatzichristofis, S. (2019). ParkChain: An IoT Parking Service Based on Blockchain. *15th International Conference on Distributed Computing in Sensor Systems (DCOSS)*, 687-693. doi: 10.1109/dcoss.2019.00123

Zyskind, G. (2016). *Efficient Secure Computation Enabled by Blockchain Technology*. Massachusetts Institute of Technology. https://dspace.mit.edu/ bitstream/handle/1721.1/ 105933/964695278-MIT.pdf?sequence=1&isAllowed=y

Zyskind, Nathan, & Pentland. (2015). Decentralizing Privacy: Using Blockchain to Protect Personal Data. *2015 IEEE CS Security and Privacy Workshops*.

About the Contributors

Amit Kumar Tyagi (GATE, NPwD-JRF, UGC-NET, and ICAR-NET) received his Ph.D degree in 2018 from Pondicherry Central University, Puducherry, India, in area of "Vehicular Ad-hoc Networks". His research interests include Formal Language Theory, Smart and Secure Computing, Privacy (including Genomic Privacy), Machine Learning with Big data, Blockchain Technology, Cyber Physical System etc. He has completed his M.Tech degree from the Pondicherry Central University, Puducherry, India. He joined the Lord Krishna College of Engineering, Ghaziabad (LKCE) for the periods of 2009-2010, and 2012-2013. With more than 08 (Eight) years of teaching and research experience across India, currently he is working as an Assistant Professor in Vellore Institute of Technology, Chennai Campus, Chennai 600127, Tamilnadu, India. Additionally, He is also the recipient/ awarded of the GATE and NPwD-JRF fellowship in 2009, 2016 and 2013. He has been published one major book titled "Know Your Technical (IT) Skills". Also He is a member of various Computer/ Research Communities like IEEE, ISOC, CSI, ISTE, DataScience, MIRLab, etc.

* * *

Abhishek Bhattacharya is a Co-founder at Whrrl and was a Product Owner for Policybazaar.com's service product. A 3x Entrepreneur and a 2x Author, he has been in Blockchain for about 3 years, commercially, and academically prior to that. At Whrrl, he's building India's first Agri-Lending blockchain that can save 25-40% of farmers' income, and protect banks from millions in frauds. He has been an Advisor to several startups such as eSports.com (who raised 5.8 Million EUR in their ICO), Vayla, Blockchain Advisory Council, NafCoin et. al. His second book (**Secure Chains: Cybersecurity and Blockchain-powered Automation**) has been published by **BPB Publications - Asia's Largest Publisher of IT Books**. He is a regular speaker in Blockchain and mostly gives 2-day (10-hour) workshops in Universities to students in 2nd, 3rd or 4th year, in an attempt to show them a path to choose a career in Blockchain when there's still time, apart from taking Lectures in Blockchain for faculty and students, including a global audience. He's an Educator with **ODEM**. He has also advised the **Certified Blockchain Professional (CBP) Course by IIB-Council which is present across 145 countries.** Lastly, he was nominated for the "**Top 50 Tech Leaders**" award by **InterCon Dubai**. He had been invited as a Speaker at one of Europe's biggest Blockchain conferences - **Decentralized 2019 in Athens, Greece;** as a Speaker at **The Blockchain World Forum in Shenzhen, China;** and as a Panelist/Speaker with a nomination for **Best Crypto Educator** in GURUS Awards by **Next Block Asia 2.0 in Bangkok, Thailand** last year, and as a panellist/judge at Govt. of India's program for startups, and has taken lectures at IIM Kashipur.

Divyangana is a research scholar in the field of Information Technology at Manipal University Jaipur.

Abhishek Kumar Gautam is an Electronics and Communication Engineer from Guru Tegh Bahadur Institute of Technology, GGSIPU, New Delhi. He had published an International Journal in Springer in the field of Rectangular Dielectric Resonator Antenna in the year 2017. Moreover, he presented and published 2 research papers in IEEE International Conference on Stacked DRA & Micro-strip Fed RDRA in the year 2016. Currently, he is pursuing an MBA from IIM Shillong from the batch of 2018-2020. His current areas of interest include- Applications of Blockchain and had recently been the Global Winner of a competition conducted by Blockchain Council for the Student Scholarship Program 2019.

N. Gayathri received her B. Tech as well as M. Tech. degree in Computer Science and Engineering from Anna University, Chennai, India. She is currently working as an Assistant Professor in Department of Computer Science and Engineering. Her research interests include cloud computing, Bigdata Analytics, and network security.

Abhishek Kumar is working as an Assistant Professor, Department of Computer Science, Institute of Science at Banaras Hindu University. He has awarded Ph.D., Doctorate in Computer Application (Research Interests: Stereoscopy, 3D Animation, Design, Computer Graphics & visual effects), Dual Master Degree in Animation & Visual Effects and in Computer Science and Bachelor of Science in Multimedia. Dr. Abhishek Kumar is Apple Certified Associate, Adobe Education Trainer & Certified by Autodesk also. Dr. Abhishek has trained over 40,000+ students across the globe from 153 Countries, top 5 countries are India, Germany, United States, Spain & Australia. His alumni have worked for several national & international movies like Ra-One, Krissh, Dhoom, Life of Pi, Avengers Series, Iron Man series, Gijoe 3D, 300, Alvin & chipmunks, Prince of Persia, Titanic 3D, Transformers series, Bahubali 1 & 2, London has fallen, Warcraft, Aquaman 3D, Alita & a lots. His experience in academic and production environment has prepared him to be an effective Team Leader & mentor of 3D Animation, Computer Graphics, Visual Effects & Design engineering Industry. His technical proficiency & research journal papers have covered a wide range of topics in various Digital Art areas (Image analysis, visual Identity, Graphics, Digital Photography, Motion graphics, 3D Animation, Visual Effects, Editing and Compositing). Through his experience as a Mentor at MAAC (Maya Academy of Advanced Cinematics) Training Centers (India) & Assistant Professor at Banaras Hindu University, He has developed confidence and an interest in teaching. He is actively involved in development of the courseware of Animation & design engineering course for various Institutions & Universities as per future industry requirement. Dr. Abhishek is actively working as a Course Coordinator of "Animations", Computer Science course running on SWAYAM. (An initiative of the MHRD under its NME-ICT being executed by the UGC). He is an active member American Association for the Advancement of Science (AAAS), The Association for Computing Machinery (ACM) and Society for Animation Studies, Singapore.

Randhir Kumar received the M.Tech degree from RGPV University, India. He is currently pursuing the Ph.D. degree in Department of Information Technology, National Institute of Technology, Raipur. His research interests includes Blockchain Technology, Information Security, and Image Processing.

V. D. Ambeth Kumar received Ph.D (Computer Science Engineering) from Sathyabama University, India in 2013. He pursued his M.E (Computer Science Engineering) degree in Annamalai University,

Chidambaram and B.E (Computer Science Engineering) in Madurai Kamaraj University, Madurai, Tamil Nadu, India in the year 2006 and 2004. He has a rich experience in the field of Computer Science close to a decade and he is currently working as an Professor at Panimalar Engineering College, Chennai, India. He has contributed in Technology initiatives and published books on Theory of Computation, Design and Analysis of Algorithms, Advanced Computer Architectures and Python Programming. His Articles are published in 25 International Journals, 6 National Journals. He has also presented papers in more than 42 National and International conferences. He is a recognized supervisor of Anna University. He is guide research scholars for Ph.D progemme. He is the recipient of the Best Teacher award of PEC in 2011. His recived 14 copytights and 3 patent puiblished . His work has been profiled broadly such as in Image Processing, pattern Recognition, Neural Network and Network. His research Interests include Computational Model, Compiler design, Data Structure and Microprocessors. He is Reviewer and Editor of many reputed Journal. He is Life Member of ISTE, IAENG and ACEEE.

P. Lalitha Surya Kumari is presently working as a Professor in the department of Computer Science and Engineering, Koneru Lakshmaiah University, Hyderabad, Telangana. She obtained her Ph.D in Computer Science and Engineering from Jawaharlal Nehru Technological University, Hyderabad, Telangana, India. Her research area includes Security in Network Security., Information Security and Algorithms

Brahim Lejdel is currently an Associate Professor in the Faculty of Exact Sciences, University of EL-Oued (Algeria). He holds a Magister Degree in Computer Science from University of Ourgla since 2009. He held his PhD in computer science in 2015. In 2017, he has its habitation which permits him to supervise research in PhD projects. He is the author of more than 50 papers published in refereed journals and International Conferences. He publishes four books in his research domain. He is the chairman of many international conferences. He works as invited editor, reviewer, and others in many journals and conference. He supervised the researches of many students at the University in the last ten years.

Agnel Livingston L. G. X., Assistant Professor, is with Department of Computer Science and Engineering, St. Xavier's Catholic College of Engineering, Chunkankadai, Kanyakumar District, TN 600127, INDIA. He has completed Master's Degree in Computer Science and Engineering from Anna University, Chennai, India. He has more than 10 years of experience in Teaching and Research and keenly interested in the areas of Image Processing, Computer Network, Computer Architecture, Data Analytics, Data Structures & Algorithms and Data Base Systems.

Merlin Livingston L. M. is the Principal of Jeppiaar Institute of Technology, Chennai. She has completed Ph.D. in the area of Image Processing from Sathyabama University, Chennai, Master of Engineering degree in Applied Electronics from Madurai Kamaraj University, Madurai and Bachelor of Engineering degree in Electronics & Communication Engineering from Bharathiar University, Coimbatore. She has nearly 20 years of teaching experience and in her tenure, she has attended many training programs, technical workshops and has published many technical research papers in renowned National / International conferences and journals. She has applied for a patent and received AICTE award from Confederation of Indian Industry (CII) for her innovation in 2016. She has been the resource person for Faculty development program in the field of Embedded Systems,Signal Processing and VLSI design.

Nitin is a member of Information Systems Area. In the past he has worked as Professor Educator in the Department of EECS at University of Cincinnati, Cincinnati, OH, and First Tier Bank Professor at Peter Kiewit Institute, University of Nebraska at Omaha (UNO), Omaha, USA. Recently he has been awarded 2017-2018 Outstanding Services to the EECS Department by UC. He has earned all of his degrees: D.Sc., Ph.D., M.Engg. and B.Engg. in the field of Computer Science & Engineering. He has work experience of more than 16 years and published more than 185 Research Papers in peer reviewed International Journals and Conferences. He has bagged more than 40 Academic and Industrial Awards and till now has guided and awarded 10 Doctoral and 19 Masters Thesis in the area of Computer Science & Engineering and Information Technology. He is a IBM certified engineer and Life Member of IAENG, Senior Member of IEEE, ACM and IACSIT and Member of SIAM and ACIS. His areas of interest include Distributed Blockchain, Knowledge Management and Information Systems.

Vengat San currently working as Professor, Department of Computer Engineering, Sanjivani College of Engineering, 13 years of teaching experience in computer science engineering. I received Ph.D Computer Science and Engineering, Bhopal 2017 Sri Satya Sai University of Technology and Medical Science, pursued my M.Tech in Information Technology (2008-2010) from Sathyabama University, Chennai, B.E in Computer Science Engineering (2001-2005) in PGP College Of Engineering And Technology (Anna University Chennai) Namakkal. He completed His research area is in Data mining, bioinformatics, clustering, correlation & Bi-clustering. Life Time Member of Indian Society for Technical Education. Reviewer following journals International Journal of Medical Engineering and Informatics (IJMEI), Interscience, Concurrency and Computation: Practice and Experience, Progress of Electrical and Electronic Engineering, Whioce Publishing Pte. Ltd.

Ashutosh Satapathy, Full Time Ph.D. Scholar, is with the School of Computing Science and Engineering, VIT University, Chennai. He has completed his Masters Degree in Information Security and Computer Forensics from SRM University, India.

Shantanu Saurabh is an Assistant Professor, Faculty of Commerce, Maharaja Sajajirao University of Baroda, Vadodara.

Rakesh Shaktivel received his B. Tech. degree in Computer Science and Engineering from Anna University Chennai in the year 2012. He received his M.E. degree in Computer Science and Engineering from Anna University Chennai in the year 2016. Currently, he is working as an Assistant Professor in Department of Computer Science and Engineering. His main thrust research areas are Bigdata Analytic network security and cloud computing.

Achintya Singhal is currently associated as Associate Professor in the department of Computer Science, Institute of Science, Banaras Hindu University, Varanasi. He has experience of more than 12 years of Post Graduate teaching and research.

Devesh Kumar Srivastava has been working as a professor in the School of Computing and Information Technology at Manipal University Jaipur. He is a professional member of ACM and have been a faculty sponsor of ACM student chapter during 2015-16. He has published total many research papers in peer reviewed referred Journals and research papers through conferences of IEEE / Springer/ ACM and Elsevier . He chaired 19 technical sessions and addressed 6 invited talks in the various international conferences. He has reviewed conference papers and journal papers. He has been honored with awards for the year 2017, 2018 and 2019 for the big contribution in the research work.

Rakesh Tripathi received the M.Tech degree from Tezpur University, India, and the Ph.D. degree in computer science and engineering from the Indian Institute of Technology Guwahati, India. He is an Assistant Professor with the Department of Information Technology, National Institute of Technology Raipur. He has over ten years of experience in academic. He has published over 20 referred article and served as a reviewer of several journals. His research interests include Mobile-Adhoc Networks, Sensor Networks, data center networks, distributed systems, and game theory in networks.

Ashok Kumar Yadav is currently working as an assistant professor at Rajkiya Engineering College Azamgarh, Uttar Pradesh. He has worked as an assistant professor (On Adhoc) in the Department of Computer Science, University of Delhi, New Delhi for 2.5 Years. He is pursuing Ph.D. from the School of Computer and Systems Sciences, Jawaharlal Nehru University, New Delhi, India. He has completed M.Tech from the School of Computer and Systems Sciences, Jawaharlal Nehru University, New Delhi, India.

Index

Ensure Quality Research is Introduced to the Academic Community

Become an IGI Global Reviewer for Authored Book Projects

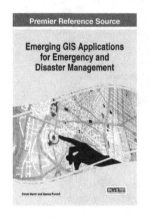

Premier Reference Source

Emerging GIS Applications for Emergency and Disaster Management

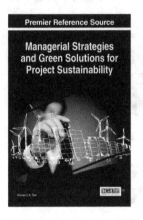

Premier Reference Source

Managerial Strategies and Green Solutions for Project Sustainability

Premier Reference Source

Comparative Approaches to Using R and Python for Statistical Data Analysis

Premier Reference Source

Solutions for High-Touch Communications in a High-Tech World

The overall success of an authored book project is dependent on quality and timely reviews.

In this competitive age of scholarly publishing, constructive and timely feedback significantly expedites the turnaround time of manuscripts from submission to acceptance, allowing the publication and discovery of forward-thinking research at a much more expeditious rate. Several IGI Global authored book projects are currently seeking highly-qualified experts in the field to fill vacancies on their respective editorial review boards:

Applications and Inquiries may be sent to:
development@igi-global.com

Applicants must have a doctorate (or an equivalent degree) as well as publishing and reviewing experience. Reviewers are asked to complete the open-ended evaluation questions with as much detail as possible in a timely, collegial, and constructive manner. All reviewers' tenures run for one-year terms on the editorial review boards and are expected to complete at least three reviews per term. Upon successful completion of this term, reviewers can be considered for an additional term.

If you have a colleague that may be interested in this opportunity, we encourage you to share this information with them.

Printed in the United States
By Bookmasters